discover
ITALY

CRISTIAN BONETTO
DAMIEN SIMONIS, ALISON BING, GREGOR CLARK, DUNCAN
GARWOOD, ABIGAIL HOLE, ALEX LEVITON, VIRGINIA MAXWELL,
JOSEPHINE QUINTERO, BRENDAN SAINSBURY

DISCOVER ITALY

Rome (p50) Italy's former Caput Mundi is a breathtaking combo of priceless ruins, vainglorious churches, sweeping piazzas and effortless cool.

Milan & the Northwest (p103) Moneyed cities and uber-romantic lakes meet snow-capped Alps, truffle-sprinkled hills and gorgeous coastal hamlets.

Venice & the Northeast (p155) Foodie-fabulous cities and glittering Byzantine churches meet villa-freckled plains and the inimitable romance of Venice.

Florence & Central Italy (p207) A classic blend of cultured Renaissance cities, brooding Gothic towns and heavenly vine-laced hills.

Naples, Pompeii & Amalfi (p263) An adrenalin-pumping mash-up of electrifying street life, bombastic baroque *palazzi*, vivid ancient ruins and tumbling coastal villages.

Sicily & the South (p297) Arabesque architecture and spicy flavours meet steamy volcanoes, stunning turquoise beaches and surreal, far-flung abodes.

⬎ CONTENTS

CONTENTS

VENICE & THE
NORTHEAST
p155

MILAN & THE
NORTHWEST
p103

FLORENCE &
CENTRAL ITALY
p207

ROME
p54

NAPLES,
POMPEII &
AMALFI
p263

SICILY &
THE SOUTH
p297

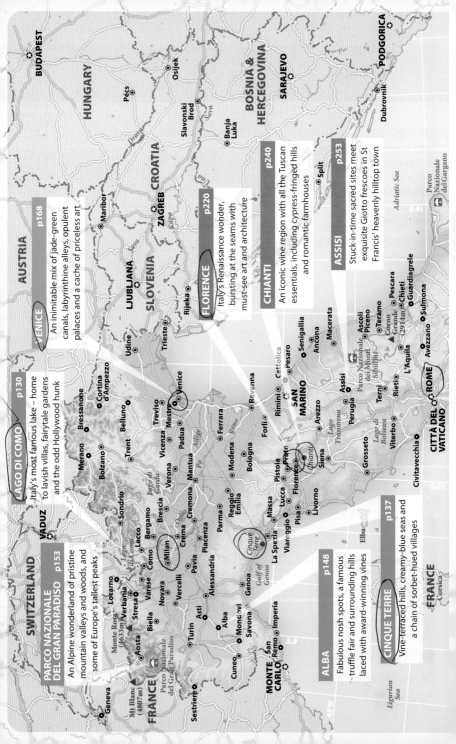

SWITZERLAND

PARCO NAZIONALE DEL GRAN PARADISO p153

An Alpine wonderland of pristine mountain valleys and woods, and some of Europe's tallest peaks

LAGO DI COMO p130

Italy's most famous lake – home to lavish villas, fairytale gardens and the odd Hollywood hunk

VENICE p168

An inimitable mix of jade-green canals, labyrinthine alleys, opulent palaces and a cache of priceless art

FLORENCE p220

Italy's Renaissance wonder, bursting at the seams with must-see art and architecture

CHIANTI p240

An iconic wine region with all the Tuscan essentials, including cypress-fringed hills and romantic farmhouses

ASSISI p253

Stuck-in-time sacred sites meet exquisite Giotto frescoes in St Francis' heavenly hilltop town

ALBA p148

Fabulous nosh spots, a famous truffle fair and surrounding hills laced with award-winning vines

CINQUE TERRE p137

Vine-terraced hills, creamy-blue seas and a chain of sorbet-hued villages

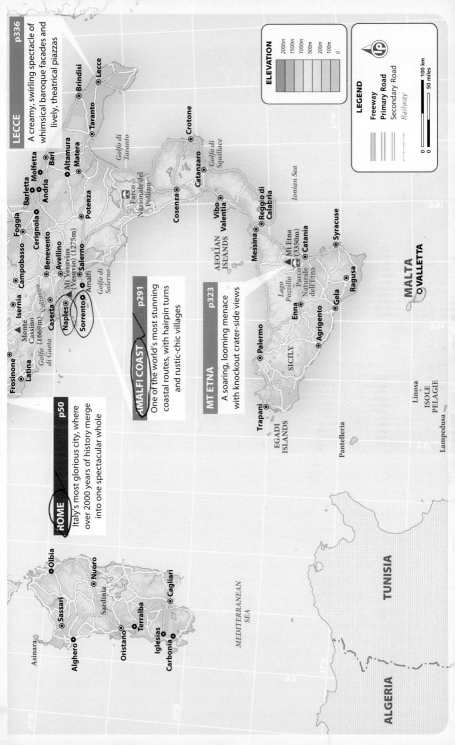

ROME p50

Italy's most glorious city, where over 2000 years of history merge into one spectacular whole

AMALFI COAST p291

One of the world's most stunning coastal routes, with hairpin turns and rustic-chic villages

MT ETNA p323

A soaring, looming menace with knockout crater-side views

LECCE p336

A creamy, swirling spectacle of whimsical baroque facades and lively, theatrical piazzas

ELEVATION

2000m
1500m
1000m
500m
200m
100m
0

LEGEND

Freeway
Primary Road
Secondary Road
Railway

0 — 100 km
0 — 50 miles

↘ THIS IS ITALY

It's not the size that matters – it's what you do with it. Italy should know. Smaller than New Mexico, this dramatic, self-assured marvel boasts art collections, culinary skills and landscapes that few nations would ever dare compete with.

Not surprisingly, the *Belpaese* (Beautiful Country) is a seasoned seducer. For millennia, foreigners have fought for a slice of Europe's sexiest boot. Goethe and Keats sipped espresso in Rome; Wagner and Wolfe waxed lyrical about the Amalfi Coast; and George Clooney continues to live *la dolce vita* on Lago di Como's elegant shores.

Italy's great *città d'arte* (cities of art) – among them Rome, Venice and Florence – count masterpieces the way most cities count cars. Beyond these cities lies an exhausting bounty of treasures, from Tuscany's vine-laced hills and Emilia-Romagna's food-obsessed cities to the raw, brooding beauty of 'deep south' Basilicata.

Not that Italy is without a dark side. Philandering politicians, Mafia dealings, illegal immigration and the country's infamous bureaucracy are as much a part of Italian life as da Vinci, Armani and long Sunday lunches.

And the country is no stranger to drama. Local history is littered with tales of self-serving viceroys, martyred saints, devastating earthquakes and volcanic eruptions. But while the peninsula's history could fill countless volumes, the country of Italy is actually quite young. After the fall of Rome, the peninsula remained divided into bickering city-states and small warring kingdoms, eventually succumbing to foreign control before finally opting for unification in 1861.

Almost 150 years on, Europe's fourth-largest economy remains a country of enormous contradictions, its 20 regions flaunting their own idiosyncratic cuisines, dialects, architecture and cultural traditions. With Napoleonic *palazzi* (palaces) in Piedmont, medieval pageants in Umbria and Arabesque domes in Sicily, Italy can feel more like a compact collection of different worlds than a single country. The contrasts might cause the odd political division, but for the rest of us it's what makes this Mediterranean diva so deliciously rewarding.

> "Italy can feel more like a compact collection of different worlds than a single country"

↘ ITALY'S TOP
25 EXPERIENCES

⤵ THE DUOMO

I grabbed her by the hand and demanded, 'Follow me! Don't argue!' A quick trail through the narrow streets and telling her to shut her eyes, I pushed her into the piazza and said, 'Look!'. Florence's **Duomo** (p221). Instantly Italy was in her blood. I'll never forget that look on her face.

Doug (Thorn Tree name mckellan), Traveller, Australia

↘ WINING THROUGH CHIANTI

2

Tuscany's **Chianti** (p240) region is much more than great wine. The landscape looks like a perfectly thought-out composition: rows of svelte cypresses, quaint farmhouses and rolling vineyards. We spent four days driving around, feasting on fabulous local food, practising our Italian and stocking up on Chianti Classico (of course).

Nathan Brewer, Traveller, Australia

3

↘ HORSE PARTY

Il Palio (p243) is Siena's annual horse race and for the Sienese it is life. Throughout the city young and old send the streets vibrating with the rhythm of drums and spinning with twirling flags in practise for the July race. Italy may be known for Catholicism, but in Siena they practise Il Palioism.

Hannah Rothstein, Traveller, USA

1 JEAN-PIERRE LESCOURRET; 2 DAMIEN SIMONIS; 3 MARKA/ALAMY

1 Duomo (p221), Florence; 2 Vineyard, Chianti (p240); 3 Il Palio (p243), Siena

↘ FREEWHEELING ALONG THE AMALFI

4

You don't often get the Amalfi Coast (p291) to yourself, but that's what happened one bright day in early March when I found myself the only passenger on the bus from Positano to Sorrento. This stretch is the least developed and most beautiful on the entire coast. It was an amazing and unforgettable ride.

Duncan Garwood, Lonely Planet Author, Italy

5

↘ LAGO DI COMO

It's no surprise that George Clooney moved to Lago di Como (p130). The lake is beyond enchanting, with dignified villas and manicured gardens. We'd planned to spend a couple of nights in Bellagio (p134) but ended up staying a week, cruising the lake and exploring its picture-book villages.

Georgia McDonald, Traveller, Australia

↘ ST PETER'S BASILICA

Stepping into the Vatican's St Peter's Basilica (p85) for the first time was a truly gob-smacking experience. The sheer size of the building aside, face-to-face with priceless treasures like Michelangelo's *Pietà* and the bronze baldachin, even the most fervent atheist could be excused for thinking twice.

Cameron Macintosh, Traveller, Australia

6

4 STEPHEN SAKS; 5 GLENN VAN DER KNIJFF; 6 WILL SALTER

4 Bridge crossing, Amalfi Coast (p291); 5 Villa Balbianello (p135), Lago di Como; 6 St Peter's Basilica (p85)

⬎ MICHELANGELO'S DAVID

Everyone says that Michelangelo's **David** (p228) is wonderful, but I had no idea just how stunning he is. Five metres tall, muscles rippling, veins pulsing – an example of perfection. If I had a regret about my trip to Italy, it's that David's not a live and single man.

Hannah Rothstein, Traveller, USA

7

8

◥ BASILICA DI SAN MARCO

Stepping into Venice's Basilica di San Marco (p172), I imagine a medieval peasant glimpsing those gold mosaic domes for the first time. Once you see those tiny gilt tesserae cohere into a singular heavenly vision, every leap of human imagination since the 12th century seems comparatively minor.

Alison Bing, Lonely Planet Author, USA & Italy

◥ MORNING IN MATERA

9

I started to explore Matera (p338) before the town got up. There were just the faintest stirrings of life and the scent of coffee in the air. It's an extraordinary town: elegant buildings developed from caves that pockmark a dizzying ravine. Tinged gold by the early morning sun, it was bleary, deserted and quiet.

Abigail Hole, Lonely Planet Author, UK

7 JOHN HAY; 8 KRZYSZTOF DYDYNSKI; 9 ALAN BENSON

7 David, Galleria dell'Accademia (p228); 8 Mosaics, Basilica di San Marco (p172); 9 The *sassi* (338), Matera

10

↘ BEAUTIFUL BOLOGNA

Unlike Rome, Florence or Venice, Bologna (p194) isn't a museum piece. Here the past is a background glow that imbues all things but leaves you free to enjoy the pleasures of the moment. And what pleasures: Italy's finest food, stylish shopping, a vibrant cultural life and easy-on-the-eye architecture.

Sandra Haywood, Traveller, UK

↘ CARNEVALE IN VENICE

11

Every February, Venice bursts with colour and festivities for Carnevale (p179). Crowds of people – both locals and tourists – swarm the city, some wearing masks and costumes, others simply basking in the lively atmosphere. The party continues until the early hours of the morning, as music and dancing fill the narrow streets.

Kristine Ortiz, Traveller, Australia

⬆ DAWN AT THE TREVI

As we approached Rome's **Trevi Fountain** (p77) in the wee morning hours, we saw something we hadn't found in our previous five days: tranquillity. We joined six others, including one man sweeping the previous day's coins into a pile. With the collection man gone, we tossed coins into the Trevi, the first of the day.

Bob & Alicia Smith, Travellers, Canada

⬆ CHOCOLATE & COFFEE IN TURIN

If you're a fan of chocolate and coffee, consider a weekend in **Turin** (p141). This overlooked city has some of Europe's best chocolate shops and cafes. You could easily spend the whole time savouring cocoa and taking in the cafe's fantastic vintage interiors. And you can enjoy it without the tourist swarms.

Rachel Joss, Traveller, Canada

10 ATLANTIDE PHOTOTRAVEL/CORBIS; 11 RUTH EASTHAM & MAX PAOLI; 12 WILL SALTER; 13 MARTIN MOOS

10 Piazza Maggiore (p195), Bologna; 11 Carnevale participants, Venice (p168); 12 Trevi Fountain (p77); 13 Cafe interior, Turin (p141)

ITALY'S TOP 25 EXPERIENCES

14

↘ PARADING IN PERUGIA

For me, Perugia (p249) is the one place that will always stand out. At dusk, people come out to wander along Corso Vannucci. People dine outside and as the night proceeds the entire town gathers on the steps of the Duomo, accompanied by guitars. Everything comes alive.

Evelien van Delft, Traveller, the Netherlands

⬎ MIDWEEK IN ASSISI

I highly recommend going to Assisi (p253) midweek in May, when there are fewer tourists around. You get to mix more with the locals. The surrounding countryside is breathtaking and peaceful: the perfect place to chill out. Get up early and watch Assisi come alive.

Elizabeth Spratt, Traveller, Australia

15

14 EIGHTFISH/GETTY; 15 FRANK WING

14 Corso Vannucci (p250), Perugia; 15 Basilica di San Francesco (p254), Assisi

⬊ CINQUE TERRE

We like to walk and did the **Cinque Terre** (p137) five-towns walk along the cliffs. Even though we're in our seventies we had a great but sweaty time. Great views, and the local townspeople were very helpful, especially when they found out where we came from.

Desmond Gardiner, Traveller, New Zealand

16

◥ SCALING MT ETNA

I'll never forget the exhausting thrill of climbing through the snow of Sicily's Mt Etna (p323) to reach the crater. Making our way around the rim, struggling to stay upright against the gale-force winds, was unforgettable. The views that lead down to Catania was a timely reminder of nature's power.

Kim Usher, Traveller, Australia

◥ FEELING ALIVE IN NAPLES

It's impossible to be unaffected by the energy, the traffic and the in-your-face human drama of Naples (p274). All the while there's Vesuvius (p288) snoozing ominously across the bay, just to add that extra degree of tension. And you haven't eaten pizza until you've tried a *vera* Neapolitan Margherita!

Mick Haus, Traveller, New Zealand

16 JOHN ELK III; 17 DIANA MAYFIELD; 18 ALAN BENSON

16 Vernazza (p139), Cinque Terre; 17 Mt Etna (p323); 18 Neapolitan Margherita pizza

↘ LEANING TOWER OF PISA

Never in my life would I have thought of actually getting to the top of Pisa's **Leaning Tower** (p237). I'm scared of heights and not fond of enclosed spaces. But I did it and it is one of the biggest accomplishments in my life. The view from the top is incredible.

Kayla Elliot, Traveller, USA

19

20

↘ BYZANTINE BEAUTY IN RAVENNA

After visiting the obvious must-sees on our first trip to Italy, my wife and I spent our second Italian adventure visiting less-obvious spots. Top of the list was **Ravenna** (p204), whose intricate, lustrous mosaics left us gob-smacked. Needless to say, the town is well worth the train trip from Bologna.

Jim Wirrell, Traveller, Australia

19 PHILIP & KAREN SMITH; 20 JOHN ELK III

19 Leaning Tower of Pisa (p237); 20 Mosaic, Basilica di San Vitale (p204), Ravenna

21

⬐ RIDING ALONG LUCCA'S WALLS

Weeks of museums, churches and indulgent eating were taking their toll. I needed to avoid annunciations, crucifixions and antipasto Toscana and find some fresh air and conscience-clearing exercise. An afternoon bike ride along the monumental medieval walls of **Lucca** (p234) was the perfect answer.

Virginia Maxwell, Lonely Planet Author, Australia

⬐ LECCESE BAROQUE

Lecce (p336) is Italy's wild child of baroque architecture, its churches and *palazzi* carved with the most incredibly intricate details. It feels like the spirit of a child designed the place, its facades so playful and alive with whimsical creatures and exotic themes. You either love it or hate it, but we were completely enamoured.

Michelle McGregor, Traveller, Canada

22

⬖ LA PESCHERIA MARKET

Walking through the fish market **La Pescheria** (p322) in Catania, Sicily, you're fixed by gleaming eyes of swordfish, you hear fishermen holler their daily catches and you see squid heaped up on top of ruby-coloured langoustines. Any fish- or seafood-lover will feel like they've died and gone to (a noisy kind of) heaven.

Vesna Maric,
Lonely Planet Author, UK

23

24

⬖ ANCIENT RUINS IN SICILY

Whether you're roaming around the **Valley of the Temples** (p329) or taking in a Greek tragedy at the **Teatro Greco** (p320) in Taormina, it's hard to wrap your head around just how many centuries these structures have seen come and go. It's a humbling, somewhat haunting feeling that never really leaves you.

Cristian Bonetto, Lonely Planet Author, Australia

21 Lucca (p234); 22 Basilica di Santa Croce (p336), Lecce; 23 La Pescheria (p322), Catania; 24 Teatro Greco (p320), Taormina

⬊ MUSIC & FIREFLIES

Verona (p191) was magical. During the day it was so hot, too hot for me (travelling in July), but in the evening I went to see the opera in **Roman Arena** (p191). The set design was beautiful, the music was magical and fireflies were flying in the spotlights. It was amazing.

MsMrd (Thorn Tree name), Finland

25

BARRY MASON/ALAMY

Roman Arena (p191), Verona

↘ ITALY'S TOP ITINERARIES

WORLD HERITAGE WONDERS

FIVE DAYS FLORENCE TO RAVENNA OR ASSISI

Italy is home to an enviable 44 Unesco World Heritage Sites, ranging from the natural to the handmade. While you'd need plenty of time to get around them all, this itinerary offers a bite-sized serve of the country's World Heritage best.

❶ FLORENCE

Not only is Florence (p220) the cradle of the Renaissance, its entire *centro storico* (historic centre) is a Unesco World Heritage Site. Hit the city's scooter-crammed streets for treasures like the Duomo (p221), the Basilica di Santa Maria Novella (p227) and the Basilica di Santa Croce (p228). Spend part of day two at either the Uffizi (p226) or the Galleria dell'Accademia (p228).

❷ SAN GIMIGNANO

On day three, head to skyscraping San Gimignano (p247), famous for its medley of medieval towers. Step into the town's basilica (p247) for 14th-century frescoes, including works by Domenico Ghirlandaio. For inspiration of the viticultural kind, drop in at the Museo del Vino (p248) to sample some of the region's tipples. Done – now to Siena.

❸ SIENA

Begin day four in the sweeping majesty of Siena's Piazza del Campo (p243), home to the art-filled Museo Civico (p243) and the setting for the nail-biting horserace Il Palio (p243). Stunning marble creations await

San Gimignano (p247)

JOHN ELK III

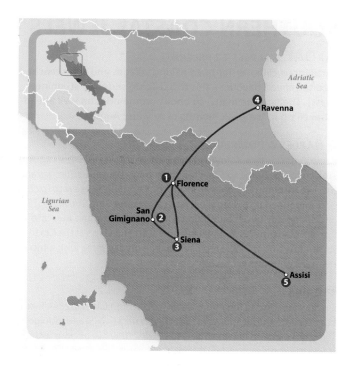

in Siena's great Gothic cathedral (p244). Stay the night to enjoy Tuscan noshing amongst ancient tombs at Antica Osteria da Divo (p246).

❹ RAVENNA

The following morning, make your way back to Florence and catch a train to Bologna, where connecting services reach glittering Ravenna (p204). The main drawcard here is the city's booty of Byzantine mosaics. Strictly unmissable are those in the Basilica di San Vitale (p204), the Battistero Neoniano (p205) and the Basilica di Sant'Apollinare Nuovo (p205). Cap your trip with a feast of regional dishes under frescoed domes at Ca' de Vèn (p206). If visiting between June and late July, treat your ears at the esteemed Ravenna Festival (p205).

❺ ASSISI

If you're pining for more rolling hills and hilltop towns, consider swapping Ravenna for the Umbrian pearl of Assisi (p253), which can be reached by train from Florence, interchanging at Terontola. A deeply spiritual place, its star attraction is the superlatively frescoed Basilica di San Francesco (p254), final resting place of St Francis of Assisi. Find inner peace at the medieval Santuario di San Damiano (p255) or hire a bicycle (p255) and lose yourself in the area's olive-grove landscapes.

SOUTHERN COASTAL JEWELS

10 DAYS NAPLES TO PALERMO

Vertiginous cliffs, pastel-hued fishing villages and sun-drenched Mediterranean flavours – this trip takes in seriously stunning coasts. The fans are many, so book accommodation well ahead if travelling in the peak months of July and August.

❶ NAPLES & POMPEII

Begin your southern sojourn in hyperactive **Naples** (p274), its **centro storico** (p275) home to Graeco-Roman ruins, baroque churches and the awe-inspiring *Cristo Velato* inside the **Cappella Sansevero** (p278). Tuck into superlative Neapolitan pizza at **Pizzeria Gino Sorbillo** (p282) and spend day two hunting down local produce at the **Mercato di Porta Nolana** (p279) and soaking up the art and views at the **Certosa di San Martino** (p279). Step back in time on day three with a trip to the ruins of **Pompeii** (p288).

❷ CAPRI

On day four, catch a ferry from Naples to dazzling **Capri** (p284). Take a boat trip into the incandescent **Grotta Azzurra** (p285) and indulge in some *dolce vita* on **Piazza Umberto I** (p285). Day five options include riding the **seggiovia** (p285) for heavenly views, snooping around imperial ruins at **Villa Jovis** (p285) or hiring a boat for coastal cruising.

❸ POSITANO

If it's summer, catch a ferry directly to **Positano** (p291) on day six. Otherwise, catch a ferry to Sorrento, from where frequent buses depart

EMILY RIDDELL

Positano (p291)

for the Amalfi Coast's most photogenic town. Short on sights per se, spend the rest of the day exploring Positano's twisting, boutique-lined streets or soaking up some rays on **Spiaggia Grande** (p291).

❹ TAORMINA

On day seven, head east to **Salerno** (p296) and catch an early afternoon train south to Messina, Sicily. From here, regular buses depart for jet-set–favourite **Taormina** (p319), getting you there just in time for dinner. Spend the following day rambling through Taormina's medieval streets. Shop for local ceramics and, if it's warm, paddle your way from Mazzaro to **Isola Bella** (p320) for lazy beachside lounging. If you can pull yourself away from the bronzed eye-candy, don't forget to drop in on Taormina's iconic **Teatro Greco** (p320).

❺ AEOLIAN ISLANDS

If the thought of island hopping takes your fancy, consider trading in Taormina for three days on the stunning **Aeolian Islands** (p316). Easily reached by ferry from Messina or nearby Milazzo, its booty of islands offer a blissful mix of crystal-clear waters, therapeutic hot springs, fiery craters and verdant, flower-sprinkled woods.

CLASSIC CITIES

TWO WEEKS ROME TO MILAN

While Italy's riches could easily take a lifetime to explore, two weeks will allow you a respectable taste of its astounding architectural, artistic, culinary and geographic diversity. The focus here is on the big-hitters, with a speedy side trip thrown in.

❶ ROME

Spend your first day exploring ancient must-see sights such as the **Colosseum** (p66) and the **Pantheon** (p73), before a well-earned spritz on buzzing **Campo De' Fiori** (p76). The following day, take in the cultural riches of the **Vatican** (p88) and the views from **Gianicolo** (p84) before feasting on Roman grub and nightlife in **Trastevere** (p82). On day three, meet masterpieces at **Museo e Galleria Borghese** (p79) and flip a coin into the **Trevi Fountain** (p77) to ensure a return visit.

❷ FLORENCE

Catch a train north to the Renaissance jewel of **Florence** (p220) on day four. Get your bearings atop the **Duomo** (p221) and spend the afternoon musing on masterpieces at the **Uffizi** (p226). Spend the following day wandering the city's atmospheric streets, saying 'ciao' to David at the **Galleria dell'Accademia** (p228) and watching the sun sink behind the **Ponte Vecchio** (p229).

LEFT: NEIL SETCHFIELD; RIGHT: IZZET KERIBAR

Left: Grand Canal (p172), Venice; Right: The Colosseum (p66), Rome

❸ CHIANTI

On day six, take a break from Italy's urban intensity with a bike tour to the vine-draped hills of **Chianti** (p240). Indulge in a little wine tasting and noshing, soak up the heavenly Tuscan countryside, and pedal back to Florence in time for a dinner at **L'Osteria di Giovanni** (p231).

❹ BOLOGNA

The following morning it's time to travel north to food-obsessed **Bologna** (p194). Take in art and medieval architecture on **Piazza Maggiore** (p195) before diving into the streets of the **Quadrilatero** (p195) for a crash-course in local produce. Kill the carbs climbing the drunken **Torre degli Asinelli** (p196), then resurrect them the next day by taking part in a cooking course at **La Vecchia Scuola Bolognese** (p197).

❺ VENICE

The trip's ninth day sees you moving on to inimitable **Venice** (p168). Spend time exploring the architectural gems flanking **Piazza San Marco** (p172) before hopping on a *vaporetto* to wander Venice's quieter neighbourhoods. Spice up day 10 with modern art at **Peggy**

Guggenheim Collection (p174) or Tintorettos at the Scuola Grande di San Rocco (p176) before Venetian 'tapas' and Prosecco at I Rusteghi (p182). Cap off the following day with a boat tour of the Venetian lagoon.

❻ VERONA

On day 12, travel west to Romeo and Juliet's hometown of Verona (p191). If you're single and looking, rub Juliet's bronze right breast at the Casa di Giulietta (p191) before falling head-over-the-heels for the city's posse of beautiful churches and *palazzi,* amongst them the Romanesque Basilica di San Zeno Maggiore (p193) and Renaissance Loggia del Consiglio (p193). Stock up on local sheep's cheese at Salumeria G Albertini (p193) and sip a local classic at Caffè Filippini (p194). If you're visiting between July and September, consider taking in an evening opera at Verona's mighty Roman Arena (p191).

❼ MILAN

On day 13, catch a westbound train to high-octane Milan (p116), home of the outlandishly Gothic Duomo (p117), the Galleria Vittorio Emanuele II (p120) and opera great La Scala (p120). Ensure you're booked in to see Leonardo Da Vinci's The Last Supper (p120) the following morning. If you miss out, get your cultural fix at the Pinacoteca di Brera (p121) before a wardrobe overhaul in the fashionista heartland Quadrilatero d'Oro (p125). Looking fabulous, hit Milan's killer aperitivo scene (p123) to toast to your two-week Italian adventure.

KRZYSZTOF DYDYNSKI

Frescoes inside the Basilica di San Zeno Maggiore (p193), Verona

➘ PLANNING YOUR TRIP

ITALY'S BEST

⬈ CLASSIC ART MUSEUMS

- **Museo e Galleria Borghese** (p79) An unmissable medley of masterpieces, including sumptuous Bernini sculptures.
- **Vatican Museums** (p88) Priceless sculptures and canvases, and the incomparable Sistine Chapel.
- **Galleria degli Uffizi** (p226) Everything from blockbuster Botticellis to lesser-known gems from antiquity to the baroque.
- **Museo Archeologico Nazionale** (p279) Pompeiian mosaics, colossal statues and ancient erotica.

⬈ MODERN ART MUSEUMS

- **Peggy Guggenheim Collection** (p174) Surrealism, futurism, abstract expressionism and Peggy's ex-husband Max Ernst.

- **Palazzo Grassi** (p174) Contemporary greats in a neoclassical palace revamped by architect Tadao Ando.
- **Galleria Nazionale d'Arte Moderna e Contemporanea** (p79) Italy's modern-art top guns mixed in with the likes of Mondrian and Duchamp.
- **MADRE** (p275) From Jeff Koons' uberkitsch *Wild Boy and Puppy* to Rebecca Horn's Neapolitan-esque *Spirits*.

⬈ FOODIE REGIONS

- **Emilia-Romagna** (p194) Italy's gastronomic holy grail, home to *prosciutto di Parma, parmigiano reggiano* (Parmesan) and balsamic vinegar.
- **Piedmont** (p141) Truffles, gorgonzola, chocolate and nougat await in the home of the Slow Food Movement.

ROBERTO GEROMETTA

Piazza del Campo (p243), Siena

- **Naples & Surrounds** (p274) Real-deal pizza and *mozzarella di bufala* (buffalo-milk mozzarella) meet crispy *sfogliatelle* (ricotta-filled pastries).
- **Sicily** (p308) Cuisine with kick and Arab undertones, from wild-caught tuna and *arancini siciliani* (risotto balls) to handcrafted marzipan and ricotta-stuffed *cannoli*.

HIKING

- **Mt Etna** (p323) Scale the slopes of Europe's volcanic alpha male.
- **Parco Nazionale del Gran Paradiso** (p153) Dizzying mountain peaks, crisp Alpine valleys and thrilling wildlife encounters.
- **Sentiero degli Dei** (p293) Heavenly vistas beckon along the Amalfi Coast's 'Path of the Gods'.
- **Cinque Terre** (p137) Choose between a gentle romantic stroll and a calf-building adventure along this ultradramatic coastline.

ANCIENT MARVELS

- **Herculaneum** (p289) Pompeii might be bigger but these nearby ruins are better preserved.
- **Pantheon** (p73) Ancient Rome's finest feat of engineering.
- **Paestum** (p296) Stoic Greek temples considered among the world's finest.
- **Valley of the Temples** (p329) Magna Grecian ruins with commanding Mediterranean views.

SHOPPING LOCATIONS

- **Milan** (p116) A fashionista must.
- **Florence** (p220) Exquisite stationery, butter-soft leathergoods, gold jewellery and heavenly scented toiletries.
- **Venice** (p168) Murano glassware and Carnevale masks.
- **Sicily** (p308) Sunny ceramics, vintage marionettes, marzipan treats and sweet Marsala wine.

HILL TOWNS

- **Assisi** (p253) The hauntingly spiritual home of St Francis of Assisi.
- **Siena** (p243) Florence's historic rival, complete with baronial buildings, a liquorice-striped cathedral and showpiece central square.
- **Matera** (p338) A ravine-clinging town with a cavernous disposition.
- **Locorotondo** (p335) Rated one of Italy's most beautiful towns by www.borghitalia.it.

PLACES TO SHOUT 'ENCORE'

- **La Fenice** (p184) From Rossini to Stravinsky, this gilded theatre has lured the world's best.
- **La Scala** (p120) Catch an opera where Verdi premiered several of his own.
- **Ravello Festival** (p295) Indulge in A-list arts in the town that once wooed Wagner.
- **Teatro San Carlo** (p282) Freshly restored, Italy's largest opera house predates La Scala.

THINGS YOU NEED TO KNOW

AT A GLANCE

- **ATMs** *Bancomats* (ATMs) readily available in cities and towns
- **Credit Cards** Visa and MasterCard widely accepted
- **Currency** Euro
- **Tipping** Optional 10% for good service
- **Visas** Not required for most nationalities

ACCOMMODATION

- **Agriturismi** Farmstays range from few-frills rustic to pool-side chic; see p380.
- **B&Bs** Affordable and increasingly popular, from a room in a family home to self-contained studio apartments; see p380.
- **Convents & Monasteries** Tranquillity and an early curfew define Italy's more spiritually inclined slumber options; p381.

- **Hotels** An extensive range of options spanning cheap-and-nasty dosshouses near stations to über-luxe retreats; p382.
- **Pensioni** Like modest, smaller-scale hotels and equally prevalent; usually family-run. See p382.
- **Villa Rentals** Self-contained accommodation in pictorial rural dwellings; see p382.

ADVANCE PLANNING

- **Three months before** Shop for the cheapest and most convenient flight available (p396), book accommodation if travelling during peak times and research courses you may fancy taking.
- **One month before** Scan local tourist websites for special events or festivals (see also p46) during your stay, and book tickets where possible.

LEFT: GIORGIO COSULICH; RIGHT: TONY BURNS

Left: Outside Palazzo Pitti (p229), Florence; Right: Colourful houses, Burano (p178)

- **One week before** If taking prescription medications, ask your physician for a signed and dated letter describing your medical condition and medication. Scan or photocopy all important documents (passport, driving licence), reconfirm your accommodation bookings and book a table at that restaurant you're dying to try.

BE FOREWARNED

- **Appropriate attire** Cover torsos, shoulders and upper legs when visiting religious sites.
- **Petty theft** Be mindful of personal possessions, especially in crowded public areas; see p385.
- **Public holidays** Many restaurants and shops close for at least a part of August; see p389.

COSTS

- **€150 per day** Simple B&B or *pensione* accommodation, *panini* for lunch and dinner in a low-frills *trattoria,* a couple of museums/ sites, regional trains.
- **€150 to €300** Mid-range hotels and dinners, a couple of museums/sites, high-speed intercity trains.
- **More than €300** Top-notch hotels and dinners, domestic flights.

EMERGENCY NUMBERS

- **Ambulance** ☎ 118
- **Carabinieri/Police** ☎ 112/113
- **Fire** ☎ 115

GETTING AROUND

- **Air** Best for time-poor travellers travelling extreme distances; see p400.
- **Boat** Frequent ferries and hydrofoils connect Italy's islands to several mainland ports; see p401.
- **Bus** Handy for smaller towns, Italy's extensive bus network spans local to intercity routes; see p401.
- **Car** Rental is limited to persons aged 25 years or over; see p401.
- **Train** Italy's extensive and affordable train network spans high-speed intercity to slower regional services; see p405.

GETTING THERE & AWAY

- **Air** Rome and Milan are Italy's main intercontinental hubs; frequent European connections serve regional capitals. See p396.
- **Bus** Regular services between major Italian cities and other European hubs; see p397.
- **Train** Direct routes to neighbouring countries depart from numerous northern Italian centres; see p397.

PLANNING YOUR TRIP

THINGS YOU NEED TO KNOW

TECH STUFF

- **Electricity** Plugs have two or three round pins. The electric current is 220V, 50Hz. Older buildings may still use 125V.
- **Internet** Irregular wi-fi hot spots often require payment. Bring ID to use internet cafes; see p389.
- **Mobile Phones** Italy uses GSM 900/1800, compatible with Europe and Australia but not with North American GSM 1900 or the Japanese system. Some GSM 1900/900 phones do work; see p393.

WHAT TO BRING

- **Clothing** Smart casual clothes: T-shirts, shorts and dusty sandals don't cut it in bars and restaurants in fashion-literate Italy.
- **ID** Passport or country ID card obligatory for hotel check-in and internet cafes. Valid driving licence and car documents required if driving.
- **Insurance** Ensure comprehensive coverage (p389) for theft, cancellations and medical expenses (p387), and car insurance if driving (p402).

WHEN TO GO

- **Best months** April, May, September and October generally offer mild conditions and fewer crowds.
- **Worst months** July and August see prices and temperatures soar, and museum queues lengthen.

MARTIN HUGHES

Tourist in front of Ponte Santa Trinita (p227), Florence

GET INSPIRED

BOOKS

- **Christ Stopped at Eboli** (1947) Carlo Levi's bitter-sweet tale of an exiled dissident doctor.
- **History** (1974) War, sexual violence and a mother's struggles define Elsa Morante's controversial novel.
- **The Betrothed** (1827) Alessandro Manzoni's historical novel is one of Italy's best-selling tales.
- **The Name of the Rose** (1980) A medieval murder mystery from literary great Umberto Eco.
- **The Snack Thief** (2000) A torrent of twists keeps a maverick cop on his toes in Andrea Camilleri's whodunnit.

FILMS

- **Il Postino** (1994) Massimo Troisi plays Italy's most adorable postman.
- **La Dolce Vita** (1960) Federico Fellini's eternally chic tale of hedonism, celebrity and suicide in 1950s Rome.
- **Pane e Tulipani** (2000) A housewife runs away to Venice, befriending an anarchist florist, an eccentric masseuse and a suicidal Icelandic waiter.
- **Caro Diario** (1994) Director/actor Nanni Moretti navigates a Vespa through Rome while obsessing over the meaning of city life, insomnia and Jennifer Beales' performance in Flashdance.
- **Gomorra** (2008) An in-your-face Camorra exposé based on Roberto Saviano's best-selling book.

MUSIC

- **Mina** (Mina) One of the best-selling albums from Italy's first female rocker.
- **Terra Mia** (Pino Daniele) A critically acclaimed fusion of Neapolitan folk, tarantella, rumba and blues.
- **Crueza de mä** (Fabrizio de Andrè) Bob Dylan–esque de Andrè pays tribute to his native Genovese language.
- **Stato di Necessità** (Carmen Consoli) Gorgeous guitar riffs and soulful lyrics from one of Sicily's finest singer/songwriters.
- **Suburb** ('A67) Neapolitan rock-crossover group 'A67 collaborate with anti-Mafia journalist Roberto Saviano.

WEBSITES

- **Delicious Italy** (www.deliciousitaly.com) Find a cooking course or simply read about Italy's fabulous food and wine.
- **Ente Nazionale Italiano per il Turismo** (www.enit.it) The Italian national tourist body's website.
- **Italia Mia** (www.italiamia.com) A plethora of links, from artists and museums to cinema and genealogy.
- **Life in Italy** (www.lifeinitaly.com) The latest Italian news in English, from current affairs to fashion.
- **Lonely Planet** (lonelyplanet.com) Country-specific information as well as a user exchange on the Thorn Tree forum.

CALENDAR

| JAN | FEB | MAR | APR |

Pope Benedict XVI before the crowds at St Peter's Sq (p85), Vatican City

OSSERVATORE ROMANO/HO/EPA/CORBIS

➤ FEBRUARY–APRIL

FESTA DI SANT'AGATA   3–5 FEB

Hysterical celebrations and spectacular fireworks mark the **Feast Day of Sant'Agata** (p322), where Catholicism collides with Sicilian passion. A million locals and out-of-towners follow a bejewelled reliquary bust of the saint through Catania's main street.

CARNEVALE

In the period leading up to Ash Wednesday, many Italian towns stage carnivals and enjoy a little pre-Lent indulgence. Of them all, Venice's **Carnevale** (p179) is the most spectacular, filled with exquisitely costumed crowds, glamorous balls and baroque-inspired revelry. See www.carnevale.venezia.it.

SETTIMANA SANTA

In Rome, the pope leads a candlelit procession to the Colosseum on Good Friday before giving his blessing on Easter Sunday. In Florence, a cartful of fireworks exploded in Piazza del Duomo on Easter Sunday for the historic Scoppio del Carro (Explosion of the Cart).

➤ MAY

FESTA DI SAN GENNARO

On the first Sunday in May, the faithful gather in Naples' cathedral to wait for San Gennaro's blood to liquefy. If it does, the city is said to be safe from disaster. Repeat performances take place on 19 September and 16 December.

CORSA DEI CERI   15 MAY

This iconic festival sees three teams, each carrying a *cero* (massive wooden pillar, bearing the statue of a rival saint) race through the streets of Gubbio in commemoration of the city's patron saint, Sant'Ubaldo.

PLANNING YOUR TRIP

CALENDAR

CICLO DI RAPPRESENTAZIONI CLASSICHE

Classical intrigue in an evocative setting, the Festival of Greek Theatre brings the stones of Syracuse's 5th-century-BC amphitheatre back to life with top-notch performances from some of Italy's acting greats from mid-May to mid-June. See www.indafondazione.org.

↘ JUNE

LA BIENNALE DI VENEZIA

Held in odd-numbered years, the **Venice Biennale** (p179) is one of the art world's most prestigious events. Celebrating cutting-edge visual arts from across the globe, exhibitions are held in venues around the city from June to October or November. See www.labiennale.org.

RUTH EASTHAM & MAX PAOLI

Masked Carnevale participants

RAVELLO FESTIVAL

From June to mid-September, the Amalfi Coast town of Ravello spoils audiences with a series of world-class music and dance concerts, exhibitions, film screenings and other cultural events in stunning locations adored by writers, actors and presidents. See www.ravellofestival.com.

FESTA DI SAN GIOVANNI   24 JUN

Florence celebrates San Giovanni's feast day with the lively **Calcio Storico** (p230), a series of medieval football-style matches played on Piazza di Santa Croce. Crackling fireworks over Piazzale Michelangelo add to the revelry.

FESTIVAL DEI DUE MONDI

Held in the Umbrian hill town of Spoleto from late June to mid-July, the **Festival of the Two Worlds** (p259) is one of the world's great arts events. Spanning

MAX CESCHIA/53RD ART BIENNALE 2009

Artwork for Venice's Biennale

CALENDAR

JAN	FEB	MAR	APR

three weeks, its international offerings include theatre, dance, music and exhibitions. See www.spoletofestival.it.

PALIO DELLE QUATTRO ANTICHE REPUBBLICHE MARINARE

Historic maritime rivals Pisa, Venice, Amalfi and Genoa battle it out at the Regatta of the Four Ancient Maritime Republics. The boat race rotates between the towns: Pisa in 2010, Venice in 2011, Genoa 2012 and Amalfi 2013. Usually held in June, it is sometimes delayed as late as September.

⬎ JULY–AUGUST

IL PALIO   2 JUL & 16 AUG

Daredevils in tights thrill the crowds at this chaotic bareback horse race (p243) around Siena's main piazza. Preceding the race is a parade in medieval costume and some rather skilful flag throwing.

FESTA DEL RENDENTORE

This popular festival (p179) features gondola regattas and fireworks over the Bacino di San Marco. A specially built pontoon bridge connects the Chiesa del Redentore on the Giudecca with the rest of Venice. Third weekend in July

TAORMINA ARTE FESTIVAL

Ancient ruins and languid summer nights set a seductive scene for Taormina's esteemed arts festival (p320), spanning July and August. Featuring film, theatre and music events, its impressive line-up includes to-notch international acts. See www.taormina-arte.com.

VENICE FILM FESTIVAL

The Mostra del Cinema di Venezia (www. labiennale.org/en/cinema) draws international film glitterati with its red-carpet premieres and paparazzi glamour. Held at the Lido in late August or early September, it's a chance for Venetians to feast on the latest offerings.

DALLAS STRIBLEY

Costumed parade for Il Palio, Siena

Maria Grazia Cucinotta, 66th Venice Film Festival

REUTERS/ALESSANDRO BIANCHI

SEPTEMBER

REGATA STORICA
On the first Sunday in September, gondoliers and other skilled rowers work those biceps in this regatta, where boats in period dress are followed by gondola and other boat races along the Grand Canal in Venice.

OCTOBER

SALONE INTERNAZIONALE DEL GUSTO
Graze away at this biennial foodie expo (p146), held in Turin in even-numbered years. Run by the home-grown, anti–fast food organisation, the Slow Food Movement, it celebrates 'real food' made by traditional producers.

NOVEMBER

FESTA DI SANTA CECILIA   22 NOV
Music and art take over Siena as the city honours the patron saint of musicians with a series of concerts and exhibitions.

DECEMBER

NATALE
The weeks preceding Christmas are studded with religious events, including the set up of elaborate *presepi* (nativity scenes) in churches and homes across the country. Naples is especially famous for these, its Via San Gregorio Armeno (p278) a hot spot for *presepe*-seeking shoppers.

Regata Storica rowers

ROBERTO GEROMETTA

PLANNING YOUR TRIP

CALENDAR

GLENN BEANLAND

Laneway in Trastevere (p82)

GREATER ROME

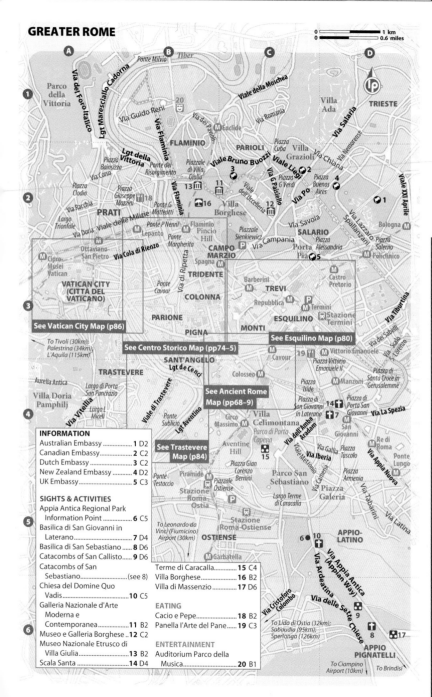

0 ——— 1 km
0 ——— 0.6 miles

INFORMATION
Australian Embassy **1** D2
Canadian Embassy **2** C2
Dutch Embassy **3** C2
New Zealand Embassy **4** D2
UK Embassy **5** C3

SIGHTS & ACTIVITIES
Appia Antica Regional Park
   Information Point **6** C5
Basilica di San Giovanni in
   Laterano **7** D4
Basilica di San Sebastiano **8** D6
Catacombs of San Callisto **9** D6
Catacombs of San
   Sebastiano .... (see 8)
Chiesa del Domine Quo
   Vadis **10** C5
Galleria Nazionale d'Arte
   Moderna e
   Contemporanea **11** B2
Museo e Galleria Borghese .. **12** C2
Museo Nazionale Etrusco di
   Villa Giulia **13** B2
Scala Santa **14** D4

Terme di Caracalla **15** C4
Villa Borghese **16** B2
Villa di Massenzio **17** D6

EATING
Cacio e Pepe **18** B2
Panella l'Arte del Pane **19** C3

ENTERTAINMENT
Auditorium Parco della
   Musica **20** B1

To Tivoli (30km);
Palestrina (34km);
L'Aquila (115km)

See Vatican City Map (p86)

See Centro Storico Map (pp74–5)

See Esquilino Map (p80)

See Ancient Rome Map (pp68–9)

See Trastevere Map (p84)

To Leonardo da
Vinci (Fiumicino)
Airport (30km)

To Lido di Ostia (32km);
Sabaudia (95km);
Sperlonga (126km)

To Ciampino
Airport (10km)

To Brindisi

ROME HIGHLIGHTS

1 MUSEO E GALLERIA BORGHESE

BY ALESSIO ZITO, TOUR GUIDE

What makes the Museo e Galleria Borghese so special is the fact there are so many important artworks in a relatively compact space. The result is less museum fatigue and a journey that takes you from the Roman period to golden-age masters like Caravaggio, Bernini, Borromini, Titian and Canova...just to name a few!

⬎ ALESSIO ZITO'S DON'T MISS LIST

❶ VENERE VINCITRICE

Antonio Canova's depiction of Napoleon's sister, Paolina Borghese, as *Venere Vincitrice* (Venus Victorious) is sublime. You could spend hours marvelling at how Canova managed to make the figure 'sink' into the cushions. The way the drapery flows so effortlessly over her body is equally impressive.

❷ RATTO DI PROSERPINA

Gian Lorenzo Bernini's sculpture *The Rape of Proserpina* (1621–2) is incred-

ible in that its twisting composition allows the simultaneous depiction of Pluto's abduction of Proserpina, their arrival in the underworld and her praying for release. To experience the narrative, start from the left, move to the front, and then view it from the right.

❸ RITRATTO DI GIOVANE DONNA CON UNICORNO

Raphael's portrait *The Young Woman with a Unicorn* (c 1506) was inspired by da Vinci's *The Lady with an Ermine*

Clockwise from top: Museo e Galleria Borghese entrance; statue in the museum gardens; Chiesa di Santa Maria del Popolo; Orangery adjacent to the museum; Canova's *Venere Vincitrice*

(1490). The painting originally depicted a woman holding a dog, a symbol of fidelity. But when the marriage did not take place, scholars believe, Raphael replaced the dog with a unicorn, a symbol of chastity or virginity.

❹ SATIRE SU DELFINO

In Sala VII, the 'Egyptian Room', you'll find the *Satyr on a Dolphin*, dating from the 2nd century and probably intended for a fountain. The piece is believed to have inspired Raphael's design for the figure of Jonah and the Whale in the Chigi Chapel inside the **Chiesa di Santa Maria del Popolo** (p79).

❺ BACCHINO MALATO

Of the many Caravaggio paintings, *Sick Bacchus* (1592–5) is particularly intrigu-

ing for its portrayal of the god of heady pleasures as a pale, tired-looking youth. Scholars believe the self-portrait was executed when Caravaggio was suffering from malaria. Cardinal Scipione Borghese, who formed the Borghese art collection, was a strong believer in the young artist's talent, buying pictures rejected by those who had commissioned them.

↘ THINGS YOU NEED TO KNOW

Only two hours? On the ground floor, check out the gladiatorial mosaics. Upstairs, focus on Canova's *Venere Vincitrice* (Sala I), Bernini's *Apollo e Daphne* (Sala III) and *Ratto di Prosperina* (Sala IV), the Caravaggios (Sala VIII) and Raphael's paintings (Sala IX) **See our author's review on p79**

ROME

ROME HIGHLIGHTS

ROME HIGHLIGHTS

2 | COLOSSEUM

BY VINCENZO MACCARRONE, COLOSSEUM STAFF MEMBER

Even before stepping foot into the ancient stadium, most visitors are gob-smacked to step out of the metro station to find the Colosseum looming before them in all its glory. Not only is this Roman arena impressive for its size and endurance, but its well-preserved condition makes for an evocative insight into ancient life.

↘ VINCENZO MACCARRONE'S DON'T MISS LIST

❶ THE ARENA

The arena had a wooden floor covered in sand to prevent combatants from slipping and to soak up blood. Gladiators arrived directly from their training ground via underground passageways, and were hoisted onto the arena by a complicated system of pulleys.

❷ THE CAVEA AND THE PODIUM

The cavea, for spectator seating, was divided into three tiers: knights in the lowest, wealthy citizens in the middle and plebs at the top. The podium – close to the action but protected by nets made of hemp – was reserved for emperors, senators and VIPs.

❸ THE FACADE

The exterior mimics the **Teatro di Marcello** (p77); the walls were once clad in travertine, with statues in the niches on the 2nd and 3rd storeys. On the top level are holes which held wooden masts supporting the Velarium (a canvas awning over the arena).

Clockwise from top: The Colosseum; Colosseum interior; Teatro di Marcello (p77); columns at the Roman Forum (p70)

➍ TEMPORARY EXHIBITIONS

The 2nd floor hosts some fantastic exhibitions, either about the Colosseum or on the wider history of Rome. Walk past the bookshop to the end of the corridor and look towards the eastern side of the **Roman Forum** (p70) – there's a wonderful view of the Tempio di Venere e Roma (Temple of Venus and Rome), hard to see from the ground.

➎ THE PERFECT PHOTO

Towards closing time, the Colosseum is bathed in a beautiful light. For great views of the building, head up Colle Oppio (Oppio Hill) right above the Colosseo metro station, or up Colle Celio (Celio Hill) opposite the Palatino and Colosseum exit.

➊ The Arena
➋ The Cavea & the Podium
➌ The Facade
➍ Temporary Exhibitions
➎ Colle Celia

0 —— 50 m
0 —— 0.02 miles

Via delle Carine
Parco San Sebastiano
Largo G Agnesi
Ⓜ Colosseo
Parco del Colle Oppio
Via Salvi
Via dei Fori Imperiali
Via Sacra
Piazza del Colosseo
Via Celio Vibenna
Viale del Parco del Celio
Parco del Celio

↘ THINGS YOU NEED TO KNOW

Best time to visit Afternoon **Best route** Take the lift to the 2nd floor for the temporary exhibitions and view of the Palatino and Roman Forum, then head down to the arena **Tickets** Buy online (www.pierreci.it) to avoid queuing **Avoid** Unofficial guides outside the entrance **See our author's review on p66**

ROME HIGHLIGHTS

3

↘ VATICAN MUSEUMS

Modesty may be a Pope-preached virtue, but it's a sentiment lost on the vainglorious **Vatican Museums** (p88), the star of which is the Sistine Chapel. While masterpieces like Botticellis, Ghirlandaios and Pinturicchios grace the walls, it's Michelangelo's ceiling and wall frescoes that take the cake, studded with terrified sinners and ravishing prophets bursting out in incredible 3-D brilliance.

4

↘ CHILLING IN TRASTEVERE

The ever-diminishing *trasteverini* (real-deal locals) consider themselves the city's true classical descendants. Fact or fiction, there's no doubt that their beloved quarter – the kicking left-bank 'hood – is a visual charmer. Crammed with ivy-tickled facades, labyrinthine laneways, vintage trattorias and buzzing squares, **Trastevere** (p82) is your best bet for a twilight Roman adventure.

5

↘ VIA APPIA ANTICA

It's hard to dispute the otherworldly lure of Rome's ancient highway, the **Via Appia Antica** (p87). Here, secret burial frescoes, saintly tombs and long-forgotten epigraphs lurk below rolling hills, crumbled mausoleums and ancient chariot racetracks. If possible, hit the strip on Sundays, when traffic is banned and Rome's 'Queen of the Roads' turns into pedal-friendly bliss.

6

↘ CULTURE AT THE AUDITORIUM

Boasting astounding acoustics – architect Renzo Piano was inspired by the interiors of lutes and violins – cutting-edge architecture and top-notch cultural offerings, **Auditorium Parco della Musica** (p99) is Europe's hottest arts venue. Culture vultures are spoilt rotten by a program as dynamic as it is democratically priced.

7

↘ CLASSICS AT THE CAPITOLINE

The **Capitoline Museums** (p72), the world's oldest public museum, is a powder keg of legend and melodrama, encapsulated in Rome's finest collection of classical treasures. Among the countless must-sees are the timid *Capitoline Venus* and the 3rd-century BC sculpture *Dying Gaul,* a moving Roman copy of a Hellenic original.

3 Sistine Chapel ceiling, Vatican Museums (p88); 4 Cafe scene, Trastevere (p82); 5 Via Appia Antica (p87); 6 Auditorium Parco dell Musica, architect Renzo Piano Building Workshop (p99); 7 Capitoline Museums artefacts (p72)

ROME'S BEST...

⬎ FREEBIES

- Watching the rain fall into the **Pantheon** (p73).
- **Vatican Museums** on the last Sunday of the month (p88).
- Crowd scanning on the **Spanish Steps** (p78).
- Il Baciccia's fresco inside the **Chiesa del Gesù** (p76).

⬎ SPOTS FOR A SWEEPING VIEW

- **Dome of St Peter's Basilica** (p85) Dizzying views of Rome and the Pope's backyard.
- **Gianicolo** (p84) A romantic jumble of spires and domes, best viewed in the late afternoon light.
- **The Vittoriano** (p72) A Roman panorama sans this hulking eyesore.
- **The Palatine** (p67) Scan the Roman Forum from the city's ancient Beverly Hills.

⬎ APERITIVO BARS

- **Freni e Frizoni** (p98) Boho-cool in a one-time garage.
- **Femme** (p98) Eye-candy crowds and lip-smacking nibbles.
- **Il Pentagrappolo** (p98) A well-versed wine list close to the Colosseum.
- **Etablì** (p98) Understated chic with a sprinkling of French antiques.

⬎ 'WHERE IT HAPPENED' HOT SPOTS

- Clarke Gable frightened Audrey Hepburn at the **Bocca della Verità** (p77) in *Roman Holiday*.
- Vestal virgins kept the sacred flame burning inside the Tempio di Vesta at the **Roman Forum** (p70).
- St Peter ran into Christ himself on the **Via Appia Antica** (p87).
- Mussolini addressed the masses from **Palazzo Venezia** (p73).

LEFT: GLENN BEANLAND; RIGHT: KRZYSZTOF DYDYNSKI

Left: Interior of the Pantheon (p73); Right: View from the Vittoriano (p72)

THINGS YOU NEED TO KNOW

⬊ VITAL STATISTICS

- **Population** 3.8 million
- **Area code** ☎06
- **Best time to visit** March to June, September & October

⬊ NEIGHBOURHOODS IN A NUTSHELL

- **Ancient Rome** Blockbuster ruins.
- **Centro Storico** Heart of the city.
- **Tridente** Catwalk couture and the Spanish Steps.
- **Villa Borghese & Around** Parklands and a superlative art museum.
- **Termini & Esquilino** An archaeological museum and the city's transport hub.
- **San Giovanni & Celio** Early Christian treasures.
- **Trastevere** Rome's lively left bank.
- **Gianicolo** Lofty city views.
- **Vatican City, Borgo & Prati** Artistic glories and media types in wine bars.
- **Via Appia & The Catacombs** Ancient burial sites.

⬊ ADVANCE PLANNING

- **One month before** Book a tour of the Tomb of St Peter (p87). Scan the Auditorium Parco della Musica (p99) website (www.auditorium. com) for upcoming events.
- **Two weeks before** Book dinner at Agata e Romeo (p94).
- **One week before** Purchase tickets online to the Vatican Museums (p88).

⬊ ONLINE RESOURCES

- **Roma Turismo** (www.roma turismo.it)
- **In Rome Now** (www.inrome now.com)
- **Pierreci** (www.pierreci.it) Online tickets for the Colosseum and other major sights.

⬊ EMERGENCY NUMBERS

- **Fire** ☎115
- **Carabinieri/Police** ☎112/113
- **Ambulance** ☎118

⬊ GETTING AROUND

- **Air** Major airlines fly to/from Leonardo da Vinci (Fiumicino). Low-cost carriers use Ciampino.
- **Bus** Handy connections between Roma Termini station and Centro Storico.
- **Metro** Useful for Ancient Rome and Vatican City.
- **Train** To or from Fiumicino airport and Ostia Antica.
- **Tram** Handy for Auditorium Parco della Musica.
- **Walk** Perfect for exploring Rome's distinct neighbourhoods.

⬊ BE FOREWARNED

- **Museums** Most close on Monday.
- **Restaurants** Many close in August for the summer break.
- **Museo e Galleria Borghese** (p79) Call ahead to pre-book tickets.
- **Pickpockets** Operate on transport and at tourist sites.

ROME

THINGS YOU NEED TO KNOW

ROME

DISCOVER ROME

In this country so blessed with exquisite cities, Rome is the daddy of them all. As addictive as a charming, exasperating lover, it will try your patience but steal your heart. There are too many reasons to fall in love with Rome: the masterpieces around every corner (the Sistine Chapel, St Peter's, the Pantheon and countless Caravaggios, to name a few), the sultry summer nights, the shade-wearing, scooter-driving Romans, the operatic piazzas and the bombastic theatrical splendour of the Vatican. Then there's the irrepressible charm of the population (fuelled by perfect coffee and bathed in perpetual sunshine), the scale of the Colosseum, the joy of getting lost in ivy-coated backstreets, the cocktail of provinciality and sophistication, and the colour palette of blue sky, ochre terracotta and deep-green umbrella pines. Rome's sheer brilliance means that you can, most of the time, forgive its less-endearing traits: the traffic, the 'every person for themself' attitude, the conservatism, the potholes, the crazy parking and the pickpockets.

DISCOVER ROME

ROME IN...

Two Days

Visit **St Peter's Basilica** (p85), the **Vatican Museums** (p88) and the **Sistine Chapel** (p88). Lunch around **Piazza Navona** (p76), before popping into the **Pantheon** (p73), en route to the **Colosseum** (p66) and the **Roman Forum** (p70). Make a night of it in vibrant **Trastevere** (p82).

After a leisurely breakfast, wander over to the **Trevi Fountain** (p77) and **Piazza di Spagna** (p78), where the **Spanish Steps** (p78) provide excellent people-watching opportunities. In the nearby **Villa Borghese** (p79), the **Museo e Galleria Borghese** (p79) is a highlight of any visit.

Four Days

Visit the **Galleria Doria Pamphilj** (p73), a mini-Versailles, or check out the fabulous **Palazzo Massimo alle Terme** (p81) before revelling in the quiet of the **Jewish Ghetto** (p76) and wandering some bijou backstreets such as Via del Governo Vecchio or Via dei Coronari.

Back on the museum trail, visit the **Capitoline Museums** (p72).

HISTORY

According to myth, vestal virgin Rhea Silva and Mars, God of War, was the dysfunctional coupling that spawned Romulus and Remus. Set adrift on the Tiber to escape King Amulius' death warrant, the twins were found and suckled by a broody she-wolf. When Remus was captured by Amulius, Romulus killed the king and rescued his brother. They began to found a new town, but squabbles led to fratricide, and Romulus went on to take sole credit. Historians proffer a more prosaic version of events, involving Romulus becoming the first king of Rome (Roma) on 21 April 753 BC and an amalgamation of Etruscan, Latin and Sabine settlements on the Palatine, Esquiline and Quirinale Hills.

Following the deposition of the last Etruscan king, Tarquin the Proud, the Roman Republic was founded in 509 BC, establishing itself as the dominant Western superpower until internal rivalries led to civil war. Julius Caesar wrested power in BC 49, and began to dramatically reform the Republic. He was assassinated five years later, leaving Mark Antony and Octavian to fight for the top job. Octavian prevailed and, with the blessing of the Senate, became Augustus, the first Roman emperor.

Augustus ruled well and a period of political stability and unparalleled artistic achievement ensued, but his successors, rulers such as Tiberius, Caligula and Nero, were contrastingly corrupt and depraved. Their efforts, and events such as the Great

ROME

HISTORY

CLOCKWISE FROM TOP: KRZYSZTOF DYDYNSKI; TONY BURNS; GREG ELMS; DAVID TOMLINSON

Clockwise from top: St Peter's Basilica (p85) facade; Staircase at the Vatican Museums (p88); Typical Via dei Coronari shop; Statue of Constantine, Capitoline Museums (p72)

Fire of AD 64, combined to leave Rome in tatters, yet the city bounced back. By 100, it had a population of 1.5 million and was the undisputed *Caput Mundi* (capital of the world). But it couldn't last and when, in 330, Constantine moved his power base to Byzantium, Rome's glory days were numbered.

By the 6th century, Rome's population had shrunk to a measly 80,000. However God was on the city's side. Christianity had been spreading since the 1st century AD thanks to the underground efforts of apostles Peter and Paul, and under Constantine it received official recognition. Pope Gregory I (590–604) did much to strengthen the Church's grip over the city and, in 774, Rome's place as centre of the Christian world was cemented when Pope Leo III crowned Charlemagne as Holy Roman Emperor.

The medieval period was marked by continuous fighting by just about anyone capable of raising an army. In the thick of things, the Papal States fought their corner as ruthlessly as anyone.

In 1309, however, Pope Clement V decided enough was enough and upped sticks to Avignon, leaving the powerful Colonna and Orsini families to contest control of the city. Once the waters had calmed, Pope Gregory XI returned to Rome in 1377 and, finding the city close to ruins, set up home in the fortified Vatican.

Out of the ruins grew the Rome of the Renaissance. At the behest of the great papal dynasties – the Barberini, Farnese and Pamphilj among others – the leading artists of the 15th and 16th centuries were summoned to work on projects such as the Sistine Chapel and St Peter's Basilica. But the enemy was never far away, and in 1527 Pope Clement VII took refuge in Castel Sant'Angelo as Charles V's Spanish forces ransacked Rome.

Another rebuild was in order, and it was to the 17th-century baroque masters Bernini and Borromini that Rome's patrons turned.

The next makeover followed the unification of Italy and the declaration of Rome as its capital. Mussolini, believing himself a modern-day Augustus, left an indelible stamp, bulldozing new imperial roads and commissioning ambitious building projects such as the monumental suburb of EUR.

Post-Fascism, the 1950s and '60s saw the glittering era of *la dolce vita* and hasty urban expansion, resulting in Rome's sometimes wretched suburbs. A cleanup in 2000 rendered the city in better shape than for decades, and in recent years some dramatic modernist building projects have given the Eternal City some edge, such as Richard Meier's Museo dell'Ara Pacis (p78) and Centro Congressi 'Nuvola' by Massimiliano Fuksas.

ORIENTATION

Rome is a sprawling city, but most sights lie within the *centro storico* (historical centre; comprising the areas around the Piazza Navona, Campo de' Fiori, Pantheon, Ghetto, Capitoline, Piazza Barberini, Trevi and Tridente). Vatican City and Trastevere are over the water on the west bank of the Tiber.

The city's major transport hub, Stazione Termini (its full name is Stazione Centrale-Roma Termini) is a useful point of reference. The majority of the city's budget hotels and *pensioni* (small hotels or guesthouses) are in this slightly sleazy area and the main city bus terminus is on Piazza Cinquecento, in front of the train station.

From Piazza Cinquecento, Via Cavour leads directly down to the Roman Forum, while from Piazza della Repubblica,

Piazza Navona (p76)

GLENN BEANLAND

a short walk to the west of Stazione Termini, Via Nazionale heads down towards Piazza Venezia. Running north from Piazza Venezia, Via del Corso leads up to Piazza del Popolo and the Villa Borghese.

INFORMATION
EMERGENCY
Ambulance (☎ 118)
Police (☎ 113/112)
Main police station (Questura; Map p80; ☎ 06 46 86; Via San Vitale 11)
Ufficio Stranieri (Foreigners' Bureau; Map p80; ☎ 06 468 63 216; Via Genova 2; ☼ 24hr) Thefts can be reported here.

MONEY
There's a bank, ATMs and several currency exchange booths at Stazione Termini (Map p80), Fiumicino airport and Ciampino airport. In town, there are loads of ATMs and numerous exchange booths, including **American Express** (Map pp74-5; ☎ 06 6 76 41; Piazza di Spagna 38; ☼ 9am-5.30pm Mon-Fri, 9am-12.30pm Sat).

POST
There are post office branches at Piazza dei Capretti 69, Via Terme di Diocleziane 30 (Map p80), Via della Scrofa 61/63 (Map pp74-5), Stazione Termini (next to platform 24) and Via Arenula (Map pp74-5).
Main post office (Map pp74-5; ☎ 06 679 37 213; Piazza di San Silvestro 20; ☼ 8.30am-6.30pm Mon-Fri, 8.30am-1pm Sat)

TOURIST INFORMATION
Enjoy Rome (Map p80; ☎ 06 445 18 43; www.enjoyrome.com; Via Marghera 8a; ☼ 8.30am-7pm Mon-Fri, 8.30am-2pm Sat Apr-Sep, 9am-5.30 Mon-Fri & 8.30am-2pm Sat Oct-Mar)
Rome Tourist Board (APT; ☎ 06 06 08; www.romaturismo.it; ☼ 9am-6pm) Has an office at Fiumicino airport in Terminal B, International Arrivals.

The Comune di Roma (city council) runs a free multilingual **tourist information line** (☎ 06 06 08; www.060608.it; ☼ 9am-9pm), providing information on culture, shows, hotels, transport etc; you can also book theatre, concert, exhibition and museum tickets on this number. If you need

ROME

SIGHTS

Cyclists in the Domus Augustana (p70)

MARTIN MOOS

practical information, the city's free ☎ 06 06 06 number is incredibly useful. The Comune also publishes the useful monthly 'What's On' pamphlet: *L'Evento* as well as *Un Ospite a Roma* (A Guest in Rome; www.unospitearoma.it, www.aguestinrome.com). These, and other information (including maps), can be picked up at the following tourist information points:

Castel Sant'Angelo (Map p86; Piazza Pia; ✦ 9.30am-7pm)

Ciampino airport (International Arrivals, baggage reclaim area; ✦ 9am-6.30pm)

Fiumicino airport (Terminal C, International Arrivals; ✦ 9am-6.30pm)

Piazza Navona (Map pp74-5; ✦ 9.30am-7pm) Near Piazza delle Cinque Lune.

Piazza Santa Maria Maggiore (Map p80; Via dell'Olmata; ✦ 9.30am-7pm)

Piazza Sonnino (Map p84; ✦ 9.30am-7pm)

Stazione Termini (Map p80; ✦ 8am-8.30pm) Next to platform 24.

Trevi Fountain (Map pp74-5; Via Marco Minghetti; ✦ 9.30am-7pm) This tourist point is nearer to Via del Corso than the fountain.

Via dei Fori Imperiali (Map pp68-9; Piazza del Tempio della Pace; ✦ 9.30am-7pm)

Via Nazionale (Map p80; ✦ 9.30am-7pm)

SIGHTS

They say that a lifetime's not long enough for Rome – *Roma, non basta una vita!* So the best plan is to choose selectively what to see, and leave the rest for next time.

ANCIENT ROME
COLOSSEUM

The **Colosseum** (Colosseo; Map pp68-9; ☎ 06 399 67 700; www.pierreci.it; Piazza del Colosseo; incl Palatine adult/EU 18-24yr/EU under 18yr & over 65yr €9/4.50/free, plus possible €3 exhibition supplement, ticket valid 2 days; ✦ 8.30am-6.15pm Apr-Aug, 8.30am-6pm Sep, 8.30am-5.30pm Oct, 8.30am-4.30pm mid-end Mar, 8.30am-4pm mid-Feb–mid-Mar, 8.30am-3.30pm Nov–mid-Feb) is the most extraordinary of all Rome's monuments. It's not just the amazing completeness of the place, or its size, but the sense of its gory history that resonates: it was here that gladiators met in mortal combat and condemned prisoners fought off hungry lions. Don't let the lengthy queue put you off: just pop down to the Palatine ticket office, buy your combined ticket there, and on returning march straight in.

Built by the emperor Vespasian (r AD 69–79) in the grounds of Nero's palatial **Domus Aurea** complex, the Colosseum was inaugurated in AD 80. To mark the occasion, Vespasian's son and successor Titus (r 79–81) held games that lasted 100 days and nights, during which some 5000 animals were slaughtered.

ARCO DI COSTANTINO

On the western side of the Colosseum, the **Arco di Costantino** (Map pp68-9) was built to honour Constantine following his victory over rival Maxentius at the battle of Ponte Milvio (Milvian bridge; northwest of Villa Borghese) in AD 312.

THE PALATINE

Just down the road overlooking the Roman Forum, the **Palatine** (Map pp68-9; ☎ 06 399 67 700; www.pierreci.it; Via di San Gregorio 30; admission incl Museo Palatino, Colosseum & Roman Forum adult/EU 18-24yr/EU under 18yr & over 65yr €9/4.50/free, plus possible €3 exhibition supplement, ticket valid 2 days, audioguide €4 or €6 incl Roman Forum; ⏲ 8.30am-6.15pm Apr-Aug, 8.30am-6pm Sep, 8.30am-5.30pm Oct, 8.30am-4.30pm mid-end Mar, 8.30am-4pm mid-Feb–mid-Mar, 8.30am-3.30pm Nov–mid-Feb) was ancient Rome's Beverly Hills. Romulus killed his brother Remus and founded Rome here in 753 BC, and from 500 BC, Rome's most affluent citizens set up residence in the area.

The largest part is covered by the remains of Emperor Domitian's vast complex, which served as the main imperial palace for 300 years.

On entering the complex from Via di San Gregorio, head uphill until you come

MAKING THE MOST OF YOUR EURO

Appia Antica Card (€7.50, valid seven days) For the Terme di Caracalla, Mausoleo di Cecilia Metella and Villa Quintili.

Archaeologia Card (€23.50, valid seven days) For entrance to the Colosseum, Palatine, Terme di Caracalla, Palazzo Altemps, Palazzo Massimo alle Terme, Terme di Diocleziano, Crypta Balbi, Mausoleo di Cecilia Metella and Villa Quintili.

Roma Pass (€23, valid three days; www.romapass.it) Includes free admission to two museums or sites (choose from a list of 38) as well as reduced entry to extra sites, unlimited public transport within Rome, access to the bike-sharing scheme and reduced price entry to other exhibitions and events. If you use this for more-expensive sights such as the Capitoline Museums and the Colosseum you'll save a considerable amount of money.

You can buy the cards at any of the monuments or museums listed (or online at www.pierreci.it) and the Roma Pass is also available at Comune di Roma tourist information points.

Note that EU citizens between the ages of 18 and 24 and over the age of 65 are entitled to significant discounts at most museums and galleries in Rome. Unfortunately student discounts don't usually apply for citizens of non-EU countries.

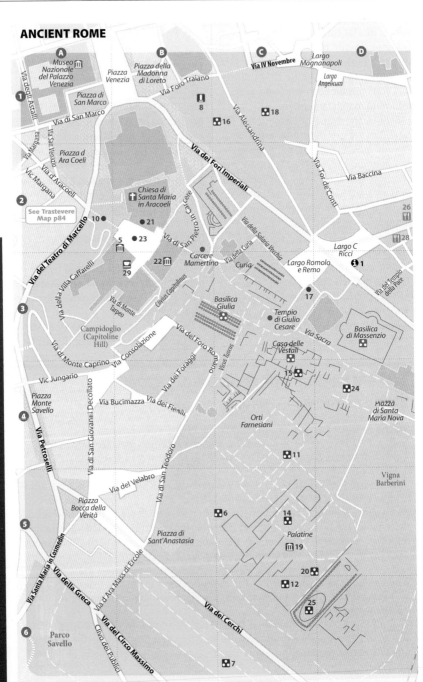

ANCIENT ROME

ANCIENT ROME

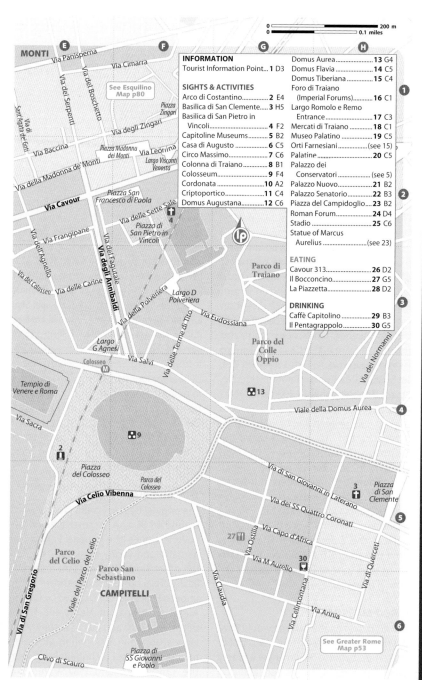

INFORMATION

Tourist Information Point... **1** D3

SIGHTS & ACTIVITIES

Arco di Costantino.............**2** E4
Basilica di San Clemente....**3** H5
Basilica di San Pietro in
  Vincoli.........................**4** F2
Capitoline Museums...........**5** B2
Casa di Augusto **6** C5
Circo Massimo....................**7** C6
Colonna di Traiano.............**8** B1
Colosseum..........................**9** F4
Cordonata.........................**10** A2
Criptoportico.....................**11** C4
Domus Augustana..............**12** C6

Domus Aurea.....................**13** G4
Domus Flavia **14** C5
Domus Tiberiana................**15** C4
Foro di Traiano
  (Imperial Forums)...........**16** C1
Largo Romolo e Remo
  Entrance.......................**17** C3
Mercati di Traiano **18** C1
Museo Palatino **19** C5
Orti Farnesiani ....(see 15)
Palatine **20** C5
Palazzo dei
  Conservatori ....(see 5)
Palazzo Nuovo...................**21** B2
Palazzo Senatorio..............**22** B3
Piazza del Campidoglio......**23** B2
Roman Forum....................**24** D4
Stadio **25** C6
Statue of Marcus
  Aurelius ....(see 23)

EATING

Cavour 313.......................**26** D2
Il Bocconcino.....................**27** G5
La Piazzetta.......................**28** D2

DRINKING

Caffè Capitolino **29** B3
Il Pentagrappolo................**30** G5

See Esquilino
Map p80

See Greater Rome
Map p53

to the first recognisable construction, the **stadio** (Map pp68-9), probably used by the emperors for private games and events.

On the other side of the stadio are the ruins of the huge **Domus Augustana** (Map pp68-9), the emperor's private residence.

The grey building near the Domus Augustana houses the **Museo Palatino** (8am-4pm) and its collection of archaeological artefacts.

North of the museum is the **Domus Flavia** (Map pp68-9), the public part of Domitian's huge palace complex.

Among the best-preserved buildings on the Palatine is the **Casa di Livia**, northwest of the Domus Flavia. Home to Augustus' wife Livia, it was built around an atrium leading onto what were once reception rooms, decorated with frescoes of mythological scenes, landscapes, fruits and flowers. In front is the **Casa di Augusto** (entry in groups of five; 11am-3.30pm Mon, Wed, Sat & Sun), Augustus' separate residence. Opened to the public in 2008 after years of restoration, it contains superb frescoes in vivid reds, yellows and blues.

Northeast of the Casa di Livia lies the **Criptoportico** (Cryptoporticus; Map pp68-9), a 128m tunnel where Caligula was thought to have been murdered, and which Nero later used to connect his Domus Aurea with the Palatine.

The area west of this was once Tiberius' palace, the Domus Tiberiana, but is now the site of the 16th-century **Orti Farnesiani**, one of Europe's earliest botanical gardens.

CIRCO MASSIMO

The emperors on the Palatine would have overlooked **Circo Massimo** (Map pp68-9), Rome's largest stadium, now a grassy basin used mainly by joggers and dog walkers, and for the occasional concert. Chariot races were held here as far back as the 4th century BC, but it wasn't until Trajan rebuilt it after the AD 64 fire that it reached its maximum grandeur.

ROMAN FORUM

In ancient Rome, a forum was a covered market, civic centre and religious complex all rolled into one. The centre of public life, it was richly decorated and grandly scaled. Today a sprawl of underlabelled ruins, the **Roman Forum** (Foro Romano; Map pp68-9; 06 399 67 700; www.pierreci.it; entrances at Largo Romolo e Remo 5-6 & Via di San Gregorio 30; admission incl Colosseum & Palatine adult/EU 18-24yr/EU under 18yr & over 65yr €9/4.50/ free, plus possible €3 exhibition supplement, ticket valid 2 days, audioguide €4 or €6 incl Palatine; 8.30am-6.15pm Apr-Aug, 8.30am-6pm Sep, 8.30am-5.30pm Oct, 8.30am-4.30pm mid-end Mar, 8.30am-4pm mid-Feb–mid-Mar, 8.30am-3.30pm Nov–mid-Feb) is still impressive – overlook it from Palazzo Senatorio behind Piazza del Campidoglio to set your imagination in gear. The oldest and most famous of Rome's forums, it was originally an Etruscan burial ground, first developed in the 7th century BC and expanding over 900 years to become the gleaming heart of the Roman Republic.

THE IMPERIAL FORUMS

The original Roman Forum got too small around 46 BC and successive emperors built new ones (the Imperial Forums) as demand and vanity required. Thus, on the other side of Via dei Fori Imperiali, lie the collection of forums known as the **Imperial Forums**. Constructed by Caesar, Augustus, Vespasian, Nerva and Trajan between 42 BC and AD 112, they were largely buried in 1933 when Mussolini bulldozed Via dei Fori Imperiali between the Colosseum and Piazza Venezia.

ROME

WILL SALTER
Roman Forum

SIGHTS

Excavations have since unearthed much of them, but work continues and visits are limited to the **Foro di Traiano** (Trajan's Forum), accessible through the Museo dei Fori Imperiali

The **Mercati di Traiano & Museo dei Fori Imperiali** (Map pp68-9; ☎ 06 820 59 127; www.mercatiditraiano.it; Via IV Novembre 94; adult/concession €6.50/4.50, audioguide €3.50; ⏰ 9am-7pm Tue-Sun, last entry 6pm) is a striking new museum that brings alive Trajan's great 2nd-century market complex. The museum's real highlight is the access it gives to Trajan's Forum. From the main hallway, a lift whisks you up to the **Torre delle Milizie** (Militia Tower; Map p80), a 13th-century red-brick tower, and the upper levels of the Mercati di Traiano (Trajan's Markets). These markets, housed in a three-storey semicircular construction, were Trajan's frenetic commercial precinct, with hundreds of traders selling everything from oil and vegetables to flowers, silks and spices.

Little recognisable remains of the forum except for some pillars from the **Basilica Ulpia** and the **Colonna di Traiano** (Trajan's Column), whose minutely detailed reliefs celebrate Trajan's military victories over the Dacians (from modern-day Romania).

CAMPIDOGLIO

Rising above the Roman Forum, the Campidoglio (Capitoline Hill) was one of the seven hills on which Rome was founded. An important political and spiritual site, it was considered the heart of the Roman Republic.

The most dramatic approach is via the **Cordonata** (Map pp68-9), Michelangelo's graceful staircase that leads up from Piazza d'Aracoeli.

Designed by Michelangelo in 1538, the beautiful **Piazza del Campidoglio** (Map pp68-9) is bordered by three *palazzi*: Palazzo Nuovo to the left, Palazzo Senatorio straight ahead and Palazzo dei Conservatori on the right. Together, Palazzo Nuovo and Palazzo dei Conservatori house the Capitoline

ROME

SIGHTS

Museums, while Palazzo Senatorio houses Rome's city council.

In the centre of the square, the bronze equestrian **statue of Marcus Aurelius** (Map pp68-9) is a copy. The original, which dates from the 2nd century AD, was in the piazza from 1538 until 1981, when it was moved to a glass annexe within Palazzo Nuovo to protect it from erosion.

The world's oldest national museums, the **Capitoline Museums** (Musei Capitolini; Map pp68-9; ☎ 06 820 59 127; www.museicapi tolini.org; Piazza del Campidoglio 1; adult/EU 18-25yr/EU under 18yr & over 65yr €6.50/4.50/free, incl exhibition €9/7/free, incl Centrale Montemartini & exhibition €11/9/free, audioguide €5; ⏰ 9am-8pm Tue-Sun, last admission 7pm) were founded in 1471 when Pope Sixtus IV donated a few bronze sculptures to the city, forming the nucleus of what is now one of Italy's finest collections of classical art.

The main entrance to the museums is in **Palazzo dei Conservatori** (Map pp68-9), where you'll find the original core of the sculptural collection and, on the 2nd floor, a masterpiece-packed art gallery.

CENTRO STORICO
PIAZZA VENEZIA

Traffic and people-thronged Piazza Venezia is dominated by a garish lapse of taste, the mammoth, white marble **Vittoriano** (Map pp74-5; ☎ 06 699 17 18; www.ambienterm.arti.beni culturali.it/vittoriano/index.htm; Piazza Venezia; admission free; ⏰ 10am-4pm Tue-Sun), nicknamed 'the typewriter'. Almost endearingly monstrous, it's official name is the Altare della Patria (Altar of the Fatherland). It was begun in 1885 to commemorate Italian unification and honour Vittorio Emanuele II, Italy's first king and the subject of the gargantuan equestrian statue. It also hosts the Tomb of the Unknown Soldier, which means that you can't sit anywhere on the monument, a rule the hawk-eyed guardians strictly enforce.

Climb up to the top though, and the 360-degree views are stunning, especially at night when the entire city is lit up beneath you. To get to the top, take the glass lift, **Roma del Cielo** (adult/concession €7/3.50; ⏰ 9.30am-6.30pm Mon-Thu, 9.30am-7.30pm Fri-Sun) from the back of the building.

Trevi Fountain (p77)

GREG ELMS

Inside the body of the structure, the **Museo Centrale del Risorgimento** (Map pp74-5; ☎ 06 679 35 98; Via di San Pietro in Carcere; admission free; ⏲ 9.30am-6pm), often referred to as the Complesso del Vittoriano, hosts temporary art exhibitions and a small collection of military knick-knacks documenting the history of Italian unification.

On the western side of the piazza is the Renaissance **Palazzo Venezia** (Map pp74-5), where Mussolini had his official residence – he used to make speeches from the balcony. To see inside, visit the sprawling, under-visited **Museo Nazionale del Palazzo Venezia** (Map pp74-5; ☎ 06 699 94 318; entrance at Via del Plebiscito 118; adult/concession €4/2; ⏲ 8.30am-7.30pm Tue-Sun) with its superb Byzantine and early Renaissance paintings and eclectic collection of jewellery, tapestries, ceramics, bronze figurines, arms and armour.

PANTHEON & AROUND

Competition is fierce, but the **Pantheon** (Map pp74-5; ☎ 06 683 00 230; Piazza della Rotonda; admission free, audioguide €4; ⏲ 8.30am-7.30pm Mon-Sat, 9am-6pm Sun) is surely ancient Rome's most astonishing building. Its current form dates to around AD 120, when the emperor Hadrian built the Pantheon over Marcus Agrippa's original temple (27 BC).

Its harmonious appearance is due to a precisely calibrated symmetry – its diameter is exactly equal to the Pantheon's interior height of 43.3m.

South of the Pantheon, the Piazza della Minerva is home to Bernini's **Elefantino** (Map pp74-5), a curious, endearing sculpture of an elephant supporting a 6th-century-BC Egyptian obelisk. On the eastern flank of the square is the 13th-century Dominican **Chiesa di Santa Maria Sopra Minerva** (Map pp74-5; ☎ 06 679 39 26; Piazza della Minerva; ⏲ 8am-7pm). Built on the

Galleria Doria Pamphilj entrance

WILL SALTER

➘ PALAZZO DORIA PAMPHILJ

Just north of Piazza Venezia is the **Palazzo Doria Pamphilj**, home to the **Galleria Doria Pamphilj**. You wouldn't know it from the grimy exterior but this *palazzo* houses one of Rome's richest private art collections, with works by Raphael, Tintoretto, Brueghel, Titian, Caravaggio, Bernini and Velázquez.

Palazzo Doria Pamphilj dates to the mid-15th century but the interior resembles a mini-Versailles, the work of the Doria Pamphilj family, who acquired it in the 18th century.

Things you need to know: Palazzo Doria Pamphilj (Map pp74-5; cnr Via del Corso & Via del Plebiscito); Galleria Doria Pamphilj (☎ 06 679 73 23; www.doria pamphilj.it; Via del Corso 305; adult/concession €9/6; ⏲ 10am-5pm daily, ticket office closes 6.15pm)

site of an ancient temple to Minerva, this is Rome's only Gothic church. Left of the high altar is one of Michelangelo's lesser-known sculptures, *Cristo Risorto* (Christ Bearing the Cross; 1520), to which blush-saving bronze drapery was later added.

An imposing, much-copied example of Counter-Reformation architecture, the

CENTRO STORICO

INFORMATION
American Express.................1 F4
Bed & Breakfast Italia............2 B6
French Embassy...............(see 27)
Main Post Office.....................3 E5
Post Office 4 D8
Post Office 5 D5
Tourist Information Point.........6 C6
Tourist Information Point.........7 F6

SIGHTS & ACTIVITIES
Barcaccia 8 F4
Battelli di Roma...............(see 34)
Campo de' Fiori......................9 C8
Castel Sant'Angelo............10 A5
Chiesa del Gesù..................11 E8
Chiesa di San Luigi dei Francesi.........12 D6
Chiesa di Santa Maria dei Miracoli.........13 D2
Chiesa di Santa Maria del Popolo.........14 D1
Chiesa di Santa Maria in Montesanto.........15 D2
Chiesa di Santa Maria Sopra Minerva.........16 E7
Chiesa di Sant'Agnese in Agone.........17 C6
Chiesa di Sant'Agostino...18 D5
Elefantino...........................19 D7
Fontana dei Quattro Fiumi.........20 C6
Galleria Doria Pamphilj..(see 26)
Keats-Shelley Memorial House.........21 F4
Museo Centrale del Risorgimento.........22 F8
Museo dell'Ara Pacis..........23 D3
Museo Nazionale del Palazzo Venezia...........(see 28)
Museo Nazionale Romano: Crypti Balbi.........24 E8
Museo Nazionale Romano: Palazzo Altemps.........25 C5
Obelisk.............................(see 30)
Palazzo Doria Pamphilj.....26 F7
Palazzo Farnese...................27 B8
Palazzo Venezia...................28 F8
Pantheon.............................29 D7
Piazza del Popolo................30 D1
Piazza di Spagna 31 F3
Piazza Navona......................32 C6
Pincio Hill Gardens 33 E1
Ponte Sant'Angelo..............34 A5
Porta del Popolo 35 D1
Spanish Steps......................36 F3
Trevi Fountain.....................37 F6
Trinità dei Monti.................38 F3
Vittoriano............................39 F8

SLEEPING
Casa Montani 40 D1
Portrait Suites......................41 E4
Teatropace 33 ....42 C6

EATING
Ara Coeli.............................43 E8
Campo de' Fiori Market ...(see 9)
Da Michele 44 F6
Forno di Campo de' Fiori..45 C8
Gelateria Giolitti 46 D6
Gino......................................47 E5
Il Margutta 48 E2
Palatium 49 E4
Pizzeria da Baffetto.............50 B7

DRINKING
Caffè Farnese 51 C8
Caffè Sant'Eustachio..........52 D7
Caffé Tazza d'Oro................53 D6
Etablì.....................................54 C6
Femme..................................55 C7
Il Goccetto............................56 B7
L'Antica Enoteca.................57 E3
Salotto 42.............................58 E6
Société Lutèce......................59 C6
Stravinskij Bar – Hotel de Russie.........60 D2

SHOPPING
Ai Monasteri.........................61 C6
Fausto Santini.......................62 F4
Officina Profumo Farmaceutica di Santa Maria Novella.........63 C7
Sermoneta.............................64 F4

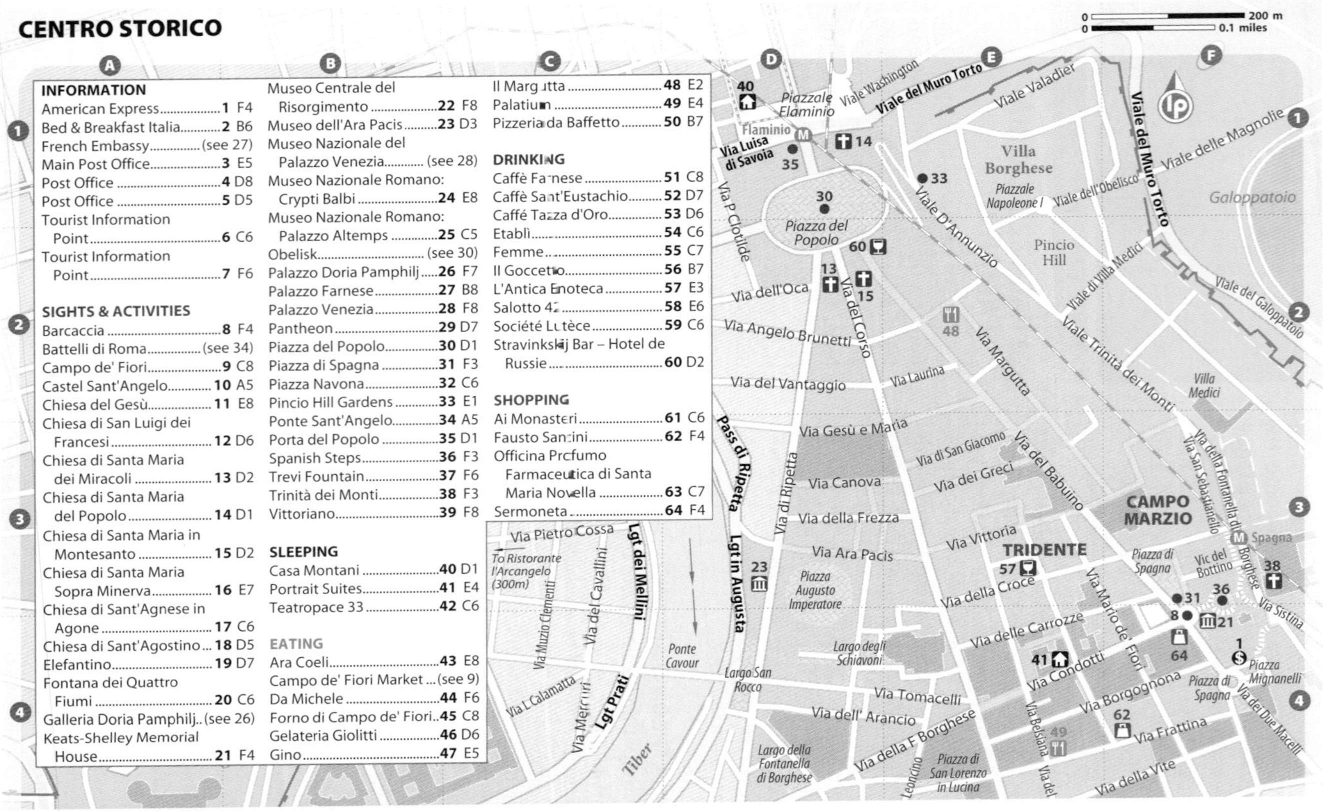

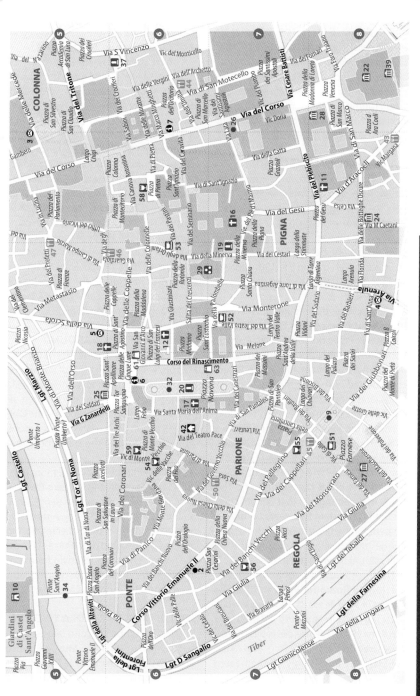

ROME

SIGHTS

Chiesa del Gesù (Map pp74-5; ☎ 06 69 70 01; www.chiesadelgesu.org; Piazza del Gesù; ⏰ 7am-12.30pm & 4-7.45pm), is Rome's most important Jesuit church. Of the art on display, the most astounding is the *Trionfo del Nome di Gesù* (Triumph of the Name of Jesus), the swirling, hypnotic vault fresco by Giovanni Battista Gaulli (aka Il Baciccia).

PIAZZA NAVONA & AROUND
With its baroque *palazzi* and extravagant fountains, pavement cafes, hawkers, and ebbing, flowing crowds, stadium-sized **Piazza Navona** (Map pp74-5) is Rome's most iconic public square. Laid out on the ruins of an arena built by Domitian in AD 86, it was paved over in the 15th century and for almost 300 years was the city's main market.

Of the piazza's three fountains, Bernini's high-camp **Fontana dei Quattro Fiumi** (Fountain of the Four Rivers; Map pp74-5) dominates. Symbolising Catholic might, it depicts the Nile, Ganges, Danube and Plate, is festooned with a palm tree, lion and horse, and topped by an obelisk. Legend has it that the figure of the Nile is shielding his eyes from the **Chiesa di Sant'Agnese in Agone** (Map pp74-5; ☎ 06 681 92 134; www.santagneseinagone.com; ⏰ 9.30am-12.30pm & 4-7pm Mon-Sat, 10am-1pm & 4-8pm Sun), designed by Bernini's bitter rival, Borromini. The truth, more boringly, is that Bernini completed his fountain two years before his contemporary started work on the facade. The gesture indicates that the source of the Nile was unknown at the time.

North of Piazza Navona, the **Museo Nazionale Romano: Palazzo Altemps** (Map pp74-5; ☎ 06 683 35 66; www.pierreci.it; Piazza Sant'Apollinare 44; adult/EU 18-24yr/EU under 18yr & over 65yr €7/3.50/free, plus possible €3 exhibition supplement, audioguide €4; ⏰ 9am-7.45pm Tue-Sun) feels surprisingly off the beaten track, and houses the best of the Museo

Nazionale Romano's formidable collection of classical sculpture, beautifully lit.

A short walk away are two churches that no art-lover should miss. The **Chiesa di Sant'Agostino** (Map pp74-5; ☎ 06 688 01 962; Piazza di Sant'Agostino; ⏰ 7.45am-noon & 4-7.30pm) contains two outstanding works of art: Raphael's 1512 fresco of Isaiah, and the *Madonna of the Pilgrims* (1604) by Caravaggio. Nearby, Caravaggio dominates the baroque **Chiesa di San Luigi dei Francesi** (Map pp74-5; ☎ 06 68 82 71; Piazza di San Luigi dei Francesi; ⏰ 10am-12.30pm & 4-7pm, closed Thu afternoon), church to Rome's French community since 1589. His three canvases make up the St Matthew cycle: *La Vocazione di San Matteo* (The Calling of Saint Matthew), *Il Martirio di San Matteo* (The Martyrdom of Saint Matthew) and *San Matteo e l'Angelo* (Saint Matthew and the Angel).

CAMPO DE' FIORI & AROUND
Noisy, colourful **Campo de' Fiori** (Il Campo; Map pp74-5) is a major focus of Roman life: by day it hosts a much-loved market, while at night it morphs into a raucous open-air pub. Towering over the square is the Obi-Wan–like form of Giordano Bruno, a monk who was burned at the stake for heresy in 1600.

Overlooking the adjoining, more tranquil Piazza Farnese, the **Palazzo Farnese** (Map pp74-5) is a magnificent Renaissance building. Started in 1514 by Antonio da Sangallo, continued by Michelangelo and finished by Giacomo della Porta, it is now the French embassy. The twin fountains in the square are enormous granite baths taken from the Terme di Caracalla.

JEWISH GHETTO & ISOLA TIBERINA
Housed in Europe's second largest synagogue, built in 1904, the **Museo Ebraico di Roma** (Jewish Museum of Rome; Map p84; ☎ 06 684 00 661; www.museoebraico.roma.it; Via Catalana;

adult/student/under 10yr €7.50/4/free; ⏱ 10am-6.15pm Sun-Thu, 10am-3.15pm Fri mid-Jun–mid-Sep, 10am-4.15pm Sun-Thu, 9am-1.15pm Fri mid-Sep–mid-Jun) chronicles the historical, cultural and artistic heritage of Rome's Jewish community. You can also book a one-hour guided walking tour of the Ghetto (adult/student €8/5) at the museum.

To the east of the Ghetto is the archaeological area of the **Portico d'Ottavia** (Map p84; Via del Teatro di Marcello; ⏱ 9am-7pm summer, 9am-6pm winter), the oldest *quadriporto* (four-sided porch) in Rome. The columns and fragmented pediment once formed part of a vast rectangular portico, supported by 300 columns, that measured 132m by 119m. Erected by a builder called Octavius in 146 BC, it was rebuilt in 23 BC by Augustus, who kept the name in honour of his sister Octavia. From the Middle Ages until the late 19th century, the portico housed the city's fish market.

Most imposing is the **Teatro di Marcello**, akin to a smaller Colosseum with later buildings tacked on top. Follow Via del Teatro di Marcello onward as it becomes

Via Petroselli and you eventually come to Piazza Bocca della Verità (Map pp68-9), where you'll find a queue of tourists waiting to put their hands in one of Rome's most famous curiosities: the **Bocca della Verità** (Mouth of Truth; ☎ 06 678 14 19; Piazza Bocca della Verità 18; ⏱ 9.30am-5pm). It's said if you put your right hand in the mouth of this mask-shaped disk while telling a lie the mouth will bite your hand off.

TREVI FOUNTAIN
The **Trevi Fountain** (Fontana di Trevi; Map pp74-5) almost fills an entire piazza and is Rome's most famous fountain, its iconic status sealed when Anita Ekberg splashed here in *La Dolce Vita*. The baroque bonanza was designed by Nicola Salvi in 1732 and depicts Neptune's chariot being led by Tritons with sea horses – one wild, one docile – representing the moods of the sea.

PIAZZA BARBERINI & AROUND
Seventeenth-century **Chiesa di Santa Maria della Concezione** (Map p80; ☎ 06 487

LEFT: MARTIN MOOS; RIGHT: NEIL SETCHFIELD

Left: Bocca della Verità; Right: Interior, Chiesa del Gesù

ROME

11 85; Via Vittorio Veneto 27; admission by donation; 🕑 9am-noon & 3-6pm Fri-Wed) is nothing special, but descend into the Capuchin cemetery below and you'll be gobsmacked. Between 1528 and 1870 the Capuchin monks used the bones of 4000 of their departed brothers in a most macabre take on interior decoration.

The spectacular 17th-century **Palazzo Barberini** (Map p80) was commissioned by Urban VIII to celebrate the Barberini family's rise to papal power. Today it houses part of the **Galleria Nazionale d'Arte Antica** (Map p80; ☎ 06 225 82 493; www.galleriaborghese.it; Via delle Quattro Fontane 13; adult/EU 18-25yr/EU under 18yr & over 65yr €5/2.50/free, plus €1 reservation fee; 🕑 9am-7.30pm Tue-Sun, ticket office closes 7pm), a Renaissance and baroque art feast.

TRIDENTE
PIAZZA DI SPAGNA & THE SPANISH STEPS
The **Spanish Steps** (Scalinata della Trinità dei Monti; Map pp74-5), a perfect auditorium for people-watching, have acted as magnets for visitors since the 18th century. The **Piazza di Spagna** (Map pp74-5) was named after the Spanish Embassy to the Holy See, although the staircase, built with a legacy from the French in 1725, leads to the French church **Trinità dei Monti** (Map pp74-5). At the foot of the steps, the 'sinking boat' fountain, the **Barcaccia** (Map pp74-5), is believed to be by Pietro Bernini, father of the famous Gian Lorenzo.

Overlooking the steps, the **Keats-Shelley Memorial House** (Map pp74-5; ☎ 06 678 42 35; www.keats-shelley-house.org; Piazza di Spagna 26; adult/under 18yr & over 65yr/under 6yr €4/3/free; 🕑 10am-1pm & 2-6pm Mon-Fri, 11am-2pm & 3-6pm Sat) is where Keats died in 1821, while on an obviously unsuccessful holiday to improve his health. The cramped apartments now form an evocative mu-

SIGHTS

seum housing poems, letters and memorabilia from Keats' fatal visit, including his death mask.

ARA PACIS
From Piazza di Spagna, if you walk to the end of Via Condotti, cross Via del Corso and continue down Via della F Borghese, turning right at Via di Ripetta, you'll come upon the **Museo dell'Ara Pacis** (Altar of Peace; Map pp74-5; ☎ 06 820 59 127; www.arapacis.it; Lungotevere in Augusta; adult/EU 18-25yr/EU under 18yr & over 65yr €6.50/4.50/free; 🕑 9am-7pm Tue-Sun), Richard Meier's glass-and-marble pavilion. Many Romans detest the first modern construction in Rome's historic centre since WWII, and Rome Mayor Gianni Alemanno even made an election promise to tear it down.

Inside is the less-controversial **Ara Pacis Augustae** (Altar of Peace), Augustus' great monument to peace. One of the most important works of ancient Roman sculpture, the vast marble altar (it measures 11.6m by 10.6m by 3.6m) was completed in 13 BC and positioned near Piazza San Lorenzo in Lucina, slightly to the southeast of its current site.

PIAZZA DEL POPOLO
For centuries the site of public executions, this elegant ellipse of a **piazza** (Map pp74-5) was laid out in 1538 to provide a suitably grandiose entrance to what was then the main northern gateway into the city.

Guarding its southern end are Carlo Rainaldi's twin 17th-century baroque churches, **Chiesa di Santa Maria dei Miracoli** (Map pp74-5) and **Chiesa di Santa Maria in Montesanto** (Map pp74-5), while over on the northern flank is the **Porta del Popolo**, created by Bernini in 1655 to celebrate Queen Christina of Sweden's defection to Catholicism. In

ROME

SIGHTS

WILL SALTER

Crowds gathering on the Spanish Steps

the centre, the 36m-high **obelisk** was brought by Augustus from Heliopolis, in ancient Egypt, and moved here from the Circo Massimo in the mid-16th century. To the east are the **Pincio Hill Gardens**.

The **Chiesa di Santa Maria del Popolo** (Map pp74-5; ☎ 06 361 08 36; Piazza del Popolo; ☺ 7am-noon & 4-7pm Mon-Sat, 8am-1.30pm & 4.30-7.30pm Sun), next to the Porta del Popolo, is one of Rome's earliest, richest Renaissance churches. In the Cappella Cerasi, to the left of the altar, are two unforgettable Caravaggio masterpieces: the *Conversion of St Paul* and the *Crucifixion of St Peter* (both 1600–01).

VILLA BORGHESE & AROUND

No one can help heeding the call of the Villa Borghese, the ravishing baroque **park** (Map p53) just north of Rome's historic centre.

Cardinal Scipione Borghese (1579–1633) was the most knowledgeable and ruthless art collector of his day, and his collection, in the **Museo e Galleria Borghese** (Map p53; ☎ 06 3 28 10; www.galleria borghese.it; Piazzale Scipione Borghese 5; adult/EU 18-25yr/EU under 18yr & over 65yr €8.50/5.25/2, audioguides €5; ☺ 8.30am-7.30pm Tue-Sun, pre-booking necessary) is as dazzling as his park. To limit numbers, visitors are admitted at two-hourly intervals, so you'll need to call to prebook, and enter at an allotted entry time, but trust us, it's worth it.

Nearby, the oft-overlooked **Galleria Nazionale d'Arte Moderna e Contemporanea** (Map p53; ☎ 06 322 98 221; www.gnam.arti.beniculturali.it; Viale delle Belle Arti 131, entrance for visitors with disabilities at Via Antonio Gramsci 73; adult/EU 18-25yr/EU under 18yr & over 65yr €10/8/free; ☺ 8.30am-7.30pm Tue-Sun) is definitely worth a visit. Set in a vast belle époque palace are works by some of the most important exponents of modern Italian art.

TERMINI & ESQUILINO

Pilgrims and art-lovers flock to the **Basilica di San Pietro in Vincoli** (Map pp68-9; ☎ 06 488 28 65; Piazza di San Pietro in

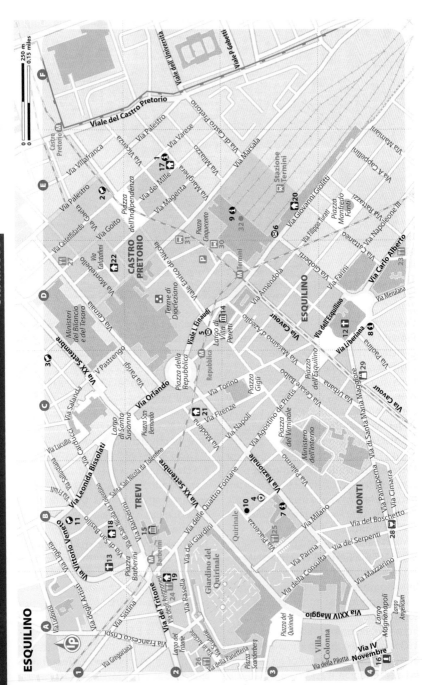

Vincoli 4a; ⏱ 8am-12.30pm & 3.30-7pm Apr-Sep, 8am-12.30pm & 3-6pm Oct-Mar) for two reasons: to see St Peter's chains and to see Michelangelo's tomb of Pope Julius II. The church was built in the 5th century specially to house the chains that bound St Peter when he was imprisoned in the Carcere Mamertino. Some time after St Peter's death, the chains were sent to Constantinople for a period before returning to Rome as relics. They arrived in two pieces and legend has it that when they were reunited they miraculously joined together. They are now displayed under the altar.

To the right of the altar is Julius' monumental tomb. At the centre of the work is Michelangelo's buff *Moses,* with magnificent beard and two small horns sticking out of his head. Subject of much curiosity, the horns were inspired by a mistranslation of a biblical passage: where the original said that rays of light issued from Moses' face, the translator wrote 'horns'. Michelangelo was aware of the mistake, but he gave Moses horns anyway.

Access to the church is via a flight of steps through a low arch that leads up from Via Cavour.

One of Rome's four patriarchal basilicas (the others being St Peter's, San Giovanni in Laterano and San Paolo Fuori-le-Mura),

the **Basilica di Santa Maria Maggiore** (Map p80; ☎ 06 698 86 800; Piazza Santa Maria Maggiore; ⏱ 7am-7pm) was built on the summit of the Esquilino in the 5th century.

MUSEO NAZIONALE ROMANO: PALAZZO MASSIMO ALLE TERME

A treasure trove of classical art, the light-filled **Museo Nazionale Romano: Palazzo Massimo alle Terme** (Map p80; ☎ 06 399 67 700; www.pierreci.it; Largo di Villa Peretti 1; adult/EU 18-24yr/EU under 18yr & over 65yr €7/3.50/free, plus possible €3 exhibition supplement, audioguide €4; ⏱ 9am-7.45pm Tue-Sun) is one of Rome's finest museums, yet receives only a smattering of visitors.

The ground and 1st floors are devoted to sculpture from the 2nd century BC to the 5th century AD. More gems, including a ravaged, voluptuous Aphrodite from Villa Adriana (see boxed text, p91) at Tivoli, are found on the 1st floor, but the sensational mosaics and frescoes on the 2nd floor blow everything else away.

But the best is still to come: the garden paintings (dating from 20-10 BC) from Villa Livia, one of the homes of Augustus' wife Livia Drusilla. Excavated in the 19th century and displayed here in 1951, these stunning frescoes depict an illusionary garden with all the plants in full bloom.

ROME

SIGHTS

SAN GIOVANNI & CELIO

For a thousand years, the **Basilica di San Giovanni in Laterano** (Map p53; ☎ 06 698 73 112; Piazza di San Giovanni in Laterano 4; ☉ 7am-6.30pm) was the most important church in Christendom. Founded by Constantine in 324 AD, it was the first Christian basilica built in the city. It is still Rome's cathedral and the pope's seat as bishop of Rome.

The **bronze doors** were moved here from the Curia in the Roman Forum, while to their right is the Holy Door, which is only opened in jubilee years.

The interior has been revamped on numerous occasions, although it owes much of its present look to Francesco Borromini, who was called in by Pope Innocent X to redecorate it for the 1650 Jubilee.

To the left of the altar, the beautiful **cloister** (admission €2; ☉ 9am-6pm) was built by the Vassalletto family in the 13th century.

Just around the corner is the fascinating octagonal **battistero** (baptistry). Built by Constantine in the 4th century, this domed building served as the prototype for later Christian churches and bell towers.

At the opposite end of Piazza di San Giovanni in Laterano is the **Scala Santa** (Holy Staircase; Map p53; ☎ 06 772 66 41; Piazza di San Giovanni in Laterano 14; admission Scala/Sancta €3.50/free, Sancta & Cappella San Silvestro €5; ☉ Scala 6.15am-noon & 3.30-6.45pm Apr-Sep, 6.15am-noon & 3-6.15pm Oct-Mar, Sancta Sanctorum 10.30-11.30am & 3-4.30pm Apr-Sep, 10.30-11.30am & 3-4pm Oct-Mar, closed Wed am & Sun year-round) and the **Sancta Sanctorum** (Holy of Holies). The Scala Santa is said to be the staircase that Jesus walked up in Pontius Pilate's palace in Jerusalem. Consequently you can only climb it on your knees. At the top of the stairs, the Sancta Sanctorum was the popes' private chapel and contains spectacular 13th-century frescoes.

Architectural time travel awaits at the **Basilica di San Clemente** (Map pp68-9; ☎ 06 774 00 21; www.basilicasanclemente.com; Via di San Giovanni in Laterano; admission church/excavations free/€5; ☉ 9am-12.30pm & 3-6pm Mon-Sat, noon-6pm Sun), which lies between San Giovanni and the Colosseum. The 12th-century church contains a stunning medieval mosaic in its apse, the *Triumph of the Cross,* with 12 doves symbolising the apostles. Though stunning, it's eclipsed by the Renaissance frescoes in the Chapel of St Catherine, to the left of the entrance.

Afterwards take steps down to a 4th-century church, mostly destroyed by Norman invaders in 1084, but with some faded 11th-century frescoes illustrating the life of San Clement. Follow the steps down another level and you'll find yourself walking an ancient lane to a 1st-century Roman house that also contains a dark, 2nd-century temple to Mithras with an altar showing the god slaying a bull.

To the southwest, Rome's most monumental ruins, the **Terme di Caracalla** (Map p53; ☎ 06 399 67 700; Viale delle Terme di Caracalla 52; admission incl Mausoleo di Cecilia Metella & Villa dei Quintili adult/EU 18-24yr/EU under 18yr & over 65yr €6/3/free, audioguide €4; ☉ 9am-7.15pm Tue-Sun Apr-Aug, 9am-7pm Sep, 9am-6.30pm Oct, 9am-5.30pm mid-end Mar, 9am-5pm mid-Feb–mid-Mar, 9am-4.30pm Nov–mid-Feb, 9am-2pm Mon year-round) show that size mattered to the Roman emperors. Covering 10 hectares, this ancient leisure centre complex could hold 1600 people and included richly decorated *caldaria* (hot rooms), a lukewarm tepidarium, a swimming pool, gymnasiums, libraries, shops and gardens.

TRASTEVERE

Trastevere's glittering heart is the beautiful **Piazza Santa Maria in Trastevere**

MARTIN MOOS

Ruins at Scavi Archeologici di Ostia Antica

ROME

SIGHTS

↘ IF YOU LIKE...

If you like **Museo Nazionale Romano: Palazzo Massimo alle Terme** (p81) we think you'll enjoy these other archaeological treasure troves:

- **Museo Nazionale Romano: Crypta Balbi** (Map pp74-5; ☎ 06 399 67 700; www. pierreci.it; Via delle Botteghe Oscure 31; adult/EU 18-24yr/EU under 18yr & over 65yr €7/3.50/ free plus possible €3 exhibition supplement; ☉ 9am-7.45pm Tue-Sun; bus to Piazza Venezia) This sophisticated archaeological museum is built around the ruins of medieval and Renaissance structures, themselves set on top of a grand Roman portico and theatre, the Teatro di Balbus (13 BC).
- **Museo Nazionale Etrusco di Villa Giulia** (Map p53; ☎ bookings 06 322 65 71; www.ticketeria.it; Piazzale di Villa Giulia 9; adult/EU 18-25yr/EU under 18yr & over 65yr €4/27free; ☉ 8.30am-7.30pm Tue-Sun; tram to Piazzale di Villa Giulia). Italy's finest collection of Etruscan treasures is considerately presented in Pope Julius III's 16th-century pleasure palace.
- **Scavi Archeologici di Ostia Antica** (☎ 06 563 52 830; www.ostiantica.info in Italian; Viale dei Romagnoli 717; adult/child €4/free, car park €2.50; ☉ 8.30am-7pm Tue-Sun Apr-Oct, to 6pm Mar, to 5pm Nov-Feb, last admission 1 hr before closing; metro line B to Piramide, then Ostia Lido train from Stazione Porta San Paolo to Ostia Antica) With preservation in places matching that of Pompeii, the ruins of this ancient port, 25km southwest of Rome, provide a vivid picture of everyday Roman life.

(Map p84), a prime people-watching spot. The central fountain is a 17th-century restoration of the Roman original.

It's overlooked by the ravishing **Basilica di Santa Maria in Trastevere** (Map p84; ☎ 06 581 48 02; www.santamariaintrastevere.org; Piazza Santa Maria in Trastevere; ☉ 7.30am-8pm),

said to be the oldest church dedicated to the Virgin Mary in Rome. Begun in AD 337, a major overhaul in 1138 saw the addition of the Romanesque bell tower and glittering mosaiced facade.

Inside, the shimmering 12th-century mosaics star.

ROME

SIGHTS

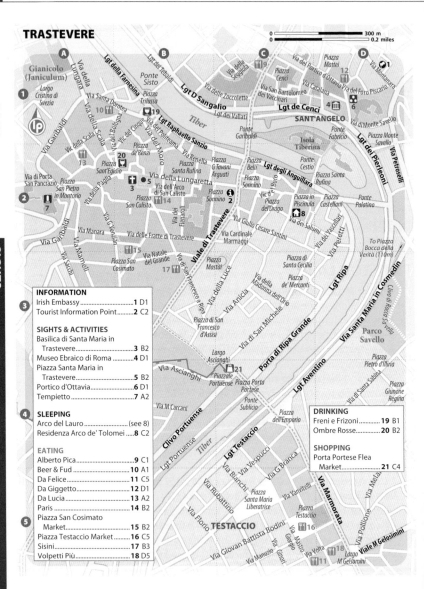

TRASTEVERE

0–300 m / 0–0.2 miles

INFORMATION
Irish Embassy **1** D1
Tourist Information Point **2** C2

SIGHTS & ACTIVITIES
Basilica di Santa Maria in
 Trastevere **3** B2
Museo Ebraico di Roma **4** D1
Piazza Santa Maria in
 Trastevere **5** B2
Portico d'Ottavia **6** D1
Tempietto **7** A2

SLEEPING
Arco del Lauro ....(see 8)
Residenza Arco de' Tolomei **8** C2

EATING
Alberto Pica **9** C1
Beer & Fud **10** A1
Da Felice **11** C5
Da Giggetto **12** D1
Da Lucia **13** A2
Paris **14** B2
Piazza San Cosimato
 Market **15** B2
Piazza Testaccio Market **16** C5
Sisini **17** B3
Volpetti Più **18** D5

DRINKING
Freni e Frizoni **19** B1
Ombre Rosse **20** B2

SHOPPING
Porta Portese Flea
 Market **21** C4

GIANICOLO

Rising up behind Trastevere, the summit of **Gianicolo** (Janiculum; Map p84) offers sweeping, bird's-eye views of Rome. It also hosts regular puppet shows, and has a small cafe-bar.

Around halfway up lies what is considered the first great building of the High Renaissance, Bramante's sublime **Tempietto** (Little Temple; Map p84; ☎ 06 581 39 40; www.sanpietroinmontorio.it; Piazza San Pietro in Montorio 2; ☉ church 8am-noon &

3-4pm Mon-Fri, tempietto 9.30am-12.30pm & 4-6pm Tue-Sun Apr-Sep, 9.30am-12.30pm & 2-4pm Tue-Sun Oct-Mar), built in the courtyard of the Chiesa di San Pietro in Montorio, on the spot where St Peter is supposed to have been crucified. More than a century later, in 1628, Bernini added a staircase, and also contributed a chapel to the adjacent church.

To reach the top of the hill is quite a climb, but you're rewarded by the views. To cheat, take bus 870 from Via Paola just off Corso Vittorio Emanuele II near the Tiber.

VATICAN CITY, BORGO & PRATI
The world's smallest sovereign state, the **Vatican City** (Città del Vaticano; Map p86) might cover an area of less than 1 sq km but it packs quite a punch.

Between the Vatican and the river lies the cobbled, medieval district of the Borgo (before Mussolini bulldozed through Via della Conciliazione, all the streets around St Peter's were like this), while north of the Vatican is Prati, a graceful residential area that's popular with media types (RAI has its headquarters here), and has some good accommodation and restaurants.

ST PETER'S SQUARE
One of the world's great public spaces, Bernini's massive **Piazza San Pietro** (Map p86) is a breathtaking work of baroque town planning.

Seen from above, it resembles a giant keyhole with two semicircular colonnades, each consisting of four rows of Doric columns, encircling a giant ellipse that straightens out to funnel believers into the basilica. The effect was deliberate – Bernini described the colonnades as representing 'the motherly arms of the church'. The 25m obelisk in the centre was brought to Rome by Caligula from Heliopolis in Egypt and later used by Nero as a turning post for the chariot races in his circus.

In the midst of all this the pope seems very small as he delivers his weekly address at noon on Sunday.

ST PETER'S BASILICA
In this city of astounding churches, **St Peter's Basilica** (Basilica di San Pietro; Map p86; ☎ 06 698 83 731; www.vatican.va; Piazza San Pietro; admission free, audioguides €5; ⏱ 7am-7pm Apr-Sep, 7am-6pm Oct-Mar) outdazzles them all. If you want enter, remember to dress appropriately – no shorts, miniskirts or bare shoulders. If you want to hire an

ROME

SIGHTS

PAPAL AUDIENCES
At 11am on Wednesdays, the pope meets his flock at the Vatican (in July and August he does so in Castel Gandolfo). For free tickets go to the ticket office of the Prefettura della Casa Pontificia (Map p86) through the bronze doors under the colonnade to the right of St Peter's. You can apply on the Tuesday before the audience or, at a push, on the Wednesday morning. Alternatively, download the application form (valid also for liturgical ceremonies) from the Vatican website (www.vatican.va/various/prefettura/en/biglietti_en.html) and send it by fax or post to the **Prefettura della Casa Pontificia** (fax 06 698 85 863; Prefecture of the Papal Household, 00120 Vatican City State). Give your Rome contact details (eg your hotel or apartment address), so that an arrangement can be made regarding delivery or collection of your tickets.

ROME

SIGHTS

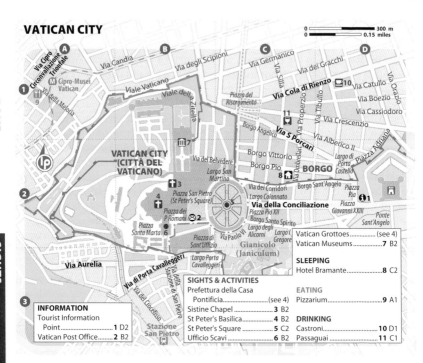

VATICAN CITY

0   300 m
0   0.15 miles

INFORMATION
Tourist Information
Point.....................................1 D2
Vatican Post Office.........2 B2

SIGHTS & ACTIVITIES
Prefettura della Casa
Pontificia...........................(see 4)
Sistine Chapel 3 B2
St Peter's Basilica.................4 B2
St Peter's Square 5 C2
Ufficio Scavi 6 B2

Vatican Grottoes...............(see 4)
Vatican Museums 7 B2

SLEEPING
Hotel Bramante....................8 C2

EATING
Pizzarium................................9 A1

DRINKING
Castroni.................................10 D1
Passaguai 11 C1

audioguide (€5), they're available at a desk in the cloakroom to the right of the entrance. Free English-language guided tours of the basilica are run from the Vatican tourist office, the Centro Servizi Pellegrini e Turisti, at 9.45am on Tuesday and Thursday and at 2.15pm every afternoon between Monday and Friday.

The first basilica was built here by Rome's first Christian emperor, Constantine, in the 4th century. Standing on the site of Nero's stadium, the Ager Vaticanus, where St Peter is said to have been buried between AD 64 and 67, it was consecrated in AD 326.

Like many early churches, it eventually fell into disrepair, and it wasn't until the mid-15th century that efforts were made to restore it, first by Pope Nicholas V and then, rather more successfully, by Julius II. In 1506 Bramante came up with a de-

sign for a basilica based on a Greek-cross plan, with a central dome and four smaller domes.

It took more than 150 years to complete the new basilica, now the second biggest in the world (the largest is in Yamoussoukro on the Côte d'Ivoire). Bramante, Raphael, Antonio da Sangallo, Giacomo della Porta and Carlo Maderno all contributed, but it is generally held that St Peter's owes most to Michelangelo, who took over the project in 1547 at the age of 72 and was responsible for the design of the dome.

The interior is 187m long and covers more than 15,000 sq metres. Decorated by Bernini and Giacomo della Porta, it can hold up to 60,000 people and contains spectacular works of art. Chief among them is Michelangelo's haunting **Pietà**, at the beginning of the right aisle.

Michelangelo's **dome** (admission with/without lift €7/5; 8am-6pm Apr-Sep, 8am-5pm Oct-Mar) soars 119m above the high altar. Entry to the dome is to the far right of the basilica. A small lift takes you halfway up but it's still a long climb to the top (320 steps). It's well worth the effort, but bear in mind it's steep, long and narrow: not recommended for those who suffer from claustrophobia or vertigo.

Accessed from the left nave of the basilica, the **Museo Storico Artistico** (Treasury; adult/child & student €6/4; 9am-6.15pm Apr-Sep, 9am-5.15pm Oct-Mar) sparkles with sacred relics and priceless artefacts, including a tabernacle by Donatello and the 6th-century Crux Vaticana, a cross studded with jewels that was a gift of the emperor Justinian II.

The **Vatican Grottoes** (Sacre Grotte Vaticane; Map p86; admission free; 9am-6pm Apr-Sep, 9am-5pm Oct-Mar) contain the tombs of numerous popes, including John Paul II, whose simple sepulchre contrasts starkly with many of the flamboyant monuments in the basilica above. You can also see several huge columns from the original 4th-century basilica. The entrance is through the right side of the portico.

Excavations beneath the basilica, which began in 1940, have uncovered part of the original church and what archaeologists believe is the **Tomb of St Peter** (admission €10, booking obligatory, over 15yrs only).

The excavations can only be visited on a 90-minute guided tour. To book a spot you'll need to email the **Ufficio Scavi** (Excavations Office; Map p86; ☎ 06 698 85 318; scavi@fsp.va), as far in advance as possible.

BORGO

The area between the Vatican and the Tiber is known as the Borgo, with its monumental landmark being **Castel Sant'Angelo** (Map pp74-5; ☎ 06 681 91 11; Lungotevere Castello 50; adult/EU 18-25yr €5/3; 9am-7pm Tue-Sun). Built as a mausoleum for the emperor Hadrian, it was converted into a papal fortress in the 6th century and named after an angelic vision that Pope Gregory the Great had in 590.

Its upper floors are filled with lavishly decorated Renaissance interiors, including, on the 4th floor, the beautifully frescoed Sala Paolina. Two stories farther up, the terrace, immortalised by Puccini in his opera *Tosca*, offers great views over Rome.

Opposite the castle, the **Ponte Sant'Angelo** (Map pp74-5) was built by Hadrian in AD 134 to provide an approach to his mausoleum. In the 17th century, Bernini and his pupils sculpted the figures of angels that line the pedestrian walkway, supplying intense drama.

VIA APPIA ANTICA & THE CATACOMBS

Heading southeast from Porta San Sebastiano, **Via Appia Antica** (the Appian Way; Map p53), one of the world's oldest roads, was known to the Romans as the *regina viarum* (queen of roads). Named after Appius Claudius Caecus, who laid the first 90km section in 312 BC, it was extended in 190 BC to reach Brindisi, some 540km away on the southern Adriatic coast.

There are several information points in the area, including the **Appia Antica Regional Park Information Point** (Map p53; ☎ 06 513 53 16; www.parcoappiaantica.org; Via Appia Antica 58-60; 9.30am-1.30pm & 2-5.30pm or 4.30pm in winter Mon-Sat, 9.30am-5.30pm or 4.30pm in winter Sun). You can also buy a map of the park here and hire bikes (per hour/day €3/10). The park authorities organise a series of free guided tours, on foot and by bike, on Sunday

ROME

GLENN BEANLAND

SIGHTS

Painting from the Stanze di Raffaello, Vatican Museums

➘ VATICAN MUSEUMS

Visiting the Vatican Museums (Musei Vaticani) is a thrilling experience, but one that will require reserves of stamina and patience. If you pre-book online at the Vatican's online ticket office (http://biglietteriamusei.vatican.va/musei/tickets/do?weblang=en&do), you will avoid some of the queues, though you will still have to pass through security checks, and make sure you bring valid ID as well as the printout email confirmation.

There are several suggested itineraries from the Quattro Cancelli area near the entrance, or you can go it alone and make up your own route. Each gallery contains priceless treasures, but for a whistle-stop tour get to the Pinacoteca, the Museo Pio-Clementino, Galleria delle Carte Geografiche, Stanze di Raffaello (Raphael Rooms) and the Sistine Chapel.

On the whole, exhibits are not well labelled so you might find it useful to hire an audioguide (€7) or buy the *Guide to the Vatican Museums and City* (€10). There are also authorised guided tours (adult/concession €30/25), which you can book at the Vatican's online ticket office.

The one place in the Vatican Museums that not one of the 4.5 million annual visitors wants to miss is the **Sistine Chapel** (Capella Sistina; Map p86). Home to two of the world's most famous works of art – Michelangelo's *Genesis* (Creation) on the barrel-vaulted ceiling and the *Giudizio Universale* (Last Judgment) on the end wall – this 15th-century chapel is where the papal conclave is locked to elect the pope.

Things you need to know: Map p86; ☎ 06 698 84 947; www.vatican.va; Viale Vaticano; adult/6yr-18yr & student/under 6yr €14/8/free, last Sun of the month free; ⊗ entry 9am-4pm Mon-Sat, closing time 6pm, 9am-12.30pm, closing time 2pm last Sun of month mornings – see the website for the latest programme.

Near the information office, the **Chiesa del Domine Quo Vadis** (Map p53; Via Appia Antica 51; ☼ 8am-6pm) is built at the point where St Peter, while fleeing Rome, is said to have met a vision of Jesus. Peter asked: *'Domine, quo vadis?'* ('Lord, where are you going?') When Jesus replied, *'Venio Roman iterum crucifigi'* ('I am coming to Rome to be crucified again'), Peter decided to join him and on his return to the city was immediately arrested and executed. In the centre of the church's aisle there are two footprints that supposedly belong to Christ; the originals are up the road in the Basilica di San Sebastiano.

The main attractions along Via Appia Antica are the catacombs – an endless-seeming warren of narrow tunnels carved out of the soft tufa rock.

The largest, most famous and busiest tunnels are the **Catacombs of San Callisto** (Map p53; ☎ 06 513 01 580; Via Appia Antica 110 & 126; www.catacombe.roma.it; adult/6-15yr/under 6yr €6/3/free; ☼ 9am-noon & 2-5pm Thu-Tue, closed Feb). Founded at the end of the 2nd century and named after Pope Calixtus I, they became the official cemetery of the newly established Roman Church.

To get to Via Appia Antica and the catacombs, catch one of the following buses: bus 218 from Piazza di San Giovanni in Laterano; bus 660 from the Colli Albani stop on metro A; or bus 118 from the Piramide stop on metro B.

TOURS
BOAT
Battelli di Roma (Map pp74-5; ☎ 06 678 93 61; www.battellidiroma.it) Offers hour-long cruises on the Tiber (tickets €12). Trips depart at 10am from Isola Tiberina, every half hour until 7pm.

BUS
Trambus Open (☎ 800 281 281; www. trambusopen.com; Piazza Cinquecento in front of Stazione Termini main entrance) Operates two tour buses: the **110open** (tickets €20; ☼ tours every 20min 8.30am-8.30pm) and the **Archeobus** (tickets €15; ☼ tours half-hourly 8.30am-4.30pm).

You can buy a joint ticket to both the 110open and Archeobus for €30 (valid 48 hours). If you have a Roma Pass (see the boxed text, p67) you receive a €5 discount on each of the bus tours.

WALKING
Enjoy Rome (Map p80; ☎ 06 445 68 90; www.enjoyrome.com; Via Marghera 8a) offers a number of choices. All guides are native or fluent English speakers who hold degrees in archaeology or related areas.

FESTIVALS & EVENTS
New Year (1 Jan) A candlelit procession in the catacombs.

Settimana dei Beni Culturale (Mar/May) Public museums and galleries open free of charge during culture week.

Procession of the Cross (Easter) A candlelit procession to the Colosseum on Good Friday evening is led by the pope. At noon on Easter Sunday he gives his traditional blessing from the balcony in St Peter's Square.

Mostra delle Azalee (Exhibition of Azaleas; late Mar/Apr) The Spanish Steps are decorated with masses of pink azaleas.

Rome's Birthday (21 Apr) To celebrate its birthday, the City of Rome provides processions, fireworks and free entry to lots of museums.

Primo Maggio (1 May) Rome's May Day rock festival attracts huge crowds and international performers to an open-air concert outside the Basilica di San Giovanni in Laterano.

ROME

SLEEPING

Circo di Massenzio ruins

PAOLO CORDELLI

➘ IF YOU LIKE...

If you like the **Catacombs of San Callisto** (p89), we think you'll like these other Appian Way sites:

- **Catacombs of San Sebastiano** (Map p53; ☎ 06 785 03 50; Via Appia Antica 136; catacombs adult/7-15yr/under 7yr €6/3/free; ⏱ 9am-noon & 2-5pm Mon-Sat, closed mid-Nov– mid-Dec) The second level features frescoes, stucco work, epigraphs and three immaculate mausoleums.

- **Basilica di San Sebastiano** (Map p53; ☎ 06 780 00 47; Via Appia Antica 136; ⏱ 8am-1pm & 2-5.30pm daily) See the arrows used to kill St Sebastian, the column to which he was tied, and a marble slab with the imprints of Jesus' footprints.

- **Villa di Massenzio** (Map p53; ☎ 06 780 13 24; www.villadimassenzio.it; Via Appia Antica 153; adult/EU 18yr-25yr/EU under 18yr & over 65yr €3/1.50/free; ⏱ 9am-1pm Tue-Sat) Further down the road, this is home to Circo di Massenzio, Rome's best-preserved ancient racetrack.

Festa di Primavera (end May–Jun) A festival of art, sport, music and theatre; for more information, check out www .provincia.roma.it.

Estate Romana (Jun–Oct) The big event in summer, this is a series of outdoor cultural events and activities for the few people who have remained in the capital – see www.romeguide.it/es tate_romana for more info.

Festa de'Noantri (3rd week in Jul) The festival 'of we others' in Trastevere is a traditional working-class festival celebrating the district's otherness, with food, wine and dancing.

Festa della Madonna della Neve (5 Aug) To celebrate the legendary snowfall that fell on 5 August 352, rose petals are showered on celebrants in the Basilica di Santa Maria Maggiore.

RomaEuropa (www.romaeuropa.net, in Italian; Sep–Nov) Top international artists take to the stage in Rome's autumn festival of theatre, opera and dance.

Christmas Market (1st Dec to 6th Jan) Christmas time in Rome sees a toy fair, with lots of handmade *presepi* (Nativity scenes), buskers, bright lights and fun in Piazza Navona.

SLEEPING

Although Rome doesn't have a low season as such, the majority of hotels offer discounts from November to March (excluding the Christmas and New Year period). Expect to pay top whack in spring and autumn and over the main holiday periods (Christmas, New Year and Easter).

Arrive without a reservation, however, and all's not lost. There's a free **hotel reservation service** (Map p80; ☎ 06 699 10 00; Stazione Termini; ⏱ 7am-10.30pm) at the main train station (opposite platform 21) and the nearby Enjoy Rome tourist office (p65) can also book a room for you.

ourpick Beehive (Map p80; ☎ 06 447 04 553; www.the-beehive.com; Via Marghera 8; dm €20-30, d without bathroom €70-95, tr €95-120) More boutique chic than backpacker crash pad, the Beehive is one of the best hostels in town. Needless to say, it's very popular, so make sure you book ahead.

Welrome Hotel (Map p80; ☎ 06 478 24 343; www.welrome.it; Via Calatafimi 15-19; s €40-100, d €50-110, tr €105-148, q €120-187) The chatty owner has a personal mission to look after her guests: not only does she take huge pride in her small, spotless hotel but she enthusiastically points out the cheapest places to eat, tells you where not to waste your time and what's good to do.

Daphne B&B (Map p80; ☎ 06 478 23 529; www.daphne-rome.com; Via di San Basilio 55; d with/ without bathroom €130-220/90-160; ✂ 🖧 💻 📶) Boutique B&B Daphne is a gem, run by an American-Italian couple, with chic, sleek, comfortable rooms, extremely helpful English-speaking staff, and top-notch breakfasts. There are 15 rooms in two locations: this one off Via Veneto (the pick, and every room is ensuite) and a second one at Via degli Avignonesi 20, towards the Trevi Fountain. Wi-fi is available.

Arco del Lauro (Map p84; ☎ 06 97840350 9am-2pm, 346 244 3212; Via Arco de' Tolomei 27; s €75-125, d €95-145, tr €120-165, q €135-180; ✂) With only six rooms, this fab B&B in an ancient *palazzo* is a find, through a

ROME

SLEEPING

A TIVOLI DOUBLE FEATURE

For millennia, the hilltop town of Tivoli has been a summer escape for rich Romans, a status amply demonstrated by its two Unesco World Heritage Sites, Villa Adriana and Villa d'Este, both incredible hedonistic playgrounds.

In Tivoli's hill-top centre, the gardens of **Villa d'Este** (☎ 199 766 166, or 0445 230310; www.villadestetivoli.info; Piazza Trento; adult/child €6.50/free; ☯ 8.30am-1hr before sunset Tue-Sun) have an *Alice in Wonderland* magic, and are a unique and superlative example of the High Renaissance garden. The villa was once a Benedictine convent, converted by Lucrezia Borgia's son, Cardinal Ippolito d'Este, into a sumptuous pleasure palace in 1550. From 1865 to 1886 it was home to Franz Liszt and inspired his compositions *To the Cypresses of the Villa d'Este,* and *The Fountains of the Villa d'Este*. The villa is a two-minute walk north from Largo Garibaldi.

Emperor Hadrian's summer residence **Villa Adriana** (☎ 06 399 67 900; adult/ child €6.50/3.25, plus €3.50 for exhibition, car park €2; ☯ 9am-1hr before sunset), 5km outside Tivoli, set new standards of luxury when it was built between AD 118 and 134, even given the excess of the Roman Empire. Consider hiring an audioguide (€4), which gives a helpful overview.

Tivoli is 30km east of Rome and is accessible by Cotral bus from outside the Ponte Mammolo station on metro line B.

Buses depart at least every 20 minutes and the one-hour journey costs €1.60 (€3.20 return). However, it's best to buy a Zone 3 BIRG ticket (€6), which will cover you for the whole day.

The easiest way to visit both sites is to visit the Villa D'Este first, then take the **CAT** (www.cattivoli.com) bus 4 or 4X (€1, 10 minutes, half-hourly Monday to Saturday, every 70 minutes Sunday) from Largo Garibaldi, asking the driver to stop at the entrance to Villa Adriana. After visiting the villa, you can then take a bus (€2, 50 minutes) to metro stop Tiburtina from outside the site.

Information is available from the **tourist information point** (☎ 07 743 13 536; ☯ 10am-1pm 4pm-6.30pm, shorter hr in winter) on Piazza Garibaldi, where the bus arrives.

Gelato varieties

WILL SALTER

large stone arch and on a narrow cobbled street, with gleaming white rooms which combine rustic charm with minimalist simplicity. The largest room has a high wood-beamed ceiling.

Suite Dreams (Map p80; ☎ 06 489 13 907; www.suitedreams.it; Via Modena 5; s €110-130, d €130-180, ste €200-250; ✗ ✗ 🖳) This popular, hip-looking place offers 15 rooms styled with neutrals, slate greys, chocolate-browns and contemporary art. Check the website for special offers.

Hotel Bramante (Map p86; ☎ 06 688 06 426; www.hotelbramante.com; Vicolo delle Palline 24-25; s €100-160, d €150-220; ✗) Borgo-set Bramante feels like a country house in the city, full of rustic elegance, oriental rugs, beams and antiques. It's housed in the 16th-century building that was home to architect Domenico Fontana before Pope

Sixtus V banished him from Rome, and has just 16 characterful rooms.

Teatropace 33 (Map pp74-5; ☎ 06 687 90 75; www.hotelteatropace.com; Via del Teatro Pace 33; s €120-160, d €150-250; ✗ ✗) Sublimely central, tucked in a lane beside Piazza Navona, this classy three-star is a top choice. In a former cardinal's residence, it has 23 beautifully appointed rooms decorated with parquet flooring, damask curtains and exposed wooden beams. There's no lift, just a monumental 17th-century stone staircase.

Residenza Arco de' Tolomei (Map p84; ☎ 06 583 20 819; www.bbarcodeitolomei.com; Via Arco de' Tolomei, 27; d €160-220; ✗ 🛜) Upstairs from Arco del Lauro, this gorgeous place has a completely different feel from its neighbour, decorated with polished antiques and rich chintz. It's also a lovely place to stay, and the owners are friendly and helpful. Wi-fi is available.

Casa Montani (Map pp74-5; ☎ 06 326 00 421; www.casamontani.it; Piazzale Flaminio 9; d €140-240) Fixtures and fittings are top quality, with rooms featuring custom-made furniture and contemporary art, yet prices are low considering the level of comfort and the position, overlooking the Porta del Popolo. It's an especially good deal if you book for three nights in low season (€120 for a deluxe room).

Portrait Suites (Map pp74-5; ☎ 06 68 28 31; www.portraitsuites.com; Via Bocca di Leone, 23; r €300-690; 🅿 ✗ ✗ 🖳) Owned by the Salvatore Ferragamo family – designer royalty – this is a discreet, exclusive boutique residence, designed by Florentine wonder-architect Michele Bonan. There are 14 exquisitely styled suites and studios across six floors in a townhouse overlooking Via Condotti, plus a dreamy 360-degree roof terrace and made-in-heaven staff. There's no restaurant, but you can have meals delivered. Breakfast is served in your room or on the terrace.

EATING

Be warned that the area around Termini has lots of substandard restaurants, and also choose carefully around the Vatican, which is packed with tourist traps.

Rome has masses of *alimentari* (grocery stores) or bars where you can get a *panino* (sandwich) made up for you for about €3, or buy *tramezzini* (premade refrigerated sandwiches; about €4). Alternatively, there are hundreds of *pizza al taglio* outlets for a takeaway slice of pizza (about €3 depending on the size and topping).

ANCIENT ROME

Cavour 313 (Map pp68-9; ☎ 06 678 54 96; Via Cavour 313; ⏰ 10am-2.30pm & 7.30pm-12.30am, closed Aug; dishes €7-14) Sink into its publike cosiness and while away hours over some sensational wine (over 1200 labels), cold cuts, cheeses, carpacci, or daily specials.

La Piazzetta (Map pp68-9; ☎ 06 699 16 40; Vicolo del Buon Consiglio 23a; meals €35) *Molto simpatico,* on a tiny medieval lane, this tucked-away, informal yet classy restaurant has a fabulous antipasti buffet and equally impressive *primi* and *secondi* – try the yolky carbonara.

CENTRO STORICO

Forno di Campo de' Fiori (Map pp74-5; ☎ 06 688 06 662; Campo de' Fiori 22; ⏰ 7am-1.30pm & 5.30-8.30pm Mon-Wed, Fri & Sat) Obscenely good, crispy, direct-from-the-oven *pizza a taglio* keeps this place permanently packed.

our pick **Pizzeria da Baffetto** (Map pp74-5; ☎ 06 686 16 17; Via del Governo Vecchio 114; pizzas €6-9; ⏰ 6.30pm-midnight) Da Baffetto offers the full-on wham-bam Roman pizza experience and some of the best pizzas in the city.

our pick **Gino** (Map pp74-5; ☎ 06 687 34 34; Vicolo Rosini 4; meals €30; ⏰ Mon-Sat) Oh, Gino! This is surely the perfect trattoria: quaint, busy and buzzing, dishing out well-executed staples such as *rigotoni alla gricia (*pasta with cured pig's cheek) and meatballs under gaudily painted vines. It's hidden away down a narrow lane close to parliament, and perennially packed by gossiping politicians. No credit cards.

ROME

EATING

GELATO AU GO GO

Here's our road-tested guide to the best gelateria in the city:

Alberto Pica (Map p84; ☎ 06 686 84 05; Via della Seggiola 12; ⏰ 8.30am-2am Mon-Sat year-round, 4pm-2am Sun, closed 2 weeks Aug) In summer, it offers flavours such as *fragolini de bosco* (wild strawberry) and *petali di rosa* (rose petal), but rice flavours are specialities whatever the season.

Ara Coeli (Map pp74-5; ☎ 06 679 50 85; Piazza d'Aracoeli 9; 🚌 Piazza Venezia) Close to the base of the Campidoglio, Ara Coeli is handily located and offers more than 40 flavours of excellent organic ice cream, semicold varieties, Sicilian granita and yoghurt.

Gelateria Giolitti (Map pp74-5; ☎ 06 699 12 43; Via degli Uffici del Vicario 40) Gregory Peck and Audrey Hepburn swung by in *Roman Holiday* and it used to deliver marron glacé to Pope John Paul II.

San Crispino (Map p80; ☎ 06 679 39 24; Via della Panetteria 42; ⏰ noon-12.30am Mon, Wed, Thu & Sun, noon-1.30am Fri & Sat) The delicate, strictly natural and seasonal flavours are served only in tubs (cones would detract from the taste).

Da Giggetto (Map p84; ☎ 06 686 11 05; Via del Portico d'Ottavia 21-22; meals €40; ☯ Tue-Sun) The atmospheric Ghetto, rustic interiors, white-jacketed waiters, *fabuloso* Roman-Jewish cooking – who needs more? Celebrate all things fried by tucking into the marvellous *carciofi alla giudia*, *fiore di zucca* (zucchini or squash flowers) and *baccalà* (cod) and follow on with a *zuppa di pesce* (fish soup) or *rigatoni alla gricia*.

Colline Emiliane (Map p80; ☎ 06 481 75 38; Via degli Avignonesi 22; meals €45; ☯ Tue-Sat, Sun lunch, closed Aug) This welcoming, tucked-away trattoria just off Piazza Barberini flies the flag for Emilia-Romagna, the well-fed Italian province that has gifted the world Parmesan, balsamic vinegar, bolognese sauce and Parma ham. On offer here are delicious meats, homemade pasta, rich *ragù*, and desserts worthy of a moment's silence.

TRIDENTE
BUDGET
Da Michele (Map pp74-5; ☎ 349 252 5347; Via dell'Umiltà 31; ☯ 8am-5am Mon-Fri, to 8pm summer) A handy address in Spagna district: buy your fresh, light and crispy *pizza a taglio* and you'll not only have a delicious lunch on the move, but also save your cents so you can – perhaps – afford that dashing designer outfit.

Palatium (Map pp74-5; ☎ 06 692 02 132; Via Frattina 94; meals €40; ☯ Mon-Sat, closed Aug) Conceived as a showcase of Lazio's bounty, this sleek *enoteca* close to the Spanish Steps serves excellent local specialities, such as *porchetta* (pork roasted with herbs), artisan cheese, and delicious salami, as well as an impressive array of Lazio wines (try lesser-known drops such as Aleatico). *Aperitivo* is a good bet too.

Il Margutta (Map pp74-5; ☎ 06 326 50 577; Via Margutta 118; meals €40) Vegetarian restaurants in Rome are rarer than parking spaces, and this art gallery/restaurant is an unusually chic way to eat your greens. Best value is the Saturday/Sunday buffet brunch (€15/25), with over 50 dishes on Sunday. It also offers a four-course vegan menu (€30).

Open Colonna (Map p80; ☎ 06 478 22 641; Via Milano 9a; meals €55; ☯ noon-midnight) The cuisine is new Roman: innovative takes on traditional dishes, cooked with wit and flair. The best thing of all? There's a more basic but still delectable fixed two-course lunch for €15, and Saturday and Sunday brunch at €28, served in the larger downstairs room, so you can live the life without splashing the cash.

TERMINI & ESQUILINO
Panella l'Arte del Pane (Map p53; ☎ 06 487 24 35; Via Merulana 54; ☯ 8am-2pm & 5-8pm Mon-Wed & Fri, 8am-2pm Thu, 8am-2pm & 4.30-8pm Sat, 8.30am-2pm Sun) With a sumptuous array of *pizza al taglio*, *supplì* (fried rice balls), focaccia, and fried croquettes, this is a great lunch stop, where you can sip a glass of chilled prosecco while eying up gastronomic souvenirs from the deli.

Trimani Wine Bar (Map p80; ☎ 06 446 96 30; Via Cernaia 37b; meals €35; ☯ Mon-Sat, closed 2 wks Aug) The best place around Termini for a quality lunch, this is a top-of-the-range wine bar, with a delectable range of dishes – from oysters to lentil soup – salami, cheeses served with mustard and jam, plus a choice of over 4500 international wines (be steered by the seriously knowledgeable waiters), and delicious bread and olive oil.

Agata e Romeo (Map p80; ☎ 06 446 61 15; Via Carlo Alberto 45; meals €120; ☯ Mon-Fri) This elegant, restrained place was one of Rome's gastronomic pioneers, and still holds its own as one of the city's most gourmet takes on Roman cuisine. Chef Agata Parisella designs and cooks menus, offering creative uses of Roman traditions;

ROME

EATING

GLENN BEANLAND

Campo de' Fiori (p76) at night

husband Romeo curates the wine cellar; and daughter Maria Antoinetta chooses the cheeses. Bookings essential.

TRASTEVERE

Sisini (Map p84; Via di San Francesco a Ripa 137; ☺ 9am-10.30pm Mon-Sat, closed Aug) Locals love this *pizza al taglio* joint (the sign outside says 'Suppli'), and you'll need to jostle with them to make it to the counter. Simple styles reign supreme – try the margherita or marinara. It's also worth sampling the *supplì* and roast chicken.

ourpick Da Lucia (Map p84; ☎ 06 580 36 01; Vicolo del Mattonato 2; meals €20; ☺ Tue-Sun) On a cobbled backstreet that is classic Trastevere, it serves up a cavalcade of Roman specialities including *trippa all romana* (tripe with tomato sauce) and *pollo con peperoni* (chicken with peppers), as well as bountiful antipasti and possibly Rome's best tiramisu.

Beer & Fud (Map p84; ☎ 06 58940 16; Via Benedetta 23; meals €25; ☺ 6.30pm-12.30am, to 2am Fri & Sat, closed Aug) This orange-and-terracotta, vaulted pizzeria, with a tented room at the back, wins plaudits for its amazingly good pizzas, *crostini* and delicious fried things (potato, pumpkin etc) and has a microbrewery on site. Save room for dessert too. Book ahead.

Paris (Map p84; ☎ 06 581 53 78; Piazza San Calisto 7a; meals €45; ☺ Tue-Sat, lunch Sun, closed 3 wks Aug) An old-school Roman restaurant set in a 17th-century building, Paris is the best place outside the Ghetto to sample Roman-Jewish cuisine, such as delicate *fritto misto con baccalà* (deep-fried vegetables with salt cod) and *carciofi alla giudia,* as well as Roman staples such as just-right *rigatoni alla carbonara.*

TESTACCIO

Volpetti Più (Map p84; ☎ 06 574 43 06; Via Volta 8; meals under €15) One of the few places in town where you can sit down and eat well for less than €15, Volpetti Più is a sumptuous *tavola calda,* offering an opulent choice of pizza, pasta, soup, meat, vegetables and fried nibbles. It adjoins Volpetti's to-die-for deli.

Da Felice (Map p84; ☎ 06 574 68 00; Via Mastro Giorgio 29; meals €30; ☼ Tue-Sun) A makeover has seen it turn all post-industrial chic, but the recited menu remains typically Roman. Try the glorious *tonnarelli cacio e pepe* (square-shaped pasta with pecorino Romano cheese and black pepper), mixed at the table, and the steaks. For those who love offal, there's also some buttery Roman soul food, and the tiramisu gets top marks.

VATICAN CITY, BORGO & PRATI

Pizzarium (Map p86; ☎ 06 397 45 416; Via della Meloria 43; pizza slice €2-3) Another contender for Rome's best *pizza al taglio,* this unassuming place offers a fluffy base and crisp crust topped by intensely flavoursome toppings. Eat standing up, and wash it down with a chilled beer.

Cacio e Pepe (Map p53; ☎ 06 321 72 68; Via Avezzana 11; meals €20; ☼ Mon-Sat) Romans flock for the home cooking at this humble trattoria, with gingham-clad tables spreading across the pavement in all di-

rections. They'll even put up with freezing winter temperatures to sit outside and dig into great steaming bowls of *cacio e pepe* – this-morning-fresh *bucatini* slicked with buttery cheese and pepper – and other classics such as spaghetti carbonara.

Ristorante l'Arcangelo (Map pp74-5; ☎ 06 321 09 92; Via Belli 59-61; meals €55; ☼ closed Sun & lunch Sat) The cuisine – surprisingly innovative – offers twists on classics, using fabulously fresh ingredients: the *amatriciana, cacio e pepe, carbonara* and *baccalá* are all contenders for the best in town.

SAN GIOVANNI & CELIO

Il Bocconcino (Map pp68-9; ☎ 06 770 791 75; Via Ostilia 23; meals €30; ☼ Thu-Tue, closed Aug) Its gingham tablecloths, outdoor seating and cosy interior look like all the others in this area, but it serves up excellent traditional pasta and other dishes, such as *insalata di finocchi arance e olive* (fennel, orange and olive salad) and *saltimbocca alla romana* ('leap in the mouth' veal with sage).

LEFT: JONATHAN SMITH; RIGHT: WILL SALTER

Left: Vegetable stall, Campo de'Fiori; **Right:** View from Caffè Capitolino

SELF-CATERING

For fresh fruit and vegetables, there are hundreds of outdoor markets, open from 7.30am to 1pm Monday to Saturday, notably:

Campo de' Fiori (Map pp74-5)
Piazza San Cosimato Market (Map p84)
Piazza Testaccio Market (Map p84)

DRINKING

Bars and cafes are an essential part of Roman life – most Romans breakfast in a cafe (a slurp of a cappuccino and a sugary bun) and pop back at least once for a pick-me-up espresso later in the afternoon. For drinks other than coffee, there are traditional *enoteche* (wine bars), a few pubs – trendy by virtue of their novelty – super-sleek designer bars, and some alternative counter-culture hang-outs.

CAFES
ANCIENT ROME

Caffè Capitolino (Map pp68-9; ☎ 06 326 51 236; Capitoline Museums, Piazza del Campidoglio 19) This well-kept-secret of a cafe is a lovely spot to take a break from the wonders of the Capitoline Museums and relax with a drink or a snack (*panini*, salads and pizza), but best are the incredible views from the rooftop terrace. You don't even need a museum ticket; you can enter from the street entrance to the right of the Palazzo dei Conservatori.

CENTRO STORICO

Caffè Sant'Eustachio (Map pp74-5; ☎ 06 686 13 09; Piazza Sant'Eustachio 82) A small stand-up place with some of Rome's best coffee, this is always three deep at the bar. The famous *gran caffè* is created by beating the first drops of espresso and several teaspoons of sugar into a frothy paste, then adding the rest of the coffee on top. It's superbly smooth and guaranteed to put some zing into your sightseeing. Specify if you want it *amaro* (bitter) or *poco zucchero* (with a little sugar).

Caffè Tazza d'Oro (Map pp74-5; ☎ 06 678 97 92; Via degli Orfani 84; ⏱ 8am-8pm Mon-Sat) A busy, stand-up bar with burnished fittings dating from the 1940s and some of the best coffee in the capital, which means it's spectacularly good.

Caffè Farnese (Map pp74-5; ☎ 06 395 61 03; Via dei Baullari 106) On a street between Campo de' Fiori and Piazza Farnese, it's ideally placed for whiling away the early afternoon hours. Try the *caffè alla casa* (house coffee) – made to a secret recipe.

VATICAN CITY, BORGO & PRATI

Castroni (Map p86; ☎ 06 687 43 83; Via Cola di Rienzo 196; ⏱ 8am-8pm Mon-Sat) Near the Vatican, this Aladdin's Cave of a gourmet food shop (it sells marrons glacés, sweets, and so on, as well as Vegemite and baked beans for homesick expats) has a bar where you can scoff a quick *cornetto* and coffee.

BARS
CENTRO STORICO

Société Lutèce (Map pp74-5; ☎ 06 683 01 472; Piazza di Montevecchio 17; ⏱ 6.30pm-2am Tue-Sat 2 weeks Aug) A group of Turin trendsters opened Société Lutèce and it's among Rome's hippest bars – grungy and art-school (expect Joy Division and hair-raising bass) rather than dressed-up and glitzy – like their other venture in Trastevere, Freni e Frizoni (p98).

Il Goccetto (Map pp74-5; ☎ 06 686 42 68; Via dei Banchi Vecchi 14; ⏱ 11.30am-2pm & 5.30pm-midnight Mon-Sat, closed Aug) Join the cast of regulars at the bar at this old-style *vino e olio* shop, and imbibe delicious drops by the glass, accompanied by a tasty assortment of snacks (cheeses, salamis, crostini etc) and large servings of neighbourhood banter.

Salotto 42 (Map pp74-5; ☎ 06 678 58 04; Piazza di Pietra 42; ♥ Tue-Sun) Run by an Italian-Swedish couple, it's as close as you'll get to a sitting-room experience in the city centre – think armchairs, sofas and coffee-table books.

Etablì (Map pp74-5; ☎ 06 97 616 694; Vicolo delle Vacche 9a; ♥ 6pm-2am Tue-Sun) Chilean-Italian brothers Massimo and Alessandro Aureli are the smiling hosts of this rustic-chic bar-cafe-restaurant in a 16th-century building.

Femme (Map pp74-5; ☎ 06 686 48 62; Via del Pellegrino 14; ♥ Tue-Sun) The splendid *aperitivo,* from 7pm to 9pm, is almost worth losing one's cool over.

TRIDENTE

L'Antica Enoteca (Map pp74-5; ☎ 06 679 08 96; Via della Croce 76; meals €25) Locals and tourists alike prop at the 19th-century wooden bar to sample the 60 wines by the glass, snack on antipasti, and generally have a good time. If antipasti won't cut it, dive into the back room and order well-priced soul food such as pasta or polenta.

Stravinskij Bar – Hotel de Russie (Map pp74-5; ☎ 06 328 88 70; Via del Babuino 9) Can't afford to stay at celeb-magnet Hotel de Russie? Then splash out on a drink in its enchanting bar, set in the courtyard, with sunshaded tables overlooked by terraced gardens.

MONTI

Ai Tre Scalini (Map p80; ☎ 06 489 07 495; Via Panisperna, 251; ♥ noon-1am Mon-Fri, 6pm-1am Sat & Sun) If you've missed out on dinner you can tuck into a heart-warming array of cheeses, salami and dishes such as *porchetta di Ariccia con patate al forno* (roasted Ariccia pork with roast potatoes).

SAN GIOVANNI & CELIO

Il Pentagrappolo (Map pp68-9; ☎ 06 709 63 01; Via Celimontana 21b; ♥ noon-3pm & 6pm-1am Tue-Sun) A few blocks from the Colosseum, these star-vaulted rooms offer 250 labels to choose from and about 15 wines by the glass. There's live jazz or soul from about 10pm and tasty *aperitivo* (6pm to 8.30pm).

TRASTEVERE

our pick Freni e Frizoni (Map p84; ☎ 06 583 34 210; Via del Politeama 4-6) The arty crowd flocks here to slurp well-priced drinks (especially mojitos) and spill into the piazza out front. You can eat breakfast here, have lunch, munch brunch at the weekend, and feast on the good-value *aperitivo.*

Ombre Rosse (Map p84; ☎ 06 588 41 55; Piazza Sant'Egidio 12; ♥ 8am-2am) The cosmopolitan clientele ranges from elderly Italian wide boys to chic city slickers. Tunes are slinky and there's live music (jazz, blues, world) on Thursday and Sunday evenings from October to May.

VATICAN CITY, BORGO & PRATI

Passaguai (Map p86; ☎ 06 874 513 58; Via Leto 1; ♥ 10am-2am Mon-Sat) A small, cavelike winebar, Passaguai has a few outdoor tables and feels pleasingly off the beaten track. There's a good wine list and a range of artisanal beers, and the food – such as cheeses and cold cuts – is tasty too.

ENTERTAINMENT

Romac'è (www.romace.it, in Italian; €1) is Rome's most comprehensive listings guide, and comes complete with a small English-language section; it's published every Wednesday. Useful websites include www.romaturismo.it and www.comune.roma.it.

PAOLO CORDELLI

Ai Monasteri

MUSIC

Free concerts are often held in many of Rome's churches, especially at Easter and around Christmas and New Year. Check newspapers and listings for programmes.

Auditorium Parco della Musica (Map p53; ☎ 06 802 41 281; www.auditorium.com; Viale Pietro de Coubertin 10; ⏰ 11am-8pm) It's supersleek and überchic, yet the excited throng is as wide a cross section as you'd see on the metro, a reflection of the democratic pricing (tickets cost from €5), and the programme, which encompasses anything from PJ Harvey to Puccini. To get to the auditorium take tram 2 from Piazzale Flaminio or bus M from Stazione Termini, which departs every 15 minutes between 5pm and the end of the last performance.

SHOPPING

Ai Monasteri (Map pp74-5; ☎ 06 688 02 783; Corso del Rinascimento 72; ⏰ 10am-1pm & 3-7.30pm Mon-Sat) This apothecary-like shop stocks all-natural cosmetics, sweets, honeys, jams and wines, all made by monks.

Fausto Santini (Map pp74-5; ☎ 06 678 41 14; Via Frattina 120) Style mavens adore Roman designer Fausto Santini for his simple, architectural shoe designs. For bargains and previous seasons' designs, check out the outlet store, Giacomo Santini (Map p80; Via Cavour 106). Both stores sell bags, too.

Officina Profumo Farmaceutica di Santa Maria Novella (Map pp74-5; ☎ 06 687 96 08; Corso del Rinascimento 47; ⏰ 9.30am-7.30pm Mon-Sat) This historic perfumery was established in Florence by Dominican friars in 1221 and has been concocting seductive scents and unguents ever since.

Porta Portese flea market (Map p84; Piazza Porta Portese) To see another side of Rome head to this mammoth flea market. Keep your valuables safe and wear your haggling hat.

Sermoneta (Map pp74-5; ☎ 06 679 19 60; Piazza di Spagna 61; ⏰ 9.30am-8pm Mon-Sat, 10.30am-7pm Sun) Buying leather gloves in Rome is a rite-of-passage for some, and this is *the* shop to do it.

ROME

GETTING THERE & AWAY

GETTING THERE & AWAY
AIR
Rome's main airport is **Leonardo da Vinci** (**FCO; Map p53; ☎ 06 6 59 51; www.adr.it**), commonly known as Fiumicino. The second smaller airport, **Ciampino** (**CIA; Map p53; ☎ 06 6 59 51; www.adr.it**), is used by many low-cost airlines and charter flights.

BUS
Long-distance national and international buses use the bus terminus on Piazzale Tiburtina, in front of Stazione Tiburtina. Take metro line B from Stazione Termini to Tiburtina and turn right when you exit the station. The long-haul buses are beyond the overpass.

Cotral buses (☎ 800 174 471; **www.cotral spa.it**) serve the Lazio region and depart from numerous points throughout the city, depending on their destination.

TRAIN
Almost all trains arrive at and depart from Stazione Termini (Map p80). There are regular connections to other European countries, all the major cities in Italy and many smaller towns.

GETTING AROUND
TO/FROM THE AIRPORT
Fiumicino is about 30km southwest of the city centre and is well connected to it. Getting to and from Ciampino is more time-consuming by public transport, despite it being only 15km southeast of the centre.

BUS
At night, from 12.30am to 6am you can catch an N2 night bus to Tiburtina metro station from where you can take a Cotral bus to Fiumicino (€4.50, 40 minutes). Buy your ticket on the bus.

Buses to Ciampino leave from Anagnina, which is accessible via metro line A. The service runs every 40 minutes from 6.30am until 10.40pm and costs €1.20 (you can buy a ticket on the bus).

Another Ciampino option is the **SIT shuttle bus service** (☎ 06 591 6826; www.sit

WILL SALTER

Bus passing the Colosseum (p66)

busshuttle.com). This travels between Stazione Termini and Ciampino from 4.30am to 9.45pm (from Termini) and 7.45am to 11.45am (from Ciampino) daily. Tickets costs €6/5 from Termini/Ciampino. The buses leave Rome from a stop on Via Marsala, and you can buy tickets on board.

TAXI & SHUTTLE SERVICE
Official taxis registered by the Comune di Roma leave from outside the arrivals halls at Fiumicino and Ciampino. They are white and have a TAXI sign on their roof, as well as an identifying number on their doors. There are fixed rates between each airport and destinations within the Aurelian Walls in central Rome: €40/30 Fiumicino/Ciampino. These rates are inclusive of luggage and apply to fares coming from and going to the airports. For destinations outside the walls, taxis use their meters and will include a surcharge for luggage (€1.04 per bag). Note that taxis registered in Fiumicino charge a set fare of €60 to travel to the centre – make sure you catch a Comune di Roma taxi instead.

Several private companies run shuttle services. **Terravision** (www.terravision.eu) has a service from Fiumicino to Stazione Termini costing €7 one-way and €12 return. It leaves about every two hours between 8.30am and 8.30pm; for tickets go to the desk in the arrivals hall.

TRAIN
The efficient Leonardo Express leaves from platform 24 at Stazione Termini and travels direct to the airport every 30 minutes from 5.52am until 10.52pm. It costs €11 (children under 12 years free) and takes about 30 minutes.

From Fiumicino, trains start at 6.36am and run half-hourly until 11.36pm. Tickets for the Leonardo Express are available at

SUMMER NIGHTS IN ROME
From mid-June to mid-September, most of the city's clubs and music joints close. Some of the clubs move to Fregene or Ostia for a summer's dancing on the sand. In town, the Estate Romana supplies ample after-dark entertainment. It's a huge umbrella festival encompassing concerts, exhibitions, theatre, open-air cinema and temporary markets and bars. Check www.estateromana.comune.roma.it for listings.

Termini from *tabacchi* and newsstands in the station, at vending machines or at the ticket desk on the platform. At Fiumicino, get tickets from the vending machines or the ticket desks at the rail terminus.

PUBLIC TRANSPORT
Tickets are valid for all forms of transport and come in various forms. The simplest is the *biglietto integrato a tempo* (BIT), which costs €1 and is valid for 75 minutes. In that time you can use as many buses or trams as you like but can take only one trip on the metro. Daily tickets (BIG) cost €4 (ask for a *biglietto giornaliero*) and give you unlimited trips; three-day tickets (BTI, *biglietto turistico integrato*) cost €11; and weekly tickets (CIS, *carta integrata settimanale*) cost €16. Children up to 1m tall, or under four years, travel free.

You can buy tickets at *tabacchi,* at newsstands and at *biglietterie* (ticket offices) at metro, bus and train stations. They must be purchased before you get on the bus or train and then validated in the yellow machine once on board, or validated at the entrance gates for the metro.

CHEAP BUS & TRAIN TICKETS

The best way to travel by public transport in Lazio is to arm yourself with a daily *biglietto integrato regionale giornaliero* (BIRG) ticket. These tickets allow unlimited travel on all city and regional transport, including buses, trams, the metro and trains (but not including Fiumicino airport services). They're priced according to zones: the most expensive, zone 7, costs €10.50; the cheapest, zone 1, costs €2.50. Tickets are available from *tabacchi*, some newsstands and *biglietterie* (ticket offices) at metro stations.

BUS & TRAM

Rome's buses and trams are run by **ATAC** (☎ 06 57003; www.atac.roma.it). The **main bus station** (Map p80; Piazza Cinquecento) is in front of Stazione Termini, where there's an **ATAC information booth** (🕙 8am-8pm) on the stand in the centre of the piazza. Largo di Torre Argentina, Piazza Venezia and Piazza San Silvestro are other important hubs. Buses generally run from about 5.30am until midnight, with limited services throughout the night on some routes.

METRO

Rome's two **metro** (☎ 06 57531, 🕙 phone line in English 8.30am-6.30pm; www.metroroma.it) lines, A and B, cross at Termini, the only point at which you can change from one line to the other. Trains run approximately every five to 10 minutes between 5.30am

and 11.30pm (one hour later on Saturday). Note that Manzoni station on line A is currently closed for works.

Construction of line C is ongoing. The service will eventually serve the city centre passing from Ottaviano (close to the Vatican), with stops at Piazza Venezia and Chiesa Nuova, and run out southeastwards to the suburbs. It is likely to open in stages after 2012.

NIGHT BUS

Rome's night buses include more than 20 lines, most of which pass Termini and/or Piazza Venezia. Buses are marked with an N after the number. Night bus stops have a blue owl symbol. Departures usually occur every 30 minutes, but can be much slower.

TAXI

Rome's taxi drivers are no better or worse than in any other city. Some will try to fleece you, others won't. To minimise the risk, make sure your taxi is licensed and metered, and always go with the metered fare, never an arranged price (the set fares to and from the airports are an exception to this rule). In town (within the ring road) flag fall is €2.33 (€3.36/4.91 Sundays/10pm-7am), then it's €0.78 per km.

You can hail a cab in Rome, but it's often easier to wait at a taxi rank or telephone for one. When you call for a cab, the meter is switched on straight away and you pay for the cost of the journey from wherever the driver receives the call. To phone a taxi, try:

La Capitale (☎ 06 49 94)
Radio Taxi (☎ 06 35 70)

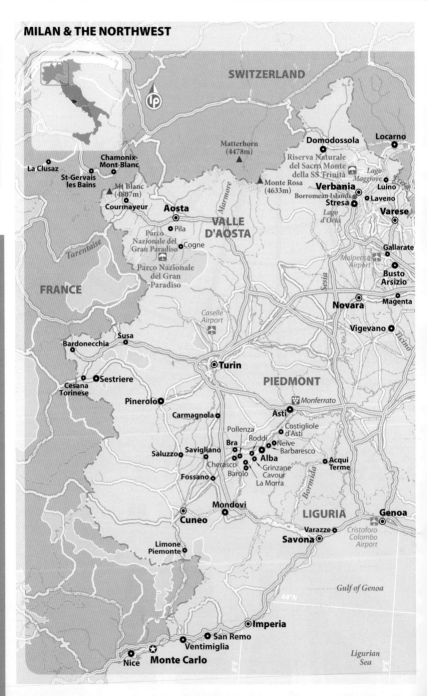

MILAN & THE NORTHWEST

SWITZERLAND

Locarno

Domodossola

Matterhorn
(4478m)

Riserva Naturale
del Sacro Monte
della SS Trinità

Lago
Maggiore

Luino

Verbania

La Clusaz

Chamonix-
Mont-Blanc

St-Gervais
les Bains

Monte Rosa
(4633m)

Borromean Islands

Stresa

Laveno

Varese

Mt Blanc
(4807m)

Marmore

Lago
d'Orta

Courmayeur

Aosta

VALLE
D'AOSTA

Pila

Gallarate

Tarentaise

Parco
Nazionale del
Gran Paradiso

Cogne

Malpensa
Airport

Busto
Arsizio

Sesia

Parco Nazionale
del Gran
Paradiso

Novara

Magenta

FRANCE

Caselle
Airport

Vigevano

Ticino

Bardonecchia

Susa

Turin

PIEDMONT

Cesana
Torinese

Sestriere

Monferrato

Pinerolo

Asti

Carmagnola

Costigliole
d'Asti

Pollenza

Roddi

Saluzzo

Savigliano

Bra

Neive
Barbaresco

Cherasco

Alba

Acqui
Terme

Fossano

Barolo

Grinzane
Cavour

La Morra

Bormida

Mondovì

LIGURIA

Genoa

Cuneo

Varazze

Cristoforo
Colombo
Airport

Limone
Piemonte

Savona

Gulf of Genoa

44°N

Imperia

San Remo

Ventimiglia

Ligurian
Sea

Nice

Monte Carlo

8°E

9°E

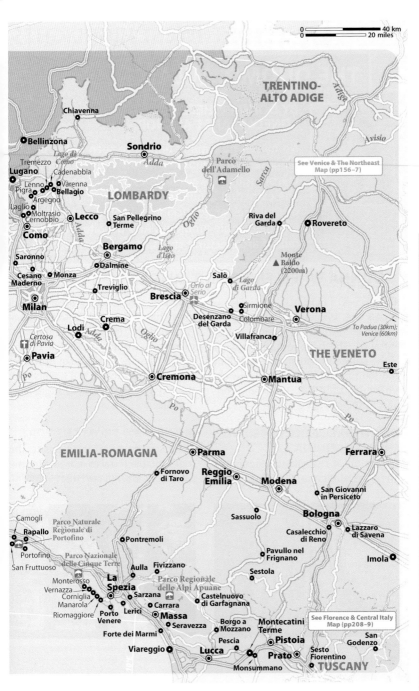

0 — 40 km
0 — 20 miles

TRENTINO-ALTO ADIGE

Avisio

Chiavenna

Bellinzona

Sondrio

Lago di Como

Adda

Parco dell'Adamello

See Venice & The Northeast Map (pp156–7)

Tremezzo
Cadenabbia
Lugano
Lenno
Varenna
Pigra
Bellagio
Argegno
Laglio
Moltrasio
Cernobbio
Como

LOMBARDY

Oglio

Sarca

Riva del Garda

Rovereto

Lecco
San Pellegrino Terme

Bergamo

Lago d'Iseo

Monte Baldo (2200m)

Saronno

Dalmine

Cesano Maderno
Monza

Treviglio

Salò

Lago di Garda

Orio al Serio

Brescia

Sirmione

Verona

Milan

Crema

Desenzano del Garda
Colombare

Lodi

Oglio

Villafranca

Adda

Certosa di Pavia

Pavia

Po

Cremona

Mantua

THE VENETO

Este

To Padua (30km);
Venice (60km)

Po

Po

EMILIA-ROMAGNA

Parma

Ferrara

Fornovo di Taro

Reggio Emilia

Modena

San Giovanni in Persiceto

Camogli
Rapallo

Parco Naturale Regionale di Portofino

Pontremoli

Sassuolo

Bologna

Casalecchio di Reno

Lazzaro di Savena

Portofino
San Fruttuoso

Parco Nazionale delle Cinque Terre

Aulla
Fivizzano

Pavullo nel Frignano

Imola

Monterosso
Vernazza
Corniglia
Manarola
Riomaggiore

La Spezia

Sarzana

Lerici

Porto Venere

Parco Regionale delle Alpi Apuane

Carrara

Castelnuovo di Garfagnana

Sestola

Massa

Seravezza

Forte dei Marmi

Borgo a Mozzano

Montecatini Terme

See Florence & Central Italy Map (pp208–9)

Pescia

Pistoia

San Godenzo

Viareggio

Lucca

Monsummano

Prato

Sesto Fiorentino

TUSCANY

MILAN & THE NORTHWEST HIGHLIGHTS

1 THE DUOMO, MILAN

**BY DONNA WHEELER,
LONELY PLANET AUTHOR**

No matter how many times I've seen it, the first glimpse of the Duomo's willowy, luminescent marble spires always inspires a quiet gasp of awe. The cathedral is quintessential Milan: a product of centuries of politicking, pillaging, graft, fashion and mercantile ambition. And despite its florid mix of architectural styles, it somehow works.

↘ DONNA WHEELER'S DON'T MISS LIST

❶ THE BATTISTERO

Access the 4th-century Baptistry via a stairwell next to the Duomo's main entrance. The back-to-basics beauty of the palaeo-Christian baptismal font and the ruins of earlier cathedrals are a haunting sight, and a touching contrast to the opulence above.

❷ FOOTBALL FANS CHEERING THE MADONNINA

Staring up at the gilded Madonnina (the little Madonna) from the piazza below as thousands of local football nuts chant 'O mia bella Mudunnina' is one of those 'only in Milano' moments. Just don't be fooled by the name: the city's traditional protector might appear tiny as she hovers over the city but she's actually more than 4m tall.

❸ THE VIEW FROM THE TOP

Make sure to climb the steps to the roof's marble terraces, not just for the panoramic view (a rare treat in Milan),

Clockwise from top: Duomo rooftop; Madonnina statue; La Rinascente; Duomo stained-glass window; Duomo exterior

but also for the fairy-tale sensation of being surrounded by the petrified marble pinnacles. It's also a must for Visconti fans – one of the most heartbreaking scenes from his 1960 film *Rocco and His Brothers* is set here. There's a lift if you can't tackle the stairs.

❹ A CATHEDRAL CONCERT

Look out for the Duomo's occasional concerts of early classical and sacred music. The Duomo's music school has been training choirboys since 1402 (expectantly, they know their stuff), and the Duomo's organ is one of the world's finest. It's also a good way to avoid the tour-group circus. You'll find details at the Cappella Musicale (Musical Chapel) page on the Duomo's website (www.duomomilano.it).

❺ A MODERN VIEW

Facing the Duomo's northern side is department store La Rinascente. Head up to Obikà on the 7th floor for a glass of local *prosecco*, a plate of fresh *bufala* mozzarella, and an unusual, close-up view of the spires.

↘ THINGS YOU NEED TO KNOW

Best time to visit During early morning mass on Sunday; some services are held in the crypt **Avoid** Wearing a singlet or mini-skirt: you'll be refused entry **Best photo** Shoot down as much as up: the graphic marble floor is gorgeous. **See our author's review on p117**

MILAN & THE NORTHWEST HIGHLIGHTS

2 | LAGO DI COMO

BY RITA ANNUNZIATA, LAKE COMO NATIVE, TOUR GUIDE & PRESIDENT OF PROMOBELLAGIO

Lago di Como is the most spectacular of Italy's northern lakes. The surrounding mountains plunge straight into the water, and their presence around the entire lake has made it difficult to build new houses and other buildings. The result is lots of small, characterful villages and the ability to always find a little peace and quiet.

⟍ RITA ANNUNZIATA'S DON'T MISS LIST

❶ WALKING TRAILS & TOURS

Walking tours of the mountains surrounding towns Bellagio (p134), Lenno (p135) and Tremezzo (p135) offer an insight into the lake's lesser-known villages and landscapes. The 6km walk from Bellano to Varenna along the ancient Viandante trail is particularly beautiful. On the western shore, head to the Chiesa di San Martino, 400m above tiny Cadenabbia, for spectacular views. You'll find information on walking trails and tours at the local tourist offices.

❷ ROMANTIC GARDENS

Quite simply, Lake Como's gardens are marvellous. To catch the spring blooming of azaleas, rhododendrons and camellias, visit before 10 May. Among the most beautiful gardens are those of Villas Serbelloni (p134), Melzi D'Eril (p134), Balbianello (p135) and Carlotta (p135). In summer, enchanting classical concerts are held in some of the gardens, mostly at Villa Carlotta. For schedules, check the villas' websites or those of the local tourist offices.

Clockwise from top: Varenna; Local fried-fish dish; Bellagio (p134); fishers on Lago di Como (p130); Villa Melzi D'Eril (p134), Bellagio

CLOCKWISE FROM TOP: ROBERTO GEROMETTA; ALAN BENSON; GLENN VAN DER KNIJFF; DENNIS JONES; ROBERTO GEROMETTA

❸ GASTRONOMIC ENCOUNTERS

You'll find lots of wonderfully atmospheric restaurants and trattorias around the lake, such as Albergo Silvio's (p133) lofty restaurant and the down-to-earth Osteria del Gallo (p132). Book a table at Locanda dell'Isola Comacina (☎ 0344 55083; www.comacina. it; return shuttle boat from Sala Comacina €6), on the lake's only island. Expect lots of fresh vegetables, local trout and fabulous fried chicken. Owner Benvenuto will tell you about the island's long and complicated history, and prepare a special coffee to 'purify' you after stepping on his 'cursed land'.

❹ BELLAGIO

Most visitors are surprised that Bellagio (p134) is even more stunning in real life than it is on postcards. Aside from its glorious lakeside gardens, there's a great selection of shops, cafes and restaurants. Every Monday, local history buff Lucia Sala runs a guided tour exploring some of the 22 hamlets, and she'll even show you her wonderful local ethnographic collection. Promobellagio can provide details.

↘ THINGS YOU NEED TO KNOW

Locanda dell'Isola Comacina Winter Most gardens and hotels close, but small, family-run hotels are a good bet for a relaxing stay See our author's review on p130

MILAN & THE NORTHWEST HIGHLIGHTS

3

⬎ SAVOUR THE LAST SUPPER

It's hard not to ask yourself whether it's worth all the fuss of phone bookings and queuing to see a mural for only 15 minutes. But once you're standing before the restored majesty of Leonardo da Vinci's **Last Supper** (p120), those doubts melt away. Eschewing convention, da Vinci ditched forward-facing figures for a table of animated disciples. Centuries later the colours may have faded but the intrigue lives on.

4

⬎ SWILL VINTAGES IN ALBA

Compare the merits of Barolo over Barbaresco with the wine quaffers of **Alba** (p148), an evocative town in the heart of Piedmont's celebrated wine region. Extending east and south of town, the green hills of the Langhe are famous for their majestic red wines, not to mention their prized white truffles. Predictably, Alba is a hit with gourmands, who head in to celebrate the pleasures of the table and the cellar.

5

⬋ LOSE YOURSELF IN BERGAMO

This staunchly independent strong-hold in the Alpine foothills was its own city-state. When you take the funicular up *città alta* (upper town), you'll enter a world apart. Bergamo (p126) is an intriguing jumble of medieval, Renaissance and baroque architecture – and the place to sample pungent yet fruity taleggio cheese.

6

⬋ SLOW FOOD SHOP IN TURIN

Treat your larder (and your taste-buds) at Turin's drool-inducing Slow Food supermarket, Eataly (p145). Housed in a vast con-verted factory, this gourmand mecca boasts a staggering array of Slow Food–affiliated food and beverages, including cheeses, breads, meats, fish, pasta, choco-late and much more.

7

⬋ ESCAPE INTO THE ALPS

Away from the metro-centric pleas-ures of Milan and Turin, the Parco Nazionale del Gran Paradiso (p153) is a tonic for the soul, a breathtaking combo of Alpine peaks and glaciers, emerald woods and grazing wildlife in sprawling mountain meadows. It's also a year-round playground, with skiing, hik-ing, cycling and horseback riding.

3 Detail, The Last Supper (p120); 4 Alba (p148); 5 Bergamo's *città alta* (126); 6 Eataly (p145), Turin; 7 Hiker, Parco Nazionale del Gran Paradiso (p153)

MILAN & THE NORTHWEST'S BEST...

↘ ROMANTIC LOCATIONS

- **Bellagio, Lago di Como** (p134) A story-book village on Lago di Como's southern shore.
- **Vernazza, Cinque Terre** (p139) A cosy hamlet wedged between the sea and rows of vineyards.
- **Isola Bella, Lago Maggiore** (p129) Tiered gardens and a baroque palace on a sparkling Lombard lake.
- **La Scala, Milan** (p120) Have a *Pretty Woman* moment in Italy's lushest opera house.

↘ NATURAL HIGHS

- Twilight cruising on the fabled **Lago di Como** (p130).
- Alpine hiking in the **Parco Nazionale del Gran Paradiso** (p153).
- Hiking the terraced coastline of Liguria's **Cinque Terre** (p137).
- Sunrise hot-air ballooning over the vineyards of **Alba** (p148).

↘ PLACES TO STOCK THE PANTRY

- **Peck, Milan** (p123) The king of gourmet delis.
- **Eataly, Turin** (p145) A temple of Slow Food treats.
- **Peyrano, Turin** (p147) The city's legendary chocolate peddler.
- **Bottega dei Quattro Vini, Neive** (p151) Local showcase wines and fantastic nibbles.

↘ APERITIVO BARS

- **Le Biciclette, Milan** (p123) Scrumptious grazing in a former bike shop.
- **Living, Milan** (p124) Crafty cocktails and an urbane crowd.
- **Lobelix, Turin** (p147) A bountiful buffet that's the talk of Turin.
- **I Tre Galli, Turin** (p147) Gourmet nosh and a lively vibe.

LEFT: JOHN ELK III; RIGHT: ROBERTO GEROMETTA

Left: Manarola (p139), Cinque Terra; Right: Isola Bella garden (p129)

THINGS YOU NEED TO KNOW

⤳ VITAL STATISTICS

- **Population** 15.7 million
- **Area codes** ☎ Milan 02, Turin 011
- **Best time to visit** April to June, September and October.

⤳ LOCALITIES IN A NUTSHELL

- **Milan** (p116) Fashion, fads and cosmopolitan fun.
- **The Lakes** (p128) Dreamy villas and snow-brushed mountains.
- **Liguria** (p135) Cinque Terre, Portofino and the meeting of mountains and sea.
- **Piedmont** (p141) Dynamic Turin meets vino-versed countryside.
- **Parco Nazionale del Gran Paradiso** (p153) Spectacular alpine scenery in the Valle D'Aosta.

⤳ ADVANCE PLANNING

- **Two months before** Book tickets to La Scala (p120) and Da Vinci's *The Last Supper* (p120).
- **One week before** Scan www.easymilano.it and www.extratorino.it to see what's on in Milan and Turin respectively. Book a table at L'Antico Ristorante Boeucc (p123).

⤳ ONLINE RESOURCES

- **Milan Tourist Bureau** (www.visitamilano.it)
- **Lombardy Tourism Board** (www.turismo.regione.lombardia.it) Covers the entire Lombardy region.
- **Piedmont Tourism Board** (www.piemontefeel.org) Itineraries, accommodation, and transport links.

- **Valle D'Aosta Tourist Board** (www.regione.vda.it/turismo)
- **Trenitalia** (www.trenitalia.it) Train times and tickets.

⤳ EMERGENCY NUMBERS

- **Fire** ☎ 115
- **Carabinieri/Police** ☎ 112/3
- **Ambulance** ☎ 118

⤳ GETTING AROUND

- **Air** International connections to/from Milan, Bergamo, Turin and Genoa.
- **Walk** Perfect for cities and towns, and coastal and alpine trails.
- **Train** Good connections between major cities and towns. Metro services in Milan and Turin.
- **Bus** Handy for towns not serviced by trains.
- **Car** Convenient for exploring Piedmont's vineyards
- **Bicycle** Ideal for alpine trails and Piedmont's wine region.

⤳ BE FOREWARNED

- **Museums** Most close Monday.
- **Restaurants** Many close in August.
- **Accommodation** Book months ahead if travelling to Milan during Fashion Week or the April Furniture Fair.
- **Pickpockets** Operate in tourist areas.

MILAN & THE NORTHWEST ITINERARIES

URBAN PLEASURES Three Days

From A-list fashion, art and dining to a refreshing hilltop day trip, this is the perfect introduction to Lombardy's cultural side.

Begin with two days in **(1) Milan** (p116), revamping your wardrobe in the Quadrilatero d'Oro, your interiors at 10 Corso Como (both boxed text, p125) and your pantry at Peck (p123). For day two, be sure to booked in for da Vinci's *The Last Supper* (p120), then jaw-drop at the Gothic Duomo (p117) and dine at L'Antico Ristorante Boeucc (p123). Assuming you've booked ahead, cap the night at the sumptuous La Scala (p120).

The next morning, escape to one-of-a-kind **(2) Bergamo** (p126) for the day. Get your bearings on Piazza Vecchia (p126) – proclaimed 'Europe's most beautiful square' by Le Corbusier – and take in the architectural mish-mash of the Basilica di Santa Maria Maggiore (p127), then ponder Raphael's *San Sebastiano* at the acclaimed Accademia Carrara (p127).

LAKESIDE LOUNGING Five Days

From quaint hamlets to regal gardens and celebrity villas, this Lago di Como sojourn is the stuff romantics and aesthetes dream about.

If you don't have your own wheels, catch a train from Milan to civilised **(1) Como** (p130). Pop into the Duomo (p132), shop for local silk at La Tessitura (p133) and drink in the views from Brunate (p132). The following day, retreat to breathtaking **(2) Bellagio** (p134) for two days of enchanted lakeside R&R. Drop into the tourist office for walking- and boating-tour information, and don't miss a visit to the enchanting gardens of Villa Serbelloni (p134).

Rejuvenated, catch a ferry across the lake to Cadenabbia or Menaggio, from where **(3) Tremezzo** (p135) and its celebrated Villa Carlotta are an easy drive or bus trip south. Soak up more romantic landscaping at Villa Balbianello in nearby **(4) Lenno** (p135) before retiring for the night at cosy Locanda Sant'Anna in **(5) Argegno** (p135).

The following day, continue south along the lake's western shore, past **(6) Laglio** (p135), George Clooney's Italian base, to silver-screen star **(7) Cernobbio** (p134), your final lakeside stop.

NORTHWESTERN FLAVOURS 10 Days

Never far from the high altar of the national *cucina* (cuisine), the northwest's gastronomic flavours and traditions are globally revered – and there's nothing better than tasting them on their home turf.

Pique your appetite with a couple of days in the fertile (1) Cinque Terre (p137), stopping in Riomaggiore (p140) for seafood and Manarola (p139) for sweet Sciacchetrà wine, then catch a train to (2) Asti (p151), famed for its Spumante Asti, Moscato d'Asti, truffles and Delle Sagre food festival. Book a winery tour of the castle-strung Monferrato (p152) area or spend two or three days chilling and sipping at Tenuta Castello di Razzano (p152).

From Asti, foodie-mecca (3) Alba (p148) is an easy train trip south-west. Spend a day exploring the town's medieval heart, noshing at Osteria dei Sognatori (p149) and deli hopping for truffles, then spend a few more days exploring the town's vine-laced surrounds. Book a guided tour of Barolo-producing vineyards, tackle a cooking course and consider a daytrip to Cherasco and Slow Food HQ Bra (boxed text, p150).

Your final stop is (4) Turin (p141), where your hit list should include chocolicious Peyrano (boxed text, p147), Slow Food mecca Eataly (p145) and some *aperitivo* bars (p147).

DISCOVER MILAN & THE NORTHWEST

Rome may don the captain's hat, but 'second city' Milan knows who steers the ship. Italy's economic and fashion powerhouse swaps Mediterranean sentimentality for shares, skyscrapers and up-to-the-second trends. It's also the capital of Lombardy (Lombardia), whose varied landscape embraces powdered Alps, medieval hill towns, and villa-strung sparkling lakes.

To the west, Piedmont has 'Made in Italy' stamped all over it. Home of Fiat and Lavazza, its showpiece metropolis, Turin, boasts a grand Napoleonic centre and a kicking aperitivo scene. Piedmont's smaller towns were once feuding fiefdoms bickering over trade and religion. Today the biggest skirmishes are over who produces the best wine or which valley showcases the finest cheese.

To the south, Liguria is where the Alps and Apennines cascade precipitously into the Mediterranean, its coastline studded with ancient, weathered settlements and chi-chi coastal resorts.

Topping the northwest is petite, French-influenced Valle d'Aosta. In the shadow of some of Europe's highest peaks, it's home to the Parco Nazionale del Gran Paradiso, one of Italy's most spectacular national parks.

MILAN

pop 1.3 million

At first glance, Milan (Milano) can appear like one of the models gracing its catwalks: great bone structure (in the shape of historic and striking new architecture), extravagant taste and no obvious soul. But Milan's style and, yes, substance, are more than skin deep.

Treasures that survived damage from Allied bombing during WWII include its elaborate cathedral, Leonardo da Vinci's *The Last Supper* and the Castello Sforzesco. The La Scala opera house also scraped through. What really sets Milan apart, however, is its creative streak and high-speed cosmopolitan feel.

HISTORY

Celtic tribes settled along the river Po in the 7th century BC, and the area encom-

passing modern-day Milan has remained inhabited since. In AD 313, Emperor Constantine made his momentous edict granting Christians freedom of worship here. The city had already replaced Rome as the capital of the empire in 286, a role it kept until 402.

A *comune* (town council) was formed by all social classes in the 11th century, and, from the mid-13th century, government passed to a succession of dynasties – the Torrianis, Viscontis and, finally, the Sforzas. It fell under Spanish rule in 1525 and Austrian in 1713.

Benito Mussolini, one-time editor of the socialist newspaper *Avanti!,* founded the Fascist Party in Milan in 1919. During WWII, allied bombings destroyed much of central Milan.

In 1992, the *Tangentopoli* scandal broke, implicating thousands of Italian (and many Milanese) politicians, officials and businesspeople, fashion designers Gianni Versace and Giorgio Armani among them.

Milan media mogul Silvio Berlusconi made the move into politics in the 1990s and has since been elected prime minister three times, most recently in 2008.

ORIENTATION

Central Milan's spider's web of streets radiates from the city's geographical and spiritual heart, the Duomo (Cathedral).

North of the Duomo is the Quadrilatero d'Oro (Golden Quad), Milan's designer shopping precinct. Northwest is the gentrified, former bohemian quarter of Brera, with narrow cobblestone streets, upmarket antique shops and alfresco cafes. The city's best nightlife is on and around Corso Como, further northwest, beyond which is the edgy Isola design district. To the Duomo's south lies the Navigli canal district, while the Castello Sforzesco stands in the Parco Sempione to the west.

INFORMATION
EMERGENCY
Police station (☎ 02 6 22 61; Via Fatebenefratelli 11)

MONEY
There are currency-exchange offices at both airports and a couple on the western side of Piazza del Duomo.

POST
Central post office (Piazza Cordusio 1)

TOURIST INFORMATION
Central tourist office (☎ 02 7740 4343; www.provincia.milano.it/turismo; lower level, Piazza del Duomo 19a; ☒ 8.45am-1pm & 2-6pm Mon-Sat, 9am-1pm & 2-5pm Sun)
Tourist office (☎ 02 7740 4318; Stazione Centrale; ☒ 9am-6pm Mon-Sat, 9am-1pm & 2-5pm Sun & holidays) In front of platform 13.

SIGHTS
Many visitors hit Milan for its shopping rather than sights, but there's plenty to see beyond the boutiques.

DUOMO & AROUND
DUOMO
A frenzy of flying buttresses, 135 spires and a staggering 3200 statues, Milan's Gothic **Duomo** (☎ 02 7202 2656; www.duomomilano.it; Piazza del Duomo) is the world's largest of its kind, and third largest in any style in Europe. This vision of pink-tinged Candoglia marble was commissioned in 1386 by Gian Galeazzo Visconti and has a capacity for a congregation of 40,000 (Milan's population at the time).

For a close-up of the forest of spires, statuary and pinnacles – and views as far as Switzerland on a clear day – you can climb 165 steps to the **cathedral roof** (admission €5; ☒ 9am-5.45pm). Alternatively,

---

DESIGNER DETAILS

Art and design intertwine at the city's groundbreaking contemporary galleries. Leading the pack is **Padiglione d'Arte Contemporanea** (PAC; ☎ 02 7600 9085; www.comune.milano.it/pac; Via Palestro 14; adult/senior & student €5/3; ☒ 2.30-7.30pm Mon, 9.30am-7.30pm Tue-Wed & Fri-Sun, 9.30am-10.30pm Thu, to 7.30pm Sun), which mounts experimental exhibitions in all media.

Retro items at **Studio Museo Achille Castiglioni** (☎ 02 7243 4231; Piazza Castello 27; ☒ tours 10am, 11am & noon Tue-Sun) range from the streetlight-turned-pendulum Arco floor lamp to early examples of Alessi's gadget wizardry. Tours are free with prepurchased Triennale di Milano tickets, but booking is required.

CENTRAL MILAN

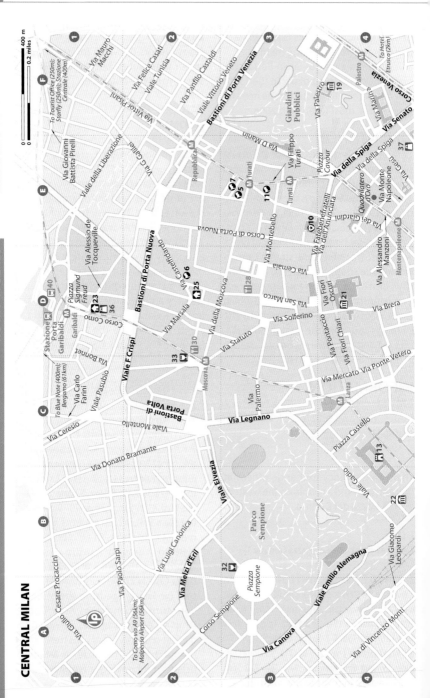

0   400 m
0   0.2 miles

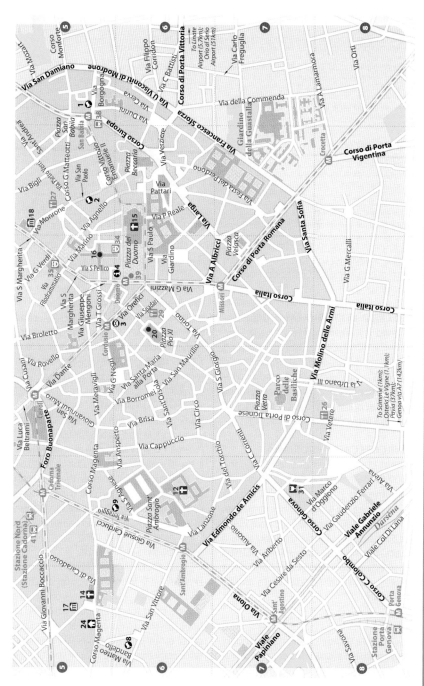

it's a quick zip up in the lift (admission €8; 9am-5.30pm) to the top. Entrances to both are outside the cathedral on the northern side.

GALLERIA VITTORIO EMANUELE II

Framed by an immense archway, the Galleria Vittorio Emanuele II opens off the Piazza del Duomo's northern flank. This glass-and-steel-roofed shopping arcade is shaped like a crucifix, and is home to elegant boutiques, cafes, and, unfortunately, a McDonald's.

PINACOTECA AMBROSIANA

Within Europe's first public library, the 1609 Biblioteca Ambrosiana, is its outstanding art gallery, the Pinacoteca Ambrosiana (02 80 69 21; www.ambrosiana. it; Piazza Pio XI 2; adult/child €8/5; 10am-5.30pm Tue-Sun). Priceless works that you should check out include Italy's first real still life, Caravaggio's *Canestro di frutta* (Fruit Basket) and Leonardo da Vinci's *Musico* (Musician).

LA SCALA

The austere facade of Milan's legendary opera house, Teatro alla Scala (La Scala) seems at odds with its sumptuous six-

tiered interior, all chandeliers and scarlet-silk-lined private boxes.

Attending a performance is incredible; see p124 for ticket details. Otherwise, you can peek inside as part of a visit to the inhouse Museo Teatrale alla Scala (La Scala Museum; 02 4335 3521; www.teatroallascala.org; Piazza della Scala; adult/child €5/4; 9am-12.30pm & 1.30-5.30pm), provided there are no performances or rehearsals in progress.

AROUND LA SCALA

Botticelli's *Madonna and Child* is the star attraction at the nearby Museo Poldi-Pezzoli (02 79 48 89; www.museopoldipezzoli. it; Via Alessandro Manzoni 12; adult/child €8/5.50; 10am-6pm Tue-Sun). Home to the city's most important private collection, it also displays some superb porcelain, jewellery, tapestries, antique furniture and paintings.

THE LAST SUPPER (IL CENACOLO VINCIANO)

Leonardo Da Vinci's depiction of Christ and his dinner companions is one of the world's most iconic images. You need to book anything from two weeks to a couple of months ahead or take a somewhat pricey city tour (see p122) to see it. Once in, you get just 15 minutes' viewing time.

The mural (☎ 02 8942 1146; www.cena colovinciano.org; adult/EU citizens 18-25 yrs/EU citizens under 18 yrs & over 65 yrs €6.50/3.25/free, plus booking fee €1.50; ☉ 8.15am-7pm Tue-Sun) is hidden away on one wall of the Cenacolo Vinciano, the refectory adjoining the Chiesa di Santa Maria delle Grazie (Corso Magenta; ☉ 8.15am-7pm Tue-Sun).

Reservations must be made by phone. You'll be allotted a visiting time and reservation number, which you present 30 minutes before your visit at the refectory ticket desk. If you turn up late, your ticket will be resold.

English-language guided tours (€3.25) take place at 9.30am and 3.30pm Tuesday to Sunday – again you'll need to reserve ahead.

CASTELLO SFORZESCO

Originally a Visconti fortress, this immense red-brick castle (☎ 02 8846 3700; www.milanocastello.it; Piazza Castello; adult/senior/child under 18yrs €3/1.50/free, after 2pm Fri free; ☉ castle grounds 7am-6pm or 7pm Tue-Sun, museums 9am-5.30pm Tue-Sun) was later home to the mighty Sforza dynasty that ruled Renaissance Milan. The castle's defences were designed by Leonardo da Vinci; Napoleon later drained the moat and removed the drawbridges. Today, it shelters a series of specialised museums, accessible on the same ticket.

AROUND CASTELLO SFORZESCO

St Ambrose, Milan's patron saint, is buried in the crypt of the Romanesque Basilica di Sant'Ambrogio (Piazza Sant'Ambrogio 15), which he founded in the 4th century. Since then, the church has been repaired, rebuilt and restored several times, resulting in a mishmash of styles.

PINACOTECA DI BRERA

Religious art amassed (or rather, purloined) by Napoleon formed the basis of the formidable collection at the 17th-century Palazzo di Brera's Pinacoteca di Brera (☎ 02 8942 1146; www.brera.beniculturali. it; Via Brera 28; adult/child €10/7.50, EU adult/child €5/free; ☉ 8.30am-7.15pm Tue-Sun).

PAOLO CORDELLI

Castello Sforzesco from Parco Sempione

Naviglio canal district at night

MARTIN MOOS

TOURS

Zani Viaggi (☎ 02 86 71 31; www.zaniviaggi. it) runs a variety of guided tours in and around the city (€25 to €55), some including admission to *The Last Supper*. Tours depart from Piazza Castello and Stazione Centrale.

FESTIVALS & EVENTS

La Scala's opera season opens on Milan's biggest feast day, the **Festa di Sant'Ambrogio**, on 7 December. Other festivals to look out for:

Carnevale Ambrosiano The world's longest carnival, this event culminates with a procession to the Duomo; held in February.

Cortili Aperti (www.italiamultimedia.com/ cortiliaperti) For one May Sunday, the gates to some of the city's most beautiful private courtyards are flung open. Print out a map and make your own itinerary.

Festa del Naviglio Parades, music and performances take place during the first 10 days of June.

SLEEPING

Finding a room in Milan (let alone a cheap one) isn't easy, particularly during the fashion weeks, furniture fair and other exhibitions, when rates skyrocket.

Hotel Etrusco (☎ 02 236 38 52; www. hoteletrusco.it; Via Porpora 56; s/d €60/80; P) This elegant little three-star features a lovely garden and pleasant rooms and is certainly the pick of the bunch around Piazza Aspromonte. Six rooms with terraces overlook the garden area.

ourpick Antica Locanda Leonardo (☎ 02 4801 4197; www.anticalocandaleonardo.com; Corso Magenta 78; s €120, d €165-245; ✗ ☎) Rooms here ooze homey comfort, from the timber beds and parquet floors in some, to the antique furniture and plush drapes in others. Take breakfast in the quiet, scented, interior garden of this 19th-century residence.

Antica Locanda Solferino (☎ 02 657 01 29; www.anticalocandasolferino.it; Via Castelfidardo 2; s €140-270, d €180-400; ✗ ☎) A genuinely charming hideway with 11 rooms, decorated in a bygone style with some nice paintings and prints, this understated Brera boutique beauty attracts artists, writers and other layabouts, so booking is essential. They have a quite decent-sized single.

3Rooms (☎ 02 62 61 63; www.3rooms-10 Corsocomo.com; Corso Como 10; d €270-310; P ⊠ ⧠ ☎) Can't drag yourself away from concept shop Corso Como? You don't have to: the villa's three guest rooms let you sleep amid Eames bedspreads, Arne Jacobsen chairs and Saarinen leather.

EATING

In the Brera area, pavement terraces open up along hip Via Fiori Chiari in summer. The canal district has a host of appealing spots.

Gelateria le Colonne (☎ 02 837 22 92; Corso di Porta Ticinese 75; gelati €2-3; ⧖ 12.30pm-1.30am Mon-Thu, 12.30pm-2am Fri & Sat, 3pm-1am Sun) Come here for artisanal ice cream in wild flavours such as rice, amaretto, orange blossom and specials like Huehuetenango coffee flavour from Guatemala.

Princi (☎ 02 87 47 97; Via Speronari 6; meals €10; ⧖ 7am-8pm Mon-Fri, 8am-8pm Sat) Equally delicious for an early-morning *cornetto* (Italian-type croissant) or *stracchino* (Lombard cow's milk cheese)-filled focaccia on the way home at midnight, Princi is perfect for a filling bite on the run.

Latteria (☎ 02 659 76 53; Via San Marco 24; meals €25-30; ⧖ Mon-Fri) If you can snare a seat in this tiny and ever-popular restaurant, you'll find old favourites like *spaghetti alla carbonara* mixed in with chef Arturo's own creations, such as *polpettine al limone* (little meatballs with lemon) or *riso al salto* (risotto fritters) on the ever-changing, mostly organic menu.

our pick **Osteria Le Vigne** (☎ 02 837 56 17; Ripa di Porta Ticinese 61; meals €25-30; ⧖ Mon-Sat) A perennially popular Navigli eatery, this place is hard to beat for value. Perusal of the menu will reveal such options as *strac-*

cetti di pasta fresca con pollo (strips of fresh pasta with chicken).

L'Antico Ristorante Boeucc (☎ 02 760 20 224; Piazza Belgioioso 2; meals €60-80; ⧖ lunch & dinner Mon-Fri, lunch only Sun) Milan's oldest restaurant (since 1696) serves up works of Lombard culinary art, from *crespelle al prosciutto* (a kind of cross between pasta and crepe with ham) to a *trancio di salmone al pepe verde* (a slice of salmon with green pepper) or Florentine steak.

SELF-CATERING

Since Milan institution **Peck** (☎ 02 802 31 61; www.peck.it; Via Spadari 7-9; ⧖ 3-7.30pm Mon, 8.45am-7.30pm Tue-Sat) opened as a deli in 1883, it's expanded to a dining room/bar upstairs and an *enoteca* (wine bar). The food hall is smaller than its reputation suggests, but what it lacks in space it makes up for in variety.

DRINKING

The Navigli canal district, the cobbled backstreets of Brera, and swish Corso Como and its surrounds are all great areas for a drink, Milan-style.

Le Biciclette (☎ 02 5810 4325; Via Torti 4; ⧖ Mon-Sat 6pm-2am & Sun 12.30pm-2am) Once a bike warehouse and now one of the

---

EAT, DRINK & BE MERRY: MILAN'S *APERITIVO* SCENE

Happy hour elsewhere in the world might mean downing cut-price pints, but not in oh-so-stylish Milan. Its nightly *aperitivi* is a two-or three-hour ritual, starting around 6pm, where for €6 to €12, a cocktail, glass of wine, or beer comes with an unlimited buffet of antipasti, bruschetta, cured meats, salads, and even seafood and pasta.

best *aperitivo* bars in Milan. Evidence of its former life includes glassed-in bicycle memorabilia.

Living (☎ 02 331 00 84; Piazza Sempione 2; ⏱ 8-2am Mon-Fri, 9-2am Sat & Sun) Living has one of the city's prettiest settings, with a corner position and floor-to-ceiling windows overlooking the Arco della Pace.

Radetzky (☎ 02 657 26 45; Corso Garibaldi 105; ⏱ 8pm-1am) Fabulous banquette and window seating make this one of the most popular places on this stylish, largely pedestrianised strip for an *aperitivo* or long Sunday sessions (well, it started with brunch…).

ENTERTAINMENT

The tourist office stocks several entertainment guides in English: *Milano Mese, Hello Milano* (www.hellomilano.it) and *Easy Milano* (www.easymilano.it).

LIVE MUSIC

Blue Note (☎ 899 700022; www.bluenotemilano.com; Via Borsieri 37; tickets €23-30; ⏱ concerts 9pm & 11pm Tue-Fri, 9pm & 11.30pm Sat, 9pm Sun) Hosts top-class jazz acts from around the world. Tickets by phone, online or at the door from 7.30pm.

Scimmie (☎ 02 8940 2874; www.scimmie.it; Via Cardinale Ascanio Sforza 49; admission €8-15; ⏱ 8pm-3am Mon-Sat) Jazz, alternative rock, and blues are the stock in trade of the emerging talents who play to overflowing crowds inside, in the garden and on its summertime jazz barge. Concerts start at 10pm.

OPERA & THEATRE

The opera season at **Teatro alla Scala** runs from November through July, but you can see theatre, ballet and concerts here year-round, with the exception of August.

You'll need perseverance and luck to secure opera tickets at La Scala (€10 to €180; up to €2000 for opening night). About two months before the first performance, tickets can be bought by telephone – ☎ 02 86 07 75 (24 hours) – and online; these tickets carry a 20% surcharge. One month before the first performance, any remaining tickets are sold (with a 10% surcharge) at the **box office** (☎ 02 7200 3744; www.teatroallascala.org; Galleria Vittorio

LEFT: MARTIN MOOS; RIGHT: DALLAS STRIBLEY

Left: 10 Corso Como; Right: Antique market stall

FASHION CAPITAL

Gucci moved to town from Florence in the 1960s, and its flagship store ushered in what is now known as the **Quadrilatero d'Oro** (Golden Quad), a quadrangle of pedestrian streets bordered by Via della Spiga, Via Sant'Andrea, Via Monte Napoleone and Via Alessandro Manzoni. The quad's narrow streets are crammed with Italian designers such as **Giorgio Armani** (☎ 02 7600 3234; www.giorgioarmani.com; Via Sant'Andrea 9), who revolutionised the industry with his prêt-à-porter (ready to wear) collection in the early 1980s.

Fashion shopping isn't confined to the Golden Quad. Ultraexclusive concept shop **10 Corso Como** (☎ 02 2900 2674; www.10corsocomo.com; Corso Como 10) was set up by former Italian *Vogue* contributor Carla Sozzani and is secluded in a vine-draped and plant-filled townhouse courtyard.

Emanuele; ☽ noon-6pm). On performance days, 140 tickets for the gallery are sold two hours before the show – one ticket per customer.

SHOPPING

Markets fill the canalside Viale Papiniano in the southwest of the city on Tuesday (7.30am-1pm) and Saturday (7.30am-5pm). There is an antique market in Brera on Via Fiori Chiari and nearby streets every third Sunday of the month.

GETTING THERE & AWAY

AIR

Most European and other international flights use **Malpensa airport** (www.sea-aeroportimilano.it), 50km northwest of the city. The majority of domestic and a handful of European flights use the more convenient **Linate airport** (www.sea-aeroportimilano.it), 7km east of the city centre.

An increasing number of budget airlines also use **Orio al Serio airport** (☎ 035 32 63 23; www.sacbo.it), near Bergamo.

BUS

Most national and international buses use the new **Lampugnano bus terminal** by the Lampugnano metro station (line 1 – the red line), west of the city centre.

TRAIN

You can catch a train from the grand **Stazione Centrale** (Piazza Duca d'Aosta) to all major cities in Italy. Ferrovie Nord Milano (FNM) trains from **Stazione Nord** (Stazione Cadorna; www.ferrovienord.it, in Italian; Piazza Luigi Cadorna) connect Milan with Como (€3.60, one hour, half hourly). Regional services to many towns northwest of Milan are more frequent from **Stazione Porta Garibaldi** (Piazza Sigmund Freud).

GETTING AROUND

TO/FROM THE AIRPORTS

LINATE AIRPORT

From Milan's Piazza Luigi di Savoia, next to Stazione Centrale, **Starfly** (☎ 02 5858 7237) runs buses to Linate airport (adult/child €4.50/2.50, 25 minutes, half-hourly between 5.40am and 9.35pm).

Local ATM bus 73 (€1, 20 minutes, every 10–15 minutes from 5.35am to 12.35am) from Piazza San Babila also does the run comfortably.

MALPENSA AIRPORT

The **Malpensa Express** (☎ 199 151152; www.malpensaexpress.it; ☽ ticket office 7am-8pm) train links Stazione Nord with Malpensa airport (adult/child €11/5.50, 40 minutes, every 30 minutes).

Malpensa Shuttle (☎ 02 5858 3185; www.malpensa-shuttle.com; ⏱ ticket office 7am-9pm) coaches depart from Piazza Luigi di Savoia (adult/child €7/3.50, every 20 minutes between 5am and 10.30pm, 50 minutes).

ORIO AL SERIO AIRPORT

Autostradale runs buses approximately every 30 minutes between 4am and 11.30pm from Piazza Luigi di Savoia to Orio al Serio airport, near Bergamo (adult/child €8.90/4.45, one hour).

PUBLIC TRANSPORT

Milan's efficient public transport system is run by **ATM** (☎ 800 808181; www.atm-mi.it). The metro consists of four underground lines (red MM1, green MM2, yellow MM3 and blue Passante Ferroviario), which run from 6am to midnight.

A ticket costs €1 and is valid for one metro ride or up to 75 minutes' travel on ATM buses and trams. You can buy a 10-ride pass for €9.20 or unlimited one-/two-day tickets for bus, tram and metro for €3/5.50. Tickets are sold at metro stations, tobacconists and newspaper stands around town.

TAXI

Head for a taxi rank or call ☎ 02 40 40, ☎ 02 69 69 or ☎ 02 85 85. The average short city ride will cost €10.

AROUND MILAN

CERTOSA DI PAVIA

One of the Italian Renaissance's most notable buildings is the splendid **Certosa di Pavia** (Pavia Charterhouse; ☎ 0382 92 56 13; www.certosadipavia.com; Viale Monumento; admission by donation; ⏱ 9-11.30am & 2.30-5.30pm Tue-Sun). Gian Galeazzo Visconti of Milan founded the monastery, 10km north of Pavia, in 1396 as a private chapel for the Visconti family and a home for 12 monks.

To reach the charterhouse (about a 10-minute walk) from the bus stop, turn right at the traffic lights and continue straight ahead. **Sila** (☎ 199 153155; www.sila.it in Italian) bus 175 (Pavia-Binasco-Milano) links **Pavia bus station** (Via Trieste) and Certosa di Pavia (15 minutes, at least seven daily).

Plenty of direct trains link Pavia train station with Milan (from €3.05, 20 to 40 minutes) and a good number run south to Genoa (from €6.75, one hour 10 minutes to 1½ hours) and beyond.

BERGAMO

pop 115,800

With its wealth of medieval, Renaissance and baroque architecture, Bergamo is one of northern Italy's most intriguing cities.

Actually, Bergamo comprises what are essentially two separate towns. The most interesting, by far, is its hilltop *città alta* (upper town), protected by more than 5km of heavy-duty walls. A funicular carries you from the western edge of the upper town up to the quaint quarter of San Vigilio. Down on the plain, the sprawling *città bassa* (lower town) is a mishmash of modern buildings and wide, traffic-filled streets.

INFORMATION

Police station (☎ 035 27 61 11; Via Noli 26)
Upper town tourist office (☎ 035 24 22 26; Via Gombito 13; ⏱ 9am-12.30pm & 2-5.30pm)

SIGHTS

PIAZZA VECCHIA

The white porticoed building on Via Bartolomeo Colleoni, which forms the northern side of the piazza, is the 17th-century **Palazzo Nuovo**, now a library. Turn south and you face the imposing arches and columns of the **Palazzo della Ragione**, built in the 12th century. The lion of St Mark is a reminder of Venice's long reign here. Across the square from the palace, the colossal **Torre del Campanone** (Piazza Vecchia; admission €3; ⊙ 9.30am-1pm & 2-5.30pm Tue-Fri, 9.30am-1pm & 2-7.30pm Sat & Sun mid-Mar–Oct, Mon-Sat by reservation Nov–mid-Mar) tolls the old 10pm curfew.

Roman remains were discovered during renovations of the modest baroque **Duomo** (cathedral; ☎ 035 21 02 23; Piazza del Duomo; ⊙ 7.30-11.45am & 3-6.30pm). A great deal more intriguing is the Romanesque **Basilica di Santa Maria Maggiore** (☎ 035 22 33 27; Piazza del Duomo; ⊙ 9am-12.30pm & 2.30-6pm Apr-Oct, 9am-12.30pm & 2.30-5pm Mon-Fri, 9am-12.30pm & 2.30-6pm Sat, 9am-12.45pm & 3-6pm Sun Nov-Mar) next door.

LOWER TOWN

Just east of the walls is one of Italy's great art repositories, **Accademia Carrara** (☎ 035 39 96 40; www.accademiacarrara.bergamo.it; Piazza Carrara 82a; adult/child €2.60/free; ⊙ 10am-1pm & 2.30-5.30pm Tue-Sun). At the time of writing it was closed for restoration, but a selection of its masterpieces was on show in the Palazzo della Ragione.

SLEEPING

Albergo Il Sole (☎ 035 21 82 38; www.ilsolebergamo.com; Via Colleoni 1; s/d €65/85) The picture windows and colourful bedspreads at Il Sole lend its rooms a countrified air, which extends to its restaurant (meals €30; ⊙ Fri-Wed Mar-Oct), set in a cool, leafy garden.

B&B Alba (☎ 349 5752596; www.bbalbachiara.info; Via Salvecchio 2; d/tr €100/120) Three spacious rooms are available in this rambling old townhouse. Mosaic and terracotta floors, high, frescoed ceilings, the odd item of antique furniture, and loads of atmosphere make this B&B attractive.

Hotel Piazza Vecchia (☎ 035 428 42 11; www.hotelpiazzavecchia.it; Via Colleoni 3; s €135-170, d €150-190; ⊙ ⊒) Carved out of

JEAN-PIERRE LESCOURRET

Certosa di Pavia ceiling

a 13th-century building a few steps off Piazza Vecchia, this hotel's 13 rooms are all quite different. All have parquet floors and baths in stone, but details vary.

EATING

Picnickers can pick up steaming-hot pizza slices, focaccias and desserts at high-quality bakeries along the upper town's main street.

Antica Hosteria del Vino Buono (☎ 035 24 79 93; Piazza Mercato delle Scarpe; meals €25; ⊙ dinner Tue, lunch & dinner Wed-Sun) Feast on typical dishes like cheese-sprinkled *casoncelli* (homemade pasta cushions filled with a spicy sausage meat and laced with a buttery sage sauce) followed by a plate of *stinco al forno con polenta* (baked beef shank with polenta).

Vineria Cozzi (☎ 035 23 88 36; www.vineria cozzi.it; Via Colleoni 22; meals €35-45; ⊗ Thu-Tue) Sample the extensive wine list by the glass and dine inside or in the tiny courtyard.

GETTING THERE & AWAY
AIR
Bergamo's airport, Orio al Serio (☎ 035 32 63 23; www.sacbo.it), is 4km southeast of the train station.

BUS
From Bergamo's bus station (☎ 800 139392, 035 28 90 00; www.bergamotrasporti.it), just off Piazzale Marconi, SAB (☎ 035 28 90 00; www .sab-autoservizi.it, in Italian) operates services to the lakes and mountains.

TRAIN
From the Piazzale Marconi train station, there are one or two trains an hour to/from Milan, although not all call at Stazione Centrale (€4.20, 50 to 65 minutes).

GETTING AROUND
TO/FROM THE AIRPORT
ATB (☎ 035 23 60 26) buses to/from Orio al Serio airport depart every 20 minutes from Bergamo bus and train stations (€1.70, 15 minutes). Direct buses also connect the airport with Milan and Brescia.

PUBLIC TRANSPORT
ATB's bus 1 connects the train station with the funicular to the upper city and Colle Aperto (going the other way, some buses stop only at the Porta Nuova stop). From Colle Aperto, either bus 21 or a funicular continues uphill to San Vigilio. Buy tickets, valid for 75 minutes' travel on buses, for €1 from machines at the train and funicular stations or at newspaper stands. Funicular tickets cost €1.50.

THE LAKES
Writers from Goethe and Stendhal to DH Lawrence and Hemingway have all lavished praise on the Italian lakes, but even their words scarcely express the lakes' beauty.

Elaborate villas attest to the roll call of celebrity visitors and residents that the lakes, which are ringed by snow-powdered mountains, have attracted over the centuries.

LAGO MAGGIORE
If you're arriving from Switzerland by train, once you emerge from the Alpine tunnels into the bright Italian sunlight, the views of the flower-filled Borromean Islands studding the dazzling blue lake are unforgettable.

The train line shadows the lake's western shore, which is its prettiest side, sprinkled with picturesque villages and towns, including the main town, Stresa.

GETTING THERE & AROUND
The daily Verbania Intra-Milan bus service operated by SAF (☎ 0323 55 21 72; www.sat duemila.com, in Italian) links Stresa with Arona (€2, 20 minutes), Verbania Pallanza (€2, 20 minutes), Verbania Intra (€2, 25 minutes) and Milan (€6.70, 1½ hours).

Ferries and hydrofoils around the lake are operated by Navigazione Lago Maggiore (☎ 800 551801; www.navigazione laghi.it, in Italian), which has its main ticket office in Arona.

Services are drastically reduced in autumn and winter.

The only car ferry connecting the western and eastern shores for motorists sails between Verbania Intra and Laveno. Ferries run every 20 minutes; one-way transport costs between €6.90 and €11.50 for a car and driver or €4.30 for a bicycle and cyclist.

MARTIN LLADO

Lago Maggiore from Isola Madre

⇲ BORROMEAN ISLANDS

Forming Lago Maggiore's most beautiful corner, Isole Borromee can be reached from various points around the lake, but Stresa and Baveno offer the best access.

Isola Bella took the name of Carlo III's wife, the *bella* Isabella, in the 17th century, when its centrepiece, Palazzo Borromeo, was built for the Borromeo family. Presiding over 10 tiers of terraced gardens, the baroque palace contains works by Tiepolo and van Dyck (to see the bulk of the art you have to buy a €16 ticket granting access to the Galleria dei Quadri), as well as Flemish tapestries and sculptures by Canova. A combined ticket covering admission to the Borromeo and Madre palaces costs €16.50/7.50 per adult/child.

All of Isola Madre is taken up by the fabulous 16th- to 18th-century Palazzo Madre. White peacocks whose fanned feathers resemble bridal gowns strut around English-style gardens that rival those of Isola Bella.

Things you need to know: Palazzo Borromeo (☎ 0323 3 05 56; www.borromeoturismo.it; adult/child €12/5; ⌚ 9am-5.30pm Apr–mid-Oct); Palazzo Madre (☎ 0323 3 05 56; adult/child €10/5; ⌚ 9am-5.30pm Mar-Oct)

STRESA

pop 5180

The town's easy access from Milan has made it a favourite for artists and writers seeking inspiration. Hemingway was one of many; he arrived in Stresa in 1918 to convalesce from a war wound. A couple of pivotal scenes towards the end of his novel *A Farewell to Arms* are set at the Grand Hotel des Iles Borromees, the most palatial of the hotels garlanding the lake.

Offshore, the Borromean Islands make an ideal ferry excursion from Stresa.

INFORMATION

Tourist office (☎ 0323 3 13 08; distrettolaghi. eu; Piazza Marconi 16; ⌚ 10am-12.30pm & 3-6.30pm mid-Mar–mid-Oct, 10am-12.30pm & 3-6.30pm Mon-Fri, 10am-12.30pm Sat mid-Oct–mid-Mar).

SIGHTS & ACTIVITIES

Captivating views of the lake unfold during a 20-minute cable-car journey on the **Funivia Stresa-Mottarone** (☎ 0323 3 02 95; www.stresa-mottarone.it; Piazzale della Funivia; adult/child return €17.50/11; ☼ 9.30am-5.30pm) to the top of 1491m-high Monte Mottarone.

Bicicò (☎ 0323 3 03 99; www.bicico.it) rents out mountain bikes at the lower Stresa cable-car station.

SLEEPING & EATING

La Stellina (☎ 0323 3 24 43; www.lastellina.com; Via Molinari 10; s/d €70/80) A couple of blocks' stroll from the main square, an early 19th-century building makes a beautiful backdrop for this charming little B&B.

Albergo Villa Mon Toc (☎ 0323 3 02 82; www.hotelmontoc.com; Viale Duchessa di Genova 67-69; s/d €55/85; ℗ ❄) Rooms have a pleasingly old-fashioned air, with dark wooden furniture, big beds and throw rugs on the tile floors.

Osteria degli Amici (☎ 0323 3 04 53; Via Anna Maria Bolongaro 33; pizzas €4.50-9, meals €25) You may need to queue (it's always packed) but it's worth it to dine under vines on one of Stresa's most delightful terraces in the centre of town.

ourpick **Il Clandestino** (☎ 0323 3 03 99; Via Rosmini 5; meals €30; ☼ Wed-Mon) An elegant corner dining room, Il Clandestino serves up great lake fish and seafood, with some of the ingredients and ideas coming from Sicily.

LAGO DI COMO

In the shadow of the snow-covered Rhaetian Alps, Lago di Como (also known as Lago Lario) is the most spectacular of the lakes. Shaped like an upside-down letter Y, its squiggly shoreline is scattered with villages, including exquisite Bellagio, in the centre of the inverted V on the lake's southern shore.

GETTING THERE & AROUND

The Como-based **ASF Autolinee** (☎ 031 24 72 47; www.sptlinea.it, in Italian) operates regular buses around the lake, which depart from the bus station.

Trains from Milan's Stazione Centrale and Porta Garibaldi station (€3.60-8.50, 40 minutes to one hour, hourly) use Como's main train station (Como San Giovanni), and some continue on into Switzerland. Trains from Milan's Stazione Nord (€3.60, one hour, hourly) use Como's lakeside Stazione FNM (listed on timetables as Como Nord Lago).

Navigazione Lago di Como (☎ 800 551801; www.navigazionelaghi.it; Piazza Cavour) ferries and hydrofoils criss-cross the lake, departing year-round from the jetty at the northern end of Piazza Cavour. One-way fares range from €1.90 (Como–Cernobbio) to €10 (Como–Lecco).

Car ferries link Cadenabbia on the west shore with Varenna on the eastern shore and Bellagio.

COMO

pop 83,170

Elegant Como is the main access town to the lake. Its twin claims to fame are the lake with which it shares its name, and its silk industry.

INFORMATION

Police station (☎ 031 31 71; Viale Roosevelt 7)
Post office (☼ 8.30am-7pm Mon-Fri, 8.30am-12.30pm Sat) Main branch (Via T Gallio 6); Old Town (Via Vittorio Emanuele II 113)
Tourist office (☎ 031 26 97 12; www.lakecomo.org; Piazza Cavour 17; ☼ 9am-1pm & 2.30-6pm Mon-Sat, plus 9.30am-1pm Sun Jun-Sep)

SIGHTS & ACTIVITIES

Como's lakeside location is stunning, and its narrow pedestrian lanes are a pleasure to explore, with some no-

COMO

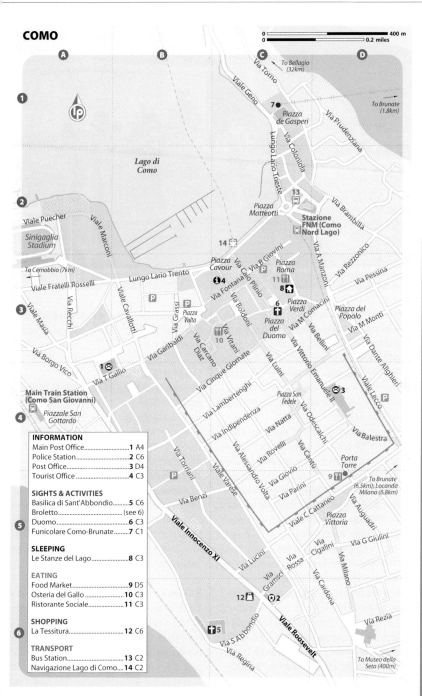

0   400 m
0   0.2 miles

To Bellagio
(32km)

To Brunate
(1.8km)

Via Torno

Viale Geno

Piazza
de Gasperi

Via Prudenziana

Lungo Lario Trieste

Via Coloniola

Lago di
Como

Via Brambilla

Piazza
Matteotti

Stazione
FNM (Como
Nord Lago)

Via A Manzoni

Via Rezzonico

Viale Puecher

Sinigaglia
Stadium

Viale Marconi

Piazza
Cavour

Via Calo Plinio

Via B Giovini

Piazza
Roma

Via Pessina

To Cernobbio (7km)

Viale Fratelli Rosselli

Lungo Lario Trento

Via Fontana

Piazza
Verdi

Via M Comacini

Piazzadel
Popolo

Viale Cavallotti

Via Recchi

Via Grassi

Piazza
Volta

Via Boldoni

Piazza
del
Duomo

Via M Monti

Via Masia

Via Garibaldi

Via Vitani

Via Luini

Via Vittorio Emanuele II

Via Dante Alighieri

Via Borgo Vico

Via Carcano
Diaz

Via Cinque Giornate

Viale Lecco

Via T Gallio

Piazza San
Fedele

Via Odescalchi

Via Balestra

Main Train Station
(Como San Giovanni)

Via Lambertenghi

Via Natta

Via Cantù

Piazzale San
Gottardo

Via Indipendenza

Via Rovelli

Via Giovio

Porta
Torre

Via Torriani

Viale Varese

Via Alessandro Volta

Via Parini

To Brunate
(6.5km); Locanda
Milano (6.8km)

Via Benzi

Piazza
Vittoria

Viale C Cattaneo

Via Auguadri

Viale Innocenzo XI

Via
Cigalini

Via G Giulini

Via Lucini

Via
Gramsci

Via
Rossa

Via Milano

Via Cardona

Via S Abbondio

Viale Roosevelt

Via Rezia

Via Regina

To Museo della
Seta (400m)

ROCCO FASANO

Swimmers in Lago di Como

table sights along the way. Elements of baroque, Gothic, Romanesque and Renaissance styles can be seen in Como's marble-clad **Duomo** (cathedral; Piazza del Duomo; ☉ 7am-noon & 3-7pm). Next door, the polychromatic **Broletto** (medieval town hall) looks like a mere appendage of the church.

About 500m south of the city walls and just beyond the busy and rather ugly Viale Innocenzo XI is the remarkable 11th-century Romanesque **Basilica di Sant'Abbondio** (Via Regina; ☉ 8am-6pm).

South of the old town, the **Museo della Seta** (Silk Museum; ☎ 031 30 31 80; www.museo setacomo.com; Via Castelnuovo 9; adult/child €8/2.60; ☉ 9am-noon & 3-6pm Tue-Fri) unravels the town's silk history, with early dyeing and printing equipment on display.

Northeast along the waterfront, past Piazza Matteotti and the train station, is the **Funicolare Como–Brunate** (☎ 031 30 36 08; www.funicolarecomo.it; Piazza de Gasperi 4; adult/child one-way €2.50/1.65, return €4.35/2.75; ☉ 6am-midnight mid-Apr–mid-Sep, to 10.30pm mid-Sep–mid-Apr), a cable car built in 1894.

It takes seven minutes to reach hill-top **Brunate** (720m), a quiet village offering splendid views.

SLEEPING

Le Stanze del Lago (☎ 339 544 65 15; www. lestanzedellago.com, Via Rodari 6; 2-/4-person apt from €70/90; ✖) Five cosy apartments, nicely decked out in modern but understated fashion, make for a good deal in the heart of Como.

Locanda Milano (☎ 031 336 50 69; www. locandamilano.it, in Italian; Via Volta 62, Brunate; s/d €80/100; P) Get away from it all in the hilltop village of Brunate, where Locanda Milano offers restful rooms in pretty yellow and blue hues, perched above its well-regarded restaurant (meals €45).

EATING

Osteria del Gallo (☎ 031 27 25 91; Via Vitani 16; meals €25; ☉ lunch Mon-Sat) This ageless *osteria* is a lunchtime must. The menu is recited and might include a first of giant ravioli stuffed with mozzarella and topped with tomatoes, followed by lightly fried fillets of agone, a local lake fish.

Ristorante Sociale (☎ 031 26 40 42; Via Rodari 6; meals €25; ☿ Wed-Mon) The Sociale is a local institution. Cooking is no-nonsense, ranging from *risotto trevisana* (with chicory) to huge Milanese *scaloppine* (veal escalopes).

Fresh fruit, vegetables and delicacies abound at Como's **food market** (☿ 8.30am-1pm Tue & Thu, 8.30am-7pm Sat) outside Porta Torre.

SHOPPING

La Tessitura (☎ 031 32 16 66; Viale Roosevelt 2; ☿ 11am-9pm Tue-Sat) Mantero, one of the biggest names in Como silk, runs this large-scale outlet-style store on the site of their former factory (which has been moved out of town).

SOUTHERN SHORE

The 32km western branch of the southern shore is a narrow, twisting, hillside drive, with a steady stream of traffic. Those with time could stop off in various villages along the way, but the 'pearl' of the lake is Bellagio (boxed text, p134) itself, suspended like a pendant on the promontory where the lake's western and eastern arms split and head south.

SLEEPING & EATING

For such an exquisite spot, there are a surprising number of affordable places to sleep and eat (and plenty of luxurious places where you can spoil yourself, too).

Bellagio Bed & Breakfast (☎ 031 95 16 80; www.bellagiobedandbreakfast.com; Salita Mella 38; s/d €50/60; ✕ ▯ ☲) Two snappy little apartments at the top end of one Bellagio's narrow stone stairway streets make for a very good deal.

Albergo Silvio (☎ 031 95 03 22; www.bellagiosilvio.com; Via Carcano 12; s/d from €65/85;

☿ Mar–mid-Nov & Christmas week; ▮P ✕ ▯ ☲) The high position over the western arm of Lago di Como is enough to recommend this spot, 1km short of the centre of Bellagio. The restaurant downstairs, with a balmy outdoor section, is one of Bellagio's badly kept secrets.

WESTERN SHORE

Without the mountains blocking the light, the western shore gets the most sunshine on the lake. For this reason, it's lined with the most lavish villas, where high-fliers from football players to film stars reside.

CERNOBBIO TO LENNO

Ocean's 11 may have been shot at Bellagio's Vegas namesake, but scenes from *Ocean's 12* were filmed in the Lago di

DAMIEN SIMONIS

Gardens of Villa Carlotta (p135)

ROBERTO GEROMETTA

Villa Melzi D'Eril

⇘ BELLAGIO

The place that inspired the Las Vegas casino (the same one involved in a heist in *Ocean's 11*) lives up to its fabled reputation. Bellagio's sapphire-blue harbour, maze of stone staircases and colourful shuttered buildings are truly enchanting.

Bellagio's **tourist office**, next to the boat landing stage, has information on water sports, mountain biking and other lake activities. Otherwise, **PromoBellagio**, in the basement of an 11th-century watchtower, also has information.

The lavish gardens of **Villa Serbelloni** cover much of the promontory on which Bellagio sits. Visits are by guided tour only and numbers are limited; tickets are sold 10 minutes in advance at PromoBellagio.

Garden-lovers can also stroll the grounds of neoclassical **Villa Melzi D'Eril**, built in 1808 for one of Napoleon's associates and coloured by flowering azaleas and rhododendrons in spring.

Things you need to know: tourist office (☎ 031 95 02 04; Piazza Mazzini; ◷ 9am-12.30pm & 2.30-5pm Mon-Tue & Thu, 9am-1pm Wed, 9am-1pm & 3-6pm Fri & Sat); PromoBellagio (☎ 031 95 15 55; www.bellagiolakecomo.com; Piazza della Chiesa 14; ◷ 9.30am-1pm Mon, 9.30am-12.30pm & 1.30-4pm Wed-Fri); Villa Serbelloni (☎ 031 95 15 55; Via Garibaldi 8; adult/child €6.50/3; ◷ tours 11am & 4pm Tue-Sun Apr-Oct); Villa Melzi D'Eril (☎ 339 4573838; www.giardinidivillamelzi.it; Lungo Lario Manzoni; adult/child €6/4; ◷ 9am-6pm Apr-Oct)

Como village of **Cernobbio**, at the 19th-century Villa Erba (Largo Luchino Visconti; closed to the public). Cernobbio is also home to the lake's most magnificent hotel, **Villa d'Este** (www.villadeste.it).

If you're driving, follow the lower lakeside road (Via Regina Vecchia) north from Cernobbio, which skirts the lake shore past a fabulous row of 19th-century villas around **Moltrasio**. Fashion designer

Gianni Versace, who was murdered in Miami Beach, Florida, in 1997, is buried in the village cemetery; his former villa is still owned by the Versace family.

A few kilometres north is the charming hamlet of Laglio, home to *Ocean's* star, George Clooney. North again, Argegno is the departure point into the mountains on the Funivia Argegno–Pigra (☎ 0318 108 44; one-way/return €2.50/3.40; ☾ 8.30am-noon & 2.30-6.30pm). The cable car makes the five-minute climb to the 860m-high village of Pigra every 30 minutes. It runs for fewer hours in winter. Argegno's Locanda Sant'Anna (☎ 031 82 17 38; www.locandasantanna.it; Via Sant'Anna 152; d €100-160; ☒ ☒ ☒) has a handful of beautiful lamp-lit guest rooms and a rustic restaurant.

In Lenno, scenes from *Star Wars: Episode II* and 2006's James Bond remake, *Casino Royale,* were shot at Villa Balbianello (☎ 0344 5 61 10; www.fondoambiente.it; Via Comoedia 5, Località Balbianello; villa & gardens adult/child €11/6, gardens only adult/child €5/2.50; ☾ 10am-6pm Tue & Thu-Sun mid-Mar–mid-Nov), a villa built by Cardinal Angelo Durini in 1787 and used for a while by Allied commanders at the tail end of WWII. Visitors are only allowed to walk the 1km from the Lenno landing stage to the estate on Tuesday and at weekends; other days, you have to take a taxi boat (☎ 333 410 38 54; €6 return) from Lenno or Sala Comacina (a few kilometres south).

TREMEZZO

pop 1300

At the 17th-century Villa Carlotta (☎ 0344 4 04 05; www.villacarlotta.it; Riva Garibaldi; adult/senior & student/child €8/4/free; ☾ 9am-6pm Easter-Sep, 9am-5pm mid-Mar–Easter & Oct–mid-Nov), the botanical gardens are filled with colour in spring from orange trees knitted into pergolas and from some of Europe's finest rhododendrons, azaleas and camellias.

Tremezzo's tourist office (☎ 0344 4 04 93; infotremezzo@tiscalinet.it; Via Statale Regina; ☾ 9am-noon & 3.30-6.30pm Wed-Mon Apr-Oct) adjoins the boat jetty.

LIGURIA

GENOA

Liguria's capital, Genoa (Genova in Italian), is a gargantuan port with a seedy underbelly whose narrow twisting streets *(caruggi)* are more reminiscent of a Moroccan medina than a romantic Venetian cityscape.

It's also a main gateway to the region's coastal hotspots, with frequent trains to Camogli (p136), the Cinque Terre (p137) and Santa Margherita, from where buses run to Portofino (p136). From June to September, Cooperativa Battellieri del Golfo Paradiso (☎ 018 577 20 91; www.golfoparadiso.it) operates boats from Genoa's Porto Antico (Old Port) to Camogli (one way/return €10/15), Portofino (€10/15), and the Cinque Terre/Porto Venere (€20/30). Consorzio Liguria Via Mare (☎ 010 26 57 12; www.liguriaviamare.it) runs a range of seasonal trips from Genoa to Camogli, San Fruttuoso and Portofino, Monterosso in the Cinque Terre, and Porto Venere.

Genoa's Stazione Principe and Stazione Brignole are linked by train to Turin (€15, 1¾ hours, seven to 10 daily), Milan (€15.50, 1½ hours, up to eight daily), Pisa (€15, two hours, up to eight daily) and Rome (€36.50, 5¼ hours, six daily).

You'll find tourist offices at the airport, ferry terminal and Stazione Principe. There's also a kiosk (Genova Informa; ☎ 010 24 87 11; www.apt.genova.it; Piazza Giacomo Matteotti; ☾ 9.30am-7.45pm) in the city centre.

Dozens of hotels are spread around town. The greatest concentration is near Stazione Principe on and around Via Balbi.

RIVIERA DI LEVANTE

Running claustrophobically from Genoa's eastern sprawl, you're quickly apprehended by the deep blue waters of the Mediterranean fringed by some of Italy's most elite resorts, including jet-set favourite Portofino. Anything but off the beaten track, this glittering stretch of coast is hugely popular, but never tacky. Heading further east, swanky resorts battle bravely with increasingly precipitous topography.

CAMOGLI

pop 5750

This still-colourful fishing village, located 25km east of Genoa, has trompe l'oeil decorating the alleys and cobbled streets, beneath a canopy of umbrella pines and voluptuous olive groves.

From the main esplanade, Via Garibaldi, boats sail to the **Punta Chiappa**, a rocky outcrop on the Portofino promontory where you can swim and sunbathe. The **tourist office** (☎ 0185 77 10 66; www.camogli.it, in Italian; Via XX Settembre 33; 9am-12.30pm & 3.30-6pm Mon-Sat, 9am-1pm Sun) has a list of diving schools and boat-rental operators.

If you'd like to stay overnight, the 16th-century villa **Hotel Cenobio dei Dogi** (☎ 0185 72 41; www.cenobio.com; Via Cuneo 34; s €111-155, d €153-208; P ⊠ ⊛) has more than 100 refined rooms yet still manages to feel intimate.

Delve down the lanes away from the water to escape the lunchtime crowd and search for some of the town's extra-crunchy focaccia.

ATP Tigullio (☎ 0185 28 88 34) runs buses to/from Rapallo and Santa Margherita at least every hour, leaving from the bus stop just past the tourist office on Via XX Settembre.

Camogli (€2.40, 40 minutes, hourly) is on the Genoa–La Spezia train line.

The Cooperativa Battellieri del Golfo Paradiso (p135) runs boats year-round to and from Punta Chiappa (one-way/return €5/7.50) and San Fruttuoso (€7/10); and boats between June and September to Genoa's Porto Antico (€10/15), Portofino (€9/15), and the Cinque Terre and Porto Venere (€18/25).

SAN FRUTTUOSO

The yin to Portofino's yang, San Fruttuoso is a slice of ancient tranquillity preserved amid some of Italy's ritziest coastal resorts.

The hamlet's extraordinary Benedictine **abbey** (Abbazia di San Fruttuoso di Capodimonte; ☎ 0185 77 27 03; adult/child €4/2.50; 10am-6pm May-Sep, to 4pm Mar, Apr & Oct, also to 4pm public holidays & day prior to public holidays only Dec-Feb) was built as a final resting place for Bishop St Fructuosus of Tarragona (martyred in Spain in AD 259).

San Fruttuoso's isolation is maintained by its lack of road access. You can walk in on foot from Camogli (a tricky, rocky hike with metal hand supports) or Portofino, a steep but easier 5km-long cliffside walk. Alternatively you can catch a boat from Camogli or Punta Chiappa (one-way/return €5/6.50).

PORTOFINO

pop 550

A byword for refined luxury, stately Portofino is beyond the wallet-stretching capabilities of most budget-minded travellers. That's not to say you can't linger over an expensive cappuccino next to its yacht-filled harbour logging the ubiquity of the Gucci handbags and Prada sunglasses.

Portofino's **tourist office** (☎ 0185 26 90 24; www.apttigullio.liguria.it; Via Roma 35; ✆ 10am-1pm & 1.30-4.30pm Tue-Sun) has free trail maps for the Parco Naturale Regionale di Portofino and information on mountain-bike rental, as well as seasonal sail and motorboat rental.

SIGHTS

From the sublime harbour, a flight of stairs signposted 'Salita San Giorgio' leads past the **Chiesa di San Giorgio** to **Castello Brown** (☎ 0185 26 71 01; www.portofinoevents.com; Via alla Penisola 13a; adult/child €3.50/free; ✆ vary), a 10-minute walk altogether (confirm the opening times with the tourist office prior to setting out, as the castle often hosts private events). The fabulous tiled staircase is one of the showpieces of the neo-Gothic interior, while there are great views from the garden.

Heading 2km north along the coastal road is the **Abbazia della Cervara** (Abbazia di San Girolamo; ☎ 800 65 21 10; www.cervara.it; Lungomare Rossetti, Via Cervara 10; ✆ guided tours by reservation), built in 1361 and surrounded by formal gardens.

SLEEPING & EATING

The least expensive accommodation options include **Eden** (☎ 0185 26 90 91; www.hoteledenportofino.com; Vico Dritto 18; d €140-270; P ✖), on a quiet cobbled side street not far from the harbour front; and **Hotel Argentina** (☎ 0185 28 67 08; www.argentinaportofino.it; Via Paraggi a Monte 56; d from €160; P ✖) on the coast road towards Santa Margherita.

Fashionable eateries overlook the port; **Magazin** (☎ 0185 26 91 78; Calata Marconi 34; meals €28-35; ✆ Fri-Wed), decked out like the

Portofino

DAVID TOMLINSON

cabin of a boat, serves authentic Ligurian luxuries.

GETTING THERE & AROUND

Regular buses run between Portofino and Santa Margherita but by far the best way is to walk. A designated path tracks the gorgeous coastline for 3km.

From April to October, Servizio Marittimo del Tigullio runs daily ferries from Portofino to/from San Fruttuoso (€7.50/10.50), Rapallo (€7/10.50) and Santa Margherita (€5.50/8.50).

CINQUE TERRE

Bar an overabundance of ogling tourists and a busy 19th-century railway line that burrows through a series of

MILAN & THE NORTHWEST

LIGURIA

PHILIP & KAREN SMITH

Cinque Terre walking path (see p140)

coastal tunnels, barely anything about these five crazily constructed Ligurian villages has changed in over three centuries. Rooted in antiquity, Cinque Terre's five towns date from the early medieval period.

Buildings aside, Cinque Terre's most unique historical feature is the steeply terraced cliffs bisected by a complicated system of fields and gardens that has been hacked, chiselled, shaped and layered over the course of nearly two millennia.

INFORMATION

Online information is available at www.cinqueterre.it and www.cinqueterre.com.

Parco Nazionale offices Corniglia (☎ 0187 81 25 23; ☯ 7am-8pm); La Spezia (☎ 0187 74 35 00; internet access per 10min €0.80; ☯ 7am-8pm); Manarola (☎ 0187 76 05 11; ☯ 7am-8pm); Monterosso (☎ 0187 81 70 59; ☯ 7am-8pm); Vernazza (☎ 0187 81 25 33; ☯ 7am-8pm)

MONTEROSSO

pop 1580

The most accessible village by car and the only Cinque Terre settlement to sport a tourist beach, Monterosso is the furthest west and least quintessential of the quintet (it was briefly ditched from the group in the 1940s).

Footsteps from the sea, **Carla** (☎ 0187 82 90 39; Via IV Novembre 75; d €60-70) has charming *affittacamere* (rooms for rent). Monterosso also has a handful of hotels, including good value for money at the four-star **Hotel Palme** (☎ 0187 82 90 13; www.hotelpalme.it; Via 4 Novembre 18; d from €140; ☯ Apr-Oct; ℗ ✖), where you can laze in the palm-filled gardens.

Along the seafront, restaurants dish up local anchovies straight out of the sea, served fried, raw with lemon juice, pickled in brine or in a *tian* (baked with potatoes and tomatoes).

To pack an authentic Ligurian beach picnic, head to **Focacceria Enoteca Antonia** (☎ 0187 82 90 39; Via Fegina 124; focaccias per slice around €2.20; ☯ 9am-8pm Fri-

Wed Mar-Oct) where Paola and her husband Giuseppe make 15 kinds of piping-hot focaccia from scratch and also stock well-priced local wines.

VERNAZZA
pop 1100

Guarding the only secure landing point on the Cinque Terre coast, Vernazza is the quaintest of the five villages. Its tiny harbour is framed by the 1318-built **Chiesa di Santa Margherita**, while the ruins of an 11th-century castle look out to sea.

To spend a romantic night here try **L'Eremo sul Mare** (☎ 339 268 56 17; Via Gerai; d €90; ⊙ mid-Mar–mid-Oct; ⊠), a charming cliffside villa with just three rooms and a lovely sun terrace a 10-minute hike up the hillside.

Traditional Cinque Terre seafood is served up at **Trattoria Gianni Franzi** (☎ 0187 82 10 03; Piazza Matteotti 5; meals €22-30; ⊙ mid-Mar-early Jan); and in the cosy stone-and-wood dining rooms of **Trattoria da Sandro** (☎ 0187 81 22 23; Via Roma 69; meals €20), whose specialities include baked stuffed mussels, and swordfish with tomatoes, capers, olives and pine nuts.

CORNIGLIA
pop 600

Corniglia, the middle village, sits atop a rocky promontory surrounded by vineyards and is the only Cinque Terre settlement with no direct sea access. The best panoramas unfold from **La Torre**, a medieval lookout reached by narrow lanes and stairways.

If you're stopping for the night, **Dai Fera'** (☎ 0187 81 23 23; Via alla Marina 39; d €60-80) offers clean and simple rooms close to the seafront. As elsewhere in the Cinque Terre, fish is the mainstay of Corniglia's restaurants – you can't go wrong by asking for whatever's fresh.

MANAROLA
pop 850

Bequeathed with more grapevines than any other Cinque Terre village, Manarola is famous for its Sciacchetrà wine and awash with priceless medieval relics supporting claims that it is the oldest of the five.

At the northern end of Via Discovolo, you'll come upon **Piazzale Papa Innocenzo IV**, dominated by a bell tower used as a defensive lookout. Opposite, the **Chiesa di San Lorenzo** dates from 1338 and houses a 15th-century polyptych.

The Cinque Terre's only hostel, **Ostello 5 Terre** (☎ 0187 92 02 15; www.cinqueterre.net/ostello; Via Riccobaldi 21; dm €20-23, d €55-65; ⊙ reception 7am-1pm, 4pm-midnight Feb-Jun & Sep-Nov, 7am-1pm, 5pm-1am Jun-Aug, hostel open Mar-Dec; ⌨), rents out mountain bikes,

MAKING THE MOST OF YOUR EURO

Easily the best way to get around the Cinque Terre is with a **Cinque Terre card**.

Two versions of the card are available: either with or without train travel. Both include unlimited use of walking paths (which otherwise cost €5) and electric village buses, as well as the elevator in Riomaggiore and cultural exhibitions. Without train travel, a basic one-/three-/seven-day card for everyone over the age of four costs €5/8/10/20. A card that also includes unlimited train trips between the towns costs €8.50/14.70/19.50/36.50.

Both versions of the card are sold at all Cinque Terre park information offices.

CINQUE TERRE WALKS

There's a reason why the Sentiero Azzurro is one of Italy's most crowded trails, and one of the few you have to pay to enter. Arguably the most drop-dead-gorgeous coastal hike in the country, the route follows an ancient network of walking paths that has linked the five Cinque Terre villages for over a millennium.

The most popular direction of traffic is east–west, beginning in Riomaggiore and finishing in Monterosso, starting on the famed Via dell'Amore. If you're not up to going the full distance, try hiking as far as the middle village, Corniglia, and getting a train back.

kayaks, Nordic walking poles and snorkelling gear.

A shoal of fish dishes and the house speciality *zuppa di datteri* (date soup) are served up at **Marina Piccola** (☎ 0187 92 01 03; www.hotelmarinapiccola.com; Via Lo Scalo 16; s/d from €87/115, meals €22-30) along with sea views. If you want to stay, the 'little marina' has good deals for half and full board.

RIOMAGGIORE

pop 1800

Cinque Terre's easternmost village, Riomaggiore, is the largest of the five, and acts as its unoffical HQ (the main park office is based here). Its peeling pastel buildings tumble like faded chocolate boxes down a steep ravine to a tiny harbour – the region's favourite postcard view – and glow romantically at sunset.

Some of the cheapest harbourside rooms are with **La Casa di Venere** (☎ 349 075 31 40; www.lacasadivenere.com; Via Sant'Antonio 114; s without bathroom €30-50, d without bathroom €40-60, d with bathroom €50-70), just off the upper stretch of the main street.

La Lanterna (☎ 0187 92 05 89; Via San Giacomo, Loc Marina; meals €25-33) is perched within pebble-lobbing distance of Riomaggiore's snug harbour that's crammed with fishing nets and over-turned boats. You can sit on the charming terrace and choose from recently caught fish chalked up on a blackboard. Across the laneway, local wine is served by the glass at **Dau Cila** (☎ 0187 76 00 32; Via San Giacomo, Loc Marina; wine & snack €10; ☼ 8am-2am Mar-Oct), accompanied by cold plates such as smoked tuna with apples and lemon or lemon-marinaded anchovies with pears and parmesan.

GETTING THERE & AROUND

BOAT

In summer Cooperativa Battellieri del Golfo Paradiso (p135) runs boats to the Cinque Terre from Genoa.

Seasonal boat services to/from Santa Margherita (one-way/return €14/21) are handled by Servizio Marittimo del Tigullio.

From late March to October, La Spezia–based Consorzio Maritimo Turistico Cinque Terre Golfo dei Poeti runs daily shuttle boats between all of the Cinque Terre villages, except Corniglia, costing €16 one-way including all stops, €21 return on weekdays and €23 on weekends.

CAR & MOTORCYCLE

Private vehicles are not allowed beyond village entrances. If you're arriving by car or motorcycle, you'll need to pay to park in designated car parks (€2.30 per hour or €19 per 24 hours).

TRAIN

Between 6.30am and 10pm, one to three trains an hour trundle along the coast between Genoa and La Spezia, stopping at each of the Cinque Terre's villages. Unlimited 2nd-class rail travel between Levanto and La Spezia is covered by the Cinque Terre Treno Card (see the boxed text, p139).

La Spezia is on the Genoa–Rome railway line and is also connected to Milan (€21, three hours, four daily), Turin (€24, three hours, several daily) and Pisa (€5, 50 minutes, almost hourly).

PIEDMONT

TURIN

pop 901,000 / elevation 240m

Here is a metropolis that harbours one of the world's biggest car companies (Fiat), a globally iconic football team (Juventus), two of Italy's finest museums (the Museo Egizio and the Mole Antonelliana), and one of history's most controversial and perplexing mysteries (the Holy Shroud).

Like all great cities, Turin has left an important mark on international culture, particularly in the field of gastronomy. Tic Tacs originated here as did solid chocolate, Lavazza coffee, breadsticks, and important elements within the Slow Food Movement.

HISTORY

Whether the ancient city of Taurisia began as a Celtic or Ligurian settlement is unknown: it was destroyed by Hannibal in 218 BC. In 1563 the Savoys abandoned their old capital of Chambéry (now in France) to set up court in Turin, which shared the dynasty's fortunes thereafter. The Savoys annexed Sardinia in 1720, but Napoleon virtually put an end to their power when he occupied Turin in 1798. Turin was occupied by Austria and Russia before Vittorio Emanuele I restored the House of Savoy and re-entered Turin in 1814. Nevertheless, Austria remained

MARTIN LLADO

Peyrano (p147)

TURIN

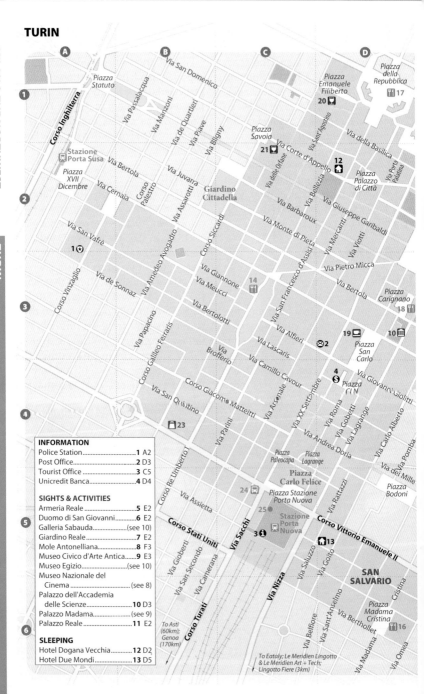

INFORMATION
Police Station 1 A2
Post Office 2 D3
Tourist Office 3 C5
Unicredit Banca 4 D4

SIGHTS & ACTIVITIES
Armeria Reale 5 E2
Duomo di San Giovanni 6 E2
Galleria Sabauda .... (see 10)
Giardino Reale 7 E2
Mole Antonelliana 8 F3
Museo Civico d'Arte Antica 9 E3
Museo Egizio .... (see 10)
Museo Nazionale del
  Cinema .... (see 8)
Palazzo dell'Accademia
  delle Scienze 10 D3
Palazzo Madama .... (see 9)
Palazzo Reale 11 E2

SLEEPING
Hotel Dogana Vecchia 12 D2
Hotel Due Mondi 13 D5

the true power throughout northern Italy until the Risorgimento (literally 'the Resurgence', referring to Italian unification) in 1861, when Turin became the nation's inaugural capital. Its capital status lasted only until 1864, and the parliament had already moved to Florence by the time full-size chambers were completed.

Turin adapted quickly to its loss of political significance, becoming a centre for industrial production during the early 20th century. The highly successful 2006 Winter Olympics were a turning point for the city. The Olympics not only ushered in a building boom, including a brand-new metro system, but transformed Turin from a staid industrial centre into a vibrant metropolis.

ORIENTATION

Via Roma, Turin's main shopping thoroughfare since 1615, runs northeast from Stazione Porta Nuova to the central square, Piazza Castello.

Busy Corso Vittorio Emanuele II is the main tram and bus route, running southeast to northwest.

The Mole Antonelliana's metallic spire dominates the horizon to the east, beyond which lies the Po and much of the city's nightlife. Just to the west of Piazza Castello, bars and bookshops fill the Quadrilatero Romano (Turin's 'Latin Quarter').

INFORMATION
EMERGENCY
Police station (☎ 011 5 58 81; Corso Vinzaglio 10)

MONEY
A 24-hour automatic banknote-change machine can be found outside Unicredit Banca (Piazza CLN).

POST

Post office (Via Alfieri 10; ⏰ 8.30am-7pm Mon-Fri, to 1pm Sat)

TOURIST INFORMATION

The tourist board's call centre (☎ 011 53 51 81; www.turismotorino.org; ⏰ 9.30am-9.30pm) can provide updated information and assistance for visitors.

Tourist office (☎ 011 53 51 81; ⏰ 9.30am-7pm) At Stazione Porta Nuova; offers free accommodation and restaurant booking service.

SIGHTS

Turin's boulevards and beautiful piazzas are lined with some outstanding museums.

PIAZZA CASTELLO

The piazza is dominated by Palazzo Madama, a part-medieval, part-baroque castle built in the 13th century on the site of the old Roman gate. Today, part of the palace houses the Museo Civico d'Arte Antica (☎ 011 443 35 01; Piazza Castello; adult/child €7.50/6; ⏰ 10am-6pm Tue-Fri & Sun, to 8pm Sat), containing a sumptuous collection of works that document the city's artistic movements post-Italian unification.

Statues of the mythical twins Castor and Pollux guard the entrance to the Palazzo Reale (☎ 011 436 14 55; Piazza Castello; adult/child €6.50/3.25; ⏰ 8.30am-7.30pm Tue-Sun), and according to local legend,

also watch over the border between the sacred ('white magic') and diabolical ('black magic') halves of the city. The surrounding Giardino Reale (Royal Garden; admission free; ⏰ 9am-1hr before sunset), east of the palace, was designed in 1697 by André le Nôtre, who also created the gardens at Versailles.

The entrance to the Savoy Armeria Reale (Royal Armoury; ☎ 011 54 38 89; www.artito.arti.beniculturali.it; Piazza Castello; adult/child €4/free; ⏰ 9am-2pm Tue-Fri, 1-7pm Sat & Sun) is under the porticoes just right of the palace gates and safeguards one of Europe's best collections of arms.

DUOMO DI SAN GIOVANNI

Turin's cathedral (Piazza San Giovanni), built between 1491 and 1498 on the site of three 14th-century basilicas, is the home of the famous Shroud of Turin (purported to be the burial cloth in which Jesus' body was wrapped). A copy of the cloth is on permanent display in front of the cathedral altar.

PALAZZO DELL'ACCADEMIA DELLE SCIENZE

The immense Palazzo dell'Accademia delle Scienze (Via Accademia delle Scienze 6) houses two outstanding museums: the 18th-century-established Museo Egizio (Egyptian Museum; ☎ 011 561 77 76; adult/child €7.50/free; ⏰ 8.30am-7.30pm Tue-Sun), with some of Europe's most important an-

---

MAKING THE MOST OF YOUR EURO

Serious sightseers will save a bundle with a Torino + Piemonte Card (2/3/5/7 days €19/22/31/35, junior 2 days €10). It covers admission to most of Turin's monuments and museums, a ride up the Mole Antonelliana panoramic lift, a return trip on the Sassi-Superga cable car, and all public transport costs including GTT boats on the Po river and the Turismo Bus Torino. You can buy the card at the tourist office.

cient Egyptian treasures; and the **Galleria Sabauda** (☎ 011 54 74 40; adult/child €4/free; ⏱ 8.30am-2pm Tue, Fri, Sat & Sun, 2-7.30pm Wed, 10am-7.30pm Thu), containing the Savoy family's incredible collection of art, which includes works by Van Dyck, Rembrandt, Poussin, Tintoretto and Jan Brueghel. A combination ticket for both museums costs €8 for adults (free for children).

VIA PO & AROUND

Trendy cafes are strung out along and around Via Po, which connects Piazza Castello with Italy's mightiest river by way of Piazza Vittorio Veneto.

The symbol of Turin is the **Mole Antonelliana** (Via Montebello 20). This 167m tower, with its distinctive aluminium spire, appears on the Italian two-cent coin. It was originally intended as a synagogue when construction began in 1862, but was never used as a place of worship.

A decade ago, the tower became home to the multifloored **Museo Nazionale del Cinema** (☎ 011 813 85 60; www.museonazion aledelcinema.org; adult/child €6.50/free; ⏱ 9am-8pm Tue-Fri & Sun, to 11pm Sat), which takes you on a fantastic tour through cinematic history – from the earliest magic lanterns, stereoscopes and other optical toys to the present day.

The Mole's glass **panoramic lift** (lift & museum ticket €8) whisks you 85m up through the centre of the museum to the Mole's roof terrace in 59 seconds.

LINGOTTO

Around 3km south of the city centre is the **Lingotto Fiere** (☎ 011 664 41 11; www.lingot tofiere.it; Via Nizza 294), Turin's former Fiat factory, which was redesigned by architect Renzo Piano into a congress and exhibition centre. In addition to two striking Le Meridien hotels (see p146), it houses the precariously perched 'treasure chest'

MARTIN LLADO

Mole Antonelliana

rooftop gallery **Pinacoteca Giovanni e Marella Agnelli** (☎ 011 006 27 13; Via Nizza 230; adult/child €4/2.50; ⏱ 10am-7pm Tue-Sun), with masterpieces by Canaletto, Renoir, Manet, Matisse and Picasso, among others.

Adjacent to the congress centre is the Slow Food Movement's 'supermarket', **Eataly** (☎ 011 195 06 811; www.eatalytorino.it; Via Nizza 230; ⏱ 10am-8pm Tue-Sun). The best time to visit is around 12.30pm to 2.30pm, when each area has its own little restaurant serving lunch. There's also a high-end restaurant here, for which you'll need to book ahead.

Some trains stop in Lingotto, but the easiest way to get here from the city centre is to take bus 1 or 35 from Stazione Porto Nuova.

Rapallo
BRUCE BL

↘ IF YOU LIKE...

If you like the villages of the Cinque Terre (p137), we think you'll like these coastal hamlets:

- **Rapallo** WB Yeats, Max Beerbohm and Ezra Pound all garnered inspiration in Rapallo and it's not difficult to see why – think bright-blue changing cabins, palm-fringed beach and a diminutive 16th-century castle perched above the sea. Trains runs to/from Genoa and La Spezia. In the warmer months, ferries sail to/from Cinque Terre and Portofino.

- **Porto Venere** A riddle of little lanes and staircases, a petite harbour and no small amount of history – the Romans built Portus Veneris as a base en route from Gaul to Spain. Catch a bus from La Spezia. Boats sail to/from Cinque Terre late March to October.

FESTIVALS & EVENTS

Salone Internazionale del Gusto Every October in even-numbered years, foodies roll into town for this festival organised by Slow Food, with traditional producers from around the world showcasing their wares in a huge market at Lingotto Fiere.

SLEEPING

Over weekends you can get some good discounted rates at various three- to five-star hotels with a 'Torino Weekend' package (www.turismotorino.org), which includes a free two-day Torino + Piemonte card (see the boxed text, p144), and an added freebie, such as a bottle of wine.

Hotel Due Mondi (☎ 011 650 50 84; www.hotelduemondi.it; Via Saluzzo 3; s/d €55/69; ✴ 🖳 🛜) A close-to-the-station bargain, the Due Mondi equips its small rooms with bright laminate floors, comfortable furnishings and ingenious shower-sauna cubicles.

Hotel Dogana Vecchia (☎ 011 436 67 52; www.hoteldoganavecchia.com; Via Corte d'Appello 4; s/d €90/110; 🅿) Mozart, Verdi and Napoleon are among those who have stayed at this historic three-star inn. Recent renovations have fortunately preserved its old-world charm, and its location in the Quadrilatero Romano is hard to beat.

Le Meridien Lingotto & Le Meridien Art + Tech (☎ 011 664 20 00; www.lemeridien lingotto.it; Via Nizza 262; Le Meridien Lingotto d €270-300, Le Meridien Art + Tech d €390-410; 🅿 ✴ 🛜) These twin hotels are both situated within the historic Fiat car factory, which was built in the 1920s and renovated by Renzo Piano in the late 1980s.

EATING

ourpick 8¾ (Ottoetre Quarti; ☎ 011 517 63 67; Piazza Solferino 8c; pizzas €3.80-10, mains €8-18; ☺ Mon-Fri; ✴) There's nothing particularly Fellini-esque about this…restaurant – but come expecting great food. Try *bistecca di vitello alla grissinopoli* (steak or veal crumbed with crunchy breadsticks), huge salads and excellent Piedmontese wines by the bottle.

Pizzeria Il Rospetto (☎ 011 669 82 21; Piazza Madama Cristina 5; pizzas €5-12; ☺) Fast, crowded and insanely popular, it has over

30 tasty thin-crust flavours to sink your teeth into here – including the dessert-style Nutella pizza!

Kuoki (☎ 011 839 78 65; Via Gaudenzio Ferrari 2h; set menus €9-25, mains €6-10; ☽ 11am-3pm & 6.30-11pm Mon-Sat; ⋈) Head around the corner from the Mole Antonelliana to this intriguing spot run by Giorgio Armani's former personal chef, Toni Vitiello.

Restaurant del Cambio (☎ 011 54 66 90; Piazza Carignano 2; set menus from €60; ☽ Mon-Sat) Crimson velvet, glittering chandeliers, baroque mirrors and a timeless air greet you at this grande dame of the Turin dining scene, regularly patronised by Count Cavour in his day. Bookings and smart dress are advised.

SELF-CATERING
Porta Palazzo (Piazza della Repubblica; ☽ 8.30am-1.30pm Mon-Fri, to 6.30pm Sat) Europe's largest open-air food market has literally hundreds of food stalls. Pick up a picnic.

DRINKING
The main drinking spots are the riverside area around Piazza Vittoria Veneto, and the Quadrilatero Romano district.

ourpick **Caffè San Carlo** (☎ 011 53 25 86; Piazza San Carlo 156; ☽ 8am-1am) Perhaps the most gilded of the gilded, this sumptuous cafe dates from 1822.

Mood (☎ 011 566 08 09; Via Battisti 3e; ☽ cafe 8am-9pm Mon-Sat, bookshop 10am-9pm Mon-Sat) An addictive coffee shop–cocktail bar–bookshop combo that you'll struggle to escape from. Flick through the design hardbacks or Dante classics while sipping a cappuccino or a €7 *aperitivo*.

I Tre Galli (☎ 011 521 60 27; Via Sant'Agostino 25; ☽ noon-midnight) Spacious and rustic, this is a fabulous spot for a drink any time, but most people come for the gourmet *aperitivi* snacks served on a buzzing pavement terrace. Meals cost about €15.

Lobelix (☎ 011 436 72 06; Via Corte d'Appello 15f; ☽ 7pm-3am Mon-Sat) Beneath the trees on Piazza Savoia, the terrace here is a favourite place for an *aperitivo* – its buffet banquet is one of Turin's most extravagant.

ENTERTAINMENT
Entertainment listings are included in 'Torino Sette', the Friday insert of the newspaper **La Stampa** (www.lastampa.it, in Italian). **Extra Torino** (www.extratorino.it) contains comprehensive, up-to-date listings in English.

GETTING THERE & AWAY
Turin airport (TRN; ☎ 011 567 63 61; www.turin-airport.com), 16km northwest of the city centre in Caselle, has connections to European and national destinations.

LA DOLCE VITA: TURINESE CHOCOLATE

Turin celebrates all things cocoa-related for two weeks every March during **CioccolaTÒ** (www.cioccola-to.com), with tastings, chocolate-making demonstrations, sculptures and dozens of creators selling their chocolates at stalls.

Year-round, you can pick up a ChocoPass from Turin's tourist office. The pass includes 10 tastings at specified stores and cafes over 24 hours (€10), or 15 tastings over 48 hours (€15).

The city's most famous chocolate house is **Peyrano** (☎ 011 53 87 65; www.peyrano.com; Corso Vittorio Emanuele II 76), creator of *Dolci Momenti a Torino* (Sweet Moments in Turin) and *grappini* (chocolates filled with grappa).

Most international, national and regional buses terminate at the **bus station** (☎ 011 433 25 25; Corso Castelfidardo).

Regular daily trains connect Turin's **Stazione Porta Nuova** (Piazza Carlo Felice) with Milan (€9.20, 1¾ hours), Aosta (€7.55, two hours), Venice (€35, five hours), Genoa (€15, 1¾ hours) and Rome (from €46.50, seven hours). Most also stop at **Stazione Porta Susa** (Corso Inghilterra), which will gradually take over as the main station in the next few years.

GETTING AROUND
TO/FROM THE AIRPORT

Sadem (☎ 011 300 01 66; www.sadem.it, in Italian) runs buses to the airport from Stazione Porta Nuova (40 minutes), also stopping at Stazione Porta Susa (30 minutes). Buses depart every 30 minutes between 5.15am and 10.30pm (6.30am and 11.30pm from the airport). Single tickets cost €5 from **Confetteria Avvignano** (Piazza Carlo Felice 50), opposite where the bus stops, or €5.50 if bought on the bus.

A taxi between the airport and the city centre will cost around €35 to €40.

PUBLIC TRANSPORT

The city boasts a dense network of buses, trams and a cable car run by **Gruppo Torinese Trasporti** (GTT; ☎ 800 01 91 52; www.gtt.to.it, in Italian), which has an **information office** (☽ 7am-9pm) at Stazione Porta Nuova. Buses and trams run from 6am to midnight and tickets cost €0.90 (€12.50 for a 15-ticket carnet, €3 for a one-day pass).

Turin's single-line metro runs from suburban Collegno to Stazione Porta Nuova.

TAXI
Centrale Radio (☎ 011 57 37)
Radio Taxi (☎ 011 57 30)

ALBA

pop 32,000 / elev 172m

In the gastronomic heaven that is Italy, Alba is an all-time highlight. The town is famous for its Ferrero Rocher chocolate factory (Kinder Surprises and Nutella), white truffles and aged wines – including the incomparable Barolo, the Ferrari of reds. All becomes clearer at the annual truffle fair and the equally ecstatic *vendemia* (grape harvest).

A historical heavyweight, Alba enjoyed prosperity that reached its apex in the Middle Ages and lasted until 1628 when Savoy took control. At its peak Alba sported more than 100 towers. A sturdy four remain along with the imposing 12th-century **Cattedrale di San Lorenzo** (Piazza Duomo).

In the town's historic centre, Alba's **tourist office** (☎ 0173 3 58 33; www.langher oero.it; Piazza Risorgimento 2; ☽ 9am-1pm & 2-6pm Mon-Fri, from 10am Sat & Sun mid-Nov–Mar, 9am-1pm & 2.30-6.30pm Mon-Fri, 9.30am-1.30pm & 2.30-6.30pm Sat & Sun Apr–mid-Sep, 9am-1pm & 2.30-6.30pm Mon-Fri, 9am-8pm Sat, to 7pm Sun mid-Sep–mid-Nov) sells walking maps and has internet access.

TOURS

Alba's tourist office (above) can organise an astounding number of Langhe/Roero valley excursions. Highlights include a 10km **walk** (2½hr walks €15) through the chestnut groves of Roero, **winery tours** (3½hr tours €80-100) in an air-conditioned minibus, **cooking courses** (half-/full-day courses €70/100), a **truffle-hunting excursion** (two hours; price depends on group size), **horse-riding** (per day €80) in the Upper Langhe, **rafting** (3hr from adult/child €20/12) on the River Tanaro, and – for the ultimate view of the vineyards – a **hot-air balloon flight** (incl transfers, wine & breakfast €220-250). Sunrise balloon flights last one hour, but you'll need to allow four hours in total.

Truffle hunting in Barolo (p150)

OLIVER STREWE

Most activities and tours need to be booked at least two days ahead (tours may be cancelled if there aren't sufficient numbers).

SLEEPING

The Langhe hills shelter some serene sleeping and eating options – see the Around Alba section (p150), or contact the tourist office's **accommodation-booking service** (Consorzio Turistico Langhe Monferrato Roero; ☎ 0173 36 25 62; www.turismo doc.it), through which you can also make restaurant reservations.

Hotel San Lorenzo (☎ 0173 36 24 06; www. albergo-sanlorenzo.it; Piazza Rossetti 6; s €65-75, d €95-100; ☰ closed 2 weeks Jan & 2 weeks Aug; P ☒) Take 11 rooms in a refurbished 18th-century house, stick it footsteps from the cathedral, call it a boutique hotel and add a unique downstairs pastry shop selling 'healthy' butter/egg/dairy-free confectionery.

EATING & DRINKING

Vincafé (☎ 0173 36 46 03; Via Vittorio Emanuele II 12; set menus €10-25) Anyone can sup on a glass of wine here, as long as you can squeeze through the door (it's small and popular) and have got the time and/or expertise to sift through a list of over 350 varieties.

ourpick Osteria dei Sognatori (☎ 0173 3 40 43; Via Macrino 8b; meals €12-20; ☰ lunch & dinner Mon-Sat) Menu? What menu? You get whatever's in the pot at this rustic beneath-the-radar place and it's always delicious.

Piazza Duomo-La Piola (☎ 0173 44 28 00; Piazza Risorgimento 4; meals €20-30, set menu €60-80; ☰ lunch & dinner, closed Mon & dinner Sun) Downstairs, La Piola sports local black-board specials, such as *vitello tonnato,* that change daily and allow diners to create their own plates. Upstairs, the theme goes more international in chef Enrico Crippa's Michelin-starred Piazza Duomo where you can eat creative food beneath colourful wall frescoes painted by contemporary artist Francesco Clemente.

GETTING THERE & AROUND

From Alba's **train station** (Piazza Trento e Trieste) there are regular trains to/from

Turin (€4.80 via Bra/Asti, 50 minutes, hourly).

Irregularity of buses makes touring the Langhe better by car or bike. For bike hire try **Cicli Gagliardini** (☎ 0173 44 07 26; Via Ospedale 7) or ask at the tourist office. Prices hover at around €15 per day. Cars go from €23 per day or the tourist office can hook you up with a driver (prices vary). Even better – hire a Vespa!

BILDAGENTUR-ONLINE/ALAMY
Bra

↘ IF YOU LIKE...

If you like **Alba** (p148), we think you'll like these other Piedmontese gourmet destinations:

- **Bra** Family-run shops replete with organic sausages, hand-crafted chocolates and fresh, local farm produce lace the hometown of the Slow Food Movement. Trains run to/from Turin.
- **Cherasco** Open wide for lumache (snails) and Baci di Cherasco ('Cherasco Kisses', made with 60% chocolate and local toasted hazelnuts). Limited bus connections; check schedules at Alba's tourist office (p148).
- **Cuneo** A gargantuan Napoleonic piazza and some of Italy's finest slow-food nosh spots. Trains run regularly to/from Turin.

AROUND ALBA

The castle-crowned Langhe hills produce some of Italy's best reds. Hire a bike and wobble freely between tasting rooms.

BAROLO & LA MORRA

Made from Nebbiolo grapes, and aged in oak barrels for three to four years, the velvety, truffle-scented reds produced around Barolo (population 680) and its 10 adjoining villages (including La Morra, Cherasco and Serralunga) are revered by critics as the 'king of wines'.

Situated at the heart of these esteemed vineyards, the diminutive village of Barolo is lorded over by its castle, the **Castello Falletti** (☎ 0173 5 62 77; www.baroloworld.it; admission €3.50; ⏲ 10am-12.30pm & 3-6.30pm Fri-Wed), which can be toured during a visit to its **Enoteca Regionale del Barolo**. Right inside the castle, the *enoteca* (wine bar) has three Barolo wines available for tasting each day, costing each/all three €2/5.

If you want to visit some of the Barolo vineyards (and taste-test some of their produce), contact **L'Insieme** (☎ 0173 50 92 12; www.linsieme.org; Cascina Nuova 51, La Morra) in La Morra (population 2670).

SLEEPING & EATING

Hotel Barolo (☎ 0173 5 63 54; www.hotelbarolo. it; Via Lomondo 2, Barolo; s/d €65/90; P ✗ 🖳 🖳) In the small town of Barolo overlooked by the famous enoteca-masquerading-as-a-castle, Hotel Barolo is a fine place to sit back on the terrace with a glass of you-know-what contemplating the 18th-century Piedmontese architecture that guards its shimmering swimming pool.

Villa Carita B&B (☎ 0173 50 96 33; www. villacarita.it; Via Roma 105, La Morra; s/d/ste €90/120/150; P ✗) This B&B not only has blink-to-be-sure-you're-not-still-dreaming daytime views from every

LEFT: MARTIN MOOS; RIGHT: ALAN BENSON

Left: Casale Monferrato (p153); Right: Tending vines, La Morra

room (and panoramic terrace), but romantic night-time views of La Morra's village lights.

Belvedere (☎ 0173 5 01 90; Piazza Castello 5, La Morra; set menus €42; ✹ lunch Tue-Sun, dinner Tue-Sat Mar-Dec, closed last week in Jul) 'Beautiful view' is no arbitrary name – it's adjacent to La Morra's lookout point. But Gian Bovio's *risotto al Barolo,* Barbera-cooked steak and triple-pyramid of chocolate all do their best to distract you from the vistas; as does the bewildering decision of choosing among more than 1000 wines.

BARBARESCO & NEIVE

You can worship Barbaresco wines at the intimate **Enoteca Regionale del Barbaresco** (☎ 0173 63 52 51; Piazza del Municipio 7, Barbaresco; ✹ 9.20am-6.30pm Mon, Tue & Thu-Sat, 9.30am-1pm & 2.30-6pm Sun), housed inside a deconsecrated church, with wines lined up where the altar once stood.

ourpick Ristorante Rabayà (☎ 0173 63 52 23; Via Rabayà 9, Barbaresco; set menus €28-40;

✹ Fri-Wed, closed mid-Feb–early Mar), on the fringe of town, is one of Barbaresco's first-rate restaurants.

If you haven't had your fill of wine yet, head a further 4km east to the pin-drop-quiet village of Neive (population 2930), where you'll find the **Bottega dei Quattro Vini** (☎ 0173 67 70 14; Piazza Italia 2, Neive; ✹ vary). Inside, you can sample wines by the glass (€1.80 to €4.50), accompanied by cold local specialities (€3.50 to €10) such as anchovies in green sauce, Langhe cheese served with *cugnà* (jam made from pressed grape residue) and *torta di nocciole* (flourless hazelnut cake, best paired with late-harvest Passito wine).

ASTI

pop 73,400 / elev 123m

Situated just 30km apart, Asti and Alba were fierce rivals in medieval times when they faced off against each other as feisty independent strongholds ruled over by feuding royal families. Asti – by far the bigger town – produces the sparkling white Asti Spumante wine made from white Muscat grapes, while Alba concocts Barolo and Barbaresco.

During the late 13th century the region became one of Italy's wealthiest, with 150-odd towers springing up in Asti alone. Of the 12 that remain today, one, the 38m-tall **Torre Troyana o Dell'Orologio** (☎ 0141 39 94 60; Piazza Medici; admission free; ☺ 10am-1pm & 4-7pm Apr-Sep, 10am-1pm & 3-6pm Sat & Sun Oct), can be climbed.

The town's two **tourist offices** (☎ 0141 53 03 57; www.astiturismo.it) – Piazza Alfieri 29 (open 9am to 1pm and 2.30pm to 6.30pm) and Corso Alfieri 328 (10am to 1pm and 3pm to 6pm) – have details of September's flurry of wine festivals.

Like Alba, the countryside around Asti contains precious black and white truffles. Asti's **truffle fair** is in November.

SLEEPING & EATING

Outside the town centre, there are some lovely spots to sleep in the nearby Monferrato vineyards – see right or ask Asti's tourist offices for a list of properties, including *agriturismi*.

Hotel Palio (☎ 0141 3 43 71; www.hotelpalio. com; Via Cavour 106; d €75-107; P ✗ 🖳 🛜) Reflecting Asti's juxtaposition of old and new, the hotel broadcasts chic, smart rooms with satellite TVs and wi-fi along with an atmospherically decorated inner sanctum.

Pompa Magna (☎ 0141 32 44 02; Via Aliberti 65; set menus €20-30; ☺ Tue-Sun; ✗) This split-level brasserie-style restaurant is a great spot for a bruschetta and glass of very good wine (the Pompa Magna also owns an *enoteca* in town at Corso Alfieri 332; closed Mondays).

GETTING THERE & AWAY

Asti is on the Turin–Genoa railway line and is served by hourly trains in both directions. Journey time is 30 to 55 minutes to/from Turin (€3.90), and 1¾ hours to/from Genoa (€6.50), stopping at Alba (€2.70, 40 minutes).

AROUND ASTI

Vineyards fan out around Asti, interspersed with castles and celebrated res-

Alba-region wine maker

OLIVER STREWE

taurants. Buses run from Asti to many of the villages; Asti's tourist offices can provide schedules.

MONFERRATO

A land of literary giants (contemporary novelist Umberto Eco and 18th-century dramatist Vittorio Alfieri hail from here) and yet another classic wine (the intense Barbera del Monferrato), the Monferrato area occupies a fertile triangle of terrain between Asti, Alessandria and its historic capital, **Casale Monferrato** (population 38,500).

The tiny hamlet of **Moncalvo** (population 3320), 15km north of Asti along the S457, makes a perfect photo stop, with a lookout above its **castle**, where you'll also find an **information office** (Piazza Antico Castello; ☺ Sat & Sun, specific hr vary) and wine tasting.

Many producers, such as Tenuta Castello di Razzano, conduct cellar tours; the **Consorzio Operatori Turistici Asti e Monferrato** (☎ 0141 59 46 98; www.terredasti. it; Piazza Alfieri 29) in Asti has a detailed list of tours and can provide directions.

ourpick **Tenuta Castello di Razzano** (☎ 0141 92 21 24; www.castellodirazzano.it; Frazione Casarello 2, Alfiano Natta; d/ste €110/200; P ✄ ⌨) is a rambling castle, which is possible to visit just to tour its working winery, and take part in a personal, seated wine tasting (from €6 for five wines, an aromatic wine and Barbera grappa plus local raw and cooked salami, bread, focaccia and pizzas; up to €15 for eight wines and a veritable feast of snacks). But to soak up the antiques-filled castle's atmosphere, you'll want to stay in one of its rooms the size of small apartments (some the size of large apartments) and roam its historic halls or curl up in its book-lined reading room. Alfiano Natta is 6km west of Moncalvo.

PARCO NAZIONALE DEL GRAN PARADISO

Gran Paradiso, formed in 1922 after Vittorio Emanuele II gave his hunting reserve to the state (ostensibly to protect the endangered ibex) is a veritable 'grand paradise'. What makes it special is a tangible wilderness feel (rare in Italy).

Gran Paradiso incorporates the valleys around the eponymous 4061m peak (Italy's 7th highest), three of which are in the Valle d'Aosta: the Valsavarenche, Val di Rhêmes and the beautiful Valle di Cogne. On the Piedmont side of the mountain, the park includes the valleys of Soana and Orco.

The main stepping stone into the park is tranquil **Cogne** (population 1474; elevation 1534m), a refreshing antidote to overdeveloped Cervinia on the opposite side of the Val d'Aosta. Aside from its plethora of outdoor opportunities, Cogne is known for its lace-making; you can buy the local fabrics at the charming craft and antique shop, **Le Marché Aux Puces** (☎ 0165 74 96 66; Rue Grand Paradis 4; ☺ closed Wed).

INFORMATION

Cogne's **tourist office** (☎ 0165 7 40 40; www. cogne.org; Piazza Chanoux 36; ☺ 9am-12.30pm & 2.30-5.30pm Mon-Sat) has stacks of information on the park and a list of emergency contact numbers.

ACTIVITIES

Gran Paradiso is one of Italy's best hiking areas with over 700km worth of trails linked by a recuperative network of *rifugi*. Guided nature walks from July to September are organised by the **Associazione Guide della Nature** (☎ 0165 7 42 82; Piazza Chanoux 36, Cogne; ☺ 9am-noon Mon, Wed & Sat).

ANDREW PEACOCK

Hiking Parco Nazionale del Gran Paradiso

Horse riding (per hr €25) and 45-minute **horse-and-carriage rides** (per carriage of up to 4 people €40) through the mountain meadows are run by **Pianta Cavalli** (☎ 3333 14 72 48) in Valnontey.

SLEEPING & EATING

Hotel Ristorante Petit Dahu (☎ 0165 7 41 46; www.hotelpetitdahu.com; Valnontey; s €36-50, d €72-100, restaurant menus €35; ✆ closed May & Oct; P ✖) Straddling two traditional stone-and-wood buildings, this friendly, family-run spot has a wonderful restaurant (also open to nonguests; advance bookings essential) cooking up rustic mountain fare using wild Alpine herbs.

ourpick Hotel Bellevue (☎ 0165 7 48 25; www.hotelbellevue.it; Rue Grand Paradis 22, Cogne; d €170-240, 2-person chalet €250-320; ✆ mid-Dec–mid-Oct; P ✆) Overlooking the meadows, this green-shuttered mountain hideaway evokes its 1920s origins with romantic canopied timber 'cabin beds', weighty cowbells strung from old beams and clawfoot baths. Its four restaurants include a Michelin-starred gourmet affair, a cheese restaurant (closed Tuesday) with cheese from the family's own cellar, a lunchtime terrace restaurant and a brasserie (closed Monday) on the village's main square a few moments' stroll away.

GETTING THERE & AROUND

There are up to seven buses daily to/from Cogne and Aosta (50 minutes). Cogne can also be reached by cable car from Pila.

Valley buses (up to 10 daily) link Cogne with Valnontey (€0.90, five minutes) and Lillaz (€0.90, five minutes).

Aosta's train station, on Piazza Manzetti, is served by trains from most parts of Italy via Turin (€7.55, two to 2½ hours, more than 10 daily). Aosta is on the A5, which connects Turin with the Mont Blanc Tunnel and France. Another exit road north of the city leads to the Great St Bernard Tunnel and on to Switzerland.

VENICE & THE NORTHEAST

VENICE & THE NORTHEAST

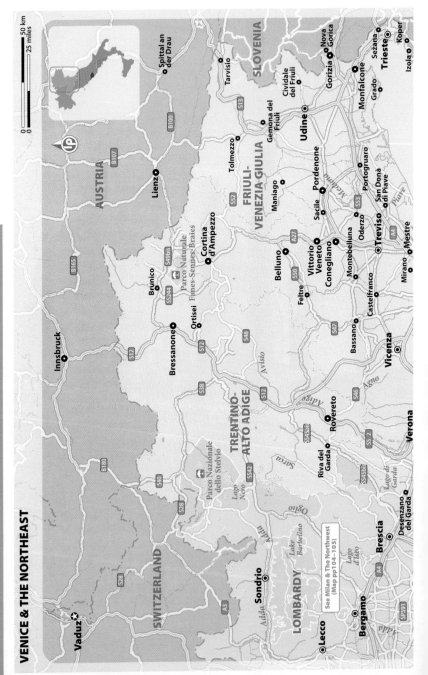

50 km
25 miles

SLOVENIA

Spittal an
der Drau

Tarvisio

Nova
Gorica
Gorizia

Sezana

Koper

Trieste

Izola

AUSTRIA

Cividale
del Friuli

Monfalcone

Grado

Gemona del
Friuli

Lienz

Udine

Tolmezzo

FRIULI-
VENEZIA GIULIA

Pordenone

Portogruaro

Maniago

Sacile

Meduna

San Donà
di Piave

Piave

Brunico

Parco Naturale
Fanes-Sennes-Braies

Cortina
d'Ampezzo

Montebelluna

Oderzo

Treviso

Mestre

Ortisei

Belluno

Vittorio
Veneto

Conegliano

Mirano

Bressanone

Feltre

Castelfranco

Innsbruck

Avisio

Bassano

Vicenza

TRENTINO-
ALTO ADIGE

Adige

Rovereto

Verona

Parco Nazionale
dello Stelvio

Sarca

Riva del
Garda

Lago
Nero

Lago di
Garda

Adda

Oglio

See Milan & The Northwest
(Map pp104–105)

Lago
d'Iseo

Desenzano
del Garda

SWITZERLAND

Sondrio

Lake
Barbellino

Brescia

Vaduz

LOMBARDY

Lecco

Bergamo

Adda

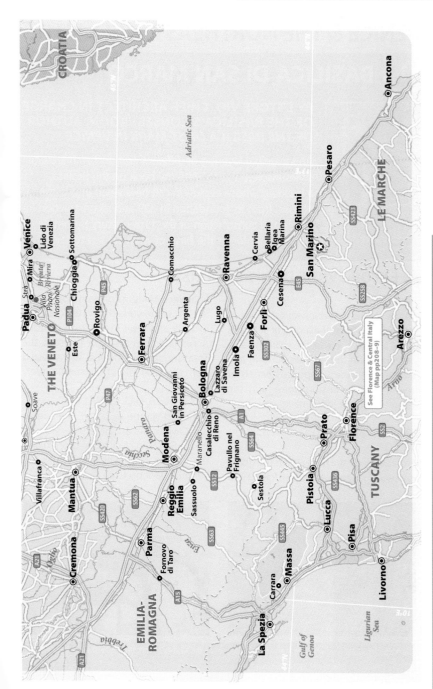

VENICE & THE NORTHEAST HIGHLIGHTS

1 BASILICA DI SAN MARCO

BY ETTORE VIO, CHIEF ARCHITECT IN CHARGE OF THE BASILICA'S CONSERVATION, AUTHOR OF *THE BASILICA OF ST MARK IN VENICE*

An incredible layering of different eras and architectural styles inspired me to write my book on the Basilica, a building whose evolution can be divided into three phases, from its foundation in 829 and reconstruction in 976 to the construction of the 11th-century Byzantine wonder that forms the basis of what we see today.

↘ ETTORE VIO'S DON'T MISS LIST

❶ MOSAICS

Above the facade's doorways, the mosaic on the left depicts the arrival of St Mark's body in Venice. Inside, the sparkling mosaics begin in the narthex (atrium) and culminate in the sumptuous panels of the central Ascension dome and the Pentecost dome in the nave.

❷ THE PALO D'ORO & THE TESORO

Sitting behind the high altar is the gold-, enamel- and jewel-encrusted Palo D'Oro altarpiece. Made in Constantinople in AD 976, it was reworked in 1105, enlarged in 1209 and reset in the 14th century. Accessible from the right transept, the Treasury houses priceless items seized from the 1204 raid of Constantinople.

❸ LOGGIA DEI CAVALLI

Accessed via the museum, the Loggia dei Cavalli has an incredible view of Piazza San Marco, plus San Giorgio and the sinuous Lido, which separates the Venetian lagoon from the sea.

Clockwise from top: Basilica di San Marco facade; Mosaics on the basilica's vault; Bronze horses in the Loggia dei Cavalli; Detail from one of the facade mosaics

CLOCKWISE FROM TOP: MARK DAFFEY; KRZYSZTOF DYDYNSKI; DAMIEN SIMONIS; KRZYSZTOF DYDYNSKI

❹ EAST MEETING WEST

The distance traversed from the entrance to the altar encapsulates the European philosophical concept of a distant God with whom communion is achieved through a long, personal journey. The Oriental domes, representing the divine, span the entire building, symbolising God's omnipresence and intimacy with humankind.

❺ THE CRYPT

Considered Venice's most scared site, the crypt harbours the 9th-century walls of the first basilica and the tomb in which St Mark's remains rested for 10 centuries. (They are now housed beneath the basilica's high altar.) Book at least a week ahead (☎ 041 270 8330; tecnico.proc@patriarcatovenezia.it).

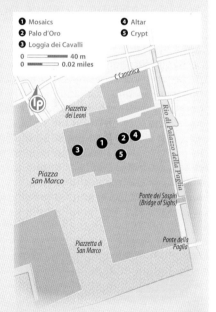

❶ Mosaics
❷ Palo d'Oro
❸ Loggia dei Cavalli
❹ Altar
❺ Crypt

0 ━━━━ 40 m
0 ━━━━ 0.02 miles

C Canonica
Piazzetta dei Leoni
Rio di Palazzo della Paglia
Piazza San Marco
Ponte dei Sospiri (Bridge of Sighs)
Piazzetta di San Marco
Ponte della Paglia

⬊ THINGS YOU NEED TO KNOW

Best time to visit Sunday mass **Best photo** Photography is forbidden inside; outside, the area between the Basilica and the Palazzo Ducale is fascinating considering the church's past role as the palazzo's chapel **See our author's review on p172**

VENICE & THE NORTHEAST HIGHLIGHTS

2 CULINARY EMILIA-ROMAGNA

BY ALESSANDRA SPISNI, CHEF, COOKING TEACHER & FOOD WRITER

There's no better place to satiate your appetite than in Emilia-Romagna. We boast the highest concentration of top-grade Italian specialities famous throughout the world. A proud Bolognese and passionate chef and teacher, I think I have the perfect job: sharing my passion for local produce and culinary traditions with hungry travellers.

⬏ ALESSANDRA SPISNI'S DON'T MISS LIST

❶ LESSER-KNOWN SPECIALITIES

Look out for highly prized Marroni di Castel Del Rio chestnuts and truffles from Savigno. The latter are celebrated each October or November at Savigno's Tartufesta. In the artisan *salumerie* (delis) of Bologna (p194) and its province, don't pass up the chance to sample *salame rosa* (pink salami). It might look like mortadella, but it's actually prepared like regular salami then steam-cooked.

❷ REGIONAL WINES

The vineyards around Modena, Reggio Emilia and Piacenza produce excellent Lambrusco, and much of Romagna is celebrated for its Sangiovese. The Colli Bolognesi (Bologna Hills) produce wonderful merlot and my personal favourite, cabernet. The latter goes perfectly with our regional dishes, whether it's *brodo da tortellini* (broth with tortellini pasta), lasagne or a fragrant *arrosto* (roast). In neighbouring Veneto, fine drops include the Amarone, a

Clockwise from top: Vegetable stall, Rialto Market (p176); Modena-produced balsamic vinegar; Venice chefs in action; Cafe tables on Piazza Maggiore (p195), Bologna; Reggio Emilia–region vineyards

Valpolicella red, the lemon-zesty Soave Classico and the nutty Recioto di Soave (the latter two are whites). Emilia-Romagna's wines tend to be lighter than their Veneto counterparts.

❸ GASTRONOMIC TOWNS

Top of the list is Bologna (p194), followed by Modena (p200), Parma (p202) and Reggio Emilia. Across the Po, the towns of Treviso, Chioggi and Rovigo are great places to try Veneto dishes, not to mention Venice (p168), home to the wonderfully historic Pescaria and Rialto Market (p176), the latter operating in one form or another for 1000 years.

❹ COOKING COURSES

One of the best ways to experience Italian culture is through food, and a cooking course offers both a fun window into the country and an investment in interesting future meals! The courses I run at La Vecchia Scuola Bolognese (p197) focus on learning how to make regional classics like *ragù alla bolognese,* tortellini, *tagliatelle* and lasagne. We run pastry courses and a bread-making course, and we collaborate with Bologna-based guides who can take you out on themed gastronomic excursions.

↘ THINGS YOU NEED TO KNOW

Cost of cooking course €80 to €250 depending on the length **Local food festivals and events** Scan www.winefoodfestivalemiliaromagna.com (in Italian) for details **For a perfect lasagne** Make sure the *sugo* (sauce) isn't too watery and don't add too much to the lasagne!

VENICE & THE NORTHEAST HIGHLIGHTS

3

↘ MEET THE VENETIAN MASTERS

The Gallerie dell'Accademia (p174) is home to the greatest collection of master-pieces by Venetian old masters, from Tintoretto's *Assunzione della Vergine* to Titian's *Presentazione di Maria al Tempio*. If that isn't impressive enough there's a veritable feast of High Renaissance, baroque and rococo wonders waiting in the wings. Put simply, the Academy is an intense one-stop lesson in Venetian artistic highlights.

4

↘ APPLAUD AN ALFRESCO ARIA

Belt-busting tenors not your shtick? Catching a summertime opera at Verona's pitch-perfect Roman Arena (p191) could change your mind. 'Think big' is the approach, from the A-list opera stars to the epic-scale sets (which have included the odd wild cat). Add a starry sky and the atmosphere that only comes with a 2000-year-old stadium, and you just might find yourself bellowing for an encore.

5

⬊ GETTING TO KNOW BOLOGNA

Nicknamed *la rossa* ('the red' – as much a political moniker as a reference to its colourful buildings), Bologna (p194) is one of Italy's unsung joys. A foodie city with a hedonistic approach to life, it's home to Europe's oldest university, an active gay scene and a stunning medieval centre laced with 40km of beautiful colonnaded sidewalks.

6

⬊ BE DAZZLED BY RAVENNA

It's a case of West meets Near East in Ravenna (p204), Italy's glittering mosaic capital. One-time seat of the Western Roman Empire and Byzantine Italy, the city's churches drip with early Christian and Byzantine mosaics that more than merit a sore neck. Not surprisingly, these technicolour wonders are on the World Heritage list.

7

⬊ VILLA-HOP ON THE BRENTA

The Brenta Riviera (p186) was the playground of 17th-century Venetian socialites. Hire a bicycle or board a restored wooden *burcio* (barge) to explore the decadent abodes. Snoop around Bacchanalian bedrooms, peer into gambling salons, see where Mussolini and Hitler first met or lose yourself in peacock-populated gardens.

3 Inside the Gallerie dell'Accademia (p174), Venice; 4 Verona's Roman Arena (p191); 5 Basilica di San Domenico (p196), Bologna; 6 Roman mosaic in Museo Arcivescovile (p204), Ravenna; 7 Villa Foscari (p186), Brenta Riviera

VENICE & THE NORTHEAST'S BEST...

⬎ FOODIE EXPERIENCES

- Perfecting your *ragù* at Bologna's Vecchia Scuola Bolognese (p197).
- Noshing on *cicheti* in Venice (boxed text, p183).
- Deli hopping on Via Garibaldi in Parma (p202).
- Touring balsamic vinegar and Parmesan producers near Modena (p200).

⬎ FREE MASTERPIECES

- Basilica di San Marco, Venice (p172) The optional extras are worth it, but the free mosaics are the undisputed highlight.
- Modena Cathedral (p201) A medieval marvel, with vigorous carvings by Wiligelmo.
- Basilica di San Vitale, Ravenna (p204) A technicolour feast of Byzantine mosaics.
- Chiesa di Santa Corona, Vicenza (p188) Three Renaissance stars in a Romanesque building.

⬎ VIEWS

- Atop Venice's Chiesa di San Giorgio Maggiore (p177) belltower.
- From Bologna's leaning Torre degli Asinelli (p196)
- Cruising down canals in an old-school Venetian gondola (p178).
- High up in Verona's Torre dei Lamberti (p193).

⬎ PLACES TO DREAM OF WINNING THE LOTTERY

- Drooling over fast cars at Galleria Ferrari (p201) in Maranello.
- Perusing art inside an heiress' palace at the Peggy Guggenheim Collection (p174).
- Inspecting decadent villas on the Brenta Riviera (p186).
- Imagining the star-studded 2009 wedding of Salma Hayek and billionaire art collector François Pinault at Palazzo Grassi (p174).

LEFT: ALAN BENSON; RIGHT: ROBERTO GEROMETTA

Left: Italian Parmesan in production; Right: Artwork inside the Gallerie dell'Accademia (p174)

THINGS YOU NEED TO KNOW

⬈ VITAL STATISTICS

- **Population** 11.3 million
- **Area codes** ☎ Venice 041, Bologna 051
- **Best time to visit** April to June, September and October

⬈ LOCALITIES IN A NUTSHELL

- **Venice** (p168) A one-of-a-kind aquatic masterpiece.
- **The Veneto** (p186) Elegant villas and salubrious towns, from the Brenta Riviera to Verona.
- **Bologna** (p194) Medieval porticoes, left-leaning politics and superlative regional cooking.
- **West of Bologna** (p200) A culinary mecca from Modena to Parma.
- **East of Bologna** (p204) Home to Byzantine-esque Ravenna.

⬈ ADVANCE PLANNING

- **Two months before** Reserve tickets to Venice's La Fenice (p184).
- **One month before** Book your Itinerari Segreti tour (p174) and your Bologna cooking course (p197).
- **One week before** Purchase tickets to Venice's Gallerie dell'Accademia (p174) online.

⬈ ONLINE RESOURCES

- **Venice Tourist Board** (www.turismo venezia.it)
- **Veneto Tourist Board** (www.veneto .to)
- **Venezia da Vivere** (www.veneziada vivere.com) Music performances, art openings, nightlife and more.

- **Emilia Romagna Tourist Board** (www.emiliaromagnaturismo.it)
- **Ravenna Mosaici** (www.ravenna mosaici.it) Historical and practical information about Ravenna's main Unesco-listed sights.
- **Trenitalia** (www.trenitalia.it) Train times and tickets.

⬈ EMERGENCY NUMBERS

- **Fire** ☎ 115
- **Carabinieri/Police** ☎ 112/113
- **Ambulance** ☎ 118

⬈ GETTING AROUND

- **Air** International connections to/from Venice, Treviso, Verona and Bologna.
- **Walk** Perfect for cities, towns and alpine trails.
- **Traghetto** Venice's commuter gondolas are a cheaper alternative to the traditional version.
- **Train** Excellent connections between major cities and towns.
- **Bus** Handy for towns not serviced by trains.
- **Bicycle** Ideal for smaller towns, the Brenta Riviera and alpine trails.

⬈ BE FOREWARNED

- **Museums** Most close Monday.
- **Restaurants** Many close in August.
- **Accommodation** Book accommodation months ahead if hitting Venice during Carnevale (p179) or Bologna during the spring and autumn trade fairs.

VENICE & THE NORTHEAST

THINGS YOU NEED TO KNOW

VENICE & THE NORTHEAST ITINERARIES

PALLADIAN TRIBUTE Three Days

Andrea Palladio, one of Italy's most celebrated Renaissance architects, redefined the Venetian landscape with his crisp, classical-inspired creations.

Begin your tribute in (1) **Venice** (p168), falling for Palladio's confident Chiesa di San Giorgio Maggiore (p177) and the Palazzo Ducale (p173), which features a Palladio-designed Collegio and a Palladio-designed ceiling in the Sala delle Quattro Porte. Cross the water to up-and-coming Giudecca (p177), where Palladio's marvellous Il Redentore shares the island with the uber-luxe Bauer Palladio & Spa (p182), set in a convent/orphanage designed by the Venetian starchitect.

On the second day, take a tour along the (2) **Brenta Riviera** (p186), home to Palladio's Villa Foscari (p186), before catching a train from Venice to (3) **Vicenza** (p187) on day three. Acknowledged by Unesco for its impressive Palladian booty, the city's treasures includes Palladio's masterpiece, La Rotonda (p190) – a template for villas worldwide.

VENETIAN SOJOURN Five Days

A city for meanders, Venice rewards every minute devoted to penetrating its cat's cradle of intertwined laneways. A short train trip away Padua houses one of Western art's most significant treasures.

Combine the obvious with the left-field in (1) **Venice**. Visits to the Basilicata di San Marco (p172) and Palazzo Ducale (p173) and a coffee at Caffè Florian (p183) could form the core of the first day, followed by a *vaporetto* ride across to San Giorgio Maggiore (p195) and then Giudecca (p177) for a wander.

Start day two with modern art at Palazzo Grassi (p174) or the Peggy Guggenheim Collection (p174) before a pilgrimage to the Chiesa di Santa Maria della Salute (p175) and a Tintoretto/Titian fest in the Scuola Grande di San Rocco (p176) and I Frari (p175).

Devote day three to exploring Cannaregio (p176) and day four to wandering around Murano (p178) and Burano (p178). On your last day, head on an out-of-town excursion to the revolutionary Cappella degli Scrovegni in (2) **Padua** (boxed text, p189).

NORTHEAST FOOD TRAIL 10 Days

A foodie foray through Italy's culinary heartland is the stuff of serious salivation. Meet artisan producers, graze in medieval cities and rediscover the meaning of life on this ten-day treat for the tastebuds.

Spend two days in (1) Parma (p202), hometown of *parmigiano reggiano* and *prosciutto di Parma*. Learn about both at the Museo del

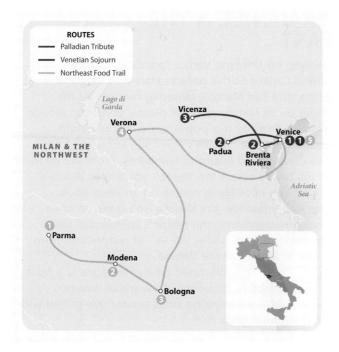

ROUTES
— Palladian Tribute
— Venetian Sojourn
— Northeast Food Trail

Lago di Garda

Vicenza ③

Verona ④

MILAN & THE NORTHWEST

Padua ② ② Brenta Riviera

Venice ① ① ⑤

Adriatic Sea

① Parma

Modena ②

Bologna ③

Parmigiano and the Museo del Prosciutto di Parma, or simply nosh on pasta stuffed with ricotta and herbs at Gallo d'Oro (p203) and stock up at Salumeria Garibaldi (p204). Spend day three in (2) Modena (p200), picking up local balsamic vinegar at Enoteca Ducale (p200) or, better still, visiting a local producer or two (see ModenaTur, p200).

From Modena, catch a train to (3) Bologna (p194), Italy's culinary capital. Raid the market stalls of Il Quadrilatero (p195), savour *tagliatelle* pasta at Osteria de' Poeti (p189) and take a cooking course (p197).

Three days later, hit the tracks for fair (4) Verona (p191), whose hinterland is awash with prize-winning grapes, from the north and northwest Valpolicella vineyards to the Soave-making grapes to the east. Stock the cellar in town, then catch a train to (5) Venice (p168), combining three days of art and architecture with produce shopping at the Rialto Market (p176) and *cicheti* (local tapas) crawls to *osterie* like I Rusteghi (p182).

DISCOVER VENICE & THE NORTHEAST

You could be forgiven for thinking Venice spends all its time primping. The Grand Canal's Gothic palaces stare admiringly at their own reflection, and San Marco's glittering mosaics let the sunset linger longer on its lavish, show-off piazza. Gorgeous though it is, make no mistake: this city is a powerhouse. At the height of its maritime trading empire, Venice's dominion stretched from Constantinople to Croatia, and inland to Lombardy. From Brenta River villas to fortified hill towns across the Veneto, you'll spot Venice's emblem: the winged lion of St Mark, resting on an open book.

Despite its fame and influence, the Veneto isn't quite an open book. With so many masterpieces, the region's splendours are constantly being revealed from under the veil of restoration, from Palladios in Vicenza to Mantegnas in Verona.

Across the mighty Po River, underrated Emilia-Romagna is a feast for the soul and the tastebuds, its booty of Byzantine mosaics, medieval squares and forward-thinking cities masterfully paired with Italy's most-lauded regional grub.

VENICE

pop 61,500

Imagine the audacity of people deciding to build a city of marble palaces on a lagoon. Instead of surrendering to *acqua alta* (high water), like reasonable folk might do, Venetians flooded the world with vivid painting in Venetian reds, baroque music and modern opera, spice-route-crossroads cuisine, bohemian-chic fashions and a Grand Canal's worth of *spritz*, the signature Prosecco-Aperol cocktail.

HISTORY

A malarial swamp seems like a strange place to found an empire, unless you consider the circumstances: from the 5th to 8th century AD, Huns, Goths and sundry barbarians repeatedly sacked Roman towns along Veneto's Adriatic coast. Crafty settlers rose above their swampy circumstances, establishing *terra semi-firma* with wood pylons driven into some 100ft of silt. The lagoon islands formed a loose federation, with each community electing representatives to a central Byzantine authority in Ravenna. When the Byzantine grip slipped, Venice seized the moment: in AD 726 the people of Venice elected their first *doge* (duke), whose successors would lead the city for more than 1000 years.

After Venice was decimated by plague, Genoa tried to take over the city in 1380. But Venice prevailed, controlling the Adriatic and a backyard that stretched from Dalmatia to Bergamo.

But events beyond Venice's control took their toll. The fall of Constantinople in 1453 and the Venetian territory of Morea (in Greece) in 1499 gave the Turks control over Adriatic Sea access. The Genovese gained the upper hand with Columbus' discovery of the Americas in

1492, calling dibs on New World trade routes. Portuguese explorer Vasco da Gama rounded Africa's Cape of Good Hope in 1498, opening up new trade routes that bypassed the Mediterranean – and Venetian taxes and duties.

As it lost its dominion over the seas, Venice began conquering Europe by charm. Venetian art was incredibly daring, bringing sensuous colour and sly social commentary even to religious subjects. The city became a playground for Europe's upper crust; nunneries in Venice held soirées rivalling those in *ridotti* (casinos) and Carnevale lasted three months.

ORIENTATION

Venice is built on 117 small islands connected by 400 bridges over 150 canals.

Since 1171, Venice has been divided into six *sestieri* (districts): Cannaregio, Castello, San Marco, San Polo, Dorsoduro and Santa Croce. Although you can take a train or bus into Venice and a car ferry to the Lido, the only ways to navigate Venice are on foot or by boat (see p186).

INFORMATION

EMERGENCY

Police station (☎ 041 112/113) Castello (Map pp170-1; Fondamenta di San Lorenzo, Castello 5053); Piazza San Marco (Map pp180-1; Piazza San Marco 67)

Ambulance ☎ 041 118

MONEY

Several bank branches with ATMs cluster around the Rialto and Piazza San Marco; several exchanges are located by the train station and San Marco.

POST

Post office (Map pp180-1; Salizada del Fondaco dei Tedeschi, nr Rialto; ⊗ 8.30am-6.30pm Mon-Sat)

TOURIST INFORMATION

Azienda di Promozione Turistica (APT; ☎ central information line 041 529 87 11; www.turismovenezia.it) branches provide information on day trips, transport, and events, shows and exhibits in the city.

Infopoint Giardini (Map pp180-1; Venice Pavilion; ⊗ 10am-6pm)

Lido (Gran Viale Santa Maria Elisabetta 6a; ⊗ 9am-12.30pm & 3.30-6pm Jun-Sep)

Marco Polo airport (arrivals hall; ⊗ 9.30am-7.30pm)

Piazzale Roma (Map pp170-1; ⊗ 9.30am-1pm & 1.30-4.30pm Nov-Mar, 9.30am-6.30pm Apr-Oct)

Piazza San Marco (Map pp180-1; Piazza San Marco 71f; ⊗ 9am-3.30pm Mon-Sat)

Stazione di Santa Lucia (Map pp180-1; ⊗ 8am-6.30pm)

KRZYSZTOF DYDYNSKI

Riding a gondola through Venice

VENICE

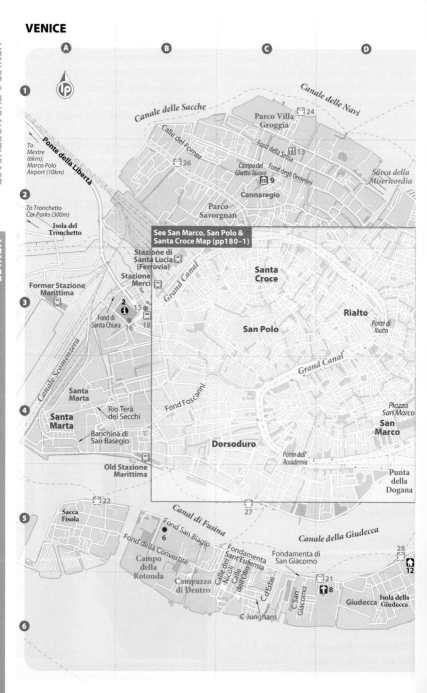

To Mestre (6km); Marco Polo Airport (10km)

Ponte della Libertà

To Tronchetto Car Parks (300m)

Isola del Tronchetto

Canale delle Sacche

Calle del Forner

Parco Villa Groggia

Canale delle Navi

Fond della Sensa

Campo del Ghetto Nuovo

Fond degli Ormesini

Sacca della Misericordia

Cannaregio

Parco Savorgnan

See San Marco, San Polo & Santa Croce Map (pp180–1)

Stazione di Santa Lucia (Ferrovia)

Stazione Merci

Former Stazione Marittima

Fond di Santa Chiara

Grand Canal

Santa Croce

Rialto

Ponte di Rialto

San Polo

Canale Scomenzera

Grand Canal

Santa Marta

Rio Terà dei Secchi

Santa Marta

Banchina di San Basegio

Fond Foscarini

Piazza San Marco

San Marco

Old Stazione Marittima

Dorsoduro

Ponte dell' Accademia

Punta della Dogana

Sacca Fisola

Canal di Fusina

Fond San Biagio

Fond della Convertite

Campo della Rotonda

Campazzo di Dentro

Fondamenta Sant'Eufemia

Fondamenta di San Giacomo

Canale della Giudecca

Calle dei Nicoli

Calle dell'Olio

C d'Erbe

C San Giacomo

C San Giacomo

Isola della Giudecca

Giudecca

C Junghans

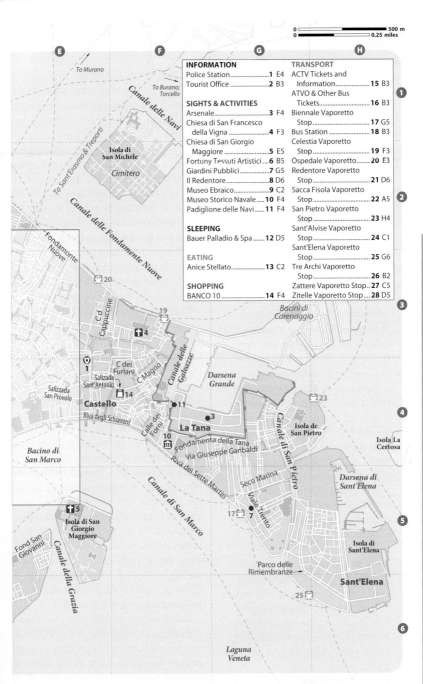

INFORMATION
Police Station..................**1** E4
Tourist Office **2** B3

SIGHTS & ACTIVITIES
Arsenale...........................**3** F4
Chiesa di San Francesco
  della Vigna **4** F3
Chiesa di San Giorgio
  Maggiore **5** E5
Fortuny Tessuti Artistici **6** B5
Giardini Pubblici..............**7** G5
Il Redentore.....................**8** D6
Museo Ebraico..................**9** C2
Museo Storico Navale **10** F4
Padiglione delle Navi **11** F4

SLEEPING
Bauer Palladio & Spa **12** D5

EATING
Anice Stellato..................**13** C2

SHOPPING
BANCO 10 ....**14** F4

TRANSPORT
ACTV Tickets and
  Information..................**15** B3
ATVO & Other Bus
  Tickets.........................**16** B3
Biennale Vaporetto
  Stop..............................**17** G5
Bus Station **18** B3
Celestia Vaporetto
  Stop..............................**19** F3
Ospedale Vaporetto........**20** E3
Redentore Vaporetto
  Stop..............................**21** D6
Sacca Fisola Vaporetto
  Stop..............................**22** A5
San Pietro Vaporetto
  Stop..............................**23** H4
Sant'Alvise Vaporetto
  Stop..............................**24** C1
Sant'Elena Vaporetto
  Stop..............................**25** G6
Tre Archi Vaporetto
  Stop..............................**26** B2
Zattere Vaporetto Stop....**27** C5
Zitelle Vaporetto Stop **28** D5

SIGHTS
GRAND CANAL

Public transport has never seemed so glamorous as the *vaporetto* No 1 route down the shimmering 3.5km stretch of the Grand Canal from the Piazzale Roma to San Marco. On the 45-minute commute, you'll pass some 50 *palazzi*, six churches, four bridges, two open-air markets and other landmarks recognis-able from scene-stealing cameos in four James Bond films.

PIAZZA SAN MARCO

Your entrance to Piazza San Marco (Map pp180-1) is heralded by live orchestras at 18th-century cafes under Napoleonic porticos flanking the square – but no amount of pomp, circumstance and decadent hot chocolate can prepare you for the otherworldly spectacle of the Basilica di San Marco (St Mark's Basilica; Map pp180-1; ☎ 041 522 56 97; www.basilicasanmarco.it; Piazza San Marco; basilica entry free, access to Pala d'Oro/Loggia dei Cavalli & Museum/Treasury €2/4/3; ☺ 9.45am-5pm Mon-Sat, 2-4pm Sun & holidays).

Luminous angels trumpet the way into San Marco in glittering mosaics above vast portals. Inside, the soaring stone structure still sets standards for razzle-dazzle, from the intricate geometry of 12th-century polychrome marble floors to 11th–15th-century mosaic domes glittering with millions of gilt-glass *tesserae* (tiles).

Alabaster chalices, icons and other Crusades booty in the Tesoro (Treasury; admission €3; ☺ 9.45am-5pm Mon-Sat Apr-Oct, to 4pm Mon-Sat Nov-Mar, 2-4pm Sun & holidays) can't quite compare to the bejewelled Pala d'Oro altarpiece (admission €2; ☺ 9.45am-5pm Mon-Sat Apr-Oct). Tucked behind the high altar that towers above St Mark's sarcophagus, this hidden treasure contains almost 2000 emeralds, amethysts, sapphires, rubies, pearls and other gemstones. More impressive still are the minuscule saints' portraits and lively biblical scenes in vibrant cloisonné, begun in Constantinople in AD 976 and elaborated by Venetian goldsmiths in 1209.

San Marco was officially the doge's chapel until 1807 and the doge's far-reaching influence is highlighted by gilt bronze horses upstairs in the Galleria (Museo di San Marco; admission €4; ☺ 9.45am-

---

MAKING THE MOST OF YOUR EURO

These passes can save you money on admissions to major Venice sights:

- helloVenezia (☎ 041 24 24; www. hellovenezia.com; ☺ call centre 8am-7.30pm daily) Offers a VENICEcard Transport & Culture Pass junior/senior per 3 days €66/73, per 7 days €87/96).
- Rolling VENICEcard allows visitors aged 14 to 29 (identification required) to buy a 72-hour public transit pass for €18 and provides discounted access to monuments and cultural events for €4. VENICEcards can be purchased at the San Marco tourist office, at helloVenezia ticket booths at the Piazzale Roma and Ferrovia *vaporetto* stops, or in advance at a 15% discount online.
- Civic Museum Pass (www.musei civiciveneziani.it; adult/child €18/12) is valid for single entry to 11 civic museums for six months, or the four museums around St Mark's Square plus one more (adult/child €13/7), and can be bought at the tourist office.

PALAZZO GRASSI SPA. FOTO: ORCH, ORSENIGO_CHEMOLLO

Moden art at Palazzo Grassi (p174)

5pm Mon-Sat, 2-4pm Sun & holidays). Through the Galleria you can access the **Loggia dei Cavalli**, where reproductions of the bronze horses gallop off the balcony over Piazza San Marco.

Note that you'll need to be dressed modestly (ie knees and shoulders covered) to enter the Basilica, and large bags must be left around the corner off Piazzetta San dei Leoni at Ateneo di San Basso, where you'll find free one-hour **baggage storage** (Map pp180-1; 9.30am-5.30pm).

The basilica's 99m-tall **Campanile** (Bell Tower; Map pp180-1; ☎ 041 522 52 05; www.basilicasanmarco.it; admission €8; 9am-9pm Jul-Sep, to 7pm Apr-Jun & Oct, 9.30am-3.45pm Nov-Mar) has been rebuilt twice since its initial construction in AD 888.

Next door to the Basilica, the splendour and intrigue of the Venetian Republic are captured in the **Palazzo Ducale** (Ducal Palace; Map pp180-1; ☎ 041 271 59 11; www.museiciviciveneziani.it; Piazzetta di San Marco 52; adult/child incl Museo Correr & 1 civic museum of choice €13/8; 9am-7pm Apr-Oct, to 5pm Nov-Mar).

Stop by the chamber featuring ominous scenes by the master of apocalyptic visions, Hieronymus Bosch, then follow the path of condemned prisoners across the covered **Ponte dei Sospiri** (Bridge of Sighs; Map pp180-1) to Venice's 16th-century **Priggione Nove** (New Prisons), dank cells covered with graffitied protestations of innocence.

To extend his royal palace, Napoleon incorporated the **Procuratie Nuove** (Map pp180-1), the building along the south end of the piazza planned by Jacopo Sansovino and completed by Vincenzo Scamozzi and Baldassare Longhena – but the job wasn't finished until the 19th century, just in time for the Hapsburgs to move in.

The **Museo Correr** (Map pp180-1; ☎ 041 240 52 11; www.museiciviciveneziani.it; Piazza San Marco 52; adult/child incl Ducal Palace & 1 civic museum of choice €13/8; 10am-7pm Apr-Oct, 9am-5pm Nov-Mar) has since taken over the royal digs with all its trophies, including ancient maps, Greco-Roman statuary and splendid medieval paintings.

STATE SECRETS REVEALED

The Ducal Palace's (p173) darkest secrets can be found through a passageway disguised as a filing cabinet in the Sala del Consiglio dei Dieci (Chamber of the Council of 10), festooned with happy cherubim and Veronese's optimistic *Triumph of Virtue over Vice*. Fascinating 1½-hour Itinerari Segreti (Secret Tours; ☎ 041 520 90 70; adult/student/child under 6yr €16/7/free; ☺ tours in English 9.55am, 10.45am & 11.35am, Italian 9.30am & 11.10am, French 10.20am, noon & 12.25pm) guide visitors into the cramped, unadorned Council of 10 headquarters, upstairs to a trial chamber lined with top-secret files, and into a windowless room with a single rope, used in perversely imaginative ways to extract information. To Venice's credit, the room was largely disused by the 17th century – but the same cannot be said for the studded cells of the Piombi, Venice's notorious attic prison. In 1756, Casanova was condemned to five years' confinement here on charges of corrupting nuns and a more serious suspicion of spreading Freemasonry – but after a few months, he slipped past the guards.

The north side of the Piazza is the Procuratie Vecchie (Map pp180-1), the former residence of the caretakers of St Mark and the Basilica, designed by Mauro Codussi. The standout feature here is the recently renovated 1497 Torre dell'Orologio (Clock Tower; Map pp180-1; ☎ 041 520 90 70; www.museicivicivenziani.it; Piazza San Marco; adult/VENICEcard-holders €12/7; age 6 & up only; ☺ visit by prebooked tour only, in English 10am, 11am & 1pm Mon-Wed, 1pm, 2pm & 3pm, in Italian noon & 4pm daily, in French 1pm, 2pm & 3pm Mon-Wed).

AROUND SAN MARCO

For avant-garde architecture, don't miss Palazzo Grassi (Map pp180-1; ☎ 041 523 16 80; www.palazzograssi.it; Campo San Samuele 3231; adult/student €15/6; ☺ 10am-7pm), a baroque palace that since 2005 has been home to the world-class contemporary art collection of French billionaire François Pinault.

Gothic Chiesa di Santo Stefano (Map pp180-1; ☺ 10am-5pm Mon-Sat, 1-5pm Sun) has a bell tower that leans disconcertingly, and a vast wood-ribbed *carena di nave*

(ship's keel) ceiling that looks like an upturned Noah's ark. Enter the cloisters museum (admission €3 or Chorus ticket) to see Canova's 1808 funerary stelae featuring gorgeous women dabbing their eyes with their cloaks, Tullio Lombardo's wide-eyed 1505 saint whom Titian is said to have referenced for his Madonna at I Frari, and three brooding Tintoretto canvases: *Last Supper*, with a ghostly dog begging for bread; the gathering gloom of *Agony in the Garden;* and the abstract, mostly black *Washing of the Feet*.

DORSODURO

Minds blown by San Marco require a bracing espresso, restorative gelato and possibly a Hail Mary before taking on the Gallerie dell'Accademia (Map pp180-1; ☎ 041 522 22 47, bookings ☎ 041 520 03 45; www.gallerie accademia.org; Campo della Carità 1050; adult/EU citizen 18-25yr/child under 12 & EU citizen under 18 or over 65yr €6.50/3.25/free, video/audio guide €6/4; ☺ 8.15am-2pm Mon, to 7.15pm Tue-Sun; last entry 45min before closing).

For a refreshingly modern take on Venice, head to Peggy Guggenheim

Collection (Map pp180-1; ☎ 041 240 54 11; www.guggenheim-venice.it; Palazzo Venier dei Leoni 701; adult/senior over 65yr/student with ID to 26yr/child under 10yr €10/8/5/free; ☒ 10am-6pm Wed-Mon). After tragically losing her father on the *Titanic,* heiress Peggy Guggenheim befriended Dadaists, dodged Nazis and amassed avant-garde works by 200 modern artists at her palatial home on the Grand Canal.

Dominating the entrance to the Grand Canal is Venice's monumental sigh of relief: **Chiesa di Santa Maria della Salute** (Map pp180-1; ☎ 041 522 55 58; www.marcianum.it/salute, in Italian; Campo della Salute 1b; sacristy admission €1.50; ☒ 9am-noon & 3-5.30pm), built by survivors of Venice's 1630 plague atop at least 100,000 pylons as thanks for salvation. Inside, you'll spot Tintoretto's surprisingly upbeat *The Wedding Feast of Cana* en route to the **sacristy**, which features no less than 12 Titians, including a vivid self-portrait in the guise of Saint Matthew and his earliest known work, the precocious vermillion *Saint Mark on the Throne* from 1510.

At the tip of Dorsoduro, Venice's old customs house has just undergone a three-year reinvention by architect Tadao Ando as Venice's splashiest contemporary art space: the **Punta della Dogana** (☎ 199 13 91 39; www.palazzograssi.it; admission adult/age 12-18yr, senior or disabled/under 11yr €15/10/free or with ticket to Peggy Guggenheim within 3 days of visit/combined ticket with Palazzo Grassi €12/20; ☒ 10am-7pm Wed-Mon).

SAN POLO & SANTA CROCE

I Frari (Map pp180-1; Campo dei Frari, San Polo 3004; admission €3 or Chorus pass; ☒ 9am-6pm Mon-Sat, 1-6pm Sun) is a soaring, sombre Italian-brick Gothic church featuring puzzlework marquetry **choir stalls,** Canova's vast **pyramid mausoleum** in the nave and Bellini's achingly sweet *Madonna with*

Chiesa di Santa Maria del Giglio

JULIET COOMBE

➤ IF YOU LIKE...

If you like the **Chiesa di Santa Maria della Salute** (left), we think you'll like these other ecclesial gems:

- **Chiesa di Santa Maria del Giglio** (Map pp180-1; Campo di Santa Maria del Giglio; admission €3 or Chorus ticket; ☒ 10am-5pm Mon-Sat, 1-5pm Sun). A 10th-century Byzantine layout, a baroque facade featuring maps of European cities c 1678, and three intriguing masterpieces by Veronese, Tintoretto and Reubens.

- **San Sebastiano** (Map pp180-1; ☎ 041 528 24 87; Campo San Sebastiano 1687; admission €3 or Chorus ticket; ☒ 10am-5pm Mon-Sat) A secret treasure, complete with floor-to-ceiling masterpieces by Paolo Veronese.

- **Chiesa di San Francesco della Vigna** (Map pp170-1; ☎ 041 520 61 02; Campo San Francesco della Vigna 2787; ☒ 8am-12.30pm & 3-7pm). Designed and built by Jacopo Sansovino, with a facade by Palladio, it's home to Bellini's glowing 1507 *Madonna and Saints* in the Capella Santa.

Child triptych in the **sacristy** – yet visitors are drawn to the small altarpiece like moths to an eternal flame. This is Titian's

1518 *Madonna of the Ascension,* capturing the moment the radiant Madonna reaches heavenward, finds her footing on a cloud and escapes this mortal coil in a swirl of Titian red cloak.

Just around the corner, you'll swear the paint is still fresh on the 50 action-packed Tintorettos painted from 1575 to 1587 for the Scuola Grande di San Rocco (Map pp180-1; ☎ 041 523 48 64; www.scuolagrandisan-rocco.it; Campo San Rocco, San Polo 3052; adult/18-26yr/under 18yr €7/5/free; ⊙ 9am-5.30pm from Easter-Oct, 10am-5pm Nov till Easter).

In Chiesa di San Polo (Map pp180-1; Campo San Polo 2118; admission €3 or Chorus ticket; ⊙ 10am-5pm Mon-Sat) Tintoretto's *Last Supper* captures apostles alarmed at Jesus' announcement that one of them will betray him and Giandominico Tiepolo (son of baroque ceiling maestro Giambattista) shows Jesus tormented by jeering onlookers in his disturbing *Stations of the Cross.*

For foodies, the star attractions of San Polo are the Rialto Market (Map pp180-1; ⊙ 7am-3.30pm) and Pescaria (fish market; Map pp180-1; ⊙ 7am-2pm) – but tempting bars and boutiques line the way to the Ponte di Rialto (Map pp180-1) along the Grand Canal.

CANNAREGIO
Behind the shopfront scenes in Cannaregio are sunny *fondamente* (canal-banks), authentic *osterie* (bistros) and the unofficial heart of Venice's maritime empire: the Ghetto (Map pp170-1). This area in Venice was once a *getto* (foundry), but its role as the designated Jewish quarter from the 16th to 18th centuries gave the word a whole new meaning.

A starting point to explore this pivotal community in Venetian arts, architecture, commerce and history is the Museo Ebraico (Map pp170-1; ☎ 041 71 53 59; www.museoebraico.it; Campo del Ghetto Nuovo, Cannaregio 2902b; adult/student €3/2, tours incl admission €8.50/7; ⊙ 10am-7pm Sun-Fri except Jewish holidays Jun-Sep, to 6pm Sun-Fri Oct-May).

Along the Grand Canal, you can't miss the stunning 15th-century Ca' d'Oro (Golden House, House of Gold; Map pp180-1; ☎ 041 522 23 49; www.cadoro.org, in Italian; Calle di Ca' d'Oro 3932; adult/EU student under 26yr/EU citizen under 18yr or over 65 €5/2.50/free; ⊙ 8.15am-2pm Mon, to 7.15pm Tue-Sun), its lacy Gothic facade resplendent even without original gold-leaf details that gave the palace its name. Ca d'Oro was donated to Venice to house the Galleria Franchetti (Map pp180-1), Baron Franchetti's art collection, plus a jackpot of bronzes, tapestries and paintings plundered from Veneto churches by Napoleon and reclaimed by Venice.

CASTELLO
You'll know you've crossed from Cannaregio into Castello when you spot Bartolomeo Colleoni galloping out to meet you. The bronze equestrian statue commemorates one of Venice's more loyal mercenary mainland commanders, and marks the entrance to the supersize Gothic Zanipolo (Chiesa dei SS Giovanni e Paolo; Map pp180-1; ☎ 041 523 59 13; Campo SS Giovanni e Paolo; admission €2.50; ⊙ 9.30am-6pm Mon-Sat, 1-6pm Sun), built by the Dominicans from 1333 to 1430 to rival the Franciscans' I Frari (p175).

The Arsenale (Map pp170-1) was founded in 1104 and soon became the greatest medieval shipyard in Europe, home to 300 shipping companies employing up to 16,000 people, and capable of turning out a new galley in a day. Venice's navy remained unbeatable for centuries, but now arty types invade the shipyards during Venice's art and architecture Biennales (p179). Giardini Pubblici (Map pp170-1) is the main site of the art

Biennale, with curators and curiosity-seekers swarming national showcases ranging from Carlo Scarpa's daring 1954 raw-concrete-and-glass **Venezuelan Pavilion** to Peter Cox's 1988 awkward **Australian Pavilion**, frequently mistaken for a construction trailer.

Museo Storico Navale (Map pp170-1; ☎ 041 520 02 76; Riva San Biagio 2148; admission €3; ⏱ 8.45am-1.30pm Mon-Fri, to 1pm Sat) is a four-storey, 42-room monument to Venice's maritime history featuring full-scale boats including the ducal barge, Peggy Guggenheim's not-so-minimalist gondola, ocean liners and WWII battleships. Museum admission includes the **Padiglione delle Navi** (Ships Pavilion; Map pp170-1) on Fondamenta della Madonna, near the Arsenale entrance.

GIUDECCA

Venice's Jewish community lived here prior to the creation of the Ghetto, but Giudecca isn't related to the word 'Jewish' (*hebrei* in Italian). Giudecca is likely derived from *Zudega*, from *giudicato*, or 'the judged', the name given to rebellious Venetian nobles banished to Giudecca.

At **Fortuny Tessuti Artistici** (Map pp170-1; ☎ 041 5224078; www.fortuny.com; Fondamenta San Biagio 805; ⏱ 9am-1pm & 2-6pm Mon-Fri, 9-11am & 2-6pm Sat & Sun), Marcel Proust waxed poetic over silken cottons printed with boho-chic art nouveau patterns.

Even from afar, you can't miss Palladio's 1577 **Il Redentore** (Chiesa del SS Redentore; Map pp170-1; Campo del SS Redentore 194; admission €3 or Chorus pass; ⏱ 10am-5pm Mon-Sat, 1-5pm Sun), a triumph of white marble along the Grand Canal celebrating the city's deliverance from the Black Death.

SAN GIORGIO MAGGIORE

Solar eclipses are only marginally more dazzling than Palladio's white Istrian marble marvel, the 1565–80 **Chiesa di San Giorgio Maggiore** (Map pp170-1; ☎ 041 522 78 27; Isola di San Giorgio Maggiore; ⏱ 9.30am-12.30pm & 2.30-6.30pm Mon-Sat May-Sep, 9.30am-12.30pm & 2.30-4.30pm Oct-Apr). The black, white and red inlaid stone floor draws the eye towards the

Brightly painted houses of Burano (p178)

EMILY RIDDELL

altar, flanked by two Tintoretto master-works: *Collecting the Manna* and *Last Supper*. Take the lift (€3) to the top of the 60m-high bell tower for a stirring panorama that takes in Giudecca, San Marco and the lagoon beyond.

JULIET COOMBE

Ca' Pesaro

⤹ IF YOU LIKE...

If you like the masterpieces of the Peggy Guggenheim Collection (p174), we think you'll like these other modern art gems:

- Ca' Pesaro (Map pp180-1; ☎ 041 72 11 27; www.museiciviciveneziani. it; Fondamenta de Ca' Pesaro, Santa Croce 2076; adult/senior, student & child €5.50/3; ☒ 10am-6pm Tue-Sun Apr-Oct, to 5pm Tue-Sun Nov-Mar) An eccentric museum featuring modern art and Asian antiques in a Longhena-designed 1710 palazzo.

- Museo della Fondazione Querini Stampalia (Map pp180-1; ☎ 041 271 14 11; www.querinistampalia.it in Italian; Campiello Querini Stampalia 5252; adult/student & senior €8/6; ☒ 10am-8pm Tue-Thu, to 10pm Fri & Sat, to 7pm Sun) Rotating contemporary art installations in the 16th-century Palazzo Querini Stampalia. Downstairs, it's all about the Carlo Scarpa–designed garden and the Mario Botta–designed bookstore and cafe.

MURANO

Venetians have been working in crystal and glass since the 10th century, but due to the fire hazards of glass-blowing, the industry was moved to the island of Murano (off Map pp170-1) in the 13th century. Today they ply their trade at workshops along Murano's Fondamenta dei Vetrai marked by Fornace (Furnace) signs, secure in the knowledge that their wares set a standard that can't be replicated elsewhere. To ensure glass you buy in Venice is handmade in Murano and not factory-fabricated elsewhere, look for the heart-shaped seal guarantee.

Since 1861, Murano has displayed its glass-making prowess at the Museum of Glass (Museo del Vetro; ☎ 041 73 95 86; www. museicivicivenezani.it; Fondamenta Giustinian 8; adult/EU senior & student 6-14yr/with Civic Museum Pass or VENICEcard & child under 6yr €5.50/3/free; ☒ 10am-6pm Thu-Tue Apr-Oct, to 4pm Thu-Tue Nov-Mar).

BURANO

The 40-minute LN ferry ride from the Fondamente Nuove is packed with photographers who bound into Burano's backstreets, snapping away at green stockings hung to dry between pink and orange houses.

Burano is traditionally famed for its lace, but at this writing the Museo del Merletto (Lace Museum; ☎ 041 73 00 34; www. museicivicivenezani.it; Piazza Galuppi 187) remained closed for restoration, and much of the stock for sale in Buranelli boutiques was imported – be sure to ask for a guarantee of authenticity.

ACTIVITIES

A gondola ride offers a view of Venice that is anything but pedestrian, with glimpses through water gates into palazzi courtyards. Official daytime rates are €80 for

40 minutes or €100 from 7pm-8am, not including songs (negotiated separately) or tips. Additional time is charged in 20-minute increments (day/night €40/50). You may negotiate a price break in overcast weather or around midday, when other travellers get hot and hungry. Agree on a price, time limit, and singing in advance to avoid surcharges.

Gondole cluster at stazi (stops) along the Grand Canal, at the train station (☎ 041 71 85 43), the Rialto (☎ 041 522 49 04) and near major monuments (eg I Frari, Ponte Sospiri and Accademia), but you can also book a pickup at a canal near you (☎ 041 528 50 75).

TOURS

APT tourist offices (see p169) offer guided tours ranging from the classic gondola circuit (€39 per person) to a 'spicy tour' with tales of Casanova dalliances and society scandal in the Rialto's former red-light district (€20 per person).

Laguna Eco Adventures (☎ 329 722 62 89; www.lagunaecoadventures.com; 2½-8hr trips per person €40-150)

Terre e Aqua (☎ 347 4205004; www.terraeacqua.com; 4-9hr trips per person incl lunch €70-120)

FESTIVALS & EVENTS

Carnevale (www.carnevale.venezia.it) Join costume parties in the streets or at La Fenice's Masked Ball (tickets start at €200).

Venezia Suona (www.veneziasuona.it) Hear medieval *campi* (squares) and baroque palaces echo with music from around the world over a glorious June weekend.

La Biennale di Venezia (www.labiennale. org) In odd years the Art Biennale usually runs June–November and in even years the Architecture Biennale kicks off

in September, but every summer the Biennale features avant-garde dance, theatre, cinema and music.

Festa del Rendentore (www.turismovenezia.it) Walk on water across the Giudecca Canal to Il Redentore via a wobbly pontoon bridge the third Saturday and Sunday in July, then watch the fireworks from the Zattere.

Venice Film Festival (www.labiennale.org/en/cinema) The only thing hotter than a Lido beach in August is this star-studded event's red carpet, usually rolled out the last weekend in August through the first week of September.

SLEEPING

The best rates are in Venice's low season, typically November, early December, January and the period between Carnevale and Easter – but you might swing deals in the heat of July-August.

Hotel Ai Do Mori (Map pp180-1; ☎ 041 528 92 93; www.hotelaidomori.com; Calle Larga San Marco 658; d €75-150, d without bathroom €50-105) Artists' garrets in an enviable location at bargain rates. Rooms with a view cost the same, so ask for No 11 with a private terrace overlooking Piazza San Marco.

Hotel Galleria (Map pp180-1; ☎ 041 523 24 89; www.hotelgalleria.it; Campo della Carità 878a; incl breakfast d from €60-195, s/d without bathroom €40-85/50-135) The bargain-hunter's Holy Grail: a family-run hotel in a 17th-century mansion smack on the Grand Canal, steps from Ponte dell'Accademia, with updated bathrooms.

ourpick Hotel Flora (Map pp180-1; ☎ 041 522 53 44; www.hotelflora.it; Calle Bergamaschi 2283a; d €130-340; 🛱 💻) Down a lane from glitzy Calle Larga XXII Marzo, this garden retreat quietly outclasses brash top-end neighbours.

Palazzo Abadessa (Map pp180-1; ☎ 041 241 37 84; www.abadessa.com; Calle Priuli 4011; d

SAN MARCO, SAN POLO & SANTA CROCE

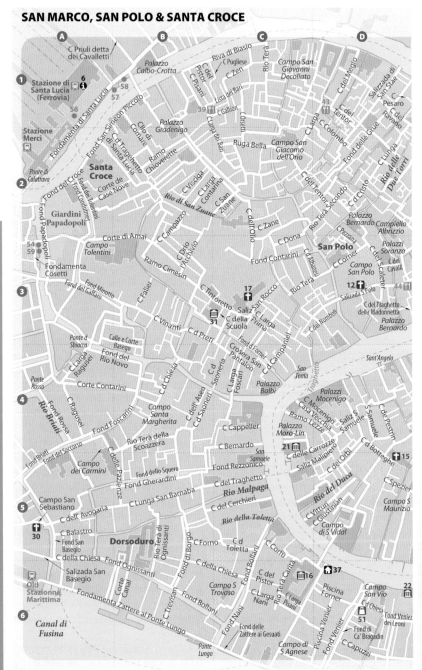

C Priuli detta
dei Cavalletti

Palazzo
Calbo-Crotta

Riva di Biasio

C Pugliese

C Zen

Campo San
Giovanni
Decollato

C del Megio

Stazione di
Santa Lucia
(Ferrovia)

58
57

56

Fondamenta di Santa Lucia

Palazzo
Gradenigo

C del
Pistor

C Pisani

Lista del Bari

C Gallion

Ruga Bella

Salizzada di
San Stae

C del
Tentor

Pesaro

C del
Ravano

C delle Grue

Stazione
Merci

Fond San Simeon Piccolo

Calle di
Cristo

Fond di
Santa Lucia

d Tragheto

Ramo
Chioverette

Campo San
Giacomo
dell'Orio

Fond delle Grue

C Lunga

C di Cristo

Ponte di
Calatrava

Santa
Croce

Fond del Croce

Fond delle Tolentini

Fond Condulmer

Corte de
Case Nove

C Visciga

C Larga
Contarina

C San
Zuane

C del Tentor

Rio Terà Secondo

Palazzo
Bernardo

Rio delle
Due Torri

Giardini
Papadopoli

Fond Papadopoli

Corte di Amai

Campazzo

Campo
Tolentini

C Dio
Archivio

Rio di San Zuane

C dell'Olio

C Zane

C Dona

Fond Contarini

Campiello
Albrizzio

Palazzo
Pezzana

C Corner

C del Cisto

San Polo

Palazzi
Soranzo

C del
Cavalli

54
59

Fondamenta
Cosetti

Fond del Gaffaro

Fond Minotto

Ramo Cimesin

C Faller

C Tintoretto

17

Saliz S
San Rocco

C Larga
Prima

Rio Terà

C dei Scaleter

Campo
San Polo

Salizada S Polo

12

44

C Vinanti

C d Preti

31

C della
Scuola

Fond d'Fomer

C Nomboli

C del Traghetto
della Madonnetta

Palazzo
Bernardo

Ponte d
Sbiacca

Calle e Corte
Basego

Fond del
Rio Novo

C d Chiesa

C d
Saoneria

Crosera San
Pantalon

C Larga
Foscari

San
Toma

Sant'Angelo

Ponte
Rosso

Fond Rosa

Rio Briati

C Ragusei

Corte Contarini

Fond Foscarini

C dell'Ased

C d Saonera

Palazzo
Balbi

Palazzi
Mocenigo

Casa
Mocenigo

Vecchia

Palazzi
Mocenigo

C de Pettrin

S Samuele

Campo
Santa
Margherita

Rio Terà della
Scoazzera

C Bernardo

C Cappeller

San
Samuele

21

Ramo Lezze

Palazzo
Moro-Lin

C delle Carrozze

Saliz S
Samuele

C del Oibo

15

Fond Briati

Fond del Socorso

C delle Pazienze

Campo
dei Carmini

Fond dello Squero

Fond Gherardini

Fond Rezzonico

Saliz Malipiero

C dei Oibo

C Spezier

Campo S
Maurizio

Campo San
Sebastiano

C dell'Avogaria

C Lunga San Barnaba

C del Traghetto

Rio Malpaga

Rio del Duca

C del Cerchieri

Rio della Toletta

C Vitturi
Giustinian

Campo
di S Vidal

30

C Balastro

Fond San
Basegio

C della Chiesa

Dorsoduro

Rio Terà di
Ognissanti

C Forno

C del Borgo

C d
Toletta

C Corfu

16

37

Piscina
Forner

Campo
San Vio

22

Old
Stazione
Marittima

Salizada San
Basegio

Fondamenta Zattere al Ponte Lungo

Corte
Canal

Fond Ognissanti

C Trevisan

Fond Bollani

Campo S
Trovaso

Fond Nani

C della Chiesa

C del
Pistor

Rio Terà
Nani

C Larga
Pisani

C Larga
Nani

Piscina
Venier

Fond di
Ca' Bragadin

51

C d Chiesa

Fond Venier
dei Leoni

Canal di
Fusina

Ponte
Lungo

Fond delle
Zattere ai Gesuati

Campo di
S Agnese

Piscina Venier

C Capuzzi

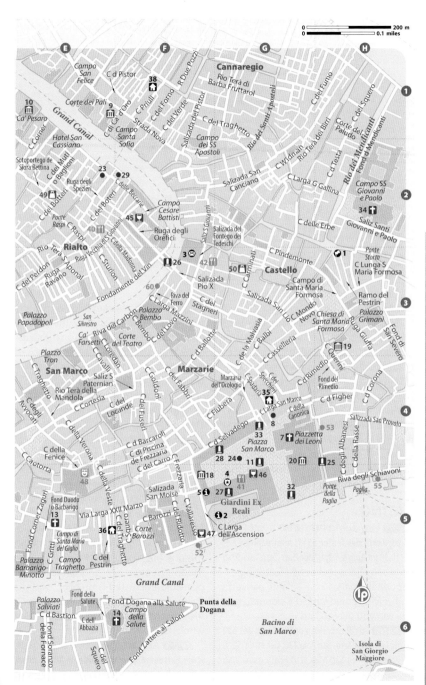

€145-325; 📷 💻 🛜) Sumptuous guestrooms feature plush beds, handmade silk-damask walls and 18th-century antique vanities; go for baroque and ask for one with original ceiling frescoes, and enjoy cocktails in the garden until you're whisked off to the opera seats on the hotel's boat.

Bauer Palladio & Spa (Map pp170-1; ☎ 041 520 70 22; www.palladiohotelspa.com; Fondamenta della Croce 33; d €210-490) Splash out in a serene, Palladio-designed former cloister with San Marco views, private solar-powered boat service and a superb spa.

EATING

ourpick I Rusteghi (Map pp180-1; ☎ 041 523 22 05; Corte del Tentor 5513; mini-panini €2-5; 🕑 10.30am-3pm & 6-9pm Mon-Sat) Outstanding wine selections and *cicheti* featuring exceptional meats – boar salami, pancetta and velvety cured *lardo di Colonnata* that will win you over to lard.

ourpick All'Arco (Map pp180-1; ☎ 041 520 56 66; Calle dell'Arco, San Polo 436; cicheti €1.50-4; 🕑 7am-5pm Mon-Sat) Maestro Francesco and his son Matteo invent Venice's best *cicheti*

daily with Rialto Market finds, and if you ask nicely and wait patiently, they'll whip up something special for you on the spot – baby artichoke topped with shavings of *bottarga,* or tuna tartare with mint, strawberries and a balsamic reduction.

Osteria La Zucca (Map pp180-1; ☎ 041 524 15 70; www.lazucca.it; Calle del Tentor, Santa Croce 1762; small plates €5-10; 🕑 12.30-2.30pm & 7-10.30pm Mon-Sat) Vegetable-centric seasonal small plates bring spice-trade influences to local produce: zucchini with ginger zing, curried carrots with yoghurt, and rice pudding with San Erasmo strawberries.

ourpick Anice Stellato (Map pp170-1; ☎ 041 72 07 44; Fondamenta della Sensa 3272; meals €25-40; 🕑 11am-3pm & 7-11pm Wed-Sun) If finding this obscure corner of Cannaregio seems like an adventure, wait until dinner arrives: pistachio-encrusted lamb fillet, wild sea bass with aromatic herbs, and perfectly fried *moecche* (soft-shelled crab) gobbled whole.

ourpick Al Gatto Nero (☎ 041 73 01 20; www.gattonero.com; via Giudecca 88; 🕑 noon-3.30pm & 7.30-10pm Tue-Sun) Once you've tried the homemade *tagliolini* with spider crab, whole grilled fish and perfect housebaked Burano biscuits, the ferry ride to Burano seems a minor inconvenience.

CAFES & GELATERIE

Caffè Florian (Map pp180-1; ☎ 041 520 56 41; www.caffeflorian.com; Piazza San Marco 56/59; drinks €8-12; 🕙 10am-midnight Thu-Tue Apr-Oct, to 11pm Thu-Tue Nov-Mar) Florian adheres to rituals established in 1720: lovers canoodle over breakfast in plush banquettes indoors, uniformed waiters serve gooey hot chocolate on silver trays, and the orchestra strikes up a dance number as fading sunlight illuminates San Marco's portal mosaics.

ourpick Pasticceria Rizzardini (Map pp180-1; ☎ 041 522 38 35; Campiello dei Meloni 1415, San Polo; 🕙 7.30am-8pm Wed-Mon) 'From 1742' reads the modest shopfront sign, and inside you'll find the secrets to the survival of this standing-room-only cafe-bakery: killer *krapfen* (doughnuts), wagging *lingue di suocere* (mother-in-law's

> ### ➥ CICHETI: VENICE'S BEST MEAL DEALS
>
> Even in unpretentious Venetian *osterie*, most dishes cost a couple of euros more than they might elsewhere in Italy. But *cicheti*, or Venetian tapas, are some of the best foodie finds in the country, served at lunch and around 6pm to 8pm with wine by the glass. For *cicheti* with ultrafresh ingredients at manageable prices, seek out *osterie* along side lanes and canals in Cannaregio, Castello, San Polo, Castello and San Marco.

tongues) and suggestively sprinkled *pallone di Casanova* (Casanova's balls).

ourpick Alaska (Map pp180-1; ☎ 041 71 52 11; Calle Larga dei Bari, Santa Croce 1159; s/d scoop €1/1.6; 🕙 9am-1pm & 3-8pm) Venetians head to Alaska for outlandish organic gelato: one glorious scoop of Venetian roasted pistachio, or two of vaguely minty *carciofi* (artichoke) with tangy lemon.

PHILIP & KAREN SMITH

Typical Venice cafe scene

TOP AVANT-GARDE ARTISANS IN VENICE

- Glass – Find witty statement jewellery in handblown glass at Marina & Susanna Sent (Map pp180-1; ☎ 041 520 81 36; www.marinaesusannasent.com; Campo San Vio, Dorsoduro 669; ⏰ 10am-1pm & 3-6.30pm Tue-Sat, 3-6.30pm Mon).
- Fashion – all the sleek jackets, tapestry handbags and diva dresses in the nonprofit boutique BANCO 10 (Map pp170-1; ☎ 041 522 14 39; Salizada Sant'Antonio, Castello 3478a; ⏰ 10am-1pm & 3-6.30pm Tue-Sat) are made in a retraining program at a women's prison on Giudecca, with remnants of sumptuous textiles donated by Fortuny and other local ateliers.
- Marbled paper – Rosanna Corró of Cartè (Map pp180-1; ☎ 320 024 87 76; 1731 Calle di Cristi; ⏰ 9am-1pm & 3-7.30pm Mon-Sat) applies modern flair to the ancient art of *carta marmorizzata* (marbled paper) in new must-haves.
- Shoes – Woven, sculpted and crested like lagoon birds: each extraordinary pair at Giovanna Zanella (Map pp180-1; ☎ 041 523 55 00; Calle Carminati, Castello 5641; ⏰ 9.30am-1pm & 3-7pm) is custom-made to treat your feet kindly as you stomp Venice's cobblestones or Film Festival red carpets.

DRINKING

Happy hour begins at 6pm with an *ombra* (small glass of wine) or *spritz,* the Venetian cocktail of Prosecco and bittersweet Aperol.

Aurora (Map pp180-1; ☎ 041 528 64 05; www. aurora.st; Piazza San Marco 48-50; ⏰ noon-2am Wed-Sun, cocktails from 6.15pm) Historic cafe by day, chilled lounge with local DJs and art openings by night.

Harry's Bar (Map pp180-1; ☎ 041 528 57 77; www.cipriano.com; Calle Vallaresso, San Marco 1323; ⏰ noon-11pm) Aspiring auteurs throng the bar frequented by Ernest Hemingway, Charlie Chaplin, Truman Capote, Orson Welles and others, enjoying a signature €18 Bellini (fresh peach juice and Prosecco) with a side of reflected glory.

Al Mercà (Map pp180-1; ☎ 393 992 47 81; Campo Bella Vienna, San Polo 213; ⏰ 9-3pm & 4-9pm Mon-Sat) Discerning drinkers throng this upbeat bar for top-notch Prosecco and DOC wines by the glass at €2 to €3.5, and *cicheti* start at just €1 for meatballs and mini-*panini*.

ENTERTAINMENT

In Venice, you can purchase tickets for major events at HelloVenezia ticket outlets (☎ 041 24 24; www.hellovenezia.it), located near key *vaporetto* stops (p186). For blockbuster events like the Biennale or La Fenice operas, you'll need to book ahead online at the appropriate website or www.vivaticket.it – though you might luck into last-minute discounts at Weekend a Venezia (http://en.venezia.waf. it).

ourpick Teatro La Fenice (Map pp180-1; ☎ 041 78 66 11; www.teatrolafenice.it; Campo San Fantin, San Marco 1965; tickets €20-1000) Tours are possible with advance booking (☎ 041 24 24), but the best way to see La Fenice is with the *loggione*, opera buffs that pass judgment on productions from on high in the top-tier cheap seats.

GETTING THERE & AWAY
AIR

Most flights arrive and depart from Marco Polo airport (VCE; off Map pp170-1; ☎ 041 260 92 60; www.veniceairport.it), 12km outside Venice, east of Mestre. Ryanair's budget flights to/from London Stansted, Dublin, Shannon and Paris currently use **San Giuseppe airport** (TSF; ☎ 0422 31 51 11; www.trevisoairport.it), about 5km southwest of Treviso and a 30km, one-hour drive from Venice.

Airport bus services link both airports with Venice's Piazzale Roma and Mestre, and the Alilaguna fast ferry runs from Marco Polo airport. ATVO's Eurobus connects to Treviso's San Giuseppe airport. For more details, see right.

BUS
Azienda del Consorzio Trasporti Veneziano (ACTV; ☎ 041 24 24; www.actv.it) buses leave from the bus station (Map pp170-1) on Piazzale Roma for Mestre and surrounding areas.

CAR & MOTORCYCLE
Once over the Ponte della Libertà bridge from Mestre, cars must be left at the car park at Piazzale Roma or Tronchetto; expect to pay €20 or more for every 24 hours. Parking stations in Mestre are cheaper.

TRAIN
Trains run frequently to Venice's Stazione Santa Lucia (signed as Ferrovia within Venice) from locations throughout Italy and major European cities; *vaporetti* (city ferries) stop right outside the station.

Venice is linked by train to Padua (€2.90 to €15.70, 30 to 50 minutes, three to four each hour) and Verona (€6.15 to €25.20, 1¼ to 2½ hours, two each hour). Regular trains run further afield to Milan (€14.50 to €38.50, 2½ to 3¼ hours), Bologna (€8.90 to €35.20, 1¾ to 2¾ hours), Florence (€21.50 to €54.50, 2¾ to 3¾ hours) and many other major points.

GETTING AROUND
TO/FROM THE AIRPORT
The **Alilaguna** (☎ 041 240 17 01; www.alilaguna.com) Orange Line ferry costs €13 from the airport ferry dock (an eight-minute walk from the terminal) to major stops at the Fondamente Nuove, near Piazza San

LEFT: JULIET COOMBE; RIGHT: ROBERTO GEROMETTA

Left: Staff outside Caffè Florian (p183); Right: Celebrating Carnevale (p179) in costume

Marco and at Zattere, making several stops along the 70-to-80-minute ride. The faster, direct Gold Line to/from San Zaccaria (near San Marco) takes 35 minutes, costs €25 and runs seven times daily on the half-hour.

ATVO (☎ 041 38 36 72; www.atvo.it) buses run to the airport from Piazzale Roma (€3, 20 minutes) about every half-hour. The trip to/from Piazzale Roma takes 65 minutes and costs €5.

VAPORETTO

The city's main mode of public transport is *vaporetto*. Tickets can be purchased from the HelloVenezia ticket booths (www.hello venezia.com) at most landing stations. You can also buy tickets when boarding; you may be charged double with luggage.

Instead of spending €6.50 for a one-way ticket, consider buying a VENICEcard (p172) or a timed pass for unlimited travel within a set time period, which begins when you validate your ticket in the yellow machine located at a ferry dock.

WATER TAXIS

The standard water taxi (☎ 041 522 23 03 or 041 240 67 11) between Marco Polo airport and Venice runs €60 to €90 for up to four people. Official rates start at €8.90 plus €1.80 per minute, €6 extra if they're called to your hotel and more for night trips, luggage and large groups.

AROUND THE VENETO

BRENTA RIVIERA

Every 13 June for 300 years, summer officially kicked off with a traffic jam along the Grand Canal, as a flotilla of fashionable Venetians headed for the Brenta. Hearts were won and fortunes lost; vendettas and villas endured.

Private ownership and privacy hedges leave much to the imagination, but four historic villas are now open as museums; others may be open to organised boat and bicycle tours and splendid villas can be visited around Vicenza (see p188).

SIGHTS

The most romantic Brenta villa is the Palladio-designed 1555–60 Villa Foscari (☎ 041 520 39 66; www.lamalcontenta.com; Via dei Turisti 9, Malcontenta; admission adult/student €10/8; ⓨ 9am-noon Tue & Sat, closed 15 Nov–31 Mar), known as 'La Malcontenta' after a grand dame of the Foscari clan allegedly exiled here for cheating on her husband – but these effortlessly light, sociable salons hardly constitute a punishment. Groups of 10 or more can book between April and 14 November at €8 per person.

To appreciate gardening and social engineering in the Brenta Riviera, stop by nearby Villa Widmann Rezzonico Foscari (☎ 041 560 06 90; www.riviera-brenta. it; Via Nazionale 420, Mira; adult/student €6/5; ⓨ 10am 5pm Sat & Sun Nov-Mar, to 6pm Tue-Sun May-Sep). The 18th-century villa originally owned by Persian-Venetian nobility captures the Brenta's last days of rococo decadence, with Murano sea-monster chandeliers, a frescoed grand salon and an upstairs ladies' gambling parlour.

TOURS

Il Burchiello (☎ 049 820 69 10; www.ilburchi ello.it; per day adult/12-17yr/6-11yr/under 6yr €66-79/52/37/free, half-day €44-48/44-48/36-37/free; ⓨ half-day cruises Tue-Fri, full-day cruises Tue-Sun Mar-Oct) is a modern luxury barge that lets you watch 50 villas drift by from cushy velvet couches with a glass of Prosecco from the onboard bar.

I Batelli del Brenta (☎ 049 876 02 33; www.battellidelbrenta.it; half-/full-day tours €44-48/66-85; ⓨ by reservation Tue-Sun Mar-

JOHN ELK III

Vicenza's Teatro Olimpico (p189)

Nov) offers full-day boat excursions covering three villas, nine swing bridges and five locks along the Brenta, including some cruises on restored wooden *burci* (barges); half-day trips may include optional lunches and transfers to/from Venice or Padua.

Rental Bike Venice (☎ 346 847 114; rental bikevenice.blogspot.com; Via Gramsci 85, Mira; bicycle per day city & mountain/foldable €10/14; ⏰ 8am-8pm) is accessible by bus from Venice, Mestre or Padua (see website for directions).

EATING
Across the road from La Malcontenta is **Ristorante da Bepi el Ciosato** (☎ 041 69 89 97; www.hotelgallimberti.it; Via Malcanton 33, Malcontenta; meals €26; ⏰ lunch & dinner), a country bistro that serves very urbane fish baked into *pasticcio di pesce* (fish pie) or wrapped in an artichoke crust.

GETTING THERE & AROUND
ACTV's **Venezia-Padova Extraurbane bus 53** leaves from Venice's Piazzale Roma

(p185) about every half-hour, stopping at key Brenta villages en route to Padua. Train service from Venice stops at Dolo (½ hour, €2.35 to €3.55) en route to Padua. By car, take SS11 from Mestre-Venezia towards Padova (Padua) and take the Autostrada A4 towards Dolo/Padova.

VICENZA
pop 113,500

If Palladio's uplifting spaces are like architectural Prozac, a walking tour of historic Vicenza is a megadose that leaves you simultaneously giddy and grounded, rational and open to possibilities.

ORIENTATION
From the train station in the gardens of Campo Marzo, Viale Roma heads into Piazzale de Gasperi. From here, Corso Andrea Palladio heads through the historic town centre.

INFORMATION
Police station (☎ 0444 54 33 33; Viale G Mazzini 213)

VENICE & THE NORTHEAST

AROUND THE VENETO

Tourist office (www.vicenzae.org) Piazza dei Signori (☎ 0444 54 41 22; Piazza dei Signori 8; 🕙 10am-2pm & 2.30-6.30pm); Piazza Matteotti (☎ 0444 32 08 54; Piazza Matteotti 12; 🕙 9am-1pm & 2-6pm)

SIGHTS

PIAZZA DEI SIGNORI

Dazzling white Piovene stone arches frame shady double arcades in the **Basilica Palladiana** (☎ 0444 32 36 81; 🕙 temporary exhibitions only), designed in 1549, while on the northwest end of the piazza, white stone and stucco grace the exposed red brick colonnade of the 1571-designed **Loggia del Capitaniato**.

CONTRÁ PORTI

North of Corso Andrea Palladio, three Palladian beauties line Contrà Porti. The finest is the newly restored **Palazzo Barbaran** (☎ 0444 32 30 14; Contrà Porti 11; www.cisapalladio.org; adult/student €5, with PalladioCard free; 🕙 10am-6pm Wed-Sun), built by Palladio (c 1569–70) with a stately double row of columns on the facade and a delightful double-height courtyard loggia that seems to usher in the sunlight.

The bank building at No 12 is **Palazzo Thiene**, begun under Palladio's supervision (c 1556–58) with rustic stone arches capped by gabled windows and elegant Corinthian pilasters, drawing the eye skyward.

Further along the street at No 21, you can't miss Palladio's blinding white, unfinished 1549–53 **Palazzo Isoppo da Porto**, rippling with eight inset Ionic columns on the first floor and crowned with sculpture and pilasters along the attic.

CONTRÀ DI SANTA CORONA

Two blocks east of Contrà Porti is another splendid sidestreet: Contrà di Santa Corona, named after **Chiesa di Santa Corona** (🕙 8.30am-noon & 3-6pm Tue-Sun, 4-6pm Mon). Built by the Dominicans in

ROBERTO GEROMETTA

Villa Pisani Nazionale

↘ VILLA PISANI NAZIONALE

To keep hard-partying nobles in line, Doge Alvise Pisani provided a monumental reminder who was in charge with the 1774 Villa Pisani Nazionale, with a labyrinthine hedge-maze and pools reflecting the doge's glory. The villa's 114 rooms saw their share of history: the gaming rooms where the Pisani racked up debts, forcing them to sell the mansion to Napoleon; the grand bathroom with a tiny wooden throne used by Napoleon; a sagging bed where Vittorio Emanuele II apparently tossed and turned as the head of independent Italy; and the reception hall where Mussolini and Hitler met for the first time in 1934, rather ironically under Tiepolo's ceiling masterpiece depicting the *Geniuses of Peace*.

Things you need to know: ☎ 041 271 90 19; www.villapisani.beniculturali.it; Via Alvise Pisani 7, Strà; adult/EU citizen 18-25yr/under 18yr €10/7.50/free, grounds only €7.50/5/free; 🕙 9am-6pm Tue-Sun Oct-Mar, to 8pm Tue-Sun Apr-Sep

PADUA'S CAPPELLA DEGLI SCROVEGNI

Just 37km west of Venice, the historic university town of Padua boasts the signature work by the artist da Vinci credited as his greatest influence: Giotto's moving, modern 1303–05 frescoes in the Scrovegni Chapel (☎ 049 201 00 20; www.cappelladegliscrovegni.it; Giardini dell'Arena; admission with PadovaCard free, adult/6-17yr & senior/under 6yr €12/8/1, night session €8/6/1; ⊙ visits daily by reservation only, minimum 3 days ahead; call centre 9am-7pm Mon-Fri & 9am-6pm Sat). Medieval churchgoers were accustomed to blank stares from flat saints on Gothic thrones – but Giotto introduced biblical figures as relatable characters in recognisable settings caught up in extraordinary circumstances.

In a new multimedia gallery, video projections and a full-scale set allow you enter each scene and experience how Giotto ended the dark ages in a blaze of glowing colour.

Booking is required online or by phone at least three days in advance, possibly weeks ahead from April to October. Chapel visits last 15 minutes, though the 'double turn' night session ticket (adult/child 7 to 17 years or senior/child under seven years €12/6/1; 7pm to 9.20pm) allows a 30-minute stay. Multimedia room visits can last 30 to 90 minutes.

The easiest way to Padua from Venice is by train (€2.90 to €15.70, 30 to 50 minutes, three or four each hour). The station is about 500m north of Cappella degli Scrovegni.

1261 to house a relic from Christ's crown of thorns, this Romanesque brick church also houses three light-filled masterpieces: Palladio's 1576 Valmarana Chapel in the crypt, Paolo Veronese's *Adoration of the Magi,* much praised by Goethe, and Giovanni Bellini's radiant *Baptism of Christ,* where the holy event is witnessed by a trio of Veneto beauties and a curious red bird.

From outside it looks like a bank, but a treasure beyond accountants' imagining awaits inside the Gallerie di Palazzo Leoni Montanari (☎ 800 57 88 75; www.palazzomontanari.com; Contrà di Santa Corona 25; adult/student €4/3; ⊙ 10am-6pm Tue-Sun).

PIAZZA MATTEOTTI

Behind a charming walled garden lies a Renaissance marvel: Teatro Olimpico (☎ 0444 22 28 00; www.olimpico.vicenza.it; com-

bined ticket with Museo Civico adult/student/child under 15yr €8/6/free, with PalladioCard adult €6; ⊙ 9am-5pm Tue-Sun), which Palladio began in 1580 with inspiration from Roman structures. Vincenzo Scamozzi finished the elliptical theatre after Palladio's death, adding a stage set modelled on the ancient Greek city of Thebes, with streets built in steep perspective to give the illusion of depth.

Save your entry ticket for access to the Museo Civico (☎ 0444 32 13 48; www.musei civicivicenza.it; Palazzo Chiericati, Piazza Matteotti 37/39; combined ticket with Teatro Olimpico adult/student/child under 15yr €8/6/free, with PalladioCard adult €6; ⊙ 9am-5pm Tue-Sun), housed in one of Palladio's finest buildings, designed in 1550 with a colonnaded ground floor and double-height loggia flanked by vast sun porches.

Giotto's frescoes in Scrovegni Chapel (boxed text, p189)

ROBERTO GEROMETTA

VICENZA SOUTH

Head down Viale X Giugno and east along Via San Bastiano and in about 20 minutes you'll reach the **Villa Valmarana 'ai Nani'** (☎ 0444 32 18 03; www.villavalmarana. com; Via dei Nani 8; admission adult/student/under 12yr €8/4/free; ☽ 10am-noon & 3-6pm Tue Sun Mar-Oct, 10am-noon & 2-4.30pm Sat & Sun Nov-Feb), covered with sublime 1757 frescoes by Giambattista Tiepolo and his son Giandomenico.

From Ai Nani, a path leads to Palladio's Villa Capra, better known as **La Rotonda** (☎ 0444 32 17 93; Via Rotonda 29; admission villa/ gardens €6/3; ☽ villa 10am-noon & 3-6pm Wed Mar-Nov, gardens 10am-noon & 3-6pm Tue-Sun Mar-Nov). No matter how you look at it, this villa is a showstopper: the namesake dome caps a square base, with colonnaded facades on all four sides. You can catch bus 8 (€1.50) to Vicenza out the front.

SLEEPING & EATING

Albergo Due Mori (☎ 0444 32 18 86; www. hotelduemori.com; Contrà do Rode 26; d €80, s/d without bathroom €48/55; ☐ ☎) Right off Piazza dei Signori on a boutique-lined cobblestone street, this historic 1854 hotel was recently restored to its period charm, with Liberty-style bedsteads and antique armoires.

Relais Santa Corona (☎ 0444 32 46 78; www.relaissantacorona.it; Contrá Santa Corona 19; s/d incl breakfast €87/104; P ☒ ☐ ☎) A boutique bargain, offering stylish stays in an 18th-century palace ideally located on a street dotted with landmarks.

ourpick Dai Nodari (☎ 0444 54 40 85; Contrà do Rode 20; meals under €10; ☽ noon-3.30pm & 7-11pm Mon-Sat) Rustic fare gets hip in the heart of historic Vicenza, packing in local crowds for €7 lunches and €9 dinner menus featuring hearty chicken with wild local mushrooms, followed by Sachertorte or local-speciality cheese plates featuring the seasoned, grappa-washed 'Bastardo di Grappo' cheese.

Antico Guelfo (☎ 0444 54 78 97; Contrà Pedemuro San Biagio 92; meals €35-40; ☽ lunch & dinner Mon-Fri, dinner Sat) This culinary hideaway is a hit with slow foodies for its inventive daily market menu, making the most of local specialities in such dishes as Amarone risotto or buckwheat crepes with Bastardo di Grappa cheese.

GETTING THERE & AWAY
BUS
FTV (☎ 0444 22 31 15; www.ftv.vi.it) buses leave for outlying areas from the bus station, located near the train station.

CAR & MOTORCYCLE
The city is on the A4 connecting Milan with Venice, while the SR11 connects Vicenza with Verona and Padua.

TRAIN
Regular trains arrive from Venice (€4.25 to €11.90, 45 minutes to 1¼ hours) and Padua (€2.90 to €10.90, 15 to 30 minutes).

VERONA
pop 264,200

Though Siena was Shakespeare's initial choice, fair Verona was where he set his scene between star-crossed lovers Romeo Montague and Juliet Capulet. As usual, the Bard got it right: romance, drama and fatal family feuds have been Verona's hallmark for centuries.

Verona was a Roman trade centre beginning in 300 BC, with ancient gates and a grand amphitheatre to prove it. After Mastino della Scala (aka Scaligeri) lost re-election to Verona's commune in 1262, he rallied the troops and claimed absolute control of the city, until his murder by a conspiracy of nobles. Under Mastino's son Cangrande I (1308–28), Verona's influence extended to Padua and Vicenza, and Dante, Petrarch and Giotto benefited from Verona's patronage and protection.

ORIENTATION
Buses leave for Verona's historic centre from outside the train station, south of town. To walk to the centre, head north past the bus station and 1.5km along Corso Porta Nuova to Piazza Brà, take Via G Mazzini northeast to Via Cappello and turn left to reach Piazza delle Erbe.

INFORMATION
Emergency medical care (☎ 118)
Police (☎ 113; Lungadige Galtarossa 11) Near Ponte Navi.
Post office (Piazza Viviani 7; 🕒 8.30am-6.30pm Mon-Sat)
Tourist office (www.tourism.verona.it) train station (☎ 045 800 08 61; 🕒 8am-7pm Mon-Sat, 9am-5pm Sun); Verona-Villafranca airport (☎ 045 861 91 63; 🕒 9am-6pm Mon-Sat, to 3pm Sun Apr-Nov, to 4pm Mon-Sat, to 3pm Sun Dec-Mar); Via degli Alpini (☎ 045 806 86 80; Via degli Alpini 9; 🕒 8.30am-7pm Mon-Sat, 9am-5pm Sun)

SIGHTS
VeronaCard (1/3 days €8/12), available at sights and tobacconists, grants access to major monuments and churches and reduced admission on minor sights, plus unlimited use of town buses.

ROMAN ARENA
The pink marble Roman amphitheatre (Roman arena; ☎ 045 800 51 51; www.arena.it; Piazza Brà, ticket office Ente Lirico Arena di Verona, Via Dietro Anfiteatro 6b; tours adult/student/child €4/3/1; 🕒 tours 1.45-7.30pm Mon & 8.30am-7.30pm Tue-Sun Oct-May, 8am-3.30pm Jun-Aug) was built in the 1st century AD and survived a 12th-century earthquake to become Verona's legendary open-air opera house, with seating for 30,000 people.

SHAKESPEARE'S VERONA
Off Via G Mazzini, Verona's main shopping street, is the legendary Casa di Giulietta (Juliet's House; ☎ 045 803 43 03; Via Cappello 23; adult/student/child €4/3/1; 🕒 8.30am-

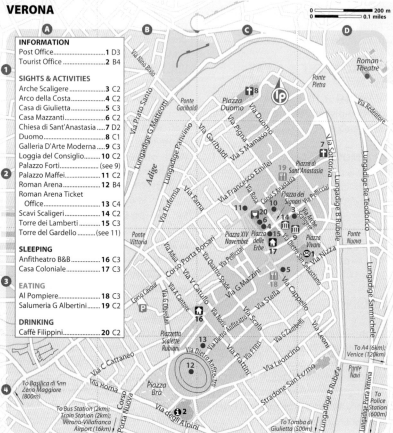

VERONA

7.30pm Tue-Sun, 1.45-7.30pm Mon). Never mind that Romeo and Juliet were completely fictional characters, and that there's hardly room for two on the narrow stone balcony: romantics flock to this 14th-century house to add their lovelorn pleas to the graffiti on the courtyard causeway and rub the right breast of the bronze statue of Juliet for better luck next time. Morbid romantics seek out the **Tomba di Giulietta** (Juliet's Tomb; ☎ 045 800 03 61; Via del Pontiere 35; adult/student/child €3/2/1; ☺ 8.30am-6.30pm Tue-Sun, 1.45-7.30pm Mon), a cloister with frescoes of minor interest.

PIAZZA DELLE ERBE
Originally a Roman forum, this piazza is ringed with cafes, buzzing with gossip and lined with some of Verona's most sumptuous buildings, including the baroque **Palazzo Maffei**, at the north end, with the adjoining 14th-century **Torre del Gardello**. On the eastern side, you can't miss the fresco-decorated **Casa Mazzanti**, former home of Verona's history-making Scaligeri clan.

Separating Piazza delle Erbe from Piazza dei Signori is the **Arco della Costa**, with a suspended whale's rib Veronese legend says will fall on the first just person to walk beneath it. Nearby, the striped Torre dei Lamberti (☎ 045 803 27 26; admission by lift/on foot €3/2; ☘ 9am-7.30pm Tue-Sun, 1.30-7.30pm Mon) is a watchtower begun in the 12th-century and finished in 1463, by which time it was too late to notice the Venetians invading – but it does offer a panoramic city view. Palazzo Forti (Palazzo della Ragione; ☎ 199 19 91 11; www. palazzoforti.it; adult/student €6/5; ☘ 10.30am-7pm Tue-Sun) is home to the new Galleria d'Arte Moderna, with 90 artworks from the 1970s to today and ambitious exhibits featuring such major modern artists as Escher and Sol LeWitt, plus well-curated photography shows in the adjoining Scavi Scaligeri.

PIAZZA DEI SIGNORI

Verona's early-Renaissance landmark is the 15th-century Loggia del Consiglio, the former city-council building, at the northern end of this square. Through the archway at the far end of the piazza are the Arche Scaligere (Via Arche Scaligere; admission incl Torre dei Lamberti by lift/on foot €4/3; ☘ 9.30am-7.30pm Tue-Sun, 1.45pm-7.30pm Mon Jun-Sep), the elaborate Gothic tombs of the Scaligeri family where murderers are interred not far from the relatives they'd killed.

CHURCHES

A masterpiece of Romanesque architecture, the striped brick and tuffo stone Basilica di San Zeno Maggiore (www. chieseverona.it; Piazza San Zeno; combined Verona church ticket/s church entry €5/2.5; ☘ 8.30am-6pm Mon-Sat & 1-6pm Sun Mar-Oct, 10am-1pm & 1.30-4pm Tue-Sat & 1-5pm Sun Nov-Feb) was built in honour of the city's patron saint from the 12th to 14th centuries.

Verona's 12th-century Duomo (Cathedral; Piazza del Duomo; combined Verona church ticket/s church entry €5/2.5; ☘ 10am-5.30pm Mon-Sat, 1.30-5.30pm Sun Mar-Oct, 10am-1pm & 1.30-4pm Tue-Sat, 1-5pm Sun Nov-Feb) is a striking striped Romanesque building, with polychrome reliefs and bug-eyed statues of Charlemagne's paladins Roland and Oliver by medieval master Nicoló on the west porch.

North of the Arche Scaligere stands the Gothic 13th-to-15th-century Chiesa di Sant'Anastasia (Piazza di Sant'Anastasia; ☘ 9am-6pm Mon-Sat, 1-6pm Sun Mar-Oct, 10am-1pm & 1.30-4pm Tue-Sat, 1-5pm Sun Nov-Feb), Verona's largest church and a showcase for Veronese art.

SLEEPING

Casa Coloniale (☎ 337 47 27 37; www.casa -coloniale.com; Via Cairoli 6; s/d incl breakfast €50-70/80-110; ☒) Snag a prime berth off Piazza Erbe in this hip new B&B, where three guestrooms have a single stripe of bold colour marked with the room number in a kind of billiard-ball decor scheme.

ourpick Anfiteatro B&B (☎ 347 24 84 62; www.anfiteatro-bedandbreakfast.com; Via Alberto Mario 5; s/d/tr or q incl breakfast €60-90/80-130/100-150) Opera divas and fashionistas rest up in the heart of the action in this recently restored 19th-century townhouse, one block from the Arena off boutique-lined Via Mazzini.

EATING & DRINKING

Salumeria G Albertini (☎ 045 803 10 74; Via Sant'Anastasia 39; ☘ 8am-2pm & 3-8pm Mon-Sat) A picture-perfect deli, featuring all the prepared pastas, cured meats, local Asiago sheep's cheese and wine you could want for an ideal picnic by the river or inside the Roman Arena.

ourpick Al Pompiere (☎ 045 803 05 37; www.alpompiere.com; Vicolo Regina d'Ungheria 5; meals €25-40; ☘ Tue-Sat & dinner Mon) The fireman's (pompiere) hat is still on the

LEFT: GLENN BEANLAND; RIGHT: DAVID TOMLINSON

Left: The famous balcony of Casa di Giulietta (p191); Right: Aerial view of Verona

wall, but the focal points at this local hot spot are the vast cheese selection and famed house-cured *salumi* platter. Reserve ahead.

Caffè Filippini (☎ 045 800 45 49; Piazza delle Erbe 26; ⊙ 8am-2am Thu-Tue) The hippest joint in town has been here since 1901, perfecting the house speciality Filippini, a killer cocktail of vermouth, gin, lemon and ice.

GETTING THERE & AWAY
Verona-Villafranca airport (VRN; ☎ 045 809 56 66; www.aeroportoverona.it) is 12km outside town and accessible by APTV Aerobus to/from the train station (€4.50, 15 minutes, every 20 minutes from 6.30am to 11.30pm).

The main intercity bus station is in front of the train station, in the Porta Nuova area.

Verona is at the intersection of the A4 (Turin–Trieste) and A22 motorways.

The trip to/from Venice is easiest by train (€6.15, two hours). Verona has rail links with Padua, Vicenza, Milan, Mantua, Modena, Florence and Rome.

GETTING AROUND
AMT (www.amt.it) city buses 11, 12, 13 and 14 (bus 91 or 92 on Sunday and holidays) connect the train station with Piazza Brà. Buy tickets from newsagents and tobacconists before you board the bus (tickets one hour/day €1/3.50).

EMILIA-ROMAGNA

BOLOGNA
pop 372,000

Boasting one of the country's great medieval cityscapes – an eye-catching ensemble of red-brick *palazzi*, Renaissance towers and arcaded porticoes – Bologna is a wonderful alternative to the north's more famous cities.

The city reached its pinnacle as an independent commune and leading European university around the 12th century. Wealth brought a building boom and every well-to-do family left its mark by erecting a tower – 180 of them in all, of which 22 still stand today.

ORIENTATION

From the train and bus stations, Via dell'Indipendenza leads to Piazza del Nettuno and Piazza Maggiore, the heart of the city.

INFORMATION

POST

Post office (Piazza Minghetti 4)

TOURIST INFORMATION

Centro Servizi per i Turisti (☎ 800 85 60 65; www.cst.bo.it; Piazza Maggiore 1e; ☽ 10am-2pm & 3-7pm Mon-Sat, 10am-2pm Sun)

Tourist office (www.bolognaturismo.info; ☽ 9am-7pm) airport (☎ 051 647 21 13); Piazza Maggiore (☎ 051 23 96 60; Piazza Maggiore 1e); train station (☎ 051 25 19 47)

SIGHTS

PIAZZA MAGGIORE & PIAZZA DEL NETTUNO

Flanked by the world's fifth-largest basilica and a series of impressive Renaissance *palazzi*, Piazza Maggiore is the city's principal focus and an obvious starting point for sightseeing. Adjacent to Piazza Maggiore, Piazza del Nettuno owes its name to the Fontana del Nettuno (Neptune's Fountain), a stirring bronze statue sculpted by Giambologna in 1566.

Forming the western flank of Piazza Maggiore, Palazzo Comunale (known also as Palazzo D'Accursio after its original resident, Francesco D'Accursio) has been home to Bologna city council since 1336. A salad of architectural styles, it owes much of its current look to makeovers in the 15th and 16th centuries. On the 2nd floor you'll find the *palazzo's* two art galleries (☎ 051 20 36 29; admission free; ☽ 9am-6.30pm Tue-Fri, 10am-6.30pm Sat & Sun).

Dominating the piazza's southern flank, the Gothic Basilica di San Petronio (☎ 051 22 54 42; ☽ 7.45am-12.30pm & 3.30-6pm) is Bologna's greatest church. Originally it was intended to be larger than St Peter's in Rome, but in 1561, some 169 years after building had started, Pope Pius IV blocked construction by commissioning a new university on the basilica's eastern flank.

THE QUADRILATERO

To the east of Piazza Maggiore, the grid of streets around Via Clavature (Street of Locksmiths) sits on what was once Roman Bologna. Known as the Quadrilatero, this bustling district is one of the centre's most enticing – colourful market stalls and delicious delis open onto cobbled medieval streets lined with trendy cafes, swish bars and neighbourhood eateries.

SOUTH & WEST OF PIAZZA MAGGIORE

Running south off Piazza Maggiore, Via dell'Archiginnasio leads to the Museo Civico Archeologico (☎ 051 275 72 11; Via dell'Archiginnasio 2; admission free; ☽ 9am-3pm Tue-Fri, 10am-6.30pm Sat & Sun) with its well-documented Egyptian and Roman artefacts and one of Italy's best Etruscan collections.

A few doors down, Palazzo dell' Archiginnasio is the result of Pope Pius IV's project to curtail the Basilica di San Petronio. Seat of the city university from 1563 to 1805 (notice the professors' coats of arms on the walls), it today houses Bologna's 700,000-volume Biblioteca Comunale (Municipal Library) and the fascinating 17th-century Teatro Anatomico (☎ 051 27 68 11; Piazza Galvani 1; admission free; ☽ 9am-6.45pm Mon-Fri, to 1.45pm Sat), where public body dissections were held under the sinister gaze of an Inquisition priest, ready to intervene if proceedings became too spiritually compromising.

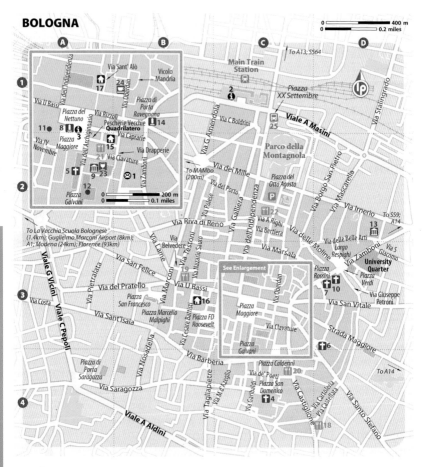

A short walk south brings you to the **Basilica di San Domenico** (☎ 051 640 04 11; Piazza San Domenico 13; ☼ 9.30am-12.30pm & 3.30-6.30pm Mon-Fri, to 5.30pm Sat & Sun), built in 1238 to house the remains of San Domenico, founder of the Dominican order, who died in 1221. His elaborate sarcophagus is in the **Cappella di San Domenico**, which was designed by Nicola Pisano and later added to by a host of artists. Michelangelo carved the angel on the right of the altar when he was only 19.

UNIVERSITY QUARTER

Towering above Piazza di Porta Ravegnana, Bologna's two leaning towers, Le Due Torri, are unmistakable landmarks. The taller of the two, the 97.6m-high **Torre degli Asinelli** (admission €3; ☼ 9am-6pm, to 5pm Oct-May) is open to the public, although it's not advisable for the weak-kneed (there are 498 steps) or superstitious students (local lore says if you climb the tower you'll never graduate). Built by the Asinelli family between 1109 and 1119, today it leans 1.3m off vertical. The neighbouring 48m **Torre Garisenda** is

INFORMATION					
Centro Servizi per i Turisti	(see 3)	Fontana del Nettuno	**8** A1	Prendiparte B&B	**17** A1
Post Office	**1** B2	Museo Civico			
Tourist Office	**2** C1	Archeologico	**9** A2	EATING	
Tourist Office	**3** A1	Museum	(see 6)	La Sorbetteria Castiglione	**18** D4
		Oratorio di Santa Cecilia	**10** D3	Mercato delle Erbe	**19** B3
SIGHTS & ACTIVITIES		Palazzo Comunale	**11** A1	Osteria de' Poeti	**20** C4
Basilica di San Domenico	**4** C4	Palazzo dell'Archiginnasio	**12** A2	Produce Market	**21** A2
Basilica di San Petronio	**5** A2	Pinacoteca Nazionale	**13** D2	Trattoria del Rosso	**22** C2
Basilica di Santo Stefano	**6** D3	Teatro Anatomico	(see 12)		
Biblioteca Comunale	(see 12)	Torre degli Asinelli	(see 14)	DRINKING	
Cappella di San Domenico	(see 4)	Torre Garisenda	**14** B1	Nu-Lounge Bar	**23** A2
Chiesa della Trinità	(see 6)			Terzi	**24** B1
Chiesa di San Giacomo		SLEEPING			
Maggiore	**7** D3	Albergo delle Drapperie	**15** A2	TRANSPORT	
		Albergo Panorama	**16** B3	Main Bus Station	**25** C1

sensibly out of bounds given its drunken 3.2m tilt.

From the two towers, head southeast along Via Santo Stefano for the **Basilica di Santo Stefano** (☎ 051 22 32 56; Via Santo Stefano 24; ☉ 9am-12.30pm & 3.30-6.30pm), an atmospheric medieval religious complex. Entry is via the 11th-century **Chiesa del Crocefisso**, which houses the bones of San Petronio and leads through to the **Chiesa del Santo Sepolcro**. Next door, the **Cortile di Pilato** is named after the central basin in which Pontius Pilate is said to have washed his hands after condemning Christ to death. In fact, it's an 8th-century Lombard artefact. Beyond the courtyard, the **Chiesa della Trinità** connects to a modest cloister and a small **museum**. The fourth church, the **Santi Vitale e Agricola** is the city's oldest. Incorporating recycled Roman masonry and carvings, the bulk of the building dates from the 11th century.

To the north of the basilica complex, along Via Zamboni, the 13th-century **Chiesa di San Giacomo Maggiore** (☎ 051 22 59 70; Piazza Rossini; ☉ 8.30am-1pm & 3.30-6.30pm) houses a noteworthy collection of paintings and artefacts. The highlight is the Bentivoglio chapel with frescoes by Lorenzo Costa and an altarpiece by Francesco Raibolini (known as Il Francia). The same pair were mainly responsible for the magnificent 16th-century frescoes in the adjacent **Oratorio di Santa Cecilia** (☎ 051 22 59 70; Via Zamboni 15; ☉ 10am-1pm & 2-6pm), one of Bologna's unsung gems.

Back on the art trail, the **Pinacoteca Nazionale** (☎ 051 420 94 11; Via delle Belle Arti 56; adult/child €4/2; ☉ 9am-7pm Tue-Sun) has a strong collection of works by Bolognese artists from the 14th century onwards, including a number of important canvases by the late-16th-century Carracci cousins Ludovico, Agostino and Annibale.

NORTH OF PIAZZA MAGGIORE

Near the northwestern edge of the historical centre, **MAMbo** (Museo d'Arte Moderna di Bologna; ☎ 051 649 66 11; Via Don Minzoni 14; admission free; ☉ 10am-6pm Tue-Sun, to 10pm Thu) is Bologna's newest museum. Housed in a cavernous former municipal bakery, its permanent and rotating exhibits showcase the work of up-and-coming Italian artists.

COURSES

La Vecchia Scuola Bolognese (☎ 051 649 15 76; www.lavecchiascuola.com; Via Malvasia 49) is one of several schools that offer courses for English speakers. Prices range from €80 for a single four-hour course to €250 for a full week of classes.

TOURS

Prima Classe (☎ 347 894 40 94; infoprima classe@libero.it) English-language tours 11am Monday and Friday, 3pm (4pm

The Quadrilatero (p195)

DAVID NOTON PHOTOGRAPHY/ALAMY

in summer) Tuesday and Thursday. German-language tours 10am Tuesday and Saturday.

Trambus Open (☎ 051 35 08 53; www.trambusopen.com) runs an hour-long hop-on-hop-off bus tour of the city departing from the train station several times daily. Tickets (€10) can be bought on board.

FESTIVALS & EVENTS

Bologna Estate A three-month (mid-June to mid-September) program of concerts, film projections, dance performances and much more. Tourist offices carry details.

Salotto del Jazz (July to August) A small-scale jazz fest organised by four venues in and around Via Mascarella in the university quarter northwest of Via Zamboni.

SLEEPING

Accommodation in Bologna is geared to the business market, with a glut of mid-range to top-end hotels and precious few budget options. Outside of fair season, some hotels offer discounts of up to 50% and attractive weekend rates.

Albergo Panorama (☎ 051 22 18 02; www.hotel panoramabologna.it; 4th fl, Via Livraghi 1; s/d/tr/q without bathroom €50/70/80/90) A cheerful old-school family *pensione* with exceptionally spacious rooms, many offering lovely views of nearby *palazzi*, towers and flowery terraces. The lone room with bathroom costs €10 extra.

Albergo delle Drapperie (☎ 051 22 39 55; www.albergodrapperie.com; Via delle Drapperie 5; s €60-105, d €75-140, breakfast per person €5 extra; ⧉) Right in the heart of the atmospheric Quadrilatero district, this welcoming three-star establishment has 21 attractive rooms with wood-beamed ceilings, the occasional brick arch and colourful ceiling frescoes.

ourpick Prendiparte B&B (☎ 051 58 90 23; www.prendiparte.it; Via Sant'Alò 7; r €300) You don't just get a room at this unique B&B, you get an entire 900-year-old tower.

EATING

ourpick **Trattoria del Rosso** (☎ 051 23 67 30; Via A Righi 30; meals €16-18; ☺ lunch & dinner) This perennially popular trattoria is said to be the oldest in the city. The daily fixed-price lunch and dinner menus (€10) are exceptional value and the vegetarian options are a welcome sight in such a meat-obsessed city.

Osteria de' Poeti (☎ 051 23 61 66; Via de' Poeti 1b; meals €30-40; ☺ closed Mon Oct-May, Sun Jun-Aug) In the wine cellar of a 14th-century *palazzo*, this historic eatery is an atmospheric place to enjoy hearty local fare.

ourpick **La Sorbetteria Castiglione** (☎ 051 23 32 57; Via Castiglione 44; ☺ 8.30am-11pm) Locals queue up day and night at this award-winning gelateria, which focuses all of its creative energy on 18 flavours.

Stock up on victuals at the **Mercato delle Erbe** (Via U Bassi 27; ☺ 7am-1.15pm Mon-Sat & 5-7.30pm Mon-Wed & Fri), Bologna's main covered market. Alternatively, the Quadrilatero area east of Piazza Maggiore harbours a daily **produce market** (Via Clavature; ☺ 7am-1pm Mon-Sat & 4.15-7.30pm Mon-Wed, Fri & Sat) and some of the city's best-known delis.

DRINKING

Terzi (☎ 051 23 64 70; Via Oberdan 10; ☺ 8am-6pm Mon-Fri, to 12.30pm Sat) A refined cafe that serves an unusual range of coffees, Terzi is a great spot to sit and toy with a *caffè con prugna e cannella* (espresso with plum and cinnamon) or *cappuccino brulé alla cannella* (cappuccino with cinnamon).

Nu-Lounge Bar (☎ 051 22 25 32; Via de'Musei 6f) One of several swish cafes in the Quadrilatero, Nu-Lounge attracts a chic, stylishly dressed crowd for everything from predinner *aperitivi* to midnight cocktails on its porticoed terrace.

GETTING THERE & AWAY

AIR

Bologna's **Guglielmo Marconi airport** (BLQ; ☎ 051 647 96 15; www.bologna-airport.it) is 8km northwest of the city.

BUS

Intercity buses leave from the **main bus station** (☎ 051 24 54 00; www.autostazionebo. it) off Piazza XX Settembre, just southeast of the train station. However, for nearly all destinations, the train's a better option.

CAR & MOTORCYCLE

Major car-hire companies are represented at Guglielmo Marconi airport and outside the train station.

TRAIN

Bologna is a major transport junction for northern Italy and has half-hourly services to Florence (regional train €5.40, 1½ hours; Eurostar €18.10, one hour), Rome (regional €23.20, five hours; Eurostar €50.40, three hours) and Milan (regional €13.50, 2¼ hours; Eurostar €37.10, one hour).

Frequent trains from Bologna serve cities throughout Emilia-Romagna.

GETTING AROUND

Aerobus shuttles (☎ 051 29 02 90; www.atc. bo.it) depart from the main train station for Guglielmo Marconi airport every 15 to 30 minutes between 5.30am and 11.10pm. The 20-minute journey costs €5 (tickets can be bought on-board).

Much of the city centre is off-limits to vehicles. Buses 25, 30 and A are among several that connect the train station with the city centre.

For taxis, phone **Cotabo** (☎ 051 37 27 27) or **CAT RadioTaxi** (☎ 051 53 41 41).

MODENA

pop 179,900

Get past the unsightly factories that ring this affluent city and you'll find a lively medieval centre, thick with market stalls, vibrant piazzas and impressive *palazzi*. The highlight, and reason enough for a visit, is the stunning Unesco World Heritage–listed cathedral.

ORIENTATION

Via Emilia is Modena's main drag. The street slices through the historic town centre from west to east.

INFORMATION

ModenaTur (☎ 059 22 00 22; www.modena tur.it, in Italian; Via Scudari 8; ⏰ 2.30-6.30pm Mon, 9am-1pm & 2.30-6.30pm Tue-Sat) A private agency that organises tours to balsamic vinegar producers and *parmigiano reggiano* dairies.

Tourist office (☎ 059 203 26 60; http://turis mo.comune.modena.it; Piazza Grande 14; ⏰ 3-6pm Mon, 9am-1pm & 3-6pm Tue-Sat, 9.30am-12.30pm Sun) Provides city maps and the useful *Welcome to Modena* brochure.

SIGHTS

Modena's main museums and galleries are housed in the **Palazzo dei Musei** (Piazzale Sant'Agostino 337) on the western fringes of the historic centre.

The most interesting, the **Galleria Estense** (☎ 059 439 57 11; admission €4; ⏰ 8.30am-7.30pm Tue-Sun) features the Este family's collection of northern Italian paintings from late medieval times to the 18th century.

SLEEPING & EATING

Hotel Cervetta 5 (☎ 059 23 84 47; www.hotel cervetta5.com; Via Cervetta 5; s/d/tr €80/110/145; P ✴ 🛜) Within a stone's throw of Piazza Grande, this welcoming boutique hotel boasts a cool, contemporary look, with modern amenities including flat-screen TVs.

Canalgrande Hotel (☎ 059 21 71 60; www. canalgrandehotel.it; Corso Canalgrande 6; s €114-132, d €154-180, jr ste €190-220; P ✴ 🖥 🛜) A venerable Modenese institution, the Canalgrande exudes old-school elegance with its acres of marble, gilt-framed paintings, sparkling chandeliers and a spacious terrace overlooking the garden out back.

Trattoria Aldina (☎ 059 23 61 06; Via Albinelli 40; meals €17; ⏰ lunch Mon-Sat) Where do locals head for lunch after a morning shopping at the produce market? Straight across the street and upstairs to this sweet, affordable trattoria, which serves the kind of no-nonsense homemade food you'd expect from a mid-1950s Italian mamma.

Ristorante da Enzo (☎ 059 22 51 77; Via Coltellini 17; meals €25-30; ⏰ closed Sun dinner & Mon) This highly regarded restaurant is known for its classic, regional cooking, which translates to dishes such as *scaloppina all'aceto balsamico* (cutlets in balsamic vinegar) and *tortelli di zucca al burro e salvia* (pumpkin tortelli with butter and sage).

SHOPPING

Load up on local wine, grappa and Modena's famous vinegar – aged anywhere from three to 100 years – at **Enoteca Ducale** (☎ 059 427 92 28; Corso Vittorio Emanuele 15; ⏰ 9am-7pm Tue-Sun).

GETTING THERE & AROUND

The bus station is on Via Molza, northwest of the centre. **ATCM** (☎ 800 11 11 01; www. atcm.mo.it, in Italian) buses connect Modena with most towns in the region.

The train station is north of the historic centre, fronting Piazza Dante.

Modena Cathedral

NEIL SETCHFIELD

◥ MODENA CATHEDRAL

One of the finest Romanesque churches in Italy, Modena's Unesco World Heritage–listed cathedral is a thrilling example of 12th-century architecture. The facade is dominated by a huge Gothic rose window, actually a 13th-century addition, under which stands the main portal; to the sides, a series of vivid bas-reliefs depict scenes from Genesis. These are the work of the 12th-century sculptor Wiligelmo, who actually autographed his work (see the panel to the left of the main door), as did the building's architect, Lanfranco (signing off in the main apse).

Opposite the entrance to the cathedral, the Musei del Duomo holds yet more of Wiligelmo's captivating stonework.

Rising above the cathedral, the early-13th-century Torre Ghirlandina (closed indefinitely for renovation at time of research) rises to 87m, culminating in a slender Gothic spire.

Things you need to know: Modena Cathedral (☎ 059 21 60 78; Corso Duomo; ☼ 7am-12.30pm & 3.30-7pm); Musei del Duomo (☎ 059 439 69 69; Via Lanfranco 6; adult/child €3/2, audioguide €1; ☼ 9.30am-12.30pm & 3.30-6.30pm Tue-Sun)

Destinations include Bologna (€3.10, 30 minutes, half-hourly), Parma (€4.30, 30 minutes, half-hourly) and Milan (regional/express train €10.55/20.40, two hours, hourly). ATCM's bus 7 links the train station with the bus station and city centre.

MARANELLO

pop 16,600

Home to Ferrari, Maranello is a motoring mecca that attracts hundreds of thousands of pilgrims each year. Most head to the Galleria Ferrari (☎ 0536 94 32 04; www.galleria.ferrari.com; Via Ferrari 43; adult/child €13/9; ☼ 9.30am-7pm May-Sep, to 6pm Oct-Apr) to

Maranello's Galleria Ferrari (p201)

HANNAH LEVY

obsess over the world's largest collection of Ferraris.

Maranello is 17km south of Modena. From Modena's bus station take bus 800 (€2.30, 30 minutes).

PARMA

pop 178,700

Rich on the back of its food industry, Parma is the perfect picture of a well-off provincial city. Well-dressed locals cycle through pretty piazzas and drink in elegant cafes, while beautifully preserved monuments adorn picturesque cobbled lanes.

Originally Etruscan, Parma achieved importance as a Roman colony astride what would become the Via Emilia.

ORIENTATION

From the train station, Via Verdi leads south to the green turf of Piazza della Pace. Continue south along Via Garibaldi to connect with Via Mazzini and Piazza Garibaldi, Parma's main square.

INFORMATION

Police station (☎ 0521 21 94; Borgo della Posta 16a)

Tourist office (☎ 0521 21 88 89; http://turismo.comune.parma.it/turismo; Via Melloni 1a; ⏱ 9am-1pm & 3-7pm Mon, 9am-7pm Tue-Sat, 9am-1pm Sun)

SIGHTS

PIAZZA DEL DUOMO & AROUND

From the outside, Parma's Duomo (☎ 0521 23 58 86; ⏱ 9am-12.30pm & 3-7pm), consecrated in 1106, is classic Lombard-Romanesque. Inside, the gilded pulpit and ornate lampholders all scream baroque bombast. But there are some genuine treasures here: up in the dome, Antonio Correggio's *Assunzione della Vergine* (Assumption of the Virgin) is a kaleidoscopic swirl of cherubims and whirling angels, while down in the southern transept, Benedetto Antelami's *Deposizione* (Descent from the Cross; 1178) relief is considered a masterpiece of its type.

Antelami was also responsible for the octagonal pink-marble battistero (☎ 0521

23 58 86; admission €5; �---9am-12.30pm & 3-6.45pm) on the south side of the piazza.

East of Piazza del Duomo, the 16th-century **Chiesa di San Giovanni Evangelista** (☎ 0521 23 53 11; Piazzale San Giovanni; �---8-11.45am & 3-7.45pm) is noted for its magnificent frescoed dome, the work of Coreggio, and a series of frescoes by Francesco Parmigianino. The adjoining **monastery** (�---8.30am-noon & 3-6pm) is known as much for the oils and unguents that its monks produce as for its Renaissance cloisters. Just around the corner, the **Spezieria di San Giovanni** (☎ 0521 50 85 32; Borgo Pipa 1; adult/child €2/free; �---8.30am-1.30pm Tue-Sun) is the monastery's ancient pharmacy, which still has its original interior.

PIAZZA DELLA PACE & AROUND

Looming over Piazza della Pace's manicured lawns and modern fountains, the monumental **Palazzo della Pilotta** is hard to miss. Heavily bombed in WWII, it has since been largely rebuilt and today houses several museums.

The most important of these, the **Galleria Nazionale** (☎ 0521 23 33 09; adult/child incl Teatro Farnese €6/free; �---8.30am-1.30pm Tue-Sun), displays Parma's main art collection. Alongside works by local artists Correggio and Parmigianino, you'll find paintings by Fra Angelico, Canaletto and El Greco. Before you get to the gallery, though, you'll pass through the **Teatro Farnese**, a copy of Andrea Palladio's Teatro Olimpico in Vicenza.

PIAZZA GARIBALDI

On the square's north side, the facade of the 17th-century **Palazzo del Governatore**, these days municipal offices, sports a giant sundial, added in 1829. Behind the palace in the **Chiesa di Santa Maria della Steccata** (☎ 0521 23

49 37; Piazza Steccata 9; �---9am-noon & 3-6pm), you'll find some of Parmigianino's most extraordinary work, notably the stunning, if rather faded, frescoes on the arches above the altar.

SLEEPING

Albergo Ristorante Leon d'Oro (☎ 0521 77 31 82; www.leondoroparma.com; Viale Fratti 4a; s/d €55/70, without bathroom €37/60) Offers no-nonsense, fan-cooled rooms with high ceilings and old-fashioned furniture. The attached restaurant is a plus, as is the location near the train station, although front rooms can get noisy.

Century Hotel (☎ 0521 03 98 00; www.centuryhotel.it; Piazza dalla Chiesa 5a; s/d/ste €80/120/200; P ✕ 🖳 🛜) Directly adjacent to the train station, this slickly remodelled hotel (formerly Albergo Moderno) sports four-star fixtures and amenities at three-star prices (all that's missing is the hotel restaurant).

EATING & DRINKING

The city's animated drinking scene is centred on Strada Farini, home to numerous wine bars, including **Tabarro** (☎ 0521 20 02 23; Strada Farini 5b; �---Tue-Sun).

Da Walter Clinica del Panino (☎ 0521 20 63 09; Borgo Palmia 2; panini from €3; �---9am-9pm Mon-Wed, to 3pm Thu, to midnight Fri & Sat) Fast food, Parma style: neon lights, deft-handed cooks and more than 100 varieties of snacks and sandwiches combined with great prices and supersonic service.

Gallo d'Oro (☎ 0521 20 88 46; Borgo Salina 3; meals €25; �---closed dinner Sun) Vintage magazine covers and artfully placed wine bottles lend the Gallo d'Oro a very agreeable bistro feel. But it's not all image: this is one of Parma's best trattorias serving consistently good Emilian cuisine. Booking is recommended.

SHOPPING

Stock up on edible goodies at Salumeria Garibaldi (☎ 0521 23 56 06; Via Garibaldi 42; ⊗ 8am-8pm Mon-Sat) and Salumeria Verdi (☎ 0521 20 81 00; Via Garibaldi 69a; ⊗ 8am-1.15pm & 4-7.45pm Mon-Wed, Fri & Sat, 8am-1.15pm Thu).

GETTING THERE & AWAY

There are frequent trains to Milan (regional/express train €8/16.20, 1¼ to 1¾ hours, hourly), Bologna (€5.80, one hour, half-hourly), Modena (€4.30, 30 minutes, half-hourly) and Piacenza (€4.30, 40 minutes, half-hourly).

GETTING AROUND

Bikes are available for hire at Parma Punto Bici (☎ 0521 28 19 79; www.parmapuntobici.pr.it, in Italian; Viale Toschi 2a; per hr/day bicycles €0.70/10, electric bikes €0.90/20; ⊗ 9am-1pm & 3-7pm Mon-Sat, 10am-1pm & 2.30-7.30pm Sun).

RAVENNA

pop 153,400

Of the region's artistic jewels, none shine brighter than Ravenna's early Christian and Byzantine mosaics. Described as a symphony of colour by Dante in his *Divine Comedy,* they date to Ravenna's golden age as an early Christian centre.

ORIENTATION

From Piazza Farini, in front of the train station, it's a 600m walk along Viale Farini and its continuation, Via Diaz, into central Piazza del Popolo.

INFORMATION

Police station (☎ 0544 48 29 99; Piazza Mameli)

Tourist office (www.turismo.ravenna.it) Via delle Industrie (☎ 0544 45 15 39; Via delle Industrie 14; ⊗ 9.30am-12.30pm & 3-6pm); Via Salara (☎ 0544 3 57 55; Via Salara 8-12; ⊗ 8.30am-6pm Mon-Sat, 10am-4pm Sun Oct-Mar, 8.30am-7pm Mon-Sat, 10am-6pm Sun Apr-Sep)

SIGHTS

BASILICA DI SAN VITALE, MAUSOLEO DI GALLA PLACIDIA & MUSEO NAZIONALE

The basilica (☎ 0544 54 16 88; Via Fiandrini, entrance on Via San Vitale; ⊗ 9am-7pm Apr-Sep, to 5.30pm Mar & Oct, 9.30am-5pm Nov-Feb) was consecrated in 547 by Archbishop Massimiano. In contrast to the sombre exterior, its interior is awash with colour as the rich greens, golds and blues of the mosaics are bathed in soft yellow sunlight.

In the same complex, the small Mausoleo di Galla Placidia (☎ 0544 54 16 88; Via Fiandrini; ⊗ 9am-7pm Apr-Sep, to 5.30pm Mar & Oct, 9.30am-5pm Nov-Feb) was constructed for Galla Placidia, the half-sister of Emperor Honorius, who initiated construction of many of Ravenna's grandest buildings.

Next door to the basilica, the Museo Nazionale (☎ 0544 54 37 39; Via Fiandrini; admission €4; ⊗ 8.30am-7.30pm Tue-Sun) is housed in the cloisters of a former Benedictine monastery. There's a wealth of pottery, bronzes, icons and vestments, plus more Madonna and Child portraits than you can shake a halo at.

MUSEO ARCIVESCOVILE & BATTISTERO NEONIANO

Next to the unremarkable 18th-century cathedral (Via Gioacchino Rasponi; ⊗ 7am-noon & 2.30-5pm), the tiny Museo Arcivescovile (Archepiscopal Museum; ☎ 0544 54 16 88; Piazza Arcivescovado; ⊗ 9am-7pm Apr-Sep, 9.30am-5.30pm Mar & Oct, 10am-5pm Nov-Feb) was closed at the time of research, but expected to reopen in early 2010; it's well worth a visit for its fine collection of mosaics and an exquisite 6th-century ivory throne.

Next door, the domed roof of the **Battistero Neoniano** (☎ 0544 54 16 88; Piazza del Duomo; ⏰ 9am-7pm Apr-Sep, 9.30am-5.30pm Mar & Oct, 10am-5pm Nov-Feb) holds another impressive set of mosaics depicting the apostles and the baptism of Christ.

BASILICA DI SANT'APOLLINARE NUOVO

Originally built by the Goths in the 6th century, the **basilica** (☎ 0544 54 16 88; Via di Roma; ⏰ 9am-7pm Apr-Sep, 9.30am-5.30pm Mar & Oct, 10am-5pm Nov-Feb) claims some of Ravenna's most beautiful mosaics.

TOMBA DI DANTE

Dante spent the last 19 years of his life in Ravenna, writing much of the *Divine Comedy* here, after Florence expelled him in 1302. As a perpetual act of penance, Florence still supplies the oil for the lamp that burns continually in his **tomb** (Via D Alighieri 9; admission free; ⏰ 9.30am-6.30pm).

BASILICA DI SANT'APOLLINARE IN CLASSE

The brilliant star-spangled apse mosaic of the **Basilica di Sant'Apollinare in Classe** (☎ 0544 47 35 69; Via Romea Sud, Classe; admission €3, Sun morning free; ⏰ 8.30am-7.30pm) is a must-see. The basilica, 5km southeast of the city centre, was built in the 6th century on the burial site of Ravenna's patron saint, who converted the city to Christianity in the 2nd century. To get there take bus 4 or 44 to Classe.

OTHER MONUMENTS

Behind the **Basilica dello Spirito Santo**, just off Via Diaz, is the **Battistero degli Ariani** (☎ 0544 54 37 11; Via degli Ariani; admission free; ⏰ 8.30am-4.30pm Oct-Mar, 8.30am-7.30pm Apr-Sep), whose breath-taking dome mosaic depicts the baptism of Christ.

JOHN ELK III

Nave of the Basilica di San Vitale

FESTIVALS & EVENTS

Renowned Italian conductor Riccardo Muti has close ties with Ravenna and is intimately involved each year with the **Ravenna Festival** (www.ravennafestival.org), one of Italy's top classical music events.

SLEEPING

Hotel Centrale Byron (☎ 0544 21 22 25; www.hotelbyron.com; Via IV Novembre 14; s €50-65, d €70-110; ❄ 🖥 🛜) The prime location is what you pay for here, a mere 20 paces from central Piazza del Popolo.

Albergo Cappello (☎ 0544 21 98 13; www.albergocappello.it; Via IV Novembre 41; s €110-130, d €130-160; 🅿 ❄ 🖥) Murano glass chandeliers, original 15th-century frescoes and coffered ceilings are set against modern fixtures and flat-screen TVs. The ample

MAKING THE MOST OF YOUR EURO

There are three combined tickets on offer in Ravenna. The first (€8.50), valid for seven days, gives entry to the five main monuments: Basilica di San Vitale, Mausoleo di Galla Placidia, Museo Arcivescovile, Battistero Neoniano and Basilica di Sant'Apollinare Nuovo. There's no individual admission price for these monuments.

A different ticket (€6) lets you into the Museo Nazionale and Mausoleo di Teodorico. Pay an extra €2 and this also includes the Basilica di Sant'Apollinare in Classe, about 5km southeast of town. Each of these sites has its own admission price.

To see the mosaics in a different light, do the rounds at night. They're open and illuminated from 9pm to 11pm Tuesday through Friday from early July to early September.

breakfast features pastries from Ravenna's finest *pasticceria*. Parking costs €13.

EATING & DRINKING

Self-caterers and sandwich-fillers should load up at the city's **covered market** (Piazza Andrea Costa).

Ca' de Vèn (☎ 0544 3 01 63; Via Corrado Ricci 24; meals €25-35; ❦ Tue-Sun) Yes, it's touristy, but the atmosphere's wonderful at this cavernous *enoteca*-cum-restaurant in a 15th-century *palazzo* with frescoed domes, vaulted brick ceilings and chequerboard marble floors.

Ristorante Cappello (☎ 0544 21 98 76; Via IV Novembre 41; tasting menu €35, meals €35-40; ❦ closed Sun dinner & Mon) The menu changes weekly, but seafood always figures prominently, in dishes such as *strozzapreti con calamaretti, zucchine,* *fiori di zucca e zafferano* (pasta with cuttlefish, courgettes, pumpkin flowers and saffron).

Locanda del Melarancio (☎ 0544 21 52 58; Via Mentana 33) A charming 16th-century stone and brick building enlivened with bold red walls forms the backdrop for this smooth, looks-conscious bar.

GETTING THERE & AROUND

ATM (www.atm.ra.it, in Italian) local buses depart from Piazza Farini. Trains connect with Bologna (€5.80, 1¼ hours, hourly), Ferrara (€5.30, 1¼ hours, 14 daily), Rimini (€3.80, one hour, hourly) and the south coast.

The main (Via Salara) branch of the tourist office offers a free bike-hire service for visitors.

FLORENCE & CENTRAL ITALY

FLORENCE & CENTRAL ITALY

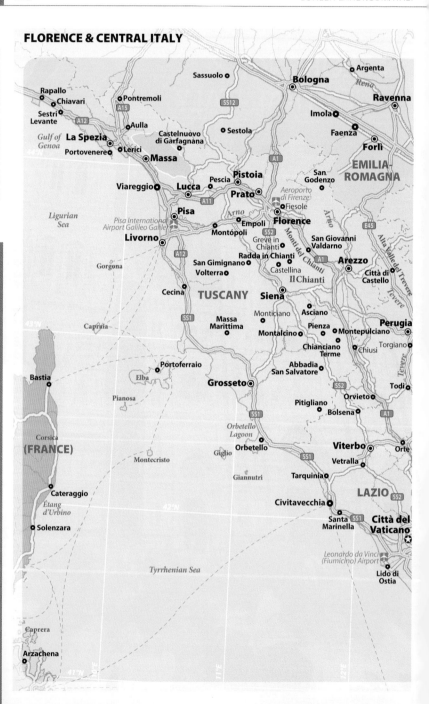

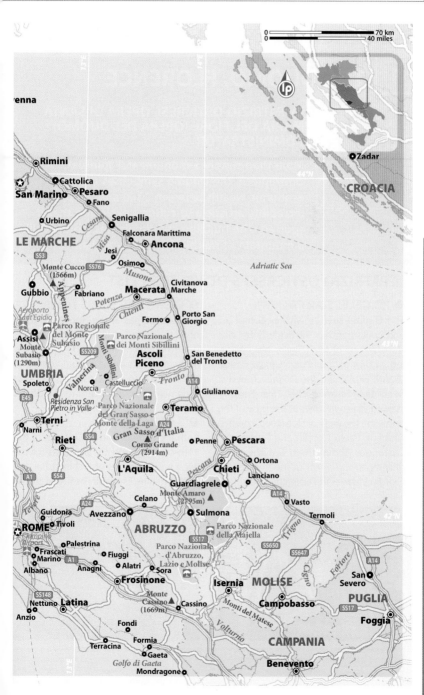

0 ——— 70 km
0 ——— 40 miles

Zadar

CROACIA

Adriatic Sea

Ravenna

Rimini
Cattolica
San Marino Pesaro
Fano
Urbino Senigallia
Falconara Marittima
LE MARCHE Ancona
SS3 Jesi
Cesano Misa
Monte Cucco SS76 Osimo
(1566m) Musone
Gubbio Fabriano Civitanova
Potenza Macerata Marche
Aeroporto Chienti
Sant'Egidio Parco Regionale Fermo Porto San
del Monte Giorgio
Assisi Subasio Parco Nazionale
Monte SS209 dei Monti Sibillini San Benedetto
Subasio Ascoli del Tronto
(1290m) Piceno
UMBRIA Castelluccio Fronto
Spoleto Norcia A14
Valnerina Giuliana
E45 Residenza San Apennines Parco Nazionale
Pietro in Valle del Gran Sasso e **Teramo**
Terni Monte della Laga A24
Narni Gran Sasso d'Italia
Rieti SS4 Corno Grande Penne Pescara
(2914m)
A1 SS4 Ortona
L'Aquila Chieti
Guardiagrele Lanciano
Guidonia Celano Monte Amaro
A24 (2795m) A14
ROME Tivoli Avezzano Sulmona Vasto
Ciampino Termoli
Airport **ABRUZZO** Parco Nazionale
Frascati Palestrina della Majella
Marino A1 Fiuggi SS17
Albano Anagni Alatri Parco Nazionale SS650 SS647
Sora d'Abruzzo, Trigno
Frosinone Lazio e Molise A14
SS148 **Isernia** **MOLISE** San
Nettuno Latina Monte Severo
Anzio Cassino Cassino Campobasso **PUGLIA**
(1669m) Monti del Matese SS17
Fondi Foggia
Terracina Formia Volturno
Gaeta **CAMPANIA**
Golfo di Gaeta
Mondragone Benevento

FLORENCE & CENTRAL ITALY

FLORENCE & CENTRAL ITALY HIGHLIGHTS

1 THE DUOMO, FLORENCE

BY PATRIZIO OSTICRESI, OPERA DI SANTA MARIA DEL FIORE (OPERA DEL DUOMO) ADMINISTRATOR

More than simply a monumental spiritual centrepiece, the Duomo symbolises the city's economic wealth between 1300 and 1500, and the incredible artistic and cultural explosion that it spurred. The building still dominates Florence, like a mountain of marble topped by a giant ruby.

↘ PATRIZIO OSTICRESI'S DON'T MISS LIST

❶ PRICELESS ARTWORK

The Duomo heaves with beautiful art and craftsmanship. Particularly famous is Domenico di Michelino's 1465 painting *La Divina Commedia illumina Firenze* (Dante Explaining the Divine Comedy). Recently restored, the 15th-century stained-glass windows at the base of the dome are the work of Donatello, Lorenzo Ghiberti, Paolo Uccello and Andrea del Castagno. Above them are the wonderful *Last Judgment* dome frescoes by Giorgio Vasari and Federico Zuccari.

❷ VIEWS FROM THE DOME

The panoramas are reason enough to head to the top of Brunelleschi's dome, but other incentives include a fine view of the interior's inlaid marble floors and the chance to get closer to the *Last Judgment* frescoes adorning the dome.

❸ BAPTISTRY

Both the exterior and the interior of the 11th-century baptistry are feasts for the eyes, and examples of architectural and artistic genius. Especially beautiful are the

Clockwise from top: The Duomo; Detail from the Baptistry's east door; Duomo interior; Dome behind the main facade and Campanile

13th-century ceiling mosaics, the inlaid marble pavement, the bronze doors and the Cossa funerary monument, created by Donatello and Michelozzo in 1428.

❹ MUSEO DELL'OPERA DEL DUOMO

Many precious works of art removed from the piazza's monuments are held at the **Museo dell'Opera del Duomo** (p224) in order to better preserve them. Highlights include Donatello's *Maddalena* statue, the original baptistry doors by Lorenzo Ghiberti, original panels from Giotto's campanile and Michelangelo's *Pietà*, which he sculpted for his own tomb but was intensely unsatisfied with.

❶ La Divina Commedia illumina Firenze
❷ Views from the Dome
❸ Baptistry
❹ Museo dell'Opera del Duomo

0 ———— 50 m
0 ———— 0.03 miles

Borgo San Lorenzo
Via de' Martelli
Via Ricasoli
Via dei Servi
Via Bufalini
Via de' Cerretani
Via de' Cerretani
SANTA CROCE
Via de' Vecchietti
Via de' Pecori
Via Roma
Piazza di San Giovanni
Via de' Calzaiuoli
Piazza del Duomo
Piazza del Adimari
Via della Canonica
Piazza delle Pallottole
Via dell'Oriuolo
Piazza de S Benedetto

↘ THINGS YOU NEED TO KNOW

Fewer crowds November to Christmas, early January to March **A magical moment** Walk around the Duomo's piazza very early in the morning **Best photo** From the back of the nave, taking in the glorious central nave and emphasising the Duomo's grandeur and spiritual aura **See our author's review on p221**

FLORENCE & CENTRAL ITALY HIGHLIGHTS

2 | SACRED ASSISI

BY FRA MIRKO, FRANCISCAN MONK

Assisi is where I live and where I had my conversion several years ago. What strikes me about the town's holy sites is their tangible links to the past, and their continued spiritual and artistic fascination. Through the life and experience of St Francis, God's 'perfume' lingers through Assisi's streets.

↘ FRA MIRKO'S DON'T MISS LIST

❶ BASILICA DI SAN FRANCESCO

Built soon after St Francis' death to house and venerate his body, the basilica (p254) is of major artistic importance. The upper church is most famous for its Giotto frescoes, while the lower church has works by Cimabue, Lorenzetti and Simone Martini. Personally, I think the lower church is the more atmospheric of the two. The crypt of St Francis is especially spiritual.

❷ SANTUARIO DI SAN DAMIANO

This convent (p255), just outside the old city walls, has beautiful views over the Valley of Spoleto. The site itself is wonderfully silent and visually arresting. Keep an eye out for the verdant, flower-filled Giardino del Cantico, where St Francis wrote his *Cantico di Frate Sole* in approximately 1225.

Clockwise from top: Detail inside the Basilica di San Francesco; Basilica di Santa Chiara; Assisi; Assisi stone house; Monk walking through Assisi

CLOCKWISE FROM TOP: MASSIMO BORCHI/4CORNERS; DIANA MAYFIELD; JAMES BRAUND; JOHN ELK III; JEFFREY BECOM

❸ EREMO DELLE CARCERI

This is a particularly fine example of a Franciscan hermitage. It's where St Francis himself would head for silent contemplation, and its location high above the town itself adds to the sense of isolation. It's particularly striking because it has changed very little since St Francis' time. See p255.

❹ BASILICA DI SANTA CHIARA

The final resting place of St Clare, this basilica (p255) is also home to the Byzantine crucifix that spoke to St Francis at the Santuario di San Damiano. The reliquary in the crypt holds some important objects, including garments and other belongings of the saint and her contemporary, St Francis.

❺ BASILICA DI SANTA MARIA DEGLI ANGELI

Unmissable, this great 16th-century basilica (p255) actually encases the tiny 10th-century Porziuncola chapel. It was on this site that St Francis lived with the original members of his order and it was at the site of the Cappella del Transito that he passed into eternal life on 3 October 1226.

↘ THINGS YOU NEED TO KNOW

Best time to visit Weekdays and outside the summer months and other holiday periods **Appropriate attire** Wear clothing that covers shoulders and knees **For more on Assisi, see p253**

FLORENCE & CENTRAL ITALY HIGHLIGHTS

3

⬦ ART-CRAM AT THE UFFIZI

The stuff art dreams are made of, Florence's **Uffizi** (p226) boasts the world's greatest collection of Renaissance art. Sheer numbers begin to tell the story: more than 1500 works distributed across 50 rooms. But it's the sustained quality of the collection that makes it truly extraordinary. From Botticelli's *Birth of Venus* to Da Vinci's *Annunciazione*, it's a case of hit after framed hit.

4

⬦ CRUISE THROUGH CHIANTI

With its gentle green hills, olive groves, stone farmhouses and prized grapes, **Chianti** (p240) is the stuff of books, movies and dreams. Long renowned for its namesake Chianti Classico, it's now the place where Brits and Americans come to buy decrepit farmhouses, fix them up and write books about their adventures. Can't stay that long? Hire a car or bike and explore for a dreamy day or two.

5

↘ TIME TRAVEL IN SIENA

Florence's historic rival Siena (p243) has no lack of devotees. An atmospheric jumble of narrow Gothic lanes and roseate stone buildings, it's also handy for forays into the Tuscan countryside. The Piazza del Campo, arguably Italy's finest square, is also the setting for Italy's wildest historic horserace, Il Palio (p243).

6

↘ FEEL SMALL IN SAN GIMIGNANO

Approaching San Gimignano (p247), the town's towers loom up like a medieval Manhattan. The legacy of one-upmanship between medieval grandees, the towers once numbered more than 70. The remaining 14 still manage to create a remarkable sense of drama in a hilltop town considered Tuscany's finest.

7

↘ BE ENTERTAINED IN PERUGIA

Don't be fooled by its perfect, stuck-in-time look: Perugia (p249) is one of Italy's most revved-up, happening towns. Boasting two universities and a kicking art scene, its calendar hums with brilliant cultural events, from regular live jams in fashionable *botteghe* (wine shop/bar) to an annual jazz fest that's one of the country's best.

3 & 6 JEAN-PIERRE LESCOURRET; 4 JOHN ELK III; 5 DAVID TOMLINSON; 7 JAMES BRAUND

3 Interior of the Uffizi (p226); 4 Chianti (p240); 5 Crowd gathering for Il Palio (p243), Siena; 6 San Gimignano (p247); 7 Waiter working the crowd, Perugia (p249)

FLORENCE & CENTRAL ITALY
FLORENCE & CENTRAL ITALY'S BEST...

FLORENCE & CENTRAL ITALY'S BEST...

⬐ FOODIE EXPERIENCES

- Tackling a no-nonsense *bistecca fiorentina* (Florentine steak) at L'Osteria di Giovanni (p231) in Florence.
- Sampling regional produce at Norcia's annual Mostra Mercato del Tartufo (boxed text, p260).
- Savouring Umbrian flavours at Orvieto's Ristorante I Sette Consoli (p262).
- Cooking classes and R&R at Alla Madonna del Piatto (p256) in beautiful Assisi.

⬐ WORLD HERITAGE TREASURES

- Florence (p220) A-list museums, architectural mavericks and a contagious, buzzing vibe.
- Siena (p243) Twisting Gothic streets and men in tights on horses.
- San Gimignano (p247) A medieval hill-town with serious tower-power.

- Basilica di San Francesco (p254) Exquisite frescoes and a profoundly spiritual aura.

⬐ UNFORGETTABLE MOMENTS

- Sunsets over Florence's Ponte Vecchio (p229).
- Evening vespers at Assisi's Santuario di San Damiano (p255).
- Cheering from the rails at Siena's Il Palio (boxed text, p243).
- Admiring/envying Michelangelo's studly David at Florence's Galleria dell'Accademia (p228).

⬐ PLACES TO PEDAL

- Past olive groves and vineyards in Chianti (p240).
- Atop mighty city walls in Lucca (p234).
- In spiritually uplifting countryside surrounding Assisi (p253).
- In the magical Monti Sibillini (boxed text, p260).

LEFT: HANNAH LEVY; RIGHT: JON DAVISON

Left: Michelangelo's David, Galleria dell'Accademia (p228), Florence; Right: Siena's Duomo (p244)

THINGS YOU NEED TO KNOW

⬐ VITAL STATISTICS

- **Population** 12.8 million
- **Area codes** ☎ Florence 055, Siena 0577, Perugia 075
- **Best time to visit** April, May, September and October

⬐ LOCALITIES IN A NUTSHELL

- **Florence** (p220) Astounding Renaissance treasures.
- **Northern & Western Tuscany** (p234) A leaning tower and fetching historic cities.
- **Central Tuscany** (p240) Famous wines, postcard-perfect landscapes and cultural gems galore.
- **Umbria** (p249) Medieval hill towns play host to worldly cultural festivals.

⬐ ADVANCE PLANNING

- **Three months before** Book accommodation and tickets to Spoleto's summer Festival dei Due Mondi (p259).
- **Two weeks before** Book online for Pisa's Leaning Tower (p237), as well as for Florence's Uffizi (p226) and Galleria dell'Accademia (p228). Make a reservation at Orvieto's Ristorante I Sette Consoli (p262).
- **One day before** Call to book your tour of Florence's Palazzo Vecchio (p226).

⬐ ONLINE RESOURCES

- **APT Firenze** (www.firenzeturismo.it) Official Florence tourism website.

- **Firenze Musei** (www.firenzemusei.it) Booking for Florentine museums.
- **Tuscany Tourist Board** (www.turismo.toscana.it)
- **Bella Umbria** (www.bellaumbria.net) Info-packed website on Umbria.
- **Trenitalia** (www.trenitalia.it) Train times and tickets.

⬐ EMERGENCY NUMBERS

- **Fire** ☎ 115
- **Carabinieri/Police** ☎ 112/113
- **Ambulance** ☎ 118

⬐ GETTING AROUND

- **Air** European routes service Pisa and, to a lesser extent, Florence and Perugia.
- **Walk** Perfect for exploring cities and towns.
- **Train** Good connections between major cities and towns.
- **Bus** Best for reaching Siena and San Gimignano.
- **Bicycle** Ideal for smaller towns and rural areas.
- **Car** Convenient for reaching villages, *agriturismi* and wineries.

⬐ BE FOREWARNED

- **Museums** Many close Monday.
- **Restaurants** Many close in August for the summer break.
- **Accommodation** Book months ahead, especially if travelling on holiday weekends, in summer or during local festivals.
- **Chianti** Vineyard visits often require reservations.

FLORENCE & CENTRAL ITALY ITINERARIES

TUSCAN VINEYARDS Three Days

Vintage vineyards, sprawling olive groves and seasonal flavours make this a must for time-pressed gourmands. Simply hire a car, muster an appetite and let Tuscany's fabled Chianti region work its magic.

From **(1) Florence** (p220), head south on the SS222 to **(2) Greve in Chianti** (p240), home to Le Cantine di Greve (p241) and its dizzying number of Chianti varieties. For lunch and larder essentials like honey and *vin santo,* drop in at nearby Castello di Verrazzano (p241) before wine tasting in a medieval abbey at the nearby Badia di Passignano (p241) and top-notch noshing at Osteria di Passignano (p241). Spend the next day cycling, walking or driving through the area's bucolic beauty before heading south to **(3) Castellina** (p242) in time for a fabulous (pre-booked) dinner at Locanda La Capannuccia (p242), your bolthole for the night. The following morning, continue east to **(4) Radda in Chianti** (p242), pairing a languid walk through picture-perfect countryside with noshing, swilling, and gourmet shopping at nearby Castello di Volpaia (p243).

UMBRIAN HILL TOWNS Five Days

Rolling hills, brooding mountains and twisting towns: Umbria gives Tuscany some serious competition. Slow down the pace and soak up the region's Gothic treasures and verdant backdrops.

Begin in cliff-clinging **(1) Orvieto** (p260), its miracle-inspired Romanesque and Gothic cathedral a shimmering technicolour marvel. Conclude the day with an Umbrian feast at Ristorante I Sette Consoli (p262) before catching a morning train to dynamic, erudite **(2) Perugia** (p249) – your home for the next two days.

Admire the efforts of homegrown artists Pinturicchio and Perugino at the Galleria Nazionale dell'Umbria (p251), eye-up ancient treasures at the Museo Archeologico Nazionale dell'Umbria (p251) and devour the region's best sweet treats at the three-centuries-old Sandri (p252). Top it all off with an evening *passeggiata* (stroll) along buzzing Corso Vannucci.

On day four, join the faithful in **(3) Assisi** (p253), a quick train ride from Perugia. Meditate on Giotto's frescoes in the Basilica di San Francesco (p254) and walk in St Francis' footsteps at the Santuario di San Damiano (p255) before heading back to Perugia for the night. The following morning, catch a bus to **(4) Gubbio** (p256), the 'City of Silence', making time to practise your ancient Umbrian at the Museo Civico (p256).

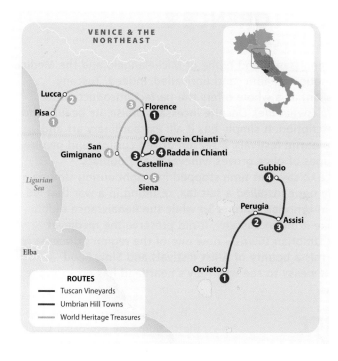

FLORENCE & CENTRAL ITALY

FLORENCE & CENTRAL ITALY ITINERARIES

WORLD HERITAGE TREASURES 10 Days

The kind of itinerary to make your friends green with envy, this trip takes in some of Italy's top World Heritage wonders, from elegant fortified towns to a Renaissance darling called Florence.

Kick-start your journey in (1) Pisa (p236), where the Leaning Tower is only one of three Romanesque marvels on Piazza dei Miracoli (p236). The following day, catch a train to (2) Lucca (p234), hometown of operameister Giacomo Puccini. Spend two days exploring the city's wealth of beautiful buildings and churches, among them the Cattedrale di San Martino (p235), and don't miss a saunter along the Passeggiata della Mura (p235).

Spoil yourself with four days in inimitable (3) Florence (p220), reserving tickets to the Uffizi (p226) in advance and admiring David at the Galleria dell'Accademia (p228).

On day eight, bus it to medieval (4) San Gimignano (p247), famed for its egotistical towers, before pushing on to (5) Siena (p243), whose cultural assets include the Duomo (p244), with vividly coloured frescoes by Bernardino Pinturicchio.

DISCOVER FLORENCE & CENTRAL ITALY

Cradle of the Renaissance and home of Michelangelo and the Medici, Firenze is magnetic, romantic, and unrivalled. Indeed, Tuscany (Toscana in Italian) as a whole offers the perfect introduction to Italy's *dolce vita* (sweet life). Despite incessant praise, its beauty and charm defy description. It simply has it all: extraordinary art and architecture; colourful festivals; a season-driven cuisine; and picture-perfect landscapes of olive groves, vineyards and poplars.

Historians like to say that time stopped in neighbouring Umbria in 1540, when the pope installed a salt tax, resulting in a war that led to a standstill in Umbrian culture. So while the Renaissance didn't flourish here like it did in Tuscany, it did preserve the medieval hearts of most Umbrian towns – now one of the region's greatest assets. Add to this a bounty of A-list festivals and Slow Food hotspots, and it's easy to see why Italy's heartland has no shortage of gushing fans.

FLORENCE

pop 364,710

There's more to this intensely absorbing place than priceless masterpieces. Towers and palaces evoke a thousand tales of its medieval past; designer boutiques and artisan workshops stud its streets; there's a buzzing cafe and bar scene; and – when the summer heat simply gets too stifling – vine-laden hills and terrace restaurants are only a short drive away.

HISTORY

Archaeological evidence suggests the presence of an earlier village founded by the Etruscans of Fiesole around 200 BC.

In the 12th century Florence became a free *comune* (town council), ruled by 12 *priori* (consuls) assisted by the Consiglio di Cento (Council of One Hundred), drawn mainly from the merchant class. Agitation among differing factions led to the appointment of a foreign governing magistrate (*podestà*) in 1207.

The first conflicts between two of the factions, the pro-papal Guelphs (Guelfi) and the pro-imperial Ghibellines (Ghibellini), started in the mid-13th century, with power passing between the two groups for almost a century. In the 14th century Florence was ruled by a caucus of Guelphs under the leadership of the Albizi family.

Cosimo il Vecchio (the Elder, also known simply as Cosimo de' Medici) emerged as head of the opposition to the Albizi in the 15th century and became Florence's ruler. His eye for talent saw a constellation of artists such as Alberti, Brunelleschi, Lorenzo Ghiberti, Donatello, Fra' Angelico and Fra' Filippo Lippi flourish.

The rule of Lorenzo il Magnifico (1469–92), Cosimo's grandson, ushered in the most glorious period of Florentine civilisation and of the Italian Renaissance. His court fostered a flowering of art, music and poetry, turning Florence into Italy's cultural capital.

ORIENTATION

Budget hotels are concentrated east of the central train station, Stazione di Santa Maria Novella, around Via Nazionale and south around Piazza di Santa Maria Novella. The main route to the centre is Via de' Panzani and Via de' Cerretani. Spot the Duomo and you're there.

From Piazza di San Giovanni around the baptistry, Via Roma leads to Piazza della Repubblica and beyond to Ponte Vecchio. From Piazza del Duomo follow Via de' Calzaiuoli for Piazza della Signoria.

INFORMATION

EMERGENCY

Police station (Questura; ☎ 055 4 97 71; Via Zara 2; ◷ 24hr)
Tourist Police (Polizia Assistenza Turistica; ☎ 055 20 39 11; Via Pietrapiana 50r, Piazza dei Ciompi; ◷ 8.30am-6.30pm Mon-Fri, to 1pm Sat)

POST

Central Post Office (Via Pellicceria)

TOURIST INFORMATION

APT Florence (www.firenzeturismo.it); Piazza Beccaria (☎ 055 233 20; Via Manzoni 16; ◷ 9am-1pm Mon-Fri); San Lorenzo (☎ 055 29 08 32; Via Cavour 1r; ◷ 8.30am-6.30pm Mon-Sat, 8.30am-1.30pm Sun); A Vespucci Airport (☎ 055 31 58 74; ◷ 8.30am-8.30pm).
Comune di Firenze Tourist Office (☎ 055 234 04 44; www.comune.fi.it, in Italian; Borgo Santa Croce 29r; ◷ 9am-7pm Mon-Sat, to 2pm Sun)
SOS Turista phoneline (☎ 055 276 03 82) Office for tourists in trouble (disputes over hotel bills etc).

SIGHTS

Florence swarms with sights, most of which are within convenient walking distance of each other.

PIAZZA DEL DUOMO

Not only is Florence's **Duomo** (☎ 055 21 53 80; www.duomofirenze.it; ◷ 10am-5pm Mon-Wed & Fri, to 3.30pm Thu, to 4.45pm Sat, to 3.30pm 1st Sat of month, 1.30-4.45pm Sun, mass in English 5pm Sat) the city's most iconic landmark, it's also one of Italy's 'Big Three' (with Pisa's Leaning Tower and Rome's Colosseum).

Begun in 1296 by Sienese architect Arnolfo di Cambio, the cathedral took almost 150 years to complete.

Scaling the 463 steep stone steps up to the cathedral **dome** (adult/child under 6yr €8/free; ◷ 8.30am-7pm Mon-Fri, to 5.40pm Sat) – an incredible feat of engineering – is a must. Allow at least half an hour up here.

Equally physical is the 414-step climb up the neighbouring 82m-high **campanile** (adult/child under 6yr €6.50/free; ◷ 8.30am-6.50pm), designed by Giotto in 1334.

MARTIN HUGHES

Basilica di Santa Maria Novella (p227)

CENTRAL FLORENCE

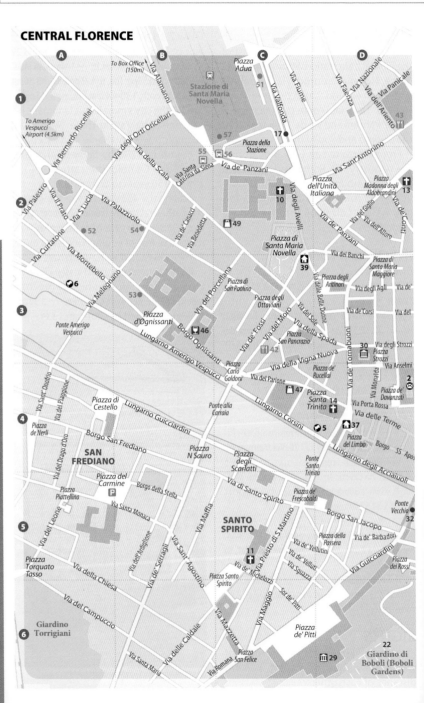

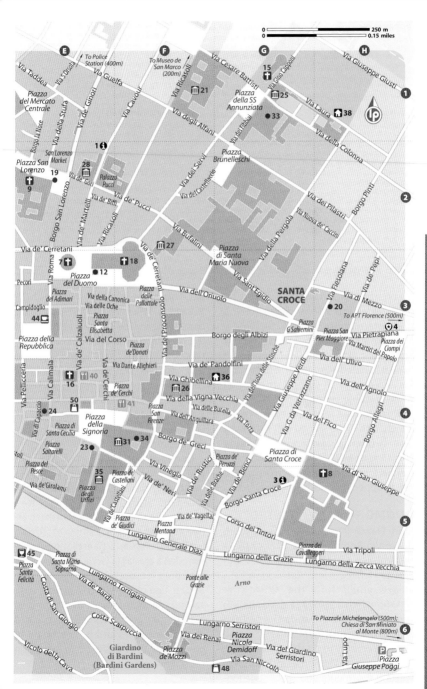

INFORMATION		
APT Florence	**1**	E2
Central Post Office	**2**	D4
Comune di Fizenze Tourist Office	**3**	G5
Tourist Police	**4**	H3
UK Consulate	**5**	D4
US Consulate	**6**	A3

SIGHTS & ACTIVITIES		
Baptistry	**7**	E3
Bascilica di Santa Croce	**8**	H5
Basilica di San Lorenzo	**9**	E2
Basilica di Santa Maria Novella	**10**	C2
Basilica di Santo Spirito	**11**	C5
Campanile	**12**	E3
Cappelle Medicee	**13**	D2
Chiesa della Santa Trinita	**14**	D4
Chiesa della SS Annunziata	**15**	G1
Chiesa di Orsanmichele	**16**	E4
City Sightseeing Firenze	**17**	C1
Duomo	**18**	F3
Entrance to Basilica di San Lorenzo	**19**	E2
Florence by Bike	**20**	H3
Galleria dell'Accademia	**21**	F1

Giardino di Boboli (Boboli Gardens)	**22**	D6
Loggia dei Lanzi	**23**	E4
Mercato Nuovo	**24**	E4
Museo Archeologico	**25**	G1
Museo del Bargello	**26**	F4
Museo dell'Opera del Duomo	**27**	F2
Palazzo del Bargello	(see 26)	
Palazzo Medici-Riccardi	**28**	E2
Palazzo Pitti	**29**	D6
Palazzo Strozzi	**30**	D3
Palazzo Vecchio	**31**	F4
Ponte Vecchio	**32**	D5
Spedale degli Innocenti	**33**	G1
Torre d'Arnolfo	**34**	F4
Uffizi Gallery	**35**	E5

SLEEPING		
Borghese Palace Art Hotel	**36**	G4
Hotel Cestelli	**37**	D4
Hotel Morandi alla Crocetta	**38**	H1
Hotel Santa Maria Novella	**39**	C3

EATING		
I Due Fratellini	**40**	E4
La Canova di Gustavino	**41**	F4

L'Osteria di Giovanni	**42**	C3
Mercato Centrale	(see 43)	
Nerbone	**43**	D1

DRINKING		
Caffè Gilli	**44**	E3
Le Volpe e L'uva	**45**	E5
Sei Divino	**46**	B3

SHOPPING		
Alberto Cozzi	**47**	C4
Alessandro Dari	**48**	G6
Officina Profumo-Farmaceutica di Santa Maria Novella	**49**	C2
Pineider	**50**	E4

TRANSPORT		
ATAF Tickets & Information Office	**51**	C1
Avis	**52**	A2
Europcar	**53**	B3
Hertz	**54**	B2
SITA Bus Station	**55**	B2
Terravision Bus Stop	**56**	C2
Train Information Counter	**57**	C1

Lorenzo Ghiberti designed the famous gilded bronze bas-reliefs adorning the eastern doors of the 11th-century Romanesque **baptistry** (battistero; Piazza di San Giovanni; admission €4; 🕐 12.15pm-6.30pm Mon-Sat, 8.30am-1.30pm 1st Sat of the month & Sun), an octagonal striped structure of white and green marble.

What you see today are copies of the panels; turn to the **Museo dell'Opera del Duomo** (www.operaduomo.firenze.it; Piazza del Duomo 9; admission €6; 🕐 9am-6.50pm Mon-Sat, to 1pm Sun) for the originals, which occupy the glass-topped ground-floor courtyard.

DUOMO TO PALAZZO STROZZI

From Piazza di San Giovanni walk south down Via Roma to reach **Piazza della Repubblica**. Continue one block south and turn left (east) into Via Orsanmichele, where you'll find the **Chiesa di Orsanmichele** (☎ 055 2 38 85; Via Arte della Lana; admission free; 🕐 10am-5pm Tue-Sun), the arcades of a grain market walled in during the 14th century to create a church.

Backtrack to Via Roma and continue walking south until you see a huge loggia. This is the **Mercato Nuovo** (New Market), a 16th-century market building commissioned by Cosimo I and called the New Market to differentiate it from the *Mercato Vecchio* (Old Market) that had occupied the site since the 11th-century. Florentines know the market as 'Il Porcellino' (The Piglet) after the bronze statue of a wild boar on its southern side. Local legend has it that rubbing its snout will ensure your return to Florence.

Continue along Via Porta Rossa until you reach **Via de' Tornabuoni**, the city's most legendary fashion street – often called the 'Salotto di Firenze' (Florence's Drawing Room). Turn right (north) to arrive at the magnificent **Palazzo Strozzi** (cnr Via de' Tornabuoni & Via degli Strozzi; admission prices & opening hr vary according to exhibition). Built for wealthy merchant Filippo Strozzi, one of the Medicis' major political and commercial rivals, this impressive 15th-century palace has been reimagined over recent years and is now home to one of the city's most exciting exhibition programs.

PIAZZA DELLA SIGNORIA

It was here that preacher-leader Savonarola set light to the city's art – books, paintings, musical instruments, mirrors, fine clothes and so on – on his famous bonfire of vanities in 1497. A year later the Dominican monk was burnt as a heretic on the same spot, marked by a bronze plaque in front of Ammannati's monumental but ugly Fontana di Nettuno (Neptune Fountain).

Far more impressive are the equestrian statue of Cosimo I by Giambologna in the centre of the piazza, the much-photographed copy of Michelangelo's David that has guarded the western entrance to the Palazzo Vecchio since 1910 (the original stood here until 1873 but is now in the Galleria dell'Accademia) and two copies of important Donatello works – Marzocco, the heraldic Florentine lion (for the original see the Museo del Bargello; p227) and Giuditta e Oloferne (Judith and Holofernes, c 1455; original inside Palazzo Vecchio). Facing this line-up is the 14th-century Loggia dei Lanzi, where works such as Giambologna's *Rape of the Sabine*

Women (c 1583), Benvenuto Cellini's bronze *Perseus* (1554) and Agnolo Gaddi's *Seven Virtues* (1384–89) are displayed.

CUT THE QUEUE

The only museums where pre-booking is necessary are the Uffizi and the Accademia – for these, pre-booking is a *really* good idea. To organise your ticket, telephone Firenze Musei (Florence Museums; ☎ 055 29 48 83, 055 265 43 21; ✆ booking line open 8.30am-6.30pm Mon-Fri, to 12.30pm Sat) or use the online booking facility at www.firenzemusei.it.

In Florence, tickets can easily be prebooked a day or two ahead of time at Firenze Musei information desks (✆ 8.30am-7pm Tue-Sun) in the Galleria Uffizi (p226), Palazzo Pitti (p229) or the ticket window at the rear of the Chiesa di Orsanmichele (p224) – if you're in town for a few days, this is the savvy thing to do.

Piazza della Signoria

JEAN-PIERRE LESCOURRET

FLORENCE & CENTRAL ITALY

FLORENCE

MARTIN HUGHES

Crowd gathering at the Uffizi

⬎ THE UFFIZI

The Palazzo degli Uffizi, designed and built by Vasari in the second half of the 16th century at the request of Cosimo I, originally housed the city's administrators, judiciary and guilds (*uffizi* means offices).

Cosimo's successor, Francesco I, commissioned the architect Buontalenti to modify the upper floor of the *palazzo* to house the Medici's growing art collection.

Housed inside the vast U-shaped *palazzo*, the Galleria degli Uffizi (Uffizi Gallery) is home to the Medici family's private collection, bequeathed to Florence in 1743 by the last of the family, Anna Maria Ludovica, on condition that it never leave the city.

The collection spans the gamut of art history from ancient Greek sculpture to 18th-century Venetian paintings and is arranged in chronological order by school. Its core is the masterpiece-rich Renaissance collection.

Allow at least four hours for your visit – many spend the entire day. The gallery's pleasant rooftop cafe is only accessible from inside the building and offers light snacks (pizza/*panino* €4.50/6.50, beer €6, cappuccino standing up/sitting down €1.60/4.50) and fabulous views.

Things you need to know: ☎ 055 238 86 51; Piazza degli Uffizi 6; adult/under 18yr with EU passport/18-25yr with EU passport €6.50/free/3.25, 85-min audioguide for 1/2 people €5.50/8; ☾ 8.15am-6.35pm Tue-Sun, to 9pm Tue Jul-Sep

As much a symbol of the city as the Duomo is the striking 94m-tall Torre d'Arnolfo that crowns the Palazzo Vecchio (☎ 055 276 82 24; www.palazzovecchio-museoragazzi.it; Piazza della Signoria; adult/child 3-17yr/18-25yr & over 65yr €6/2/4.50, family of 4/5 €14/16, visit & guided tour €8/3/6.50, each additional tour €1; ☾ 9am-7pm Fri-Wed, to 2pm Thu), the traditional seat of Florentine government.

The best way to tour this building is by guided tour (🕙 9.30am, 12.30pm, 3.30pm & 6.30pm Mon-Wed & Fri, 9.30pm & 12.30pm Thu, 10am, 1.30pm, 3pm & 6.30pm Sat & Sun).

PALAZZO DEL BARGELLO
It was behind the stark exterior of the Palazzo del Bargello, Florence's earliest public building, that the *podestà* meted out justice from the late 13th century until 1502. Today the building, which is northeast of the Uffizi, is home to the **Museo del Bargello** (☎ 055 238 86 06; Via del Proconsolo 4; adult/concession €7; 🕙 8.15am-5pm Tue-Sun & 1st & 3rd Mon of the month), Italy's most comprehensive collection of Tuscan Renaissance sculpture.

SANTA MARIA NOVELLA AREA
From the Uffizi, walk west along the Lungarno, passing the Ponte Vecchio (p229), until you reach the **Ponte Santa Trìnita**.

Turning right (north) into Via de' Tornabuoni, you arrive at 14th-century **Chiesa della Santa Trìnita** (Piazza Santa Trìnita), rebuilt in Gothic style and later graced with a mannerist facade.

Further north again is the **Basilica di Santa Maria Novella** (☎ 055 21 59 18; Piazza di Santa Maria Novella; admission €2.50; 🕙 9am-5pm Mon-Thu, 1-5pm Fri), begun in the late 13th century as the Dominican order's Florentine base. The highlight of the Gothic interior, halfway along the north aisle, is Masaccio's superb fresco *Trinity* (1424–25), one of the first artworks to use the then newly discovered techniques of perspective and proportion.

SAN LORENZO AREA
In 1425 the Medici commissioned Brunelleschi to rebuild what would become the family's parish church and funeral chapter: 50-odd Medici are buried inside **Basilica di San Lorenzo** (Piazza San Lorenzo; admission €3.50, joint ticket covering basilica & biblioteca €6; 🕙 10am-5pm Mon-Sat, 1.30-5pm Sun), one of the most harmonious examples of Renaissance architecture.

Nowhere is Medici conceit expressed so explicitly as in their mausoleum, the **Cappelle Medicee** (Medicean Chapels; ☎ 055 238 86 02; Piazza Madonna degli Aldobrandini; adult/concession €6/3; 🕙 8.15am-4.50pm Tue-Sat & 1st & 3rd Sun & 2nd & 4th Mon of month). Principal burial place of the Medici rulers, it's sumptuously adorned with granite, the most precious marble, semiprecious stones and some of Michelangelo's most beautiful sculptures.

Just off Piazza San Lorenzo is the **Palazzo Medici-Riccardi** (☎ 055 276 03 40; www.palazzo-medici.it; Via Cavour 3; adult/concession €7/4; 🕙 9am-7pm Thu-Tue), principal Medici residence until 1540 and the prototype for other *palazzi* in the city. Inside, the **Capella di Benozzo** (Chapel of the Magi) houses one of the supreme achievements of Renaissance painting and is an absolute must-see for art lovers. The tiny space is covered in a series of wonderfully detailed and recently restored frescoes (c 1459–63) by Benozzo Gozzoli, a pupil of Fra' Angelico. Only 10 visitors are allowed into the chapel at a time for a maximum of just five minutes; reserve your slot in advance at the palace ticket desk.

SAN MARCO AREA
Chiesa della SS Annunziata (Piazza della SS Annunziata; 🕙 7.30am-12.30pm & 4-6.30pm), established in 1250 and rebuilt by Michelozzo and others in the mid-15th century, is dedicated to the Virgin Mary. It houses frescoes by Andrea del Castagno, Perugino, Andrea del Sarto and Jacopo Pontormo.

On the piazza's southeastern side, the **Spedale degli Innocenti** (Hospital of the Innocents; Piazza della SS Annunziata 12) was founded in 1421 as Europe's first orphanage (hence the 'innocents' in its name). Inside, the **Museo dello Spedale degli Innocenti** (☎ 055 203 73 08; www. istitutodeglinnocenti.it; adult/concession €4/2.50; ☾ 8.30am-7pm Mon-Sat, to 2pm Sun) on the 2nd floor is home to works by Florentine artists, including Marco della Robbia, Sandro Botticelli and Domenico Ghirlandaio.

About 200m southeast of the piazza is the **Museo Archeologico** (☎ 055 23 57 50; Via della Colonna 38; adult/concession €4/2; ☾ 2-7pm Mon, 8.30am-7pm Tue & Thu, 8.30am-2pm Wed & Fri-Sun). Its rich collection of finds, including most of the Medici hoard of antiquities, plunges you deep into the past and offers an alternative to all that Renaissance splendour.

Ponte Vecchio
JOHN ELK III

Sweets at Caffè Gilli (p232)
JULIET COOMBE

The **Galleria dell'Accademia** (☎ 055 29 48 83; Via Ricasoli 60; adult/concession €6.50/3.25; ☾ 8.15am-6.50pm Tue-Sun) displays paintings by Florentine artists spanning the 13th to 16th centuries. But its main draw is Michelangelo's **David**, carved from a single block of marble when the artist was only 29.

SANTA CROCE AREA

When Lucy Honeychurch, the heroine of E M Forster's *A Room With a View*, is stranded in the Santa Croce without a Baedeker, she first panics and then, looking around, wonders why the basilica is thought to be such an important building. After all, doesn't it look just like a barn?

On entering, many visitors to the massive Franciscan **Basilica di Santa Croce** (☎ 055 246 61 05; adult/concession incl Museo dell'Opera €5/3; ☾ 9.30am-5.30pm Mon-Sat, 1-5.30pm Sun) share the same reaction. The church was designed by Arnolfo di Cambio between 1294 and 1385 and owes its name to a splinter of the Holy Cross donated by King Louis of France in 1258.

Though most visitors come to see the tombs of famous Florentines buried inside this church – including Michelangelo, Galileo, Ghiberti and Machiavelli – it's the frescoes by Giotto and his school in the chapels to the right of the altar that are the real highlight.

The **Museo dell'Opera di Santa Croce** (admission incl basilica adult/concession €5/3; ☾ 9.30am-5.30pm Mon-Sat, 1-5.30pm Sun) is located off the first cloister.

THE OLTRARNO

Literally 'Beyond the Arno', the atmospheric Oltrarno takes in all of Florence south of the river.

MARTIN HUGHES

Fresco inside Museo di San Marco

⬎ IF YOU LIKE...

If you like the artwork inside the **Palazzo Medici-Riccardo** (p227), we think you'll like these other Florence art spots:

- **Basilica di Santo Spirito** (Piazza Santo Spirito; ☽ 9.30am-12.30pm & 4-5.30pm Thu-Tue) Designed by Brunelleschi, and home to Filippino Lipi's *Madonna and Saints* (1493-94) in the Cappella Nerli and a poignant wooden crucifix attributed by some critics to Michelangelo in the sacristy.
- **Chiesa di San Miniato al Monte** (Via Monte alle Croce; admission free; ☽ 8am-7pm May-Oct, 8am-noon & 3-6pm Nov-Apr) Head in for 13th- to 15th-century frescoes, intricate inlaid marble designs, a Romanesque crypt and a sacristy (donation €1) featuring frescoes by Spinello Arentino.
- **Museo di San Marco** (☎ 055 238 86 08; Piazza San Marco 1; adult/concession €4/2; ☽ 8.15am-1.50pm Tue-Fri, 8.15am-4.50pm Sat, 8.15am-4.50pm 2nd & 4th Sun & 1st, 3rd & 5th Mon of month) A showcase of Fra' Angelico's work and one of Florence's most spiritually uplifting museums.

PONTE VECCHIO

This famous bridge has twinkled with the glittering wares of jewellers ever since the 16th century, when Ferdinando I de' Medici ordered them here to replace the often malodorous presence of the town butchers, who were wont to toss unwanted leftovers into the river.

The bridge as it stands was built in 1345 and was the only one in Florence saved from destruction by the retreating Germans in 1944.

PALAZZO PITTI

Begun in 1458 for the Pitti family, rivals of the Medici, the original nucleus of this **palace** (☎ 055 94 48 83; Piazza de' Pitti 1) took up the space encompassing the seven sets of windows on the 2nd and 3rd storeys.

Raphaels and Rubens vie for centre stage in the enviable collection of 16th- to 18th-century art amassed by the Medici and Lorraine dukes in the 1st-floor **Galleria Palatina** (☽ 8.15am-6.50pm

PALAZZO PITTI TICKETING

There are two tickets on sale at the office to the far right of the main entrance. The first (adult/concession €6/3) gives you entrance to the Costume Gallery, Boboli Gardens, Silver Museum, Porcelain Museum and Bardini Gardens. The second (€8.50/4.25) covers the Royal Apartments, Palatine Gallery and Gallery of Modern Art. Note that tickets are more expensive if temporary exhibitions are being staged. If there are no temporary exhibitions, you may purchase a combined ticket (€11.50, valid three days), which gives access to all sights. To do everything here justice, you'll need a full day.

Tue-Sun), reached by a staircase from the palace's central courtyard.

Past the Sala di Venere is the **Appartamenti Reali** (Royal Apartments; 8.15am-6.50pm Tue-Sun Feb-Dec), a series of rooms presented as they were c 1880–91, when they were occupied by members of the House of Savoy.

The palace's expansive **Giardino di Boboli** (Boboli Gardens; 8.15am-7.30pm Jun-Aug, to 6.30pm Mar-May & Sep, to 5.30pm Oct, to 4.30pm Nov-Feb, closed 1st & last Mon of the month) were laid out in the mid-16th century according to a design by architect Niccolò Pericoli, aka Il Tribolo.

PIAZZALE MICHELANGELO

Turn your back on the bevy of ticky-tacky souvenir stalls and take in the soaring city panorama from Piazzale Michelangelo, pierced by one of Florence's two *David* copies. The square is a 10-minute uphill walk along the winding route that scales

the hillside from the river and Piazza Giuseppe Poggi.

Bus 13 links Stazione di Santa Maria Novella with Piazzale Michelangelo.

TOURS

City Sightseeing Firenze (055 29 04 51; www.firenze.city-sightseeing.it; Piazza Stazione 1; tickets incl audioguide adult/child 5-15yr/family €22/11/66) Tickets are valid for 24 hours.

Freya's Florence (349 074 8907; freyasflorence@yahoo.com) Highly recommended tours by an Australian-born, Florence-based private tour guide introducing the art, history and magic of Florence.

FESTIVALS & EVENTS

Maggio Musicale Fiorentino (www.maggiofiorentino.com, in Italian) This month-long arts festival held in Florence's Teatro del Maggio Musicale Fiorentino is the oldest in Italy; it stages world-class performances of theatre, classical music, jazz and dance between late April and June.

Festa di San Giovanni (Feast of St John) Florence celebrates its patron saint with a *calcio storico* match on Piazza di Santa Croce and fireworks over Piazzale Michelangelo; 24 June.

Jazz & Co (www.santissima.it, in Italian) On summer nights, Piazza Santissima Annunziata is filled with tables of people enjoying an *aperitivo* or dinner catered by Slow Food International while listening to live jazz musicians from Italy and overseas perform; late June to September.

SLEEPING

Hotel Cestelli (055 21 42 13; www.hotelcestelli.com; Borgo SS Apostoli 25; s €40-60, d €50-80, d with bathroom €70-100; closed 2 weeks Jan, 3 weeks Aug) The scent of joss sticks and flicker of night lights add a soothing Zen air to this eight-room hotel on the first floor of a 12th-century *palazzo*.

Hotel Morandi alla Crocetta (☎ 055 234 47 47; www.hotelmorandi.it; Via Laura 50; s €70-90, d €90-170; P ✗ ⊗) This medieval convent-turned-hotel away from the madding crowds is a stunner. A couple of rooms have handkerchief-sized gardens to laze in, but the pièce de résistance is frescoed room 29 – the former chapel.

Borghese Palace Art Hotel (☎ 055 28 43 63; www.borghesepalace.it; Via Ghibellina 174r; s €120, d €140-190, ste €230-240; P ✗ ⊗) A key address for art lovers, this stylish ode to design with a glass-topped courtyard and sculptures looming large in the reception showcases original works of art from the 18th century to present day.

ourpick Hotel Santa Maria Novella (☎ 055 27 18 40; www.hotelsantamarianovella. it; Piazza di Santa Maria Novella 1; d €135-200, ste €180-235; P ✗ ▯ ⊗) The bland exterior of this excellent four-star choice gives no hint of the spacious and elegant rooms within.

EATING

Nerbone (☎ 055 21 99 49; Mercato Centrale, Piazza del Mercato Centrale; primi/secondi €4/7; ⊗ 7am-2pm Mon-Sat) This unpretentious market stall has been serving its rustic dishes to queues of shoppers and stall-holders since 1872.

I Due Fratellini (☎ 055 239 60 96; www. iduefratellini.com; Via dei Cimatori 38r; panini €2.50; ⊗ 9am-8pm Mon-Sat, closed Fri & Sat 2nd half Jun & all Aug) A legend since 1875, this hole in the wall whips out *panini* (sun-dried tomato with goat cheese, wild boar salami, truf-fled *pecorino* (sheep's milk cheese) and rocket etc), freshly filled as you order.

La Canova di Gustavino (☎ 055 239 98 06; Via della Condotta 29r; meals €24; ⊗ noon-midnight) The emphasis here is on Tuscan classics – *ribollita, trippa alla fiorentina, baccalà alla livornese* (salted cod in a to-mato sauce) – but it's perfectly fine if you choose to limit yourself to a simple cheese and meat platter or a bruschetta.

ourpick L'Osteria di Giovanni (☎ 055 28 48 97; Via del Moro 22; meals €49; ⊗ lunch & dinner Wed-Mon) Our number-one choice

GIORGIO COSULICH

I Due Fratellini

FLORENCE & CENTRAL ITALY

FLORENCE

for Florentine dining is – insert drum roll – this wonderfully friendly neighbourhood eatery, where everything is delicious and where the final reckoning will be within most budgets.

SELF-CATERING

Mercato Centrale (Piazza del Mercato Centrale; 🕑 7am-2pm Mon-Fri, to 5pm Sat) Central food market inside an iron-and-glass structure dating to 1874.

DRINKING

Caffè Gilli (☎ 055 21 38 96; Piazza della Repubblica 3r; 🕑 8am-1am Wed-Mon) Utterly delectable cakes, excellent coffee and a beautifully preserved Art Nouveau interior make this the best of Piazza della Repubblica's cafes.

our pick **Le Volpe e L'uva** (☎ 055 239 81 32; Piazza dei Rossi 1; 🕑 11am-9pm Mon-Sat) Florence's best *enoteca* – bar none.

Sei Divino (☎ 055 21 77 91; Borgo Ognissanti 42r; 🕑 8am-2am; 🛜) This bar is known for its great wine, mood music, DJs, video projections, wi-fi, no-fuss lunch deal and *aperitivo* spread.

ENTERTAINMENT

Newsstands sell *Firenze Spettacolo* (€1.80; www.firenzespettacolo.it, in Italian), the city's definitive entertainment publication, which is published monthly.

Tickets for cultural events are sold through **Box Office** (www.boxol.it, in Italian; Via Luigi Alamanni 39; 🕑 10am-7.30pm Tue-Fri, 3.30-7.30pm Mon) and **Ticket One** (www.ticketone.it, in Italian).

SHOPPING

Via de' Gondi and Borgo de' Greci, east of Piazza della Signoria, seethe with leather shops selling jackets, trousers, shoes and bags, as do the street markets.

For paper products, go to **Pineider** (☎ 055 28 46 55; www.pineirder.com; Piazza della Signoria 13-14r) or **Alberto Cozzi** (☎ 055 29 49 68; Via del Parione 35r; 🕑 Mon-Fri).

For jewellery, head to **Alessandro Dari** (☎ 055 24 47 47; www.alessandrodari.com; Via San Niccolò 115r) and for natural pharmaceuticals and perfumes go to **Officina Profumo-Farmaceutica di Santa Maria Novella** (☎ 055 21 62 76; Via della Scala 16; 🕑 9.30am-7.30pm Mon-Sat, 10.30am-8.30pm Sun).

JULIET COOMBE

Goods for sale at Pineider

GETTING THERE & AWAY

AIR

Amerigo Vespucci Airport (FLR; ☎ 055 306 13 00; www.aeroporto.firenze.it), 5km northwest of the city centre, caters for domestic and a handful of European flights. The much larger **Pisa International Airport Galileo Galilei** (☎ 050 84 93 00; www.pisa-airport.com) is one of northern Italy's main international and domestic airports. It is closer to Pisa (p236), but is well linked with Florence by public transport (see right).

BUS

From the **SITA bus station** (☎ 800 37 37 60; www.sitabus.it, in Italian; Via Santa Caterina da Siena 17r; information office ⏰ 8.30am-12.30pm & 3-6pm Mon-Fri, to 12.30pm Sat), just west of Piazza della Stazione, there are *corse rapide* (express services) to/from Siena (€6.80, 1¼ hours, at least hourly between 6.10am and 9.15pm). To get to San Gimignano (€6) you need to go to Poggibonsi (50 minutes, at least hourly between 6.10am and 7.50pm) and catch a connecting service (30 minutes, at least hourly between 6.05am and 8.35pm). Direct buses also serve Castellina in Chianti, Greve in Chianti and other smaller cities throughout Tuscany.

CAR & MOTORCYCLE

Florence is connected by the A1 northwards to Bologna and Milan, and southwards to Rome and Naples.

TRAIN

Florence's central train station is **Stazione di Santa Maria Novella** (**Piazza della Stazione**). There are regular trains to/from Rome (€16 to €40, 1¾ to 3¾ hours), Bologna (€5.40 to €24.70, one hour to 1¾ hours), Milan (€22.50 to €44.70, 2¼ to 3½ hours) and Venice (€19 to €53.20, 2¾ to 4½ hours).

Frequent regional trains run to Pistoia (€3, 45 minutes to one hour, half-hourly), Pisa (€5.60 to €11.40, one to 1½ hours, frequent) and Lucca (€5, 1½ hours to 1¾ hours, half-hourly).

GETTING AROUND

TO/FROM THE AIRPORT

A **Volainbus shuttle** (one-way/return €5/8, 25 min) travels between Amerigo Vespucci airport and Florence's Santa Maria Novella train station/SITA bus station every 30 minutes between 6am and 11.30pm.

Terravision (www.terravision.eu) runs daily shuttle services (adult one-way/return €10/16, child €4/8, 70 minutes, up to 13 daily) between the bus stop outside Florence's Stazione di Santa Maria Novella on Via Alamanni and Pisa International Airport Galileo Galilei. In Florence, tickets are sold at the Conzorzio ITA inside the train station and at the **Terravision desk** (Via Alamanni 9r; ⏰ 6am-7pm) located inside Deanna Bar oppoite the Terravision bus stop.

Regular trains link Florence's Stazione di Santa Maria Novella with Pisa International Airport Galileo Galilei (€5.60, 1½ hours, at least hourly from 4.30am to 10.25pm).

A taxi between Amerigo Vespucci airport and central Florence costs a flat rate of €20, plus surcharges of €2 on Sundays and holidays, €3.30 between 10pm and 6am and €1 per bag.

CAR & MOTORCYCLE

Most traffic is banned from the historic centre. Car-rental agencies:

Avis (☎ 199 10 01 33; Borgo Ognissanti 128r)
Europcar (☎ 055 29 04 38; Borgo Ognissanti 53-57r)
Hertz (☎ 199 11 22 11; Via Maso Finiguerra 33r)

PUBLIC TRANSPORT

ATAF (Azienda Trasporti Area Fiorentina; ☎ 800 42 45 00; www.ataf.net, in Italian) buses and electric *bussini* (minibuses) serve the city and its periphery. Most start/terminate at the ATAF bus stops opposite the south-eastern exit of Stazione di Santa Maria Novella.

Tickets cost €1.20 (€2 on board) and are sold at the **ATAF ticket & information office** (Piazza Adua; ☉ 7.30am-7.30pm Mon-Fri, to 1.30pm Sat), next to the bus stops outside the train station. A carnet of 10/21 tickets costs €10/20, a *biglietto multiplo* (four-journey ticket) is €4.50 and a one-/ three-day pass is €5/12.

TAXI

For a taxi call ☎ 055 42 42 or ☎ 055 43 90.

Lucca

RACHEL LEWIS

NORTHERN & WESTERN TUSCANY

FIESOLE

With its cooler air, olive groves, scattering of Renaissance-styled villas and spectacular views, the bijou village of Fiesole – perched 9km northeast of Florence – has seduced the best of them, from Boccaccio to Gertrude Stein. The **tourist office** (☎ 055 597 83 73; www.comune.fiesole.fi.it, in Italian; Via Portigiani 3; ☉ 9.30am-6.30pm Mon-Fri, 10am-1pm & 2-6pm Sat & Sun Mar-Oct, 9.30am-6pm Mon-Sat, 10am-4pm Sun Nov-Feb), just off the main square, can supply maps and information about walks and sights, including the **Area Archeologica** (☎ 055 5 94 77; www.fiesolemusei. it; Via Portigiani 1; adult/child under 6/concession €12/ free/8; ☉ 10am-7pm Wed-Mon Apr-Sep, to 6pm Wed-Mon Oct & Mar, to 4pm Thu-Mon Nov-Feb).

LUCCA

pop 83,228

This beautiful old city elicits love at first sight with its rich history, handsome churches and excellent restaurants. Hidden behind imposing Renaissance walls, it is an essential stopover on any Tuscan tour.

INFORMATION

APT Lucca (www.luccatourist.it) Piazza Napoleone (☎ 0583 91 99 41; ☉ 10am-1pm & 2-6pm Mon-Sat); Piazza Santa Maria (☎ 0583 91 99 31; ☉ 9am-8pm Apr-Oct, 9am-12.30pm & 3-6.30pm mid-Nov–mid-Dec, 9am-12.30pm & 3-6.30pm Mon-Sat mid-Dec–Mar)

Città di Lucca (☎ 0583 58 31 50; www.lucca itinera.it; Piazzale Verdi; ☉ 9am-7pm) Operates an info point that rents bicycles (per hour €2.50) and excellent city audioguides in English (1/2 persons €9/12), sells concert tickets and has a left-luggage service (per hour €1.50).

COMBINED TICKET

Those choosing to visit the Cathedral's Sacristy, the Cathedral Museum and the Baptistry of the nearby SS Giovanni e Reparata can save money by purchasing a combined ticket (adult/child €6/4) at any of the venues.

SIGHTS

Lucca's biggest attraction is its 12m-high city walls, built snug around the old city in the 16th and 17th centuries, defended by 126 canons and crowned with a wide silky-smooth footpath just made for a leafy Passeggiata della Mura.

CATHEDRAL

Lucca's mainly Romanesque Cattedrale di San Martino (☎ 0583 95 70 68; www.museo cattedralelucca.it, in Italian; Piazza San Martino; 9.30am-5.45pm Mon-Fri, to 6.45pm Sat, to 10.45am & noon-6pm Sun mid-Mar-Oct, to 4.45pm Mon-Fri, to 6.45pm Sat, to 10.45am & noon-5pm Sun Nov–mid-Mar), dedicated to San Martino, dates to the 11th century.

Lucca-born Matteo Civitali designed the pulpit and the 15th-century *tempietto* (small temple) in the north aisle that contains the Volto Santo.

The cathedral's many other artworks include a magnificent *Last Supper* by Tintoretto above the third altar of the south aisle; and the marble tomb of Ilaria del Carretto, a masterpiece of funerary sculpture, in the sacristy (adult/concession €2/1.50). Many more 15th- and 16th-century treasures from the cathedral are displayed in the adjacent Museo della Cattedrale (Cathedral Museum; ☎ 0583 49 05 30; Piazza Antelminelli; adult/concession €4/2.50; 10am-6pm mid-Mar-Oct, to 2pm Mon-Fri, to 5pm Sat & Sun Nov–mid-Mar).

CHIESA DI SAN MICHELE IN FORO

This dazzling Romanesque church (☎ 0583 4 84 59; Piazza San Michele; 7.40am-noon & 3-6pm Apr-Oct, 9am-noon & 3-5pm Nov-Mar) was built on the site of its 8th-century precursor over a period of nearly 300 years, beginning in the 11th century.

EAST OF VIA FILLUNGO

Piazza Anfiteatro is a huge oval just east of Via Fillungo. The houses, raised upon the foundations of the one-time Roman amphitheatre, retain the shape of this distant original. Nearby, the Museo Nazionale di Villa Guinigi (☎ 0583 49 60 33; Via della Quarquonia; adult/concession €4/2; 8.30am-7.30pm Tue-Sat, to 1.30pm Sun) showcases the city's art collection and archaeological remnants from Roman Lucca.

WEST OF VIA FILLUNGO

The facade of the Basilica di San Frediano (☎ 0583 49 36 27; Piazza San Frediano; 8.30am-noon & 3-5.30pm Mon-Fri, 9-11.30am & 3-5pm Sat & Sun) has a unique (and muchrestored) 13th-century mosaic in a markedly Byzantine style.

The privately owned Palazzo Pfanner (☎ 0583 95 40 29; Via degli Asili 33; palace or garden adult/concession €3/2.50, both €4.50/3.50; 10am-6pm Apr-Oct) is a 17th-century palace where parts of *Portrait of a Lady* (1996) with Nicole Kidman and John Malkovich were shot.

FESTIVALS & EVENTS

Lucca's Summer Festival (www.summer -festival.com) in July pulls in top international performers in a variety of musical genres.

SLEEPING & EATING

To track down a bed and breakfast in or around Lucca, surf Lucca: B&B 'n' Guesthouses (www.welcomeinlucca.it). For luxurious options at the top end of the budget spectrum, go to www.villeluc chesi.net.

Affittacamere Stella (☎ 0583 31 10 22; Via Pisana Traversa 2; www.affittacamerestella.com; s €45-55, d €60-70; P ✕ 🕸) Just outside the Porta Sant'Anna, this well-regarded guest house in an early 20th-century apartment building offers comfortable and attractive rooms with wooden ceilings, a kitchen for guests' use and private parking.

La Bohème (☎ 0583 46 24 04; www.boheme. it; Via del Moro 2; d €90-140; ✕) A hefty dark-wood door located on a peaceful back street marks the entrance to this five-room B&B, run with charm and style by former architect Ranieri.

ourpick **Forno Giusti** (Via Santa Lucia 20; pizza & filled focaccia €7-16 per kg; 🕑 7am-1pm & 4-7.30pm, closed Wed afternoon & Sun) Join the crowd queuing in front of this excellent bakery to purchase fresh-from-the-oven pizza and focaccia with a variety of fillings and toppings.

La Corte dei Vini (☎ 0583 58 44 60; Corte Campana 6; meals €24, platters €7-12; 🕑 lunch & dinner Mon-Sat) Strategically placed between Piazza Napoleone and Piazza San Michele, this friendly 'enoteca e picola cucina' (wine bar and small kitchen) is a great choice for an *aperitivo* or casual meal.

GETTING THERE & AROUND

Regional train services connect Lucca with surrounding cities and towns. Destinations include Florence (€5, 1¼ to 1¾ hours, hourly), Pisa (€2.40, 30 minutes, every 30 minutes) and Viareggio (€2.40, 25 minutes, hourly).

Bike rental is offered by two shops – Cicli Bizzarri and Biciclette Bianchi – located on either side of the tourist information office on Piazza Santa Maria. These are both open from 9am to 7pm daily and charge €2.50 per hour.

PISA

pop 87,461

Once a maritime power to rival Genoa and Venice, Pisa now draws its fame from an architectural project gone terribly wrong. But the world-famous Leaning Tower is just one of many noteworthy sights in this compact and compelling city.

INFORMATION

APT Pisa (www.pisaturismo.it); Airport (☎ 050 50 25 18; 🕑 11am-11pm); Piazza dei Miracoli (☎ 050 4 22 91; entrance foyer, Museo dell'Opera del Duomo; 🕑 10am-7pm); Piazza Vittorio Emanuele II (☎ 050 4 22 91; 🕑 9am-7pm Mon-Fri, to 1.30pm Sat)

SIGHTS

Many visitors to Pisa limit their sightseeing to the Piazza dei Miracoli monuments, but those in the know tend to stay an extra day or two to explore the historic centre. This inclination to linger will become even more pronounced when the **Museum of the Ancient Ships of Pisa** (Museo Navi Antiche Romane di Pisa, www.cantierenavipisa.it, in Italian) on Lungarno Simonelli opens in early 2010. The museum will display a remarkable collection of nine Roman cargo ships excavated from Pisa's silted-up harbour in 1998 and restored over the past decade.

PIAZZA DEI MIRACOLI

The piazza's expansive green lawns provide an urban carpet on which Europe's most extraordinary concentration of Romanesque buildings – in the form of Cathedral, Baptistry and Tower – are arranged.

TICKETING

Ticket pricing for Piazza dei Miracoli sights is complicated. Tickets to the **Tower** (€15 at ticket office, €17 booked online) and **Duomo** (€2 Mar-Oct, free Nov-Feb) are sold individually,

JEAN-PIERRE LESCOURRET

Piazza dei Miracoli

but for the remaining sights combined tickets are available. These cost €5/6/8/10 for one/two/three/five sights and cover the Duomo, Baptistry, Camposanto, Museo dell'Opera del Duomo and Museo delle Sinópie. Children aged under 10 are free for all sights except the Tower. Any ticket will also give access to the multimedia and information areas located in the Museo Dell'Opera Del Duomo and Museo delle Sinópie.

Tickets are sold at two **ticket offices** (www.opapisa.it) on the piazza: the central ticket office is located behind the tower and a second office is located in the entrance foyer of the Museo delle Sinópie. To ensure your visit to the tower, book tickets via the website at least 15 days in advance.

LEANING TOWER

Yes, the **Torre Pendente** (☎ ticket reservations 050 387 22 10; www.opapisa.it/boxoffice/index; ⏰ 8.30am-8.30pm Apr–mid-Jun & last 2 weeks Sep, 8.30am-11pm mid-Jun–mid-Sep, 9am-7pm Oct, 10am-5pm Nov-Feb, 9am-6pm or 7pm Mar) really *does* lean.

Work began in 1173 but ground to a halt a decade later, when the structure's first three tiers were observed to be tilting. In 1272 work started again, with artisans and masons attempting to bolster the foundations but failing miserably. Despite this, they kept going, compensating for the lean by gradually building straight up from the lower storeys and creating a subtle curve.

Access to the tower is limited to 40 people at one time, and children aged under eight are not admitted. If you don't want to wait for hours, book in advance (online or by telephone); otherwise go straight to a ticket office when you arrive at the piazza and book the first available slot.

DUOMO

Construction of Pisa's **Cathedral** (⏰ 10am-8pm Apr-Sep, 10am-7pm Oct, 10am-1pm & 2-5pm 1 Nov-24 Dec & 8 Jan-28 Feb, 9am-6pm 25 Dec-7 Jan, 10am-6pm or 7pm Mar) began in 1063 and continued until the 13th century, when the main facade was added. The elliptical dome, the first of its kind in Europe, dates from 1380.

BAPTISTRY

The unusual round **battistero** (☙ 8am-8pm Apr-Sep, 9am-6pm or 7pm Mar & Oct, 10am-5pm Nov-Feb) has one dome on top of another, each roofed half in lead, half in tiles. Construction began in 1152 but it was remodelled and continued by Nicola and Giovanni Pisano more than a century later and was finally completed in the 14th century – hence its hybrid architectural style.

CAMPOSANTO & MUSEO DELLE SINÓPIE

Soil shipped from Calvary during the Crusades is said to lie within the white walls of the hauntingly beautiful **Camposanto** (Cemetery; ☙ 8am-8pm Apr-Sep, 9am-6pm or 7pm Mar & Oct, 10am-5pm Nov-Feb), a cloistered quadrangle where prominent Pisans were once buried. Some of the sarcophagi here are of Graeco-Roman origin, recycled in the Middle Ages.

During WWII, Allied artillery destroyed many of the precious 14th- and 15th-century frescoes that covered the cloister walls. A program of restoration of those frescoes damaged rather than totally destroyed by the bombs is currently underway and the *sinópie* (preliminary sketches) drawn by the artists in red earth pigment on the walls of the Camposanto before the frescoes were overpainted are now on display in the **Sinópie Museum** (☙ 8am-8pm Apr-Sep, 9am-6pm or 7pm Mar & Oct, 10am-5pm Nov-Feb), on the opposite side of the square.

MUSEO DELL'OPERA DEL DUOMO

Housed in the cathedral's former chapter house, the **Museum of the Cathedral** (☙ 8am-8pm Apr-Sep, 9am-6pm or 7pm Mar & Oct, 10am-5pm Nov-Feb) is a repository for works of art once displayed in the cathedral and baptistry.

THE CITY

From Piazza dei Miracoli, head south along Via Santa Maria and turn left at

JEAN-PIERRE LESCOURRET

Horse-drawn carriage in Piazza dei Cavalieri

Piazza Cavallotti for the splendid **Piazza dei Cavalieri**, remodelled by Vasari in the 16th century. **Palazzo dell'Orologio**, located on the northern side of the piazza, occupies the site of a tower where, in 1288, Count Ugolino della Gherardesca, his sons and grandsons were starved to death on suspicion of having helped the Genovese enemy at the Battle of Meloria, an incident recorded in Dante's *Inferno*.

From Piazza Garibaldi, veer east along the Lungarno to visit the **Museo Nazionale di San Matteo** (☎ 050 54 18 65; Piazza San Matteo in Soarta, Lungarno Mediceo; adult/concession €5/2.50; ☿ 8.30am-7pm Tue-Sat, to 1.30pm Sun), a repository of medieval masterpieces housed in a 13th-century former Benedictine convent.

ACROSS THE ARNO

Cross the Ponte di Mezzo to reach Pisa's major shopping boulevard, **Corso Italia**.

Continuing west you'll come to one of Pisa's architectural gems, the **Chiesa di Santa Maria della Spina** (Lungarno Gambacorti; adult/concession €2/1.50; ☿ 10am-1.45pm & 3-5.45pm Tue-Fri, 10am-1.45pm & 3-6.45pm Sat Mar-Oct, 10am-2pm Tue-Sun Nov-Feb). A fine example of Pisan-Gothic style, this now-deconsecrated church was built between 1230 and 1223 to house a reliquary of a *spina* (thorn) from Christ's crown.

FESTIVALS & EVENTS

The **Palio delle Quattro Antiche Repubbliche Marinare** (Regatta of the Four Ancient Maritime Republics) sees a procession of boats and a dramatic race between the four historical maritime rivals: Pisa, Venice, Amalfi and Genoa. The event rotates between the four towns: it's Pisa's turn in 2010 and 2014. Although usually held in June, it has on occasion been delayed till as late as September.

SLEEPING & EATING

Hotel di Stefano (☎ 050 55 35 59; www.hoteldistefano.pisa.it; Via Sant'Apollonia 35-37; s with shared bathroom €45-65, d with shared bathroom €65-80, s with bathroom €65-140, d with bathroom €75-170; ☒) There are three reasons to stay at this friendly three-star: its location in a quiet backstreet in the medieval quarter; its smart, simple rooms; and its terrace with views of the tower's top half.

Royal Victoria Hotel (☎ 050 94 01 11; www.royalvictoria.it; Lungarno Pacinotti 12; r with shared bathroom €80, r with bathroom €100-150; ℗ ☒) This doyen of Pisan hotels, run with love and tender care by the Piegaja family for five generations, offers old-world luxury accompanied by warm, attentive service.

Il Montino (Vicolo del Monte 1; pizza slice €1.20-1.50, full pizza €3.80-7.20; ☿ 10.30am-3pm & 5-10pm Mon-Sat) Students and sophisticates alike adore the *cecina* (chickpea pizza) and *spuma* (a sweet, non-alcoholic drink) that are the specialities of this famous pizzeria.

ourpick Ristoro al Vecchio Teatro (☎ 050 20 21 0; Piazza Dante Alighieri; set menu €35; ☿ lunch Mon-Sat, dinner Tue-Sat) The four courses are dominated by local seafood specialities and diners will encounter delights such as *torta di ceci infranti con le arselle* (an unusual savoury cake of smashed chickpeas with mussels) and risotto with prawns and orange.

GETTING THERE & AWAY
AIR
Pisa International Airport Galileo Galilei (PSA; ☎ 050 84 93 00; www.pisa-airport.com), 2km south of town, is Tuscany's main international airport and handles flights to most major European cities.

CAR & MOTORCYCLE

The SCG FI-PI-LI is a toll-free alternative for Florence and Livorno, while the north–south SS1, the Via Aurelia, connects the city with La Spezia and Rome.

TRAIN

Destinations include Florence (€5.60 to €11.40, one to 1½ hours, frequent), Rome (€17.65 to €37.10, 2½ to four hours, 16 daily), Livorno (€1.80, 15 minutes, frequent) and Lucca (€2.40, 30 minutes, every 30 minutes).

GETTING AROUND

TO/FROM THE AIRPORT

For Pisa airport, take a train to/from Stazione Pisa Centrale (€1.10, five minutes, 33 per day) or the LAM Rossa (red) line (€1, 10 minutes, every 10 to 20 minutes), which is operated by CPT and passes through the city centre and train station on its way to/from the airport. A taxi between the airport and the city centre will cost between €8 and €10.

Terravision (www.terravision.eu) runs buses between the airport and Florence's Stazione di Santa Maria Novella (adult €10/16 one-way/return, child €5/9, 70 minutes, up to 13 daily). **TRAIN S.p.A.** (☎ 0577 20 42 46; www.trainspa.it) runs two services daily between the airport and Siena (€14/26 one-way/return).

Local company **Ecovoyager** (☎ 050 56 18 39, 339 760 76 52; www.ecovoyager.it; Via della

> ### ⬎ WARNING
>
> There is a strict Limited Traffic Zone (ZTL) in Pisa's historic centre for all nonresidents, and this is rigorously enforced. For maps of the ZTL, go to https://secure.comune.pisa.it/tzi/info.jsp.

Faggiola 41; ☺ 9am-midnight Mon-Fri) offers city bike hire for €12 per day.

For a taxi call ☎ 050 54 16 00 (airport), ☎ 050 41 25 2 (Pisa railway station) or ☎ 050 561 878 (Piazza dei Miracoli).

CENTRAL TUSCANY

CHIANTI

When people imagine classic Tuscan countryside, they usually conjure up images of Chianti – gentle hills, sun-baked farmhouses and lots of vines.

Bus-hopping is feasible, but having your own wheels – two or four – is the only real way to discover the region. You can rent wheels from **Ramuzzi** (☎ 055 85 30 37; www.ramuzzi.com; Via Italo Stecchi 23; bike/50cc scooter per day €20/30; ☺ 9am-1pm & 3-7pm Mon-Fri, 9am-1pm Sat) in Greve in Chianti. **Florence by Bike** (☎ 055 48 89 92; www.florencebybike.it; Via San Zanobi 120-122r) offers a 32km-long day tour of northern Chianti (including lunch and wine tasting, €76) leaving Florence at 9.30am and returning by 4pm.

GREVE IN CHIANTI

pop 14,087

This small town, 20km south of Florence on the SS222 and the only one in Chianti easily accessible from Florence by SITA bus (€3.10, one hour, half-hourly), has two claims to fame. They are the historic *macellerìa* (butcher shop) **Antica Macellerìa Falorni** (☎ 055 85 30 29; www.falorni.it; Piazza Matteotti 71; ☺ closed Wed pm & daily 1-4pm), known for its mean cuts since 1729; and Giovanni da Verrazzano (1485–1528). Local-boy-made-good and discoverer of New York harbour, Verrazzano was commemorated there by the Verrazano Narrows bridge linking Staten Island to Brooklyn.

ROBERTO GEROMETTA
Le Cantine di Greve in Chianti

In the first or second week of September, the town's main square, Piazza Matteotti, hosts Greve's annual wine fair. At other times, head to **Le Cantine di Greve in Chianti** (☎ 055 854 64 04; www.lecantine.it; Piazza delle Cantine 2; ☻ 10am-7pm), a vast commercial *enoteca* stocking more than 1200 varieties of wine.

Three kilometres north of the town is the ancestral home of Greve's New York pioneer, **Castello di Verrazzano** (☎ 055 85 42 43; www.verrazzano.com; ☻ guided tours 10am & 11am Mon-Fri), the castle of an estate where Tuscan produce – Chianti Clàssico, *Vin Santo,* grappa, honey, olive oil and balsamic vinegar – has been produced for centuries. You can tour its historic wine cellar and gardens and enjoy a tasting of its wines (1½ hours, €14, Monday to Friday only) or go the whole hog and lunch on five estate-produced courses in the company of five different wines (three hours, €48, Monday to Friday only). On Saturdays, there's a 2½-hour 'Chianti Tradition' option including a tour, tasting and light repast (€28).

In the nearby 11th-century abbey of **Badia di Passignano**, another famous wine estate can be visited. Guided **wine tours** (2hr visit €25; ☻ 3.30pm Mon-Wed, Fri & Sat) visit the estate's cellar and vineyard and taste four Antinori wines; bookings must be made in advance at the **Osteria di Passignano** (☎ 055 807 12 78; www.osteria dipassignano.com; Via Passignano 31; ☻ wine shop 10am-11pm Mon-Sat), the Antinori wine shop and restaurant situated below the abbey. You don't need to make a reservation to enjoy a **wine-tasting** (€15, €20 & €30 for three wines depending on what you taste) in the *osteria.*

The **tourist office** (☎ 055 854 62 87; Piazza Matteotti 11; ☻ 9am-1pm & 2-6pm Mon-Fri, & on Sat May-Sep) stocks a mine of electronic info on wineries to visit and trails to cycle or stroll.

SLEEPING

Agrifuturismo (☎ 339 5019849; www.agrifu turismo.com; Strada San Silvestro 11, Barberino Val d'Elsa; 2-/4-/6-bed apt €70/100/120; ☞) Woods filled with oak, juniper, cypress and pine

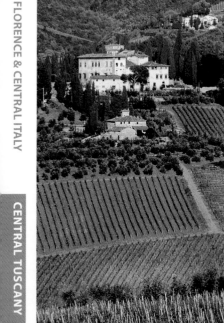

Greve in Chianti (p240)

OLIVER STREWE

trees sit next to ancient terraces of olive trees on this farm estate 13km southwest of Greve. The apartments are charming, with a strong and attractive design ethos. No credit cards.

Fattoria di Rignana (☎ 055 85 20 65; www.rignana.it; Val di Rignana 15, Rignana; d in villa €130-140, d in fattoria €95-105; P 및 ☎) This old farmstead and noble villa 3.8km from Badia di Passignano offers a textbook Chianti experience – namely, great views, wine and food in a tranquil and comfortable vineyard environment.

EATING

Osteria Le Pazanelle (☎ 0577 73 35 11; Lucarelli; meals €25; ☺ lunch & dinner Tue-Sun) Swiss-born chef Angelo cooks up a straightforward choice of around six

dishes per course. Don't miss his crostini topped with *lardo* and orange peel, or his pasta dressed in a *pecorino* and pear sauce. Find it 5km south of Panzano on the SP2 to Radda in Chianti.

our pick **Osteria di Passignano** (☎ 055 807 12 78; www.osteriadipassignano.com; Via di Passignano 33; meals €65, degustation menus €60 & €100; ☺ lunch & dinner Mon-Sat) The delectable food utilises local produce and is decidedly Tuscan in inspiration, but its execution is refined rather than rustic.

CASTELLINA

The area's Etruscan roots form the focus of the modern **Museo Archeologico del Chianti Sienese** (☎ 055 74 20 90; www.museoarcheologicochianti.it; Piazza del Comune 18; adult/concession €3/2; ☺ 10am-1pm & 3.30-6.30pm Thu-Tue).

The privately run **tourist office** (☎ 0577 74 13 92; www.essenceoftuscany.it; Via Ferruccio 26; ☺ 10am-1pm & 2-6pm daily Mar-Nov, 10am-1pm & 2-4pm Mon-Sat Dec & Feb) can help with maps, tours, accommodation and information.

Down a valley at the end of a 1.5km dirt road, **Locanda La Capannuccia** (☎ 0577 74 11 83; www.lacapannuccia.it; Borgo di Pietrafitta; d €95-125; ☺ Mar–mid-Oct; P ☎) is a charming Tuscan getaway. Reserve in the morning for one of Daniela's very special dinners (€24 to €28, Monday to Saturday). To get there, head north along the SS222 from Castellina and turn left to Pietrafitta.

RADDA IN CHIANTI

Shields and escutcheons add a dash of drama to the facade of 16th-century **Palazzo del Podestà** (Piazza Ferrucci), facing the church on the main square of this popular tourist spot 11km east of Castellina. The volunteer-staffed **Ufficio Pro Loco** (☎ 0577 73 84 94; Piazza Castello 6; ☺ 10am-1pm & 3-7pm Mon-Sat, 10.30am-1pm Sun mid-Apr–mid-Oct, 10.30am-12.30pm & 3.30-6.30pm Mon-Sat mid-Oct–mid-Apr) supplies tourist information, including ample information on walking in the area, including several pretty half-day walks.

Alternatively, head 6km north to the gorgeous old-stone hill-top hamlet of **Castello di Volpaia** (☎ 0577 73 80 66; www.volpaia.it; Piazza della Cisterna 1, Volpaia), where particularly lovely wines, olive oils and vinegars have been made for aeons.

SIENA
pop 53,881

The rivalry between historic adversaries Siena and Florence continues to this day, and every traveller seems to strongly identify with one over the other. It often boils down to aesthetic preference: while Florence saw its greatest flourishing during the Renaissance, Siena's enduring artistic glories are largely Gothic.

ORIENTATION

Historic Siena, still largely surrounded by its medieval walls punctuated by the eight original city gates, is small and easily tackled on foot, although the way streets swirl in semicircles around Piazza del Campo (known as Il Campo) can be confusing.

INFORMATION

Police station (☎ 0577 20 11 11; Via del Castoro 23)
Post office (Piazza Matteotti 1)
Tourist office (☎ 0577 28 05 51; www.terresiena.it; Piazza del Campo 56; ☾ 9am-7pm) Reserves accommodation and sells direct bus tickets to Pisa Airport (€14/26 one-way/return).

SIGHTS
PIAZZA DEL CAMPO

In the upper part of the square is the 15th-century **Fonte Gaia** (Happy Fountain), now clad in reproductions of the original panels by Jacopo della Quercia.

At the lowest point of the square (or the tap of the above mentioned metaphorical sink), the spare, elegant **Palazzo Comunale** is also known as the Palazzo Pubblico, or town hall. From the *palazzo* soars its graceful bell tower, the **Torre del Mangia** (admission €7; ☾ 10am-7pm mid-Mar-Oct, to 4pm Nov–mid-Mar), 102m high, completed in 1297.

The lower level of the *palazzo*'s facade features a characteristic Sienese-Gothic arcade. Inside is the **Museo Civico** (☎ 0577 29 22 63; adult/student €7.50/4.50, museum & tower €12; ☾ 10am-7pm mid-Mar-Oct, to 5.30pm

---

IL PALIO

Dating from the Middle Ages, this spectacular event stages a series of colourful pageants and a wild horse race around Il Campo on 2 July and 16 August. Ten of Siena's 17 *contrade* (town districts) compete for the coveted *palio* (silk banner).

From about 5pm representatives from each *contrada* (district) parade in historical costume, all bearing their individual banners. For scarcely one exhilarating minute, the 10 horses and their bareback riders tear three times around Il Campo with a speed and violence that makes spectators' hair stand on end.

Join the crowds in the centre of Il Campo at least four hours before the start (7.45pm in July, 7pm in August) if you want a place on the rails.

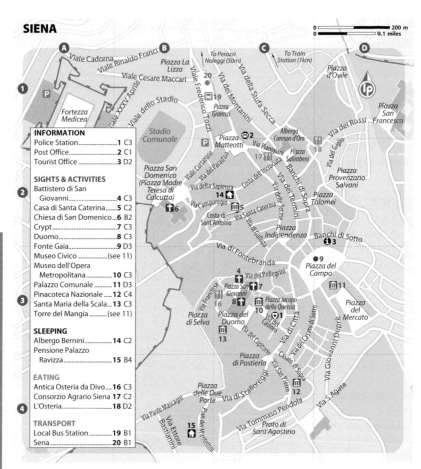

SIENA

0 ——— 200 m
0 ——— 0.1 miles

INFORMATION
Police Station......................1 C3
Post Office.........................2 C1
Tourist Office 3 D2

SIGHTS & ACTIVITIES
Battistero di San
    Giovanni.......................4 C3
Casa di Santa Caterina......5 C2
Chiesa di San Domenico...6 B2
Crypt................................7 C3
Duomo.............................8 C3
Fonte Gaia........................9 D3
Museo Civico ....(see 11)
Museo dell'Opera
    Metropolitana 10 C3
Palazzo Comunale 11 D3
Pinacoteca Nazionale 12 C4
Santa Maria della Scala...13 C3
Torre del Mangia ....(see 11)

SLEEPING
Albergo Bernini...............14 C2
Pensione Palazzo
    Ravizza.......................15 B4

EATING
Antica Osteria da Divo....16 C3
Consorzio Agrario Siena 17 C2
L'Osteria.........................18 D2

TRANSPORT
Local Bus Station 19 B1
Sena 20 B1

or 6.30pm Nov–mid-Mar), occupying rooms richly decorated by artists of the Sienese school.

DUOMO

Siena's **cathedral** (☎ 0577 4 73 21; www.operaduomo.siena.it; Piazza del Duomo; admission €3; ☷ 10.30am-7.30pm Mon-Sat, 1.30-6.30pm Sun Mar-Oct, 10.30am-6.30pm Mon-Sat, 1.30-5.30pm Sun Nov-Feb) is one of Italy's greatest Gothic churches. Begun in 1196, it was completed by 1215, although work continued on features such as the apse and dome well into the 13th century.

The most precious feature of the cathedral's interior is the inlaid marble floor, decorated with 56 panels depicting historical and biblical subjects. The most valuable are kept covered and are revealed only from 21 August through 27 October each year (admission is €6 during this period).

MUSEO DELL'OPERA METROPOLITANA

This **museum** (☎ 0577 28 30 48; www.operaduomo.siena.it Piazza del Duomo 8; admission €6; ☷ 9.30am-7pm Mar-May & Sep-Nov, to 8pm Jun-

Aug, 10am-5pm Dec-Feb), also known as Museo dell'Opera del Duomo, is in what would have been the southern aisle of the nave of the Nuovo Duomo.

Inside, formerly adorning the cathedral, are the 12 statues of prophets and philosophers by Giovanni Pisano that decorated the facade.

For a great panoramic view haul yourself up the 131-step, narrow corkscrew stairway to the Panorama del Facciatone (admission €6) at the top of the facade of the putative Nuovo Duomo. A combined admission ticket for the museum and panorama costs €10 and is valid for three days.

CRYPT

Just north of the cathedral and down a flight of steps is the crypt (admission incl audioguide €6; ☉ 9.30am-7pm Mar-May, to 8pm Jun-Aug, to 7pm Sep-Oct), a room below the cathedral's pulpit discovered in 1999. Its walls are completely covered with *pintura a secco* ('dry painting') dating back to the 1200s.

BATTISTERO DI SAN GIOVANNI

Opposite the crypt is the Battistero di San Giovanni (Piazza San Giovanni; admission €3; ☉ 9.30am-7pm Mar-May, to 8pm Jun-Aug, to 7pm Sep-Oct).

The centrepiece is a marble font by Jacopo della Quercia, decorated with bronze panels in relief and depicting the life of St John the Baptist.

SANTA MARIA DELLA SCALA

In the basement of this former pilgrims' hospital (☎ 0577 22 48 11; Piazza del Duomo 2; admission €6; ☉ 10.30am-6.30pm Apr-Oct, to 4.30pm Nov-Mar) is the Sala dei Pellegrinaio clad in vivid secular frescoes (quite a relief after so much spirituality all around town) by Domenico di Bartolo, lauding the good works of the hospital and its patrons.

PINACOTECA NAZIONALE

Within the 15th-century Palazzo Buonsignori, this art gallery (☎ 0577 28 11 61; Via San Pietro 29; adult/child €4/free; ☉ 10am-6pm Tue-Sat, 9am-1pm Sun, 8.30am-1.30pm Mon) is a showcase for the greatest of Sienese artists.

CHIESA DI SAN DOMENICO

Santa Caterina di Siena took her vows within this imposing church (Piazza San Domenico; ☉ 7.30am-1pm & 3-6.30pm). In the Cappella di Santa Caterina are frescoes by Sodoma depicting events in her life – as well as the saint's head, held in a 15th-century tabernacle above the altar.

For more of Santa Caterina – figuratively speaking – visit Casa di Santa Caterina (☎ 0577 22 15 62; Costa di Sant'Antonio 6;

DAVID TOMLINSON
Town district banquet before Il Palio (p243)

San Gimignano

ROBERTO GEROMETTA

admission free; ⏲ 9am-6.30pm Mar-Nov, 10am-6pm Dec-Feb), where the saint was born and lived with her parents plus, says the legend, 24 siblings.

SLEEPING & EATING

Albergo Bernini (☎ 0577 28 90 47; www.albergobernini.com; Via della Sapienza 15; s €50, d with shared bathroom €30-65, d with bathroom €45-85; 💻) A welcoming, family-run hotel with a tiny terrace sporting views across to the cathedral and the Chiesa di San Domenico.

Pensione Palazzo Ravizza (☎ 0577 28 04 62; www.palazzoravizza.com; Pian dei Mantellini 34; s €95-150, d €115-200; 🅿 🞄 💻) Occupying a delightful Renaissance *palazzo,* frescoed ceilings and antique furniture co-exist with flatscreen TVs and comprehensive wi-fi coverage.

L'Osteria (☎ 0577 28 75 92; Via dei Rossi 79-81; meals €27) We promised a local we wouldn't put this one in the book. We lied. It was just too good.

our pick Antica Osteria da Divo (☎ 0577 28 43 81; www.osteriadadivo.it; Via Franciosa 29;

meals €50) The inventive menu includes dishes such as cannelloni with ricotta, spinach, grilled sweet peppers, tomatoes and Tuscan pesto sauce.

SELF-CATERING

Consorzio Agrario Siena (Via Pianagini 13) An enticing emporium of local food and wines.

GETTING THERE & AWAY
BUS

The **local bus station** is on Piazza Gramsci. Both TRAIN S.p.A and SITA have ticket offices underneath the piazza, where there's also a left-luggage office (per day €5.50). Express buses race up to Florence (€6.80, 1¼ hours, up to 30 daily). Other regional TRAIN S.p.A destinations include San Gimignano (€5.30, one to 1½ hours, 10 daily either direct or changing in Poggibonsi), Montalcino (€3.30, 1½ hours, six daily), Montepulciano (€4.70, 1¾ hours) and Colle di Val d'Elsa (€2.60, 30 minutes, hourly). **Sena** (☎ 0577 28 32 03; www.sena.it) buses run to/from Rome (€20, three hours, eight daily) and Milan (€29, 4¼ hours, three daily).

CAR & MOTORCYCLE
For Florence, take the SS2, the *super-strada,* or the more attractive SS222, also known as the Strada Chiantigiana, which meanders its way through the hills of Chianti.

TRAIN
Siena isn't on a major train line so buses are generally a better alternative.

GETTING AROUND
TRAIN S.p.A operates city bus services (€0.90). Buses 8, 9 and 10 run between the train station and Piazza Gramsci.

Perozzi Noleggi (☎ 0577 28 83 87; www. perozzi.it; Via dei Gazzani 16-18; ⊙ 8.30am-12.30pm & 3pm-7pm) rents mountain bikes (per day/week €10/50) and 125cc scooters (per day/week €45/260). If there's no-one in the showroom, pop round the corner to Via del Romitorio 5.

Cars are banned from the town centre, though visitors can drop off luggage at their hotel, then get out (don't forget to have reception report your licence number or risk receiving a 'souvenir' fine).

SAN GIMIGNANO
pop 7735

Within easy reach of both Siena and Florence, San Gimignano is a tourist magnet. Come in winter or early spring to indulge your imagination a little; in summer you'll spend your time dodging fellow visitors. Even then, though, you'll discover a different, almost peaceful San Gimignano once the last bus has pulled out.

Originally an Etruscan village, the town was named after the bishop of Modena, San Gimignano, who is said to have saved the city from Attila the Hun.

ORIENTATION
From the main gate, Porta San Giovanni, at the southern end of the town, Via San Giovanni heads northwards to central Piazza della Cisterna and the connecting Piazza del Duomo.

The **tourist office** (☎ 0577 94 00 08; www. sangimignano.com; Piazza del Duomo 1; ⊙ 9am-1pm & 3-7pm Mar-Oct, 9am-1pm & 2-6pm Nov-Feb) hires out audioguides of the town (€5) and organises Vernaccia di San Gimignano vineyard visits (two-hour tours, Tuesdays and Thursdays, from May to October; €20). Advance reservations are essential.

SIGHTS
COLLEGIATA
The 13th-century **Palazzo del Podestà** and its tower, the **Torre della Rognosa**, look across to the town's Romanesque **basilica** (adult/child €3.50/1.50; ⊙ 9.30am-7.30pm Mon-Sat, 12.30-5pm Sun Apr-Oct, 9.30am-5pm Mon-Sat, 12.30-5pm Sun Nov–mid-Jan & Mar). Its bare facade belies the remarkable 14th-century frescoes that stripe the interior walls like some vast medieval comic strip.

The **Cappella di Santa Fina** is adorned with naive and touching frescoes by Domenico Ghirlandaio depicting events in the life of the saint, and a superb alabaster and marble altar picked out in gold.

MONEYSAVERS
If you're an assiduous sightseer, two combined tickets may be worth your while. One (adult/child €7.50/5.50) gives admission to the Palazzo Comunale and its Museo Civico, the archaeological museum, Torre Grossa and some secondary sights. The other (adult/child €5.50/2.50) gets you into the Collegiata and nearby Museo d'Arte Sacra.

DAVID TOMLINSON

Montalcino

⇘ IF YOU LIKE...

If you like **San Gimignano** (p247), we think you'll like these other Tuscan hill towns:

- **Montalcino** Home to the internationally coveted Brunello wine, this retiring hill town is also known for its Jazz & Wine Festival, held in the second and third weeks of July. Catch a bus to/from Siena.
- **Pienza** A World Heritage–listed gem where Renaissance buildings meet the renowned ewe-milk cheese *pecorino di pienza*. Buses run to/from Siena and Montepulciano.
- **Montepulciano** Renaissance buildings and dizzying views await in the home of Vino Nobile, one of Tuscany's most reputed drops.
- **Volterra** Well-preserved medieval ramparts and a windswept, forbidding air set the scene for the planet's principal vampire coven in writer Stephanie Meyer's hit series *Twilight*. From Pisa, catch a bus to Seline, then one to Volterra. From Florence, Siena and San Gimignano, change at Colle di Val d'Elsa (no services Sundays).

Across the square, the **Museo d'Arte Sacra** (☎ 0577 94 03 16; Piazza Pecori 1; adult/child €3/1.50; ⏲ 9.30am-7.30pm Mon-Fri, to 5pm Sat, 12.30-5pm Sun Apr-Oct, 9.30am-5pm Mon-Sat, 12.30-5pm Sun Nov–mid-Jan & Mar) has some fine works of religious art, collected in the main from the town's churches.

PALAZZO COMUNALE

From the internal courtyard, climb the stairs to the **Pinacoteca** (☎ 0577 99 03 12;

Piazza del Duomo; museum & tower adult/child €5/4; ⏲ 9.30am-7pm Mar-Oct, 10am-5.30pm Nov-Feb), which features paintings from the Sienese and Florentine schools of the 12th to 15th centuries. In the main room, the great poet **Dante** addressed the town's council, urging it to support the Guelph cause.

MUSEUMS

In an unmarked gallery just outside the town's fortress is **Museo del Vino** (Wine

Museum; ☎ 0577 94 12 67; Parco della Rocca; admission free; ⏰ 11.30am-6.30pm Thu-Mon, 3-6.30pm Wed Mar-Oct). A sommelier is usually on hand to lead an informed – and paid – tasting of some of the choice local white wines.

The **Museo Archeologico & Speziera di Santa Fina** (☎ 0577 94 03 48; Via Folgore da San Gimignano 11; adult/child both museums €3.50/2.50; ⏰ 11am-5.45pm mid-Mar-Dec) complex is home to the town's small archaeological museum and a reconstructed 16th-century pharmacy and herb garden. There's also a **modern art gallery** that in itself merits a visit.

OTHER SIGHTS

At the northern end of the town is the **Chiesa di Sant'Agostino** (Piazza Sant'Agostino; ⏰ 7am-noon & 3-7pm Apr-Oct, to 6pm Nov-Mar). Its main attraction is the fresco cycle in the apse by Benozzo Gozzoli, depicting the saint's life.

SLEEPING & EATING

Hotel Leon Bianco (☎ 0577 94 12 94; www.leonbianco.com; Piazza della Cisterna 13; s €65-80, d €85-135; 🍴 💻 🛜) This smoothly run hotel is welcoming and friendly with a ground-floor abundance of plants, a pretty inner courtyard, a breakfast patio, a billiard table and a fitness room.

Hotel La Cisterna (☎ 0577 94 03 28; www.hotelcisterna.it; Piazza della Cisterna 24; s €62-78, d €88-145; 🍴 💻 🛜) Located in a splendid 14th-century building, this accommodation option now offers 21st-century comfort in quiet, spacious rooms.

Osteria al Carcere (☎ 0577 94 19 05; Via del Castello 5; meals €35; ⏰ closed Thu lunch & Wed) There are a half-dozen soups, including zuppa di farro e fagioli (spelt and white bean soup) and creative flashes like tacchina al pistacchi e arance (turkey with pistachios and orange sauce).

Dorando (☎ 0577 94 18 62; www.ristorante dorando.it; Vicolo dell'Oro 2; meals €60; ⏰ daily Easter-Oct, Tue-Sun Oct-Easter) Recognised by the Slow Food Movement, Dorando runs a classic five-course menu with dishes based on authentic Etruscan recipes. The menu is otherwise brief and focused (only four primi and four secondi).

GETTING THERE & AWAY

Buses run to/from Florence (€6, 1¼ hours, over 30 daily) but almost always require a change at Poggibonsi. Buses also run to/from Siena (€5.30, one to 1½ hours, 10 daily).

There are car parks (per hour €2 or per day €5 to €20) outside the city walls and beside and below Porta San Giovanni.

UMBRIA
PERUGIA
pop 163,287

One of Italy's best-preserved hill towns replete with museums and churches, Perugia is also a hip student town with a never-ending stream of cultural events and concerts. Within the city walls, little has changed architecturally for over 400 years, and a few hotels and restaurants are in triple-digit ages. Culturally, however, Perugia is on the edge.

ORIENTATION

Urbano (city) buses originate from Piazza Italia while extraurbano (intercity) buses originate at Piazza Partigiani. From here, take a few sets of scale mobili (elevators) through the Rocca Paolina to reach Piazza Italia. If you have heavy luggage, watch out: scale mobili interchange with staircases up the steep hillside. From the train station it's an enormous hike, especially with that luggage, or a quick €1 bus ride or €10 taxi, 1.5km up the hill to Piazza Italia.

FLORENCE & CENTRAL ITALY

UMBRIA

PERUGIA

INFORMATION
InfoUmbria **1** C4
Police Station **2** C2
Post Office **3** C2

SIGHTS & ACTIVITIES
Cathedral of San
  Lorenzo **4** C1
Chiesa di San Domenico ...**5** D3
Fontana Maggiore **6** C2
Galleria Nazionale
  dell'Umbria .... (see 8)
Museo Archeologico
  Nazionale dell'Umbria....**7** D3
Nobile Collegio del
  Cambio .... (see 8)
Nobile Collegio della
  Mercanzia .... (see 8)
Palazzo dei Priori **8** C2

SLEEPING
Albergo Anna **9** B2
Hotel Brufani Palace **10** C3

EATING
Al Mangiar Bene **11** C2
Il Gufo **12** D2
Sandri **13** C2

DRINKING
Bottega del Vino **14** C1

TRANSPORT
Ferrovia Centrale
  Umbra **15** C3
Intercity Bus Station **16** C4
Via dei Priori Scale
  Mobile **17** B1
Via dei Priori Scale
  Mobile **18** B2

INFORMATION

Banks line Corso Vannucci. All have ATMs, known as *bancomats*.

InfoUmbria (☎ 075 57 57; www.infoumbria. com in Italian; Piazza Partigiani Intercity bus station, Largo Cacciatori delle Alpi 3; ☽ 9am-1pm & 2.30-6.30pm Mon-Fri, 9am-1pm Sat)

Police station (☎ 075 572 32 32; Palazzo dei Priori)

Post office (Piazza Matteotti; ☽ 8am-6.30pm Mon-Fri, 8am-noon Sat)

SIGHTS
CORSO VANNUCCI

The centre of Perugia – and therefore the centre of all of Umbria – is Piazza IV Novembre.

On the north end of the piazza is the Cathedral of San Lorenzo (☎ 075 572 38 32; Piazza IV Novembre; ☽ 10am-1pm & 2.30-5.30pm Tue-Sun). Although a church has been on this land since the 900s, the version you see was begun in 1345 from designs created by Fra Bevignate in 1300.

In the very centre of the piazza stands the Fontana Maggiore (Great Fountain). It was designed by Fra Bevignate, and father-son team Nicola and Giovanni Pisano built the fountain between 1275 and 1278.

The Palazzo dei Priori houses some of the best museums in Perugia. The foremost art gallery in Umbria is the stunning Galleria Nazionale dell'Umbria (National Gallery of Umbria; ☎ /fax 800 69 76 16; Palazzo dei Priori, Corso Vannucci 19; adult/concession €6.50/3.25; ☽ 8.30am-7.30pm), entered from Corso Vannucci.

Also in the same building is what some consider the most beautiful bank in the world, the Nobile Collegio del Cambio (Exchange Hall; ☎ 075 572 85 99; Corso Vannucci 25; adult/concession €4.50/2.60; ☽ 9am-12.30pm & 3-7pm Mon-Sat summer, 2.30-5.30pm winter). The Nobile Collegio della Mercanzia (Merchant's Hall; ☎ 075 573 03 66; Corso Vannucci 15; admission €3.10; ☽ 9am-12.30pm & 2.30-5.50pm Tue-Sun summer, often closed afternoon winter) highlights an older audience chamber, from the 13th century, covered in wood panelling by northern craftsmen.

DOWN CORSO CAVOUR

The city's largest church is the early 14th–century Chiesa di San Domenico (☎ 075 573 15 68; Piazza Giordano Bruno; ☽ 8am-noon & 4pm-sunset). It has a Romanesque interior, lightened by the immense stained-glass windows, that was replaced by austere Gothic fittings in the 16th century.

The adjoining convent is home to the Museo Archeologico Nazionale dell'Umbria (☎ 075 572 71 41; Piazza Giordano Bruno 10; adult/concession €4/2; ☽ 8.30am-7.30pm Tue-Sun, 10am-7.30pm Mon), which will boggle the mind with its collection of Etruscan and prehistoric artefacts – carved funerary urns, coins, Bronze Age statuary – dating back to the 16th century BC.

Just past the Porta di San Pietro is the 10th-century Chiesa di San Pietro (☎ 075 3 47 70; Borgo XX Giugno; ☽ 8am-noon & 4pm-sunset), entered through a frescoed doorway in the first courtyard. The interior is an incredible mix of gilt and marble and contains a *pietà* (a painting of the dead Christ supported by the Madonna) by Perugino.

FESTIVALS & EVENTS

Umbria Jazz (☎ 800 46 23 11, 075 500 11 07; www.umbriajazz.com in Italian) This attracts topnotch international performers for 10 days each July, usually around the middle of the month.

SLEEPING

Albergo Anna (☎ /fax 075 573 63 04; www.albergoanna.it; Via dei Priori 48; s €30-50, d €50-80,

FLORENCE & CENTRAL ITALY

UMBRIA

JOHN ELK III

Piazza IV Novembre

tr €60-90, all incl breakfast) If you want central and quiet and don't have a lot of heavy luggage (think: fourth floor walk-up), this antiqued option is a fabulous bet.

Hotel Brufani Palace (☎ 075 573 25 41; www.sinahotels.com; Piazza Italia 12; s/d €215/320, ste €440-850; P ⊠ 🖳 🛜 🛒 ♿) One of Umbria's two five-star hotels (the second is Le Tre Vaselle in Torgiano) and a truly spectacular experience, the palace's special touches include frescoed main rooms, impeccably decorated bedrooms and suites, a garden terrace for summer dining, and helpful trilingual staff.

EATING

Al Mangiar Bene (☎ 075 573 10 47; Via della Luna 21; pizzas €5-8, meals €25) Pizzas and calzones, baked in a hearth-like brick oven, are all made with organic ingredients.

Il Gufo (☎ 075 573 41 26; Via della Viola 18; meals €29; ☽ 8pm-1am Tue-Sat) Try dishes such as *cinghiale* (wild boar) with fennel (€12.50) or *riso nero* (black rice) with

---

A TASTE OF TORGIANO

If you're a food and wine connoisseur, consider a daytrip to Torgiano, home to Europe's most important wine museum, the **Museo del Vino** (☎ 075 988 02 00; Corso Vittorio Emanuele 31; adult/concession €4.50/2.50, incl Museo dell'Olivo e dell'Olio €7, audioguide €2; ☽ 9am-1pm & 3-7pm summer, to 6pm winter). The village is also home to the **Museo dell'Olivo e dell'Olio** (☎ 075 988 03 00; Via Garibaldi 10; adult/concession €4.50/2.50; ☽ 10am-1pm & 3-7pm summer, to 6pm winter), which is dedicated to olives and olive oil. **APM Perugia** (☎ 800 51 21 41; www.apmperugia.it) buses head to/from Perugia (€1.80, 25 minutes, nine daily).

---

grilled vegetables and brie (€12.50). No credit cards.

Sandri (☎ 075 572 41 12; Corso Vannucci 32; ☽ 10am-8pm Tue-Sun) Known for delectable chocolate cakes, candied fruit, espresso and pastries.

DRINKING

Bottega del Vino (☎ /fax 075 571 61 81; Via del Sole 1; ☽ 7pm-1am Mon-Sat) A fire or candles burn atmospherically on the terrace, while inside, live jazz and hundreds of bottles of wine lining the walls add to the romance of the setting.

GETTING THERE & AWAY
AIR
Aeroporto Sant'Egidio (PEG; ☎ 075 59 21 41; www.airport.umbria.it), 13km east of the city, offers at least three daily **Alitalia** (www.alitalia.it) flights to Milan, plus a new **Ryanair** (www.ryanair.co.uk) service to London Stansted thrice weekly. An extremely convenient white shuttle-bus (€3.50) leaves from Piazza Italia about an hour and 10 minutes before a scheduled departure, stopping at the train station 15 minutes into the journey.

BUS
Intercity buses leave from Piazza Partigiani (take the *scale mobili* through the Rocca Paolina from Piazza Italia). Most routes within Umbria are operated by **APM** (☎ 800 51 21 41; www.apmperugia.com) in the north and **SSIT** (☎ 0742 67 07 47; www.spoletina.com) or **ATC Terni** (☎ 0744 40 94 57; www.atcterni.it) in the south.

CAR & MOTORCYCLE
You'll find three car-rental companies at the main train station. All are open from 8.30am to 1pm and 3.30pm to 7pm Monday to Friday, and from 8.30am to 1pm Saturday.

Sandri

MASSIMO BORCHI/4CORNERS

Avis (☎ /fax 075 500 03 95; alvalrent@hotmail.com)

Hertz (☎ 075 500 24 39; hertzperugia@tiscali.it)

TRAIN

Regular trains run to Rome (€10.50 to €29.50, 2¼ to three hours), Florence (€9.20 to €15, two hours) and Arezzo (€4.50 to 6.85, one hour and 10 minutes, every two hours). Within Umbria, it's easy to reach Assisi (€2.05, 25 minutes, hourly), Gubbio (€4.75, 1½ hours, seven daily), Spello (€2.65, 30 minutes, hourly) and Orvieto (€6.15 to €9.60, 1¼ hours, at least every other hour).

GETTING AROUND

It's a steep 1.5km climb uphill from Perugia's train station, so a bus is highly recommended, essential for those with luggage.

CAR & MOTORCYCLE

Perugia is humorously difficult to navigate and most of the city centre is only open to residential or commercial traffic (although tourists may drive to their hotels to drop off luggage).

METRÒ

These single-car people-movers traverse between the train station and Pincetto (just below Piazza Garibaldi) every minute. The same €1 tickets work for the bus and Minimetrò.

TAXI

Call ☎ 075 500 48 88 to arrange pick-up. A ride from the city centre to the main train station, Stazione Fontivegge, will cost about €10 to €15. Tack on €1 for each suitcase.

ASSISI

pop 27,279

The spiritual capital of Umbria is Assisi, a town more tied to its most famous son than anywhere else on earth. St Francis of Assisi was born here in 1182 and preached his message throughout Umbria until his death in 1226.

Basilica di San Francesco from Piazza di San Francesco

JOHN ELK III

ORIENTATION

Piazza del Comune is the centre of Assisi. At the northwestern edge of this square, Via San Paolo and Via Portica both eventually lead to the Basilica di San Francesco. Via Portica also leads to the Porta San Pietro and the Piazza Unita d'Italia, where most intercity buses stop, although APM buses from smaller towns in the area terminate at Piazza Matteotti. Train riders arrive at Piazza Matteotti by shuttle bus (€1) from Santa Maria degli Angeli.

INFORMATION

Police station (☎ 075 81 28 20; Piazza del Comune)

Post office Porta Nuova (☺ 8am-1.30pm Mon-Fri, 8am-12.30pm Sat); Porta San Pietro (☺ 8.10am-6.30pm Mon-Fri, 8am-1pm Sat & Sun)

Tourist office (☎ 075 813 86 80; www.assisi. regioneumbria.eu; Piazza del Comune 22; ☺ 8am-2pm & 3-6pm Mon-Sat, 10am-1pm & 2-5pm Sun summer, 9am-1pm Sun winter)

SIGHTS
BASILICA DI SAN FRANCESCO

The **Basilica di San Francesco** (☎ 075 81 90 01; Piazza di San Francesco) has a separate **information office** (☎ 075 819 00 84; www. sanfrancescoassisi.org; ☺ 9am-noon & 2-5pm Mon-Sat) opposite the entrance to the lower church where you can schedule a tour in, at the very least, English or Italian, led by a resident Franciscan friar.

The **upper church** (☺ 8.30am-6.45pm Easter-Oct, to 6pm Oct-Easter) was built just after the lower church, between 1230 and 1253, and the change in style and grandiosity is readily apparent.

The **lower church** (☺ 6am-6.45pm Easter-Oct, to 6pm Oct-Easter) was built between 1228 and 1230. In the centre of the lower church, above the main altar, are four frescoes attributed to Maestro delle Vele, a pupil of Giotto, that represent what St Francis called 'the four greatest allegories'. The first was the victory of Francis over evil, and the other three were the precepts his order was based on: poverty, obedience and chastity.

One of the most moving locations in the basilica complex is downstairs from the lower church: the **crypt of St Francis**, where the saint's body has been laid to rest. Bench seating around the tomb allows time for quiet reflection.

The basilica's **Sala delle Reliquie** (Relics Hall; ☎ 075 81 90 01; 9am-6pm daily, 1-4.30pm holidays) contains items from St Francis's life, including his simple tunic and sandals and fragments of his celebrated *Canticle of the Creatures*.

CHURCHES & MUSEUMS

Basilica di Santa Chiara (☎ 075 81 22 82; Piazza Santa Chiara; 6am-noon & 2-7pm summer, to 6pm winter) is 13th-century Romanesque, with steep ramparts and a striking facade. The daughter of an Assisian nobleman, St Clare was a spiritual contemporary of St Francis and founded the Sorelle Povere di Santa Chiara (Order of the Poor Ladies), now known as the Poor Clares. She is buried in the church's crypt.

From the basilica, take Via Santa Chiara or Corso Mazzani back to Piazza del Comune, which once was the site of a partially excavated **Foro Romano** (Roman Forum; ☎ 075 81 30 53; Via Portica; adult/child incl Pinacoteca €3/2; 10am-6pm summer, to 5pm winter). The **Chiesa Nuova** (☎ 075 81 23 39; Piazza Chiesa Nuova; 6.30am-noon & 2.30-6pm summer, 6.30am-noon & 2-5pm winter) was built by King Philip III of Spain in the 1600s on the spot reputed to be the house of St Francis's family.

Dominating the city is the massive 14th-century **Rocca Maggiore** (☎ 075 81 52 92; Via della Rocca; adult/concession €5/3.50; 10am-sunset), an oft-expanded, pillaged and rebuilt hill-fortress offering 360-degree views of Perugia.

The 13th-century Romanesque **Duomo di San Rufino** (☎ 075 81 60 16; Piazza San Rufino; 7am-noon & 2.30-7pm, to 6pm in winter), remodelled by Galeazzo Alessi in the 16th century, contains the fountain where St Francis and St Clare were baptised.

FRANCISCAN SITES

Walk the 1.5km olive tree-lined stroll to the **Santuario di San Damiano** (☎ 075 81 22 73; admission free; 10am-noon & 2-6pm summer, 10am-noon & 2-4.30pm winter, vespers 7pm summer, 5pm winter), where St Francis first heard the voice of God and where he wrote his *Canticle of the Creatures*.

Find out why St Francis chose the caves of **Eremo delle Carceri** (☎ 075 81 23 01; admission free; 6.30am-7pm Easter-Oct, to sunset Oct-Easter) as his hermitage. The *carceri* (isolated places, or 'prisons') along the slopes of Monte Subasio are as peaceful today as in St Francis's time. It's a 4km drive (or walk) east, and a dozen nearby hiking trails are well signposted.

A quick walk from the train station is the imposing **Basilica di Santa Maria degli Angeli** (☎ 075 8 05 11; Santa Maria degli Angeli; 6.15am-12.50pm & 2.30-7.30pm summer), built between 1565 and 1685 around the first Franciscan monastery and tiny Porziuncola Chapel. Perugino fans will appreciate his intact crucifixion, painted on the rear wall.

ACTIVITIES

A popular spot for hikers is nearby **Monte Subasio**. Local bookstores sell all sorts of walking and mountain-biking guides and maps for the area and the tourist office can help with brochures and maps as well.

Bicycle rentals are available at **Angelucci Andrea Cicli Riparazione Noleggio** (☎ 075 804 25 50; www.angelucci cicli.it; Via Risorgimento 54a) in Santa Maria degli Angeli.

FESTIVALS & EVENTS

The Festa di San Francesco falls on 3 and 4 October and is the main religious event in the city.

SLEEPING & EATING

Alla Madonna del Piatto (☎ 075 819 90 50; www.incampagna.com; Pieve San Nicolo 18; d incl breakfast €85-120; ☺ Mar-mid Nov; ℗) As beautiful as it is seemingly isolated, this *agriturismo* is less than 15 minutes from the Basilica. But the real reason to stay here is the intimate cooking classes Letizia runs (in Italian or English). Two-night minimum.

Trattoria Pallotta (☎ 075 81 26 49; Vicolo della Volta Pinta; meals €25; ☺ Wed-Mon) They cook all the Umbrian classics here: rabbit, homemade *strangozzi,* even pigeon.

Medio Evo (☎ 075 81 30 68; Via Arco dei Priori 4; meals €28; ☺ Thu-Tue) Traditional Umbrian dishes are served in fabulous vaulted 13th-century surroundings, including rabbit stew (€12) and truffle omelettes (€10).

GETTING THERE & AWAY

Assisi is on the Foligno–Terontola line with regular services to Perugia (€1.80, 25 minutes, hourly). You can change at Terontola for Florence (€9.40 to €15.20, 1¾ to 2¾ hours, 10 daily) and at Foligno for Rome (€9.40 to €16, two to 2½ hours, hourly).

To reach Assisi from Perugia by road, take the SS75, exit at Ospedalicchio and follow the signs.

GETTING AROUND

A shuttle bus (€0.80) operates every half-hour between Piazza Matteotti and the train station. Six car parks dot the city walls (they are connected to the centre by orange shuttle buses), or head for Via della Rocca where, for the price of a short but fairly steep walk, you should be able to find free parking.

For a taxi, dial ☎ 075 81 31 00.

GUBBIO

pop 32,804

While most of Umbria feels soft and rounded by the millennia, Gubbio is angular, sober and imposing. Perched along the steep slopes of Monte Ingino, the Gothic buildings wend their way up the hill towards Umbria's closest thing to an amusement park ride, its open-air funicular.

ORIENTATION

The immense traffic circle known as Piazza Quaranta Martiri, at the base of the hill, is where buses to the city terminate, and it also has a large car park. From here it is a short, if somewhat steep, walk up Via della Repubblica to the main square, Piazza Grande, also known as Piazza della Signoria. Or, you can take the lift from the Palazzo del Podestà to the Palazzo Ducale and the cathedral.

INFORMATION

Police station (☎ 075 927 37 70; Via Mazzatinti)

Tourist office (☎ 075 922 06 93; info@iat. gubbio.pg.it; www.gubbio-altochiascio.umbria 2000.it; Via Repubblica 2; ☺ 8am-2pm & 3-6pm Mon-Fri, 9am-1pm & 3-6pm Sat, 9.30am-12.30pm & 3-6pm Sun & holidays)

SIGHTS

PIAZZA GRANDE

The piazza is dominated above all by the 14th-century Palazzo dei Consoli, attributed to Gattapone. The building houses the Museo Civico (☎ 075 927 42 98; Piazza Grande; adult/concession incl gallery €4/2.50; ☺ 10am-1pm & 3-6pm Apr-Oct, 10am-1pm & 2-5pm Nov-Mar), which displays the

Eugubian Tablets, discovered in 1444. The seven bronze tablets are the main source for research into the ancient Umbrian language.

FUNIVIA COLLE ELETTO

Although the Basilica di Sant'Ubaldo – where you'll find the body of St Ubaldo, the 12th-century bishop of Gubbio – is a perfectly lovely church, the adventure is in the getting there. Take the Funivia Colle Eletto (☎ 075 922 11 99; adult/child return €5/4; ☺ 9am-8pm Jul-Aug, 9.30am or 10am-1.15pm & 2.30-5.30pm or 7pm Mar-Jun, Sep & Oct, 10am-1.15pm & 2.30-5pm Nov-Feb, closed Wed winter), where your first rule is to believe the man when he tells you to stand on the dot. He will then throw you into a moving metal contraption. The ride up is as frightening as it is utterly beautiful.

Just below the Funivia Colle Eletto is the Museo della Ceramica a Lustro e Torre Medioevale di Porta Romana (☎ 075 922 11 99; Via Dante 24; admission €2.50; ☺ 10.30am-1pm & 3.30-7pm). The *a lustro* ceramic style has its origins in 11th-century Muslim Spain. On the 2nd floor, ceramics from prehistoric times share space with medieval and Renaissance pieces.

VIA FEDERICO DA MONTEFELTRO

Walk up Via Ducale to a triumvirate of ancientness, the 13th-century pink cathedral (Via Federico da Montefeltro; donations welcome; ☺ 10am-5pm), with a fine 12th-century stained-glass window and a fresco attributed to Bernardino Pinturicchio. Opposite, the 15th-century Palazzo Ducale (☎ 075 927 58 72; Via Federico da Montefeltro; adult/concession €2/1; ☺ 9am-7.30pm Tue-Fri & Sun, 9am-10.30pm Sat) was built by the Duke of Montefeltro's family as a scaled-down version of their grand *palazzo* in Urbino. Next door is the Museo Diocesano (☎ 075 922 09 04; Via Federico da Montefeltro; ☺ 10am-7pm

FRANK WING

Riding the Funivia to Gubbio

summer, 10am-6pm Mon-Sat winter, 10am-6pm Sun & holidays all year), a winding homage to Gubbio's medieval history.

FOUNTAIN OF LUNATICS

In the western end of the medieval section is the 13th-century Palazzo del Bargello, the city's medieval police station and prison. In front of it is the Fontana dei Pazzi (Fountain of Lunatics), so-named because of a belief that if you walk around it three times, you will go mad.

FESTIVALS & EVENTS

The Corsa dei Ceri (Candles Race) is a centuries-old event held each year on 15 May to commemorate the city's patron saint, Sant'Ubaldo.

On the last Sunday in May, there's the annual **Palio della Balestra**, an archery competition involving medieval crossbows, in which Gubbio competes with its neighbour San Sepolcro.

SLEEPING & EATING

our pick **Residenza di Via Piccardi** (☎ 075 927 61 08; www.agriturismocolledelsole.it; Via Piccardi 12; s/d/apt incl breakfast €30/55/60; ⏰ closed Jan-Feb) Family owned, the characteristically medieval stone building has cosy rooms decorated in cheery florals with all the basic comforts.

Bosone Palace (☎ 075 922 06 88; www.mencarelligroup.com; Via XX Settembre 22; r €160-190, ste €184-230, all incl breakfast; P ✦) Fancy looking at a fresco during breakfast? How about staying in a room once frequented by Dante Alighieri?

our pick **Ristorante La Fornace di Mastro Giorgio** (☎ 075 922 18 36; Via Mastro Giorgio 2; meals €46; ⏰ Wed-Mon) Named after Gubbio's most famous medieval ceramicist (whose oven still graces one of the restaurant's ancient walls), Mastro Giorgio is our favourite place for a special occasion.

Taverna del Lupo (☎ 075 927 43 68; Via Ansidei 21; meals €42; ⏰ Tue-Sun) Most meals are locally produced in the surrounding Apennines, including its cheese, truffles and olive oil. Plan at least two hours for a meal.

GETTING THERE & AROUND

APM (☎ 800 51 21 41; www.apmperugia.it) buses run to Perugia (€4.40, one hour and 10 minutes, 10 daily). Walking is the best way to get around, but APM buses connect Piazza Quaranta Martiri with the funicular station and most main sights.

SPOLETO

pop 38,909

Spoleto was one of those sleepy Umbria hill towns until, in 1958, Italian-American composer Gian Carlo Menotti changed everything when he founded the Festival dei Due Mondi, known around the world now as, simply, the Spoleto Festival.

ORIENTATION

The old part of the city is about 1km south of the main train station.

INFORMATION

Police station (☎ 0743 2 32 41; 191 Via Marconi)

Tourist office (☎ 0743 23 89 20/1; www.visitspoleto.it; Piazza della Libertà 7; ⏰ 8.30am-1.30pm & 4-7pm Mon-Fri, 9.30am-12.30pm Sat & Sun Apr-Oct, 8.30am-1.30pm & 3.30-6.30pm Mon-Sat, 9.30am-12.30pm Sun Nov-Mar)

SIGHTS

ROMAN SPOLETO

Make your first stop the **Museo Archeologico** (☎ 0743 22 32 77; Via S Agata; adult/concession/child €4/2/free; ⏰ 8.30am-7.30pm), located on the western edge of Piazza della Libertà. Then step outside to view the mostly intact 1st-century **Teatro Romano** (Roman Theatre), which often hosts live performances during the summer. Check with the museum or the tourist office.

East of Piazza della Libertà, around the Piazza Fontana, are more Roman remains, including the **Arco di Druso e Germanico** (Arch of Drusus and Germanicus; sons of the Emperor Tiberius), which marks the entrance to the old forum. The excavated **Casa Romana** (Roman House; ☎ /fax 0743 23 42 50; Via di Visiale; adult/child €2.50/2; ⏰ 10am-6pm 15 Oct-31 Mar closed Tue, 10am-8pm daily 1 Apr-14 Oct) isn't Pompeii, but it gives visitors a peek into what a typical Roman house of the area would have looked like in the 1st century BC.

The **cathedral** (☎ 0743 4 43 07; Piazza Duomo; ⏰ 7.30am-12.30pm & 3-6pm summer,

RUSSELL MOUNTFORD

Rocca Albornoziana

7.30am-12.30pm & 3-5pm winter) was conse-crated way back in 1198, but later-day (17th century) remodelling included a striking Renaissance porch.

OTHER SIGHTS

The Rocca Albornoziana (☎ /fax 0743 22 30 55; Piazza Campello; adult/child incl tour €4/3; 🕙 10am-8pm summer & weekends, 10am-1pm & 3-6pm late Mar-Jun, Sep & Oct, 10-11.45am & 2-4.15pm Mon-Fri, 10am-4pm Sat & Sun Nov-Feb) dominates the city. It's a former papal for-tress that until 1982 was a high-security prison housing such notables as Pope John Paul II's attempted assassin, Mehmet Ali Agca. Reservations for tours are essen-tial as entry is only by guided tour.

An hour-long stroll or an all-day hike can be made along the Via del Ponte to the Ponte delle Torri, which was erected in the 14th century on the foundations of a Roman aqueduct. Cross the bridge and follow the lower path, Strada di Monteluco, to reach the Chiesa di San Pietro (☎ 0743 4 48 82; Località San Pietro; ad-mission free; 🕙 9.30-11am & 3.30-6.30pm). The 13th-century facade, the main attraction of the church, is liberally bedecked with sculpted animals.

To check out more modern artwork, head towards the Galleria D'Arte Moderna (☎ 0743 4 64 34; Palazzo Collicola; adult/child €4/3; 🕙 10.30am-1pm & 3-5.30pm 16 Oct-14 Mar, 10.30am-1pm & 3.30-7pm Wed-Mon 15 Mar-15 Oct) a homage to Spoleto's commit-ment to its ongoing artistic support.

FESTIVALS & EVENTS

The Italian-American composer Gian Carlo Menotti conceived the Festival dei Due Mondi (Festival of Two Worlds) in 1958. For details, phone ☎ 800 56 56 00 or look for further details and book tickets online at www.spoletofestival.it.

SLEEPING & EATING

Hotel Aurora (☎ 0743 22 03 15; www.hotel auroraspoleto.it; Via Apollinare 3; s/d/tr incl break-fast from €40/55/70; P 🖳) Just off Piazza della Libertà, the Aurora is very central and is fabulous value.

NORCIA, THE VALNERINA & MONTI SIBILLINI

Many consider this the most beautiful area in the region, and we heartily agree. It's near impossible to reach using public transport, but those with a car could easily fill an entire week here. Norcia produces the country's best salami – the word 'Norcineria' is synonymous with 'butcher' throughout all of Italy – and the surrounding area is one of the largest producers of the elusive black truffle. Indeed, truffle lovers, foodies and moochers should head to Norcia on the last weekend in February and the first weekend in March for the **Mostra Mercato del Tartufo Nero** (www.neronorcia.it).

One of the most scenic roads in all of Umbria is the SS209, where the medieval convent **Residenza San Pietro in Valle** (☎ 0744 78 01 29; www.sanpietroinvalle.com; SS209 Valnerina km20; s/d incl breakfast 98-109/129-139; ⊙ Easter-Oct; ℗) beckons travellers with its historical charm. Spend a few nights or simply stop by for lunch or dinner at its famed restaurant, **Il Cantico** (☎ 0744 78 00 05; meals €31; ⊙ mid-Mar-Oct), tucked under the abbey in a centuries-old subterranean stone vault.

Visit the **Casa del Parco** (☎ 0743 81 70 90; Via Solferino 22, Norcia; ⊙ 9.30am-12.30pm & 3-6pm Mon-Fri, 9.30am-12.30pm & 3.30-6.30pm Sat & Sun) for tourist information about the area, including the myriad walking trails that traverse the magical Monti Sibillini.

---

ourpick **Hotel Charleston** (☎ 0743 22 00 52; www.hotelcharleston.it; Piazza Collicola 10; s incl breakfast €40-75, d €52-135; ℗ ✗ ▯ 🛜) Named after Charleston, South Carolina (home of a sister Spoleto Festival), the hotel is covered in distinguished modern art and provides wine tastings or aperitifs every evening. Parking costs €10.

Pizzeria Zeppelin (☎ 0743 4 77 67; Corso Giuseppe Mazzini 81; pizzas & snacks €0.80-3; ⊙ 10.30am-9.30pm; ▯) A meeting point in town, where you can get a filling slice of pizza for less than €1, plus check your email (one hour costs €3).

Apollinaire (☎ 0743 22 32 56; Via S Agata 14; tasting menus incl veg €30-48; ⊙ Wed-Sun) California cuisine meets Umbrian tradition at this restaurant that somehow manages to figure out that squid-ink pasta does go with pesto and crayfish, and rabbit feels quite at home in a black olive sauce.

GETTING THERE & AROUND

From the train station, take city buses A, B or C for €0.80 (make sure the bus reads 'Centro').

Trains from the main station connect with Rome (€7.10 to €11.60, 1½ hours, hourly), Perugia (€3.70, one hour, nine daily – take care not to land on one of the €9.10 Eurostars).

ORVIETO

pop 20,955

Orvieto is placed precariously on a cliff made of tufaceous stone, a craggy porous limestone that seems imminently ready to crumble under the weight of the magnificent Gothic cathedral (or at least under all the people who come to see it).

ORIENTATION

Trains pull in at Orvieto Scalo and from here you can catch bus 1 up to the old town or board the funicular to take you up the steep hill to Piazza Cahen. Those with cars should head to the free parking behind the train station.

INFORMATION

Campo della Fiera tourist office (☎ 0763 30 23 78; bottom of funicular; ⏲ 9am-4pm) Buy funicular, bus and Carta Unica tickets here.

Police station (☎ 0763 39 21 1; Piazza Cahen)

Tourist office (☎ 0763 34 17 72; info@iat.or vieto.tr.it; Piazza Duomo 24; ⏲ 8.15am-1.50pm & 4-7pm Mon-Fri, 10am-1pm & 3-6pm Sat, Sun & holidays)

SIGHTS

Next to the cathedral is the **Museo dell' Opera del Duomo** (☎ 0763 34 24 77; Palazzo Soliano, Piazza Duomo; adult/concession €5/4; ⏲ 10am-1pm & 3-7pm Jul & Aug, 10am-6pm Apr-Jun, Sep & Oct, 10am-5pm Nov-Mar, closed Tue in winter), which houses a clutter of religious relics from the cathedral, as well as Etruscan antiquities and works by artists such as Simone Martini and the three Pisanos: Andrea, Nino and Giovanni.

The fantastic **Museo Claudio Faina e Civico** (☎ 0763 34 15 11; www.museofaina. it; Piazza Duomo 29; adult/concession €4.50/3; ⏲ 9.30am-6pm Apr-Sep, 10am-5pm Tue-Sun Oct-Mar), opposite the cathedral, houses one of Italy's most important collections of Etruscan archaeological artefacts, as well as some significant Greek ceramic works, mostly found near Piazza Cahen in tombs dating back to the 6th century BC.

Head northwest along Via del Duomo to Corso Cavour and the **Torre del Moro** (Moor's Tower; ☎ 0763 34 45 67; Corso Cavour 87; adult/concession €2.80/2; ⏲ 10am-8pm May-Aug, 10am-7pm Mar, Apr, Sep & Oct, 10.30am-1pm & 2.30-5pm Nov-Feb). Climb all 250 steps for sweeping views of the city. Back on ground level, continue west to

Piazza della Repubblica and to the 12th-century **Chiesa di Sant'Andrea** (Piazza della Repubblica; ⏲ 8.30am-12.30pm & 3.30-7.30pm) and its curious decagonal bell tower.

At the northwestern end of town is the **Chiesa di San Giovenale** (Piazza Giovenale; ⏲ 8am-12.30pm & 3.30-6pm), a church constructed in the year 1000. Its Romanesque-Gothic art and later frescoes from the medieval Orvieto school are an astounding contrast.

DIANA MAYFIELD
Facade detail, Duomo di Orvieto

⚓ ORVIETO CATHEDRAL

Little can prepare you for the visual feast that is this cathedral. Started in 1290, this remarkable edifice was originally planned in the Romanesque style but, as work proceeded and architects changed, Gothic features were incorporated into the structure.

Inside, Luca Signorelli's fresco cycle *The Last Judgement* shimmers with life. Look for it to the right of the altar in the **Cappella di San Brizio**.

Things you need to know: Orvieto Cathedral (☎ 0763 34 11 67; Piazza Duomo; ⏲ 7.30am-12.45pm year-round, 2.30-7.15pm Apr-Sep, 2.30-6.15pm Mar & Oct, 2.30-5.15pm Nov-Feb); Cappella di San Brizio (admission €3; ⏲ closed during Mass)

MAKING THE MOST OF YOUR EURO

Pick up an Orvieto Unica Card (adult/concession valid 1 yr €18/15). It entitles its owner to entrance to the nine main attractions (including the Cappella di San Brizio in the cathedral, Museo Claudio Faina e Civico, Orvieto Underground, Torre del Moro, Museo dell'Opera del Duomo and the Crocifisso del Tufo necropolis) and either five hours' free car parking at the Campo della Fiera car park next to the funicular, or a round trip on the funicular and city buses. It can be purchased at the Campo della Fiera car park, many of the attractions, the tourist office or the funicular car park.

FESTIVALS & EVENTS

Umbria Jazz Winter takes place from the end of December to early January, with a great feast and party on New Year's Eve.

SLEEPING & EATING

B&B La Magnolia (☎ 0763 34 28 08, mobile ☎ 338 902 74 00; www.bblamagnolia.it; Via del Duomo 29; r €65-75, apt for 2 people €75, for 3 people €90 & 4 people €105) In the absolute centre of Orvieto is this light-filled historic residence with six delightful rooms, an English-speaking owner and a large shared kitchen.

Hotel Maitani (☎ 0763 34 20 11; www.hotelmaitani.com; Via Lorenzo Maitani 5; s/d/ste €77/126/170, breakfast €10; P 🛜) Every detail is covered, from a travel-sized toothbrush and toothpaste in each room to chocolates (Perugino, of course) on your pillow. Several rooms have cathedral or countryside views.

Ristorante La Pergola (☎ 0763 34 30 65; Via dei Magoni 9b; meals €26; 🕑 Thu-Tue) The food at this restaurant is typically Umbrian – good and filling – but the real draw here is the flower-filled garden in the back.

Ristorante I Sette Consoli (☎ 0763 34 39 11; Piazza Sant'Angelo 1/a; meals €45; 🕑 Thu-Tue) With dishes like pan-fried pigeons with caramelized grapes, it's no wonder it's considered a leader in nouvelle cuisine. Reservations highly recommended for dinner.

GETTING THERE & AWAY

Main train connections include Rome (€7.10 to €15, 1¼ hours, hourly), Florence (€10.80 to €16.90, 1½ to 2½ hours, hourly), Perugia (€6.10 to €14.20, 1¼ to 2½ hours, at least every other hour). Buses depart from the station on Piazza Cahen, stopping at the train station. The city is on the A1.

GETTING AROUND

A century-old cable car connects Piazza Cahen with the train station, with carriages leaving every 10 minutes from 7.20am to 8.30pm Monday to Friday and every 15 minutes from 8am to 8pm Saturday and Sunday (€1.80 round trip, including the bus from Piazza Cahen to Piazza Duomo). Bus 1 also runs up to the old town from the train station (€0.95).

⬎ NAPLES, POMPEII & AMALFI

NAPLES, POMPEII & AMALFI

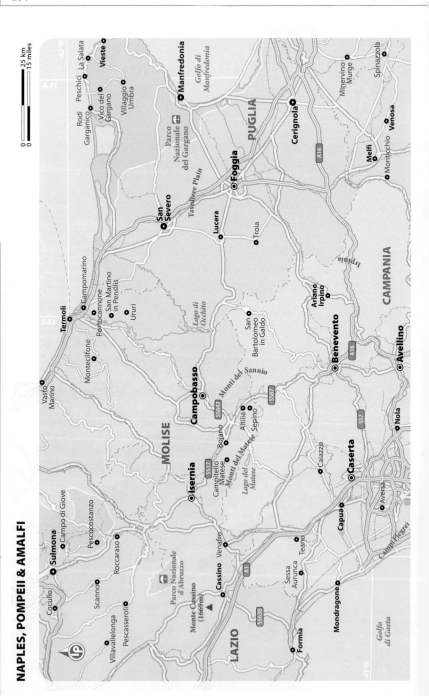

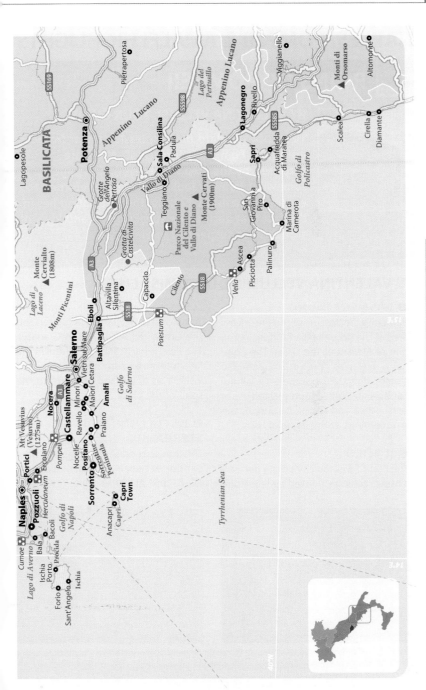

NAPLES, POMPEII & AMALFI HIGHLIGHTS

1 RUINS OF POMPEII

BY VALENTINA VELLUSI, TOUR GUIDE

The stock-standard first impression I hear from visitors to Pompeii is 'Amazing!'. Many are surprised by the area's vastness and assume a somewhat faraway look, as if they've returned to another dimension. For me, the fascination lies in the fact that each stone speaks of life and love, of stories since suspended in eternity.

↘ VALENTINA VELLUSI'S DON'T MISS LIST

❶ CASA DEL FAUNO

Pompeii's greatest mosaics were uncovered at The House of the Faun, including one of Alexander the Great. The original is in Naples' **Museo Archeologico Nazionale** (p279), but there's a faithful copy on site. With a sophisticated use of perspective and colour, it captures the last moments of the Battle of Issos.

❷ IL FORO

The Forum was the city's main piazza – a huge rectangle flanked by limestone columns. To the north stands the Tempio di Giove (Temple of Jupiter) and the Grano del Foro (Forum Granary). The Foro is particularly beautiful in the late afternoon sun, when exhausted visitors sit down and open up to the spirit of the place.

❸ LA FULLONICA DI STEPHANUS

This house represents Pompeii's final period, between the earthquake of AD 63 and AD 79 Vesuvius' eruption.

Clockwise from top: Crossing a Pompeii street; Pompeii ruins; Alexander the Great depicted in a mosaic from Casa del Fauno; Cast of a victim of the Vesuvius eruption;

Transformed into a wash house, you can still see the vats used to wash, rinse and dye clothes. Urine was commonly used to bleach clothes and assist in the dyeing process – opposite the entrance is the phallic-shaped spot where people were encouraged to relieve themselves to contribute to supplies.

❹ ORTO DEI FUGGIASCHI

The plaster casts here capture the final moments of two family groups trying to flee the eruption: the screams, the hopeless attempt to shield themselves from the falling lapilli (burning pumice stone). The very moment of their demise has been frozen forever.

THINGS YOU NEED TO KNOW

Guides Official guides outside the entrances allow visitors to form groups to cut the cost of a tour (total cost €100 to €120) **Bring** Comfortable shoes, water, a hat in summer and a windbreaker in cooler months **Photos** Flash photography damages the precious frescoes **See our author's review on p288**

NAPLES, POMPEII & AMALFI HIGHLIGHTS

↘ LOSE YOURSELF IN NAPLES

Packed with secret cloisters, cultish shrines and bellowing *pizzaioli* (pizza makers), Naples' **centro storico** (p275) is a bewitching blend of washing-strung streets harbouring fresco-laced churches, operatic staircases to heirloom trattorias, heaving market stalls, secret artisan studios and Greco-Roman ruins. Topping it off is Naples' inimitable, theatrical street life.

↘ BE INSPIRED BY RAVELLO

Perched high above the Amalfi Coast, petite **Ravello** (p294) is the stuff of romantic proposals and lingering, love-struck sighs. Wagner fell head over heels for the gardens of **Villa Rufolo** (p295), while former local Gore Vidal proclaimed the town's views the finest in the world. Add one of the country's best summer arts festivals, and you too will want to head up to find your muse.

4

⭧ WALK WITH THE GODS

The Amalfi Coast is more than piazzas and cobalt seas. Pushing up against the coast, the Lattari Mountains harbour some spectacular walking trails. The enticingly named **Path of the Gods** (boxed text, p294) is a meandering trek where ancient vineyards and verdant valleys meet some of the finest views this side of heaven.

5

⭧ FALL FOR THE GROTTA AZZURRA

As you're rowed into Capri's iconic **Grotta Azzurra** (p285), you may be tempted to pinch yourself. Don't. It's real, though we'd understand if you thought you were dreaming. Bathed in a glowing, electric-blue light, this celebrated sea cave is pure magic, seducing everyone from a Roman emperor to Grand Tour tourists.

6

⭧ EXPLORE TEMPLES IN PAESTUM

Long before the Romans swooped on southern Italy, the cultured Greeks set up camp, building civilised cities and adorning them with temples. Of those that survive, few match the majesty of the temples at **Paestum** (see boxed text, p296). These Unesco World Heritage wonders are a testament to Hellenic ingenuity.

2 & 4 GREG ELMS; 3 GLENN BEANLAND; 5 SHANIA SHEGEDYN; 6 HOLGER LEUE

2 Antique shop in Naples' centro storico (p275); 3 View from Ravello's Villa Rufolo (p295); 4 Praiano (p292), end of the Amalfi Coast's Path of the Gods; 5 Capri's Grotta Azzurra (p285); 6 One of Paestum's (p296) temples

NAPLES, POMPEII & AMALFI'S BEST...

TASTEBUD TREATS

- Epic Neapolitan pizzas at Pizzeria Gino Sorbillo (p282).
- Superlative seafood and a serenading owner at Naples' Dora (p282).
- Hardcore espresso at Caffè Mexico (p282), also in Naples.
- Fresh tuna and zesty anchovies in the tiny town of Cetara (p296).

PLACES TO WHISPER 'TI AMO'

- On the terrace at Ravello's Villa Rufolo (p295).
- Before the end of of the third act at Teatro San Carlo (p282) in Naples.
- Strolling the lush, elegant grounds of Naples' Certosa di San Martino (p279)
- Riding Capri's commanding seggiovia (p285)

BAROQUE BEAUTIES

- Chiesa e Chiostro di San Gregorio Armeno (p278) Interior design at its overstated best.
- Cappella Sansevero (p278) Home to an incomparable marble masterpiece.
- The Duomo, Naples (p275) Naples' cathedral boasts astounding cupola frescoes.
- Palazzo Reale, Caserta (boxed text, p281) Italy's 'Versailles' is a fitting epilogue to Naples' golden age.

NEAPOLITAN EXPERIENCES

- Noshing with lively locals at Nennella (p282).
- Late-night lounging with the boho crowd at Il Caffè Arabo (p282).
- An evening passeggiata (stroll) along the Lungomare (p280).
- Hunting for bargains at Mercato di Porta Nolana (p279).

LEFT: JEAN-BERNARD CARILLET; RIGHT: KARL BLACKWELL

Left: Fishmonger at Mercato di Porta Nolana (p279); Right: Coffee at Caffè Mexico (p282)

THINGS YOU NEED TO KNOW

⤳ VITAL STATISTICS

- **Population** 5.8 million
- **Area codes** ☎ Naples & Capri 081, Amalfi Coast 089
- **Best time to visit** April, May and mid-September to October

⤳ LOCALITIES IN A NUTSHELL

- **Naples** (p274) Gritty, contradictory and bewitching.
- **Capri** (p284) The Mediterranean's island *celebrant*, where sun and sea meet serious chic.
- **South of Naples** (p288) Urban sprawl meets Mt Vesuvius, incredible ruins and the Amalfi Coast gateway of Sorrento.
- **Amalfi Coast** (p291) Italy's most celebrated coastline.

⤳ ADVANCE PLANNING

- **Three months before** Book accommodation, especially if hitting Capri or the Amalfi Coast between June and mid-September.
- **One to two months before** Book tickets to the Ravello Festival (p295).
- **One week before** Reserve a table at Dora (p282) in Naples.

⤳ ONLINE RESOURCES

- **Naples Tourist Board** (www.inaples.it)
- **Pompeii Sites** (www.pompeiisites.org) Covers Pompeii and Herculaneum.
- **Capri** (www.capri.net) Listings, itineraries and ferry schedules.

- **Campania Trasporti** (www.campaniatrasporti.it) Comprehensive transport website (in Italian).

⤳ EMERGENCY NUMBERS

- **Fire** ☎ 115
- **Carabinieri/Police** ☎ 112/113
- **Ambulance** ☎ 118

⤳ GETTING AROUND

- **Air** International flights service Naples.
- **Walk** Ideal in Naples, smaller towns and along coastal trails.
- **Train** Naples is a major rail hub, with frequent connections between Naples, Pompeii, Ercolano (Herculaneum) and Sorrento.
- **Bus** Regular services between Naples and the Amalfi Coast.
- **Ferries & Hydrofoils** Regular summer services between Naples and the Bay islands, as well as to/from the Amalfi Coast and Salerno. Reduced winter services.

⤳ BE FOREWARNED

- **Museums** Many close Monday or Tuesday.
- **Restaurants** In Naples, many close in August. On Capri and the Amalfi Coast, many close November to March.
- **Accommodation** Many hotels close November to March on Capri and along the Amalfi Coast.
- **Pickpockets and bag snatchers** Particularly active in Naples.

NAPLES, POMPEII & AMALFI ITINERARIES

NEAPOLITAN BAROQUE Three Days

A magnet for the baroque's greatest artists, Campania's capital bursts at the seams with exuberant, over-the-top art and architecture.

Day one's highlights in **(1) Naples** might include the Chiesa del Gesù Nuovo (p278), whose barrel-vaulted interior features work by baroque greats Cosimo Fanzago, Luca Giordano and Francesco Solimena, and the outrageous Chiesa e Chiostro di San Gregorio Armeno (p278). Nearby, the Cappella Sansevero (p278) features a masterpiece of rococo sculpture, while the Duomo (p275) boasts breathtaking dome frescoes by Giovanni Lanfranco in the Cappella di San Gennaro. After lunch, catch a funicular up to the Certosa di San Martino (p279), whose church lays testament to Cosimo Fanzago's skill with marble.

You could easily spend most of day two feasting on masterpieces inside the Palazzo Reale di Capodimonte (p280), a baroque royal palace surrounded by parkland high above the city. Yet even this palace's grandiosity pales beside the monumental Palazzo Reale (see boxed text, p281) in **(2) Caserta** – your day trip for the last day.

STEP BACK IN TIME Five Days

Naples and Campania have no shortage of archaeological wonders, from Magna Graecian temples to Europe's most evocative Roman ruins.

In **(1) Naples**, begin your time travels with a Napoli Sotterranea tour (p281) before exploring ancient shops and laundries at the Chiesa e Scavi di San Lorenzo Maggiore (p278). On day two, tackle exquisite mosaics and ancient erotica at the Museo Archeologico Nazionale (p279) and spot early Christian frescoes in the Catacombe di San Gennaro.

The following day, take a day trip to **(2) Pompeii** (p288), where you'll need the best part of a morning to investigate the ancient streets, fossilised by ash from the nearby volcano. **(3) Mt Vesuvius** (p288) itself is easily reached from Pompeii by bus.

Combine ruins and sea breezes on day four with a trip to **(4) Capri** (p284), where you'll find kinky emperor Tiberius' Villa Jovis (p285). On day five, catch a train to Salerno, from where buses reach the breathtaking Greek temples of **(5) Paestum** (boxed text, p296).

COASTAL AFFAIR 10 Days

Neon-blue grottoes, fabled fishing villages and piercingly beautiful vistas: Campania isn't short on 'dream factor' appeal. For a slice of

seaside heaven without the hassle, avoid the high-season madness of July and August.

After two electrifying days in (1) Naples (p274), catch a ferry to VIP darling (2) Capri (p284), home to the spectacular Grotta Azzurra (p285) and your base for two days. Be seen on Capri Town's Piazzetta (p285) and ride a chairlift to Monte Solaro (p285) for mesmerising views.

On day five, catch a ferry across to (3) Sorrento (p290), from where buses run regularly to gorgeous (4) Positano (p291). Spend a couple of days exploring its boutique-laced lanes, hiring a boat to escape the hordes, or trekking along the Sentiero degli Dei (p293).

Continue east along the coast to (5) Amalfi (p293). Dive into its historic streets, explore its enlightening Museo della Carta (p293) then retreat to lofty (6) Ravello (p294), home to Villa Rufolo (p295) and its inspiring gardens. Stay overnight to soak up Ravello's aristocratic air, then hit the coast again in time for lunch in (7) Cetara (p296) and ceramics shopping in (8) Vietri sul Mare (p296). Bags and stomach full, push on to the handy transport hub of (9) Salerno (p296).

DISCOVER NAPLES, POMPEII & AMALFI

From hyperactive laneways to VIP islands and tumbling coastal villages, Campania's coastline is an intense, addictive brew of ancient legends, faded glamour, and gastronomic brilliance.

At its heart is big, boisterous Naples, a sprawling love-it-or-hate-it city theatrically set on a sweeping bay. Mt Vesuvius broods darkly in the background, a reminder of the fate it cruelly dealt Pompeii and Herculaneum 2000 years ago. Further down the coast, the magnificent temples at Paestum predate Roman times, testament to the region's Greek colonial past.

A short ferry ride from Naples, Capri is the most celebrated of Naples' three bay islands. A byword for Med chic, it's the darling of permatanned celebrities and starry eyed day-trippers, all after a fix of sun-soaked *dolce vita*.

For many, however, the region's crown jewel is the Amalfi Coast, a vertical world of plunging cliffs, cobalt seas, romantic hamlets and mesmerising views. Hidden to the world until 'discovered' in the mid-20th century, it's now one of Italy's must-see destinations.

NAPLES

pop 3.1 million

Italy's most misunderstood city is also one of its finest – an exhilarating mess of crumbling baroque churches, bellowing baristas and electrifying street life.

HISTORY

Originally called Parthenope in honour of the siren whose body had earlier washed up there (she drowned herself after failing to seduce Ulysses), it was eventually incorporated into a new city, Neapolis, founded by Greeks from Cumae (Cuma) in 474 BC. However, within 150 years it was in Roman hands, becoming something of a VIP resort favoured by emperors Pompey, Caesar and Tiberius.

After the fall of the Roman Empire, Naples became a duchy, originally under the Byzantines and later as an independent dukedom, until it was captured in 1139 by the Normans and absorbed into the Kingdom of the Two Sicilies. The Normans, in turn, were replaced by the German Swabians, whose charismatic leader Frederick II injected the city with new institutions, including its university.

In 1503 Naples was absorbed by Spain, which sent viceroys to rule as virtual dictators. Despite their heavy-handed rule, Naples flourished artistically and acquired much of its splendour.

ORIENTATION

The historic heart is centred on two parallel east–west roads: Via San Biagio dei Librai and its continuation Via Benedetto Croce (together these are known as Spaccanapoli); and, to the north, Via dei Tribunali.

On the seafront at the castle, Molo Beverello is the terminal for ferries to Capri, Ischia and Procida; next door, long-

MAKING THE MOST OF YOUR EURO

If you're planning to blitz the sights, the **Campania artecard** (☎ 800 600601; www.campaniartecard.it) is an excellent investment. A cumulative ticket that covers museum admission and transport, it comes in various forms. The tickets can be bought at train stations, newsagents, participating museums, via the internet or through the call centre.

centuries, including the addition of a late 19th-century neo-Gothic facade, have created a melange of styles and influences.

Halfway down the north aisle and beyond the 17th-century Basilica di Santa Restituta is the fascinating **archaeological zone** (admission €3; ⊙ 9am-noon & 4.30-7pm Mon-Sat, 9am-noon Sun).

A short walk to the north, **MADRE** (Museo d'Arte Contemporanea Donnaregina; ☎ 081 19 31 30 16; www.museomadre.it; Via Settembrini 79; admission €7, free Mon; ⊙ 10am-9pm Mon & Wed-Fri, to midnight Sat & Sun) has the city's best collection of contemporary art.

SPACCANAPOLI

Following the path of the ancient Roman *decumanus inferior* (minor road), **Via San Biagio dei Librai** (becoming

distance ferries sail to Sicily and beyond from the Stazione Marittima.

Follow the seafront west for the districts of Santa Lucia, Chiaia, Mergellina and Posillipo.

INFORMATION

Police station (☎ 081 794 11 11; Via Medina 75). To report a stolen car, call ☎ 113.
Post office (☎ 081 428 95 85; Piazza Matteotti; ⊙ 8am-1.30pm Mon-Fri, to 12.30pm Sat)

TOURIST INFORMATION

Piazza del Gesù Nuovo 7 (☎ 081 552 33 28; ⊙ 9am-7pm Mon-Sat, 9am-2pm Sun)
Stazione Centrale (☎ 081 26 87 79; ⊙ 9am-7pm Mon-Sat)
Via San Carlo 9 (☎ 081 40 23 94; ⊙ 9.30am-1.30pm & 2.30-6pm Mon-Sat, 9am-1.30pm Sun)

SIGHTS

CENTRO STORICO

DUOMO & AROUND

Naples' spiritual centrepiece, the **Duomo** (☎ 081 44 90 97; Via Duomo; ⊙ 8am-12.30pm & 4.30-7pm Mon-Sat, 8.30am-1pm & 5-7pm Sun) sits on the site of earlier churches, themselves preceded by a temple to the god Neptune. Copious nips and tucks over the

GREG ELMS

Centro Storico shoppers

NAPLES

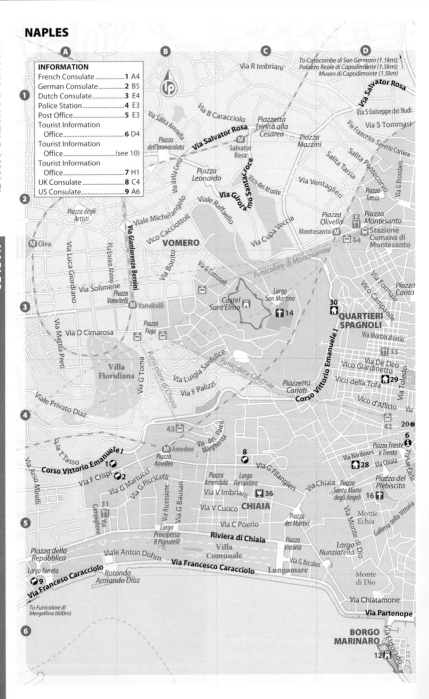

INFORMATION

French Consulate	**1** A4
German Consulate	**2** B5
Dutch Consulate	**3** E4
Police Station	**4** E3
Post Office	**5** E3
Tourist Information Office	**6** D4
Tourist Information Office	(see 10)
Tourist Information Office	**7** H1
UK Consulate	**8** C4
US Consulate	**9** A6

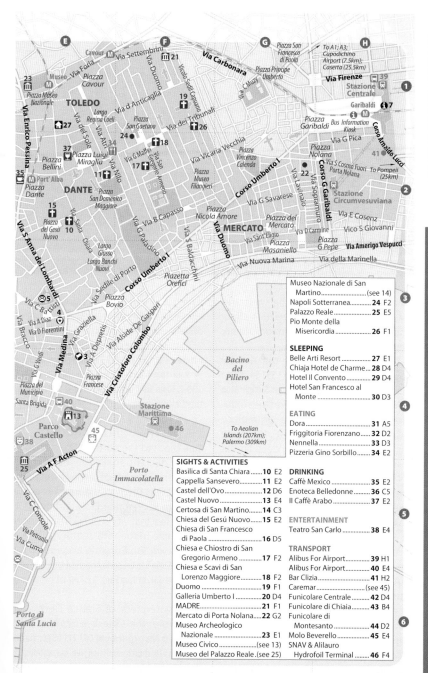

SIGHTS & ACTIVITIES

Basilica di Santa Chiara **10** E2
Cappella Sansevero **11** E2
Castel dell'Ovo **12** D6
Castel Nuovo **13** E4
Certosa di San Martino **14** C3
Chiesa del Gesú Nuovo **15** E2
Chiesa di San Francesco
  di Paola **16** D5
Chiesa e Chiostro di San
  Gregorio Armeno **17** F2
Chiesa e Scavi di San
  Lorenzo Maggiore **18** F2
Duomo **19** F1
Galleria Umberto I **20** D4
MADRE **21** F1
Mercato di Porta Nolana **22** G2
Museo Archeologico
  Nazionale **23** E1
Museo Civico ....(see 13)
Museo del Palazzo Reale .(see 25)

Museo Nazionale di San
  Martino ....(see 14)
Napoli Sotterranea **24** F2
Palazzo Reale **25** E5
Pio Monte della
  Misericordia **26** F1

SLEEPING

Belle Arti Resort **27** E1
Chiaja Hotel de Charme **28** D4
Hotel Il Convento **29** D4
Hotel San Francesco al
  Monte **30** D3

EATING

Dora **31** A5
Friggitoria Fiorenzano **32** D2
Nennella **33** D3
Pizzeria Gino Sorbillo **34** E2

DRINKING

Caffè Mexico **35** E2
Enoteca Belledonne **36** C5
Il Caffè Arabo **37** E2

ENTERTAINMENT

Teatro San Carlo **38** E4

TRANSPORT

Alibus For Airport **39** H1
Alibus For Airport **40** E4
Bar Clizia **41** H2
Caremar ....(see 45)
Funicolare Centrale **42** D4
Funicolare di Chiaia **43** B4
Funicolare di
  Montesanto **44** D2
Molo Beverello **45** E4
SNAV & Alilauro
  Hydrofoil Terminal **46** F4

JEAN-BERNARD CARILLET

Courtyard, Certosa di San Martino

Via Benedetto Croce to the west and Via Vicaria Vecchia to the east) is affectionately known as Spaccanapoli (Break Naples).

The simple exterior of the nearby **Cappella Sansevero** (☎ 081 551 84 70; Via de Sanctis 19; admission €6; ☉ 10am-5.40pm Mon & Wed-Sat, 10am-1.10pm Sun) belies the sumptuous sculpture inside. The centrepiece is *Cristo Velato* (Veiled Christ), Giuseppe Sanmartino's jaw-dropping depiction of Jesus covered by a veil so realistic that it's tempting to try and lift it. Downstairs are two meticulously preserved human arterial systems, testament to the bizarre obsession of alchemist Prince Raimondo di Sangro, the man who financed the chapel's 18th-century makeover.

PIAZZA DEL GESÙ NUOVO & AROUND

Characterised by the pyramid-shaped ashlar stones on its facade, whose carvings are said to be esoteric symbols, the **Chiesa del Gesù Nuovo** (☎ 081 551 86 13; Piazza del Gesù Nuovo; ☉ 7am-1pm & 4-7.30pm),

dating back to the 16th century, is considered one of the city's greatest examples of Renaissance architecture.

To the east, the Gothic **Basilica di Santa Chiara** (☎ 081 195 759 15; Via Benedetto Croce; ☉ 9am-1pm & 4.30-7.30pm Mon-Sat, 8am-1pm & 5.30-7.30pm Sun) is famous for its majolica-tiled cloisters.

VIA DEI TRIBUNALI & AROUND

One block to the north of Spaccanapoli is Via dei Tribunali, the *decumanus maior* (main road) of ancient Neapolis. Connecting the two, **Via San Gregorio Armeno** is celebrated for its shops selling *presepi* (nativity scenes). The street is also home to the 16th-century **Chiesa e Chiostro di San Gregorio Armeno** (☎ 081 420 63 85; Via San Gregorio Armeno 44; ☉ 9.30am-noon Mon-Sat, to 1pm Sun), a blast of bombastic baroque.

A masterpiece of French Gothic architecture, the **Chiesa e Scavi di San Lorenzo Maggiore** (☎ 081 211 08 60; Via dei Tribunali 316; church admission free, excavations €5; ☉ 9.30am-5.30pm Mon-Sat, to 1.30pm Sun) dates to the late 13th century. Beneath the complex are some remarkable *scavi* (excavations) of the original Graeco-Roman city.

To the east, the 17th-century **Pio Monte della Misericordia** (☎ 081 44 69 44; Via dei Tribunali 253; admission €5; ⊗ 9am-2pm Thu-Tue) is home to Caravaggio's masterpiece *Le sette opere di Misericordia* (The Seven Acts of Mercy), considered by many to be the single most important painting in Naples.

MERCATO DI PORTA NOLANA

Naples at its vociferous, gut-rumbling best, the **Mercato di Porta Nolana** (⊗ 8am-6pm Mon-Sat, to 2pm Sun) is a heady street market where bellowing fishmongers and green grocers collide with fragrant delis and bakeries, industrious Chinese traders and contraband cigarette stalls.

TOLEDO & QUARTIERI SPAGNOLI

The magnificent **Museo Archeologico Nazionale** (☎ 081 44 01 66; Piazza Museo Nazionale 19; admission €6.50; ⊗ 9am-7.30pm Wed-Mon) houses one of the world's finest collections of Graeco-Roman artefacts.

To avoid getting lost in its rambling galleries (numbered in Roman numerals), invest €7.50 in the green quick-guide *National Archaeological Museum of Naples* or, to concentrate on the highlights, €4 for an audioguide in English.

VOMERO

Visible from all over Naples, the stunning Certosa di San Martino is the one compelling reason to take the funicular (p283) up to Vomero (*vom*-e-ro), an area of spectacular views and Liberty mansions.

CERTOSA DI SAN MARTINO

The high point (quite literally) of Neapolitan baroque, this stunning charterhouse is home to the **Museo Nazionale di San Martino** (☎ 848 80 02 88; Largo San Martino 5; admission €6; ⊗ 8.30am-7.30pm Thu-Tue). Founded as a Carthusian monastery in the 14th century, the Certosa owes most of its present look to facelifts in the 16th and 17th centuries, the latter by baroque maestro Cosimo Fanzago.

SANTA LUCIA & CHIAIA
CASTEL NUOVO

Known to Neapolitans as the Maschio Angioino (Angevin Keep) and to everyone else as the **Castel Nuovo**, this crenellated 13th-century castle is a hulking Neapolitan landmark. Built as part of the city makeover that Charles I of Anjou launched in the late 13th century, it was erected in three years from 1279 and christened the Castrum Novum (New Castle) to distinguish it from the Castel dell'Ovo.

The walls of the **Cappella Palatina** were once graced by Giotto frescoes, of which only fragments remain on the splays of the Gothic windows. To the left of the cappella, the glass-floored **Sala dell'Armeria** (Armoury Hall) showcases Roman ruins discovered during restoration works on the **Sala dei Baroni** (Hall of the Barons) above.

Nowadays, they all form part of the **Museo Civico** (☎ 081 795 58 77; admission €5; ⊗ 9am-7pm Mon-Sat), spread across several halls on three floors.

PIAZZA DEL PLEBISCITO & AROUND

The undisputed star of Piazza del Plebiscito, Naples' largest square, is the **Chiesa di San Francesco di Paola** (☎ 081 74 51 33; ⊗ 8am-noon & 3.30-6pm Mon-Sat, 8am-1pm Sun), a later addition to the colonnade that formed the highlight of Joachim Murat's original piazza (1809).

Across Via San Carlo is one of the four entrances to the palatial glass atrium of the **Galleria Umberto I** shopping centre.

PALAZZO REALE

Flanking Piazza del Plebiscito, the rusty red **Palazzo Reale** (Royal Palace; ☎ 081 40 04 54; Piazza Trieste e Trento; admission €4; ☼ 9am-7pm Thu-Tue) was built around 1600. It was completely renovated in 1841 and suffered extensive damage during WWII.

From the courtyard, a monumental double staircase leads to the royal apartments, now home to the **Museo del Palazzo Reale** and its rich collection of baroque and neoclassical furnishings, porcelain, tapestries, statues and paintings.

THE LUNGOMARE

Marking the eastern end of the 2.5km *lungomare* (seafront), **Castel dell'Ovo** (☎ 081 240 00 55; Borgo Marinaro; admission free; ☼ 9am-6pm Mon-Fri, to 1pm Sat & Sun) sits atop the rocky Borgo Marinaro. Naples' oldest castle, it was built by the Normans in the

12th century and became a key fortress in the defence of Campania.

CAPODIMONTE
PALAZZO REALE DI CAPODIMONTE
On the northern edge of the city, this colossal palace took more than a century to build. It was originally intended as a hunting lodge for Charles VII of Bourbon, but as construction got under way in 1738, the plans kept on getting grander and grander. The result was the monumental *palazzo* that since 1759 has housed the art collection that Charles inherited from his mother Elisabetta Farnese.

The **Museo di Capodimonte** (☎ 081 749 91 11; Parco di Capodimonte; admission €7.50; ☼ 8.30am-7.30pm Thu-Tue, last entry 90min before closing) is spread over three floors and 160 rooms. You'll never see the whole place in one day, but a morning should be enough for an abridged best-of tour.

CATACOMBE DI SAN GENNARO
The oldest and most famous of Naples' ancient catacombs, the **Catacombe di San**

JEAN-BERNARD CARILLET

A Naples *pizzaiolo* (pizza maker)

Gennaro (☎ 081 741 10 71; Via di Capodimonte 13; admission €5; ⊗ 1hr tours 9am, 10am, 11am, noon, 2pm, 3pm Tue-Sat, 9am, 10am, 11pm, noon Sun), date to the 2nd century.

TOURS

Napoli Sotterranea (Underground Naples; ☎ 081 29 69 44; www.napolisotterranea.org; Piazza San Gaetano 68; tours €9.30; ⊗ tours noon, 2pm & 4pm Mon-Fri, extra tours 10am & 6pm Sat & Sun, 9pm Thu) runs 1½-hour guided tours of the city's underworld.

SLEEPING

Belle Arti Resort (☎ 081 557 10 62; www.belleartiresort.com; Via Santa Maria di Costantinopoli 27; s €65-99, d €80-160; ✗ 🖳) More boutique than B&B, this urbane hideaway melds contemporary cool with vintage touches. Four of the impeccable rooms (some as big as small suites) have ceiling frescoes, while all feature marble bathrooms and funky painted headboards.

Hotel Il Convento (☎ 081 40 39 77; www.hotelilconvento.com; Via Speranzella 137a; s €55-110, d €65-160; ✗ 🖳) Taking its name from the neighbouring convent, this lovely hotel is a soothing blend of antique Tuscan furniture, erudite book collections and candle-lit stairs.

Chiaja Hotel de Charme (☎ 081 41 55 55; www.hotelchiaia.it; Via Chiaia 216; s €95-105, d €99-145, superior d €140-165; ✗ 🖳 ⊗) The look is effortlessly noble – think gilt-framed portraits on pale lemon walls, opulent table lamps and heavy fabrics. Rooms facing Via Chiaia come with a jacuzzi.

ourpick Hotel San Francisco al Monte (☎ 081 423 91 11; www.hotelsanfrancesco.it; Corso Vittorio Emanuele I 328; s €160-190, d €170-225; 🅿 ✗ 🖳 ⊗ 🕿) The monks in this 16th-century monastery never had it as good as the hotel's pampered guests. The cells have been converted into stylish rooms, the ancient cloisters house an open-air

CUBOIMAGES SRL/ALAMY

Palazzo Reale, Caserta

⇘ IF YOU LIKE...

If you like **Palazzo Reale di Capodimonte** (p280), we think you'll like this even bigger palatial beauty:

- **Palazzo Reale** (☎ 0823 44 80 84; Via Douhet 22; admission €10; ⊗ palace 8.30am-7pm Wed-Mon, park 8.30am-7pm Jun-Aug, to 5.30pm May & Sep, to 6pm Apr, to 4.30pm Oct, to 4pm Mar, to 3.30pm Nov-Feb, last entry 1hr before closing Wed-Mon; train to Caserta) Known locally as the Reggia di Caserta, this vast palace is one of the greatest – and last – achievements of Italian baroque architecture. Follow a route through the art-filled royal apartments, before escaping into its lavish, landscaped park.

bar and the barrel-vaulted corridors are cool and atmospheric.

EATING

Pizza was created here and nowhere will you eat it better.

Friggitoria Fiorenzano (☎ 081 551 27 88; Piazza Montesanto; snacks from €1; ⊗ Mon-Sat) Here you'll find piles of crunchy deep-fried aubergines and artichokes, croquets filled with prosciutto and mozzarella, and a whole lot more.

GREG ELMS

Teatro San Carlo

Pizzeria Gino Sorbillo (☎ 081 44 66 43; Via dei Tribunali 32; pizzas from €3; ☽ Mon-Sat) Head in for gigantic, wood-fired perfection, best followed by a velvety *semifreddo;* the chocolate and *torroncino* (almond nougat) combo is divine.

Nennella (☎ 081 41 43 38; Vico Lungo Teatro 103-105; meals €10; ☽ Mon-Sat) Roguish waiters serve up uncomplicated gems like crispy fried sardines, lip-smacking *spaghetti con lupine* (spaghetti with lupin) or *insalatona nennella* (rocket, bresaola and radish salad).

Dora (☎ 081 68 05 19; Via Palasciano 30; meals €60; ☽ lunch Tue-Sun, dinner Mon-Sat) Don't be fooled by the humble front on a forlorn street: Dora's is one of Naples' finest fish restaurants. Reservations are essential.

DRINKING

The city's student and alternative drinking scene is around the piazzas and alleyways of the *centro storico*. For a chicer vibe, hit the cobbled lanes of upmarket Chiaia.

Caffè Mexico (☎ 081 549 93 30; Piazza Dante 86; ☽ 7am-8.30pm Mon-Sat) Make a beeline for Naples' best-loved espresso bar, where old-school baristas serve up the city's mightiest espresso.

Enoteca Belledonne (☎ 081 40 31 62; Vico Belledonne a Chiaia 18) One of the best-loved wine bars in Chiaia. All exposed brick walls and bottle-lined shelves, it's a stalwart of the area's well-trodden *aperitivo* (happy hour) circuit.

Il Caffè Arabo (☎ 081 442 06 07; Piazza Bellini) One of the squareside cafes on bohemian Piazza Bellini, this raffish spot is good for a laid-back wine (the cheapest on the piazza) and a Middle Eastern nibble or two.

ENTERTAINMENT

For cultural listings pick up the monthly *Qui Napoli* (at the tourist offices) or a local newspaper; for the latest club news check out the free minimag *Zero* (in Italian), available from many bars.

Teatro San Carlo (☎ 081 797 23 31; www.teatrosancarlo.it; Via San Carlo 98; ☽ box office

10am-7pm Tue-Sat) For opera, count on €50 for a place in the sixth tier and €100 for a seat in the stalls. If you're under 30 (and can prove it), last-minute tickets are available one hour before performances for €15.

GETTING THERE & AWAY
AIR
Capodichino airport (NAP; ☎ 081 789 62 59; www.gesac.it), 7km northeast of the city centre, is southern Italy's main airport, linking Naples with most Italian and several major European cities, as well as New York.

BOAT
In Naples, ferries and hydrofoils leave for Capri, Sorrento, Ischia, Procida and Forio from **Molo Beverello** in front of Castel Nuovo; hydrofoils for Capri, Ischia and Procida also sail from Mergellina; longer-distance ferries for Palermo, Cagliari, Milazzo, the Aeolian Islands (Isole Eolie) and Tunisia leave from the Stazione Marittima.

Qui Napoli lists timetables for Bay of Naples services. **Caremar** (☎ 081 551 38 82; www.caremar.it; Molo Beverello) runs services from Naples to Capri (ferry/hydrofoil €9.60/11, five daily), Ischia (€9.10/16, 13 daily) and Procida (€7/8.60, 12 daily); also between Sorrento and Capri (€7.50, four daily).

BUS
Regional bus services are operated by a number of companies, the most useful of which is **SITA** (☎ 199 730749; www.sitabus.it, in Italian), which runs buses from Naples to Pompeii (€2.40, 40 minutes, half-hourly), Sorrento (€3.30, one hour 20 minutes, twice daily), Positano (€3.30, two hours, twice daily), Amalfi (€3.30, two hours, twice daily) and Salerno (€3.30, one hour 10 minutes, every 25 minutes). You can buy SITA tickets and catch buses either from Porto Immacolatella, near Stazione Marittima, or from Via Galileo Ferraris, near Stazione Centrale; you can also buy tickets at **Bar Clizia** (Corso Arnaldo Lucci 173).

TRAIN
Most national trains arrive at or depart from Stazione Centrale or, underneath the main station, Stazione Garibaldi.

The **Stazione Circumvesuviana** (☎ 081 772 24 44; www.vesuviana.it; Corso Garibaldi), southwest of Stazione Centrale (follow the signs from the main concourse), operates trains to Sorrento (€3.30, 70 minutes) via Ercolano (€1.80, 20 minutes), Pompeii (€2.40, 40 minutes) and other towns along the coast.

GETTING AROUND
TO/FROM THE AIRPORT
By public transport you can take either the regular **ANM** (☎ 800 639525; www.anm.it, in Italian) bus 3S (€1.10, 45 minutes, every 15 minutes) from Piazza Garibaldi or the **Alibus** (☎ 800 5311705) airport shuttle (€3, 45 minutes, every 30mins) from Piazza del Municipio or Piazza Garibaldi.

Official taxi fares to the airport are as follows: €21 from a seafront hotel or from Mergellina hydrofoil terminal; €18 from Piazza del Municipio; and €14.50 from Stazione Centrale.

BUS
There's no central bus station, but most buses pass through Piazza Garibaldi, the city's chaotic transport hub.

FUNICULAR
Funicolare Centrale Ascends from Via Toledo to Piazza Fuga.
Funicolare di Chiaia From Via del Parco Margherita to Via Domenico Cimarosa.

TICKETS PLEASE

Tickets for public transport in Naples and the surrounding Campania region are managed by **Unico Campania** (www.unicocampania.it). Both the Unico Napoli 90-minute ticket (€1.10) and the 24-hour ticket (€3.10, reduced to €2.60 at weekends) offer unlimited travel by bus, tram, funicular, metro, Ferrovia Cumana or Circumflegrea. If you plan to do much travelling by **SITA** bus and/or **Circumvesuviana** train in the Bay of Naples and Amalfi Coast area, then save money by investing in a **Unico Costiera** card, available between April and October for durations of 45 minutes (€2), 90 minutes (€3), 24 hours (€6) or 72 hours (€15). Aside from the SITA buses, the 24- and 72-hour tickets also allow you to hop on the City Sightseeing tourist bus that travels between Amalfi and Ravello and Amalfi and Maiori. All Unico Campania tickets are sold at stations, ANM booths and tobacconists.

Funicolare di Montesanto From Piazza Montesanto to Via Raffaele Morghen.

METRO
Line 1 Runs north from Piazza Dante stopping at Museo (for Piazza Cavour and Line 2), Materdei, Salvator Rosa, Cilea, Piazza Vanvitelli, Piazza Medaglie D'Oro and seven stops beyond.
Line 2 Runs from Gianturco, just east of Stazione Centrale, with stops at Piazza Garibaldi (for Stazione Centrale), Piazza Cavour, Montesanto, Piazza Amedeo, Mergellina, Piazza Leopardi, Campi Flegrei, Cavaleggeri d'Aosta, Bagnoli and Pozzuoli.

TAXI
Official taxis are white and have meters. The minimum taxi fare is €4.75, of which €3.10 is the starting fare.

CAPRI
pop 13,100

A stark mass of limestone rock that rises sheerly through impossibly blue water, Capri (pronounced *ca*-pri) is the perfect microcosm of Mediterranean appeal –

a smooth cocktail of chichi piazzas and cool cafes, Roman ruins and rugged seascapes.

Already inhabited in the Palaeolithic age, Capri was briefly occupied by the Greeks before the Emperor Augustus made it his private playground and Tiberius retired here in AD 27.

ORIENTATION
All hydrofoils and ferries arrive at Marina Grande, the island's transport hub. From here the quickest way up to Capri Town is by funicular, but there are also buses and taxis.

INFORMATION
EMERGENCY
Police station (☎ 081 837 42 11; Via Roma 70, Capri Town)

POST
Post office Capri Town (☎ 081 978 52 11; Via Roma 50); Anacapri (☎ 081 837 10 15; Via de Tommaso 8)

TOURIST INFORMATION
Tourist office Marina Grande (☎ 081 837 06 34; ⏰ 9am-1pm & 3.30-6.45pm Jun-Sep, 9am-

3pm Mon-Sat Oct-May); Capri Town (☎ 081 837 06 86; Piazza Umberto I; ⏲ 8.30am-8.30pm Jun-Sep, 9am-1pm & 3.30-6.45pm Mon-Sat Oct-May); Anacapri (☎ 081 837 15 24; Via Orlandi 59; ⏲ 8.30am-8.30pm Jun-Sep, 9am-3pm Mon-Sat Oct-Dec & Mar-May)

SIGHTS
CAPRI TOWN
With its whitewashed stone buildings and tiny car-free streets, Capri Town evokes a film set. Central to the action is **Piazza Umberto I** (aka the Piazzetta), the showy, open-air salon where tanned tourists pay eye-watering prices to sip at one of four square-side cafes.

To the east of the Piazzetta, Via Vittorio Emanuele and its continuation, Via Serena, lead down to the picturesque **Certosa di San Giacomo** (Charterhouse of San Giacomo; ☎ 081 837 62 18; Viale Certosa 40; admission free; ⏲ 9am-2pm Tue-Sun), a 14th-century monastery with two cloisters and some fine 17th-century frescoes in the chapel.

From the *certosa*, Via Matteotti leads down to the colourful **Giardini di Augusto** (Gardens of Augustus; ⏲ dawn-dusk), founded by the Emperor Augustus.

VILLA JOVIS & AROUND
East of Capri Town, a comfortable 2km walk along Via Tiberio, is **Villa Jovis** (Jupiter's Villa; ☎ 081 837 06 34; Via Tiberio; admission €2; ⏲ 9am to 1hr before sunset), also known as the Palazzo di Tiberio. Standing 354m above sea level, this was the largest and most sumptuous of the island's 12 Roman villas and Tiberius' main Capri residence.

ANACAPRI & AROUND
Coming up from Capri Town, the bus deposits you in Piazza Vittoria, from where it's a short walk to **Villa San Michele di Axel Munthe** (☎ 081 837 14 01; Via Axel Munthe; admission €5; ⏲ 9am-6pm May-Sep, 10.30am-3.30pm Nov-Feb, 9.30am-4.30pm Mar, 9.30am-5pm Apr & Oct), the former home of self-aggrandising Swedish doctor Axel Munthe. If you are here between July and September, you may be able to catch one of the classical concerts that take place in the gardens.

From Piazza Vittoria, the **seggiovia** (chair lift; ☎ 081 837 14 28; single/return €5/6.50; ⏲ 9.30am-5pm Mar-Oct, 10.30am-3pm Nov-Feb) carries you to the summit of **Monte Solaro** (589m), Capri's highest point.

GROTTA AZZURRA
Capri's single most famous attraction is the **Grotta Azzurra** (Blue Grotto; admission €10.50; ⏲ 9am to 1hr before sunset), a stunning sea cave illuminated by an other-worldly blue light.

NAPLES, POMPEII & AMALFI

CAPRI

MUNICIPIO

TOD'S

GREG ELMS

Cafe in Piazza Umberto I

GREG ELMS

La Mortella gardens, Ischia

⇲ IF YOU LIKE...

If you like **Capri**, we think you'll like the Bay of Naples' other two island destinations:

- **Ischia** Natural spas, botanical gardens, hidden coves and exceptional dining define the Bay's largest island. Regular ferries and hydrofoils connect Ischia to Naples, Capri and Procida.
- **Procida** A soulful blend of hidden lemon groves, weathered fishermen and pastel-hued abodes, the Bay's smallest island was used to shoot scenes for Michael Radford's award-winning film *Il Postino*. Ferries and hydrofoils run to/from Naples, Ischia and Capri.

The easiest way to visit is to take a boat tour from Marina Grande. A return trip will cost €18.50, comprising a return motorboat to the cave, a rowing boat into the cave and admission fee; allow a good hour.

ACTIVITIES

Marina Grande is the hub of Capri's thriving water-sports business. **Sercomar** (☎ 081 837 87 81; www.caprisub.com; Via Colombo 64; ☯ closed Nov) offers various diving packages, costing from €100 for a single dive

to €350 for a four-session beginners course.

Capri also offers some memorable hiking.

SLEEPING

Hotel La Tosca (☎ 081 837 09 89; www.latosca hotel.com; Via Birago 5; s €45-80, d €65-125; ☯ Apr-Oct; ⚇) This charming one-star *pensione* is hidden away down a quiet back lane overlooking the Certosa di San Giacomo and the surrounding mountains. The rooms are plain but comfortable, with pine furniture, striped fabrics and large bathrooms.

OURPICK Hotel Villa Eva (☎ 081 837 15 49; www.villaeva.com; Via La Fabbrica 8; r €100-120; ☯ Mar-Oct; ▣ ⚇) Rooms at this gorgeous retreat, which is hidden among fruit trees, have unusual trappings, including a tiled fireplace, a brick well, domed ceilings and a boxed radio (room 6).

Relais Maresca (☎ 081 837 96 19; www.relaismaresca.it; Via Marina Grande 284; r incl breakfast €130-220; ☯ Mar-Dec; ⚇) A delightful four-star, this is the top choice in Marina Grande, with acres of gleaming ceramic in turquoise, blue and yellow. Minimum two-day stay on weekends in July and August.

Hotel Villa Sarah (☎ 081 837 06 89; www.villasarah.it; Via Tiberio 3a; s €90-140, d €140-210; ☯ Easter-Oct; ⚇ ⚇) Surrounded by its own fruit-producing gardens, it has 19 airy rooms, all decorated in classical local style with ceramic tiles and old-fashioned furniture. Best of all, though, is the small swimming pool.

EATING

Many restaurants, like the hotels, close over winter.

Trattoria Il Solitario (☎ 081 837 13 82; Via G Orlandi 96; pizzas from €4.50, meals €20; ☯ Apr-Oct) One of the better trattorias in the heart of Anacapri's touristy centre,

Il Solitario serves large helpings of tasty local food at honest prices.

Le Grottelle (☎ 081 837 57 19; Via Arco Naturale 13; meals €28; ⏲ Apr-Oct) About 150m from the Arco Naturale, Capri's most atmospheric place has two dining areas: one set in a cave, the other on a terrace perched above a wooded hillside sloping down to the sea.

La Pergola (☎ 081 837 74 12; Via Traversa Lo Palazzo 2; meals €30; ⏲ Thu-Tue Nov-Sep) The vine-shaded terrace and sea views provide a wonderful setting for La Pergola's delicious, innovative food.

Le Arcate (☎ 081 837 33 25; Via de Tommaso 24; meals €30) This is the restaurant that the locals recommend – and frequent. A real show-stopper is the *risotto con polpa di granchio, rughetta e scaglie di parmigiano* (risotto with crab meat, rocket and shavings of Parmesan).

DRINKING & ENTERTAINMENT

The main evening activity is styling up and hanging out, ideally on Capri Town's Piazzetta. Up in Anacapri, **Caffè Michelangelo** (Via Orlandi 138) is a laid-back cafe good for people-watching.

GETTING THERE & AWAY

See p283 for details of year-round ferries and hydrofoils to the island. In summer hydrofoils connect with Positano (€16.50, 30 to 40 minutes), Amalfi (€17), Salerno (€17.50) and Ischia (€15.50, one hour).

GETTING AROUND

Operating from Capri Town bus station, **Sippic** (☎ 081 837 04 20) runs regular buses to/from Marina Grande, Anacapri and Marina Piccola.

From Anacapri bus terminal, **Staiano Autotrasporti** (☎ 081 837 24 22; www.staiano-capri.com) buses serve the Grotta Azzurra and Faro.

Single tickets cost €1.40 on all routes, as does the funicular that links Marina Grande with Capri Town.

You can hire a scooter from **Ciro dei Motorini** (☎ 081 837 80 18; Via Marina Grande 55) at Marina Grande.

DAVID TOMLINSON

View from Belvedere di Tragara on Capri's southern coast

From Marina Grande, a **taxi** (☎ in Capri Town 081 837 05 43, in Anacapri 081 837 11 75) costs around €20 to Capri and €25 to Anacapri; from Capri to Anacapri costs about €15.

SOUTH OF NAPLES

MT VESUVIUS

Towering darkly over Naples and its environs, Mt Vesuvius (Vesuvio; 1281m) is the only active volcano on the European mainland.

From a car park at the summit, an 860m path leads up to the **crater** (admission, incl tour €6.50,; ⏰ 9am-6pm Jul & Aug, to 5pm Apr-Jun, to 4pm Mar & Oct, to 3pm Nov-Feb; ticket office closes 1hr before closing).

The easiest way to visit Vesuvius is to get a bus from Pompeii up to the crater car park. **Vesuviana Mobilità** (☎ 081 963 44 20) operates buses (€8.90 return, one hour, eight to 10 daily) from Piazza Anfiteatro.

By car, exit the A3 at Ercolano Portico and follow signs for the Parco Nazionale del Vesuvio.

POMPEII

pop 25,723

A stark reminder of the malign forces that lie deep inside Vesuvius, Pompeii (Pompei in Italian) is Europe's most compelling archaeological site. In AD 63, a massive earthquake hit the city, causing widespread damage and the evacuation of much of the 20,000-strong population. Many had not returned when Vesuvius blew its top on 24 August AD 79, burying the city under a layer of lapilli and killing some 2000 men, women and children.

ORIENTATION

The Circumvesuviana train drops you at Pompeii-Scavi-Villa dei Misteri station, beside the main Porta Marina entrance.

By car, signs direct you from the A3 to the *scavi* and car parks.

INFORMATION

Police station (☎ 081 856 35 11; Piazza Porta Marina Inferiore)

Tourist office Porta Marina (☎ 081 536 32 93; www.pompeiturismo.it; Piazza Porta Marina Inferiore 12; ⏰ 8am-3.30pm Mon-Fri, to 2pm Sat); Pompeii town (☎ 081 850 72 55; Via Sacra 1; ⏰ same as above)

SIGHTS

Of Pompeii's original 66 hectares, 44 have now been excavated. Of course, that doesn't mean that you'll have unhindered access to every inch of the Unesco World Heritage–listed **ruins** (☎ 081 857 53 47; entrances at Porta Marina & Piazza Anfiteatro; adult/EU national 18yr-25yr/EU national under 18yr & over 65yr €11/5.50/free; combined ticket incl Herculaneum, Oplontis, Stabiae & Boscoreale & 3 minor sites €20/10/ free; ⏰ 8.30am-7.30pm Apr-Oct, last entry 6pm, & 8.30am-5pm Nov-Mar, last entry 3.30pm); you'll come across areas cordoned off for no apparent reason, the odd stray dog and a noticeable lack of clear signs. Audioguides (€6.50) are a sensible investment, and a good guidebook will help – try the €8 *Pompeii* published by Electa Napoli.

The **Museo Vesuviano** (☎ 081 850 72 55; Via Bartolomeo 12; admission free; ⏰ 9am-1pm Mon-Fri), southeast of the excavations, contains an interesting array of artefacts.

TOURS

Reputable tour operators include: **Casting** (☎ 081 850 07 49), **Gata** (☎ 081 861 56 61) and **Promo Touring** (☎ 081 850 88 55). Expect to pay between €100 and €120 for a two-hour tour, whether you're alone or in a group.

SLEEPING & EATING

The ruins are best visited on a day trip from Naples, Sorrento or Salerno, and

GREG ELMS

Mosaic on display at Herculaneum

↘ ERCOLANO & HERCULANEUM

In contrast to modern Ercolano, classical Herculaneum was a peaceful fishing and port town of about 4000 inhabitants, and something of a resort for wealthy Romans and Campanians.

Destroyed by an earthquake in AD 63, it was completely submerged in the AD 79 eruption of Mt Vesuvius. However, as it was much closer to the volcano than Pompeii, it drowned in a 16m-thick sea of mud rather than in the lapilli (burning pumice stone) and ash that rained down on Pompeii. This essentially fossilised the town, ensuring that even delicate items, like furniture and clothing, were discovered remarkably well preserved.

From the Circumvesuviana Ercolano-Scavi station, it's a simple 500m downhill walk to the ruins – follow the signs for the *scavi* (excavations) down the main street, Via IV Novembre. From the site's main gateway on Corso Resina, head down the wide boulevard, where you'll find the new **ticket office** on the left. Covering 4.5 hectares, the ruins are easily visited in a morning.

The best way to get to Ercolano is by Circumvesuviana train (get off at Ercolano-Scavi). Trains run regularly to/from Naples (€1.80), Pompeii (€1.40) and Sorrento (€1.90).

By car take the A3 from Naples, exit at Ercolano Portico and follow the signs to car parks near the site's entrance.

Things you need to know: ☎ 081 732 43 38; Corso Resina 6; adult/EU national 18-25yr/EU national under 18yr & over 65yr €11/5.50/free, combined ticket incl Pompeii, Oplontis, Stabiae & Boscoreale €20/10/free; ☯ 8.30am-7.30pm Apr-Oct, to 5pm Nov-Mar, last entry 90 min before closing

Statue among Pompeii ruins

GUY MOBERLY

once the excavations close for the day, the area around the site becomes decidedly seedy.

Ristorante Lucullus (☎ 081 861 30 55; Via Plinio 129; pizzas from €6, meals €28; 10.30am-10pm Jun-Sep, 10.30am-4pm Tue-Sun Oct-May) Near the ruins and set back from the main road down an oleander-fringed drive, Lucullus does good pizzas as well as classic meat dishes and a delicious *penne Lucullus* (pasta with squash and prawns).

GETTING THERE & AWAY

Frequent Circumvesuviana trains run from Pompeii-Scavi-Villa dei Misteri station to Naples (€2.40, 40 minutes) and Sorrento (€1.90, 30 minutes).

To get here by car, take the A3 from Naples. Use the Pompeii exit and follow signs to Pompeii Scavi.

SORRENTO

Gateway between Naples and the Amalfi Coast, Sorrento is – on paper – a place to avoid: a package-holiday centre with few must-see sights, no beach to speak of and a glut of English-style pubs. In reality, it's a strangely appealing place, its laid-back southern Italian charm resisting all attempts to swamp it in souvenir tat.

If you do decide to linger a day or two, **Sorrento Tour** (www.sorrentotour.it) offers extensive online tourist and transport information, while the **tourist office** (☎ 081 807 40 33; Via Luigi De Maio 35; 8.45am 6.15pm Mon-Sat, plus 8.45am-12.45pm Sun Aug) in the Circolo dei Forestieri (Foreigners' Club) offers a hotel reservation service.

The town is the main jumping-off point for Capri and also has excellent ferry connections to Naples, Ischia and Amalfi coastal resorts. Frequent **Circumvesuviana** (☎ 081 772 24 44; www.vesuviana.it) trains run between Sorrento and Naples (€3.30), via Pompeii and Ercolano (€1.90 to each). **SITA** (☎ 199 73 07 49; www.sitabus.it, in Italian) buses to the Amalfi Coast leave from outside the Circumvesuviana train station. Buy tickets at the station bar or from shops bearing the blue SITA sign.

AMALFI COAST

Stretching about 50km along the southern side of the Sorrentine Peninsula, the Amalfi Coast (Costiera Amalfitana) is one of Europe's most breathtaking. Cliffs terraced with scented lemon groves sheer down into sparkling seas; sherbet-hued villas cling precariously to unforgiving slopes while sea and sky merge in one vast blue horizon.

GETTING THERE & AWAY

BOAT

Boat services to the Amalfi Coast towns are generally limited to the period between April and October.

BUS

Bus services along the coast are year-round and efficient. SITA (☎ 199 730749; www.sitabus.it, in Italian) operates a frequent service along the SS163 between Sorrento and Salerno (€3), via Amalfi.

CAR & MOTORCYCLE

If driving from the north, exit the A3 autostrada at Vietri sul Mare and follow the SS163 along the coast. From the south leave the A3 at Salerno and head for Vietri sul Mare and the SS163.

TRAIN

From Naples you can take either the Circumvesuviana to Sorrento or a Trenitalia train to Salerno, then continue along the Amalfi Coast, eastwards or westwards, by SITA bus.

POSITANO

pop 3872

The pearl in the pack, Positano is the coast's most photogenic and expensive town. An early visitor, John Steinbeck wrote in 1953: 'Positano bites deep. It is

a dream place that isn't quite real when you are there and becomes beckoningly real after you have gone.' More than 50 years on, his words still ring true.

ORIENTATION

Positano is split in two by a cliff bearing the Torre Trasita (tower). West of this is the smaller, less crowded Spiaggia del Fornillo beach and the less expensive side of town; east is Spiaggia Grande, backing up to the town centre.

INFORMATION

Police station (☎ 089 87 50 11; cnr Via Marconi & Viale Pasitea)

Tourist office (☎ 089 87 50 67; www.aziendaturismopositano.it; Via del Saracino 4; ☿ 8am-2pm & 3.30-8pm Mon-Sat Apr-Oct, 9am-3pm Mon-Fri Nov-Mar)

SIGHTS & ACTIVITIES

The lofty, ceramic-tiled dome of the **Chiesa di Santa Maria Assunta** (Piazza Flavio Gioia; ☿ 8am-noon & 3.30-7pm) is the town's most famous, and pretty much only, major sight.

It's a short hop to the nearby beach, **Spiaggia Grande**. Although it's no one's dream beach, with greyish sand covered by legions of brightly coloured umbrellas, the water's clean and the setting is memorable.

Operating out of a kiosk on Spiaggia Grande, **Blue Star** (☎ 089 81 18 89; www.bluestarpositano.it; Spiaggia Grande; ☿ 9am-8pm Easter-Nov) hires out small motorboats for around €55 per hour and also organises excursions to Capri and the Grotta dello Smeraldo.

Over on Spiaggia del Fornillo the **Centro Sub Costiera Amalfitana** (☎ 089 81 21 48; www.centrosub.it) runs dives (€60 for two hours) and lessons for adults and children.

Granita stand, Positano

DALLAS STRIBLEY

SLEEPING & EATING

Ask at the tourist office about rooms or apartments in private houses.

ourpick **Pensione Maria Luisa** (☎ 089 87 50 23; www.pensionemarialuisa.com; Via Fornillo 42; s €50, d €70-80; 🖳) The best budget choice in town, Maria Luisa's rooms and bathrooms have recently been updated with shiny new blue tiles and fittings; those with private terraces are well worth the extra €10 for the bay view.

Hotel Palazzo Murat (☎ 089 87 51 77; www.palazzomurat.it; Via dei Mulini 23; s €120-250, d €150-375; 🕸 🛜) This upmarket treat is housed in the *palazzo* that Gioacchino Murat, Napoleon's brother-in-law and one-time king of Naples, used as his summer residence. Beyond the lush gardens, rooms are traditional, with antiques, original oil paintings and plenty of lavish marble.

ourpick **Da Costantino** (☎ 089 87 57 38; Via Montepertuso; pizzas from €4, meals €20; 🕑 closed Wed) One of the few authentic places in town, it serves honest, down-to-earth Italian grub, including excellent pizzas and delicious *scialatielli* (ribboned pasta) served with aubergines, tomato and mozzarella.

Ristorante Bruno (☎ 089 87 53 92; Via Colombo 157; meals €28; 🕑 closed Thu lunch & Nov-Jan) Bag a table across the street and enjoy *the* view of Positano while swooning over house specialities like the antipasto of marinated fish with vegetables, orange and Parmesan; for a main course try the grilled fish with a wedge of local lemon.

GETTING THERE & AROUND

SITA runs frequent buses to/from Amalfi (€1.40, 40 to 50 minutes) and Sorrento (€1.40, 60 minutes).

Between April and October, daily ferries link Positano with Amalfi (€6, 15 minutes, six daily), Sorrento (€9, five daily), Salerno (€8.50, 70 minutes, five daily), Naples (€14, four daily) and Capri (€15.50, 45 minutes, five daily).

If your knees can handle them, there are dozens of narrow alleys and stairways that make walking relatively easy and joyously traffic-free. Otherwise, an orange bus follows the lower ring road every half hour, passing along Viale Pasitea, Via Colombo and Via Marconi.

AROUND POSITANO
NOCELLE & PRAIANO

A tiny, still-isolated mountain village, Nocelle (450m) affords some of the most spectacular views on the entire coast. The easiest way to get here is by local bus from Positano (€1.10, 30 minutes, 17 daily).

An ancient fishing village, **Praiano** has one of the coast's most popular beaches, Marina di Praia.

AMALFI

pop 5527

It is hard to grasp that pretty little Amalfi, with its sun-filled piazzas and small beach, was once a maritime superpower with a population of more than 70,000. Just around the headland, neighbouring Atrani is a picturesque tangle of white-washed alleys and arches centred on a lively, lived-in piazza and popular beach.

ORIENTATION

Buses and boats drop you off at Amalfi's main transport hub, Piazza Flavio Gioia. On the seafront Corso delle Repubbliche Marinare follows the coast eastwards, becoming Via Pantaleone Comite as it leads to the Saracen tower and Atrani.

INFORMATION

Tourist office (☎ 089 87 11 07; www.amalfitouristoffice.it; Corso delle Repubbliche Marinare 33; ☘ 8.30am-1.30pm & 3-5.15pm Mon-Fri, 8.30am-noon Sat Sep-Jun, 1.30pm & 3-7.15pm Mon-Fri, 8.30am-noon Sat Jul & Aug)

SIGHTS & ACTIVITIES

Dominating Piazza del Duomo, the iconic **Cattedrale di Sant'Andrea** (☎ 089 87 10 59; Piazza del Duomo; ☘ 9am-7pm Apr-Jun, 9am-9pm Jul-Sep, 9.30am-5.15pm Oct & Mar, 10am-1pm & 2.30-4.30pm Nov-Feb) makes an imposing sight at the top of its sweeping flight of stairs.

To the left of the cathedral's porch, the pint-sized **Chiostro del Paradiso** (☎ 089 87 13 24; admission €2.50; ☘ 9am-7pm Jun-Oct, 9am-1pm & 2.30-4.30pm Nov-May) was built in 1266 to house the tombs of Amalfi's prominent citizens.

In the town hall, the one-room **Museo Civico** (☎ 089 87 10 66; Piazza Municipio; admission free; ☘ 8.30am-1pm Mon-Fri) contains the *Tavole Amalfitane,* an ancient manuscript draft of Amalfi's maritime code, and other historical documents.

Amalfi's other museum of note is the fascinating **Museo della Carta** (Paper Museum; ☎ 089 830 45 61; www.museodellacarta.it; Via delle Cartiere; admission €4; ☘ 10am-6.30pm Apr–mid-Nov, 10am-3pm Tue, Wed & Fri-Sun mid-Nov–Mar).

NAPLES, POMPEII & AMALFI

AMALFI COAST

GREG ELMS

Amalfi's Piazzo del Duomo

Housed in a 13th-century paper mill (the oldest in Europe), it lovingly preserves the original paper presses, which are still in full working order, as you'll see during the 15-minute guided tour (in English).

FESTIVALS & EVENTS

The **Regatta of the Four Ancient Maritime Republics**, which rotates between Amalfi, Venice, Pisa and Genoa, is held on the first Sunday in June. Amalfi's turn comes round again in 2013.

SLEEPING & EATING

Hotel Centrale (☎ 089 87 26 08; www.hotelcentraleamalfi.it; Largo Duchi Piccolomini 1; s €60-120, d €70-140; P ✘ 🖥) This is one of the best-value hotels in Amalfi. The entrance is on a tiny little piazza in the *centro storico,* but many rooms actually overlook Piazza del Duomo (24 is a good choice).

Hotel Luna Convento (☎ 089 87 10 02; www.lunahotel.it; Via Pantaleone Comite 33; s €220-280, d €240-300; P ✘ 🛜 🛋) This

---

> ## WALK THE COAST
>
> Rising steeply from the coast, the densely wooded Lattari mountains provide some stunning walking opportunities.
>
> Probably the best-known walk, the 12km **Sentiero degli Dei** (Path of the Gods; 5½ to six hours) follows the steep, often rocky paths linking Positano to Praiano. Pick up a map of the walk at local tourist offices, included in a series of three excellent booklets containing the area's most popular hikes, including the equally famed (and lyrically named) **Via degli Incanti** (Trail of Charms) from Amalfi to Positano.

---

former convent was founded by St Francis in 1222. Rooms in the original building are in the former nuns cells, but there's nothing pokey about the bright tiles, balconies and sea views. The newer wing is equally beguiling, with religious frescoes over the bed (to stop any misbehaving).

Trattoria Il Mulino (☎ 089 87 22 23; Via delle Cartiere 36; pizzas €6, meals €20) The *scialatiella alla pescatore* (pasta ribbons with prawns, mussels, tomato and parsley) is fabulous.

Ristorante La Caravella (☎ 089 87 10 29; Via Matteo Camera 12; meals €60, tasting menu €75; ⏲ Wed-Mon Jan–mid-Nov) One of the few places in Amalfi where you pay for the food rather than the location, this celebrated dining den serves a mix of simple, soulful classics and regional grub with a nouvelle twist. The 15,000-label wine list is an aficionado's dream.

GETTING THERE & AWAY

SITA buses run from Piazza Flavio Gioia to Sorrento (€2.50, 1½ hours, at least 11 daily) via Positano (€1.40, 40 minutes), and also to Ravello (€1.10, 25 minutes, every 30 minutes), Salerno (€2.50, 1¼ hours, at least hourly) and Naples (€3.30, two to three hours depending on the route, twice daily).

Between April and October there are daily ferry sailings to Salerno (€6.50), Naples (€15), Positano (€8) and Capri (€15).

RAVELLO

pop 2500

Sitting high in the hills above Amalfi, refined Ravello is a polished town almost entirely dedicated to tourism. Most people visit on a day trip from Amalfi – a nerve-tingling 7km drive up the Valle del Dragone – although to best enjoy Ravello's romantic other-worldly atmosphere you'll need to stay overnight.

Villa Cimbrone

The **tourist office** (☎ 089 85 70 96; www. ravellotime.it; Via Roma 18bis; ⌚ 10am-8pm) has some general information on the town, plus walking maps.

SIGHTS & ACTIVITIES

Forming the eastern flank of Piazza del Duomo, the **cathedral** (⌚ 8.30am-1pm & 4.30-8pm) was originally built in 1086 but has since undergone various facelifts.

To the south of the cathedral, **Villa Rufolo** is famous for its fabulous 19th-century **gardens** (☎ 089 85 76 57; admission €6; ⌚ 9am-sunset). Commanding mesmerising views, they are packed with exotic colours, artistically crumbling towers and luxurious blooms.

Some way east of Piazza del Duomo, the 20th-century **Villa Cimbrone** (☎ 089 85 80 72; adult/under 12yr & over 65yr €6/3; ⌚ 9am-sunset) is worth seeking out for the vast views from the delightfully ramshackle gardens.

FESTIVALS & EVENTS

Between June and mid-September the **Ravello Festival** (☎ 089 85 83 60; www. ravellofestival.com) turns much of the town centre into a stage.

SLEEPING

Hotel Villa Amore (☎ /fax 089 85 71 35; Via dei Fusco 5; s €50-60, d €75-100; 🖳) This welcoming *pensione* is the best budget choice in town. The garden restaurant (meals about €20) is a further plus.

Hotel Toro (☎ /fax 089 85 72 11; www. hoteltoro.it; Via Roma 16; r €85-118; ⌚ Easter-Nov; 🐾 🛜) A hotel since the late 19th century, the Toro is just off Piazza del Duomo, within easy range of the clanging cathedral bells. The not-huge rooms are decked out in traditional style with terracotta or light-marble tiles and soothing cream furnishings.

EATING

Take Away Da Nino (☎ 089 858 62 49; Viale Parco della Rimembranza 41) Fast food Ravello-style – come here for takeaway pizza and crunchy fried nibbles.

Ristorante Pizzeria Vittoria (☎ 089 85 79 47; Via dei Rufolo 3; meals €30; ⌚ closed Nov–mid-Mar) Exceptional pizzas aside,

PERFECT PAESTUM

Easily reached from Salerno, Paestum's **ruins** (☎ 0828 81 10 23; admission €4, incl museum €6.50; ◷ 8.45am-7.45pm, last entry 7pm) include some of Magna Graecia's best-preserved temples, which are utterly unmissable. Founded in the 6th century BC by Greek settlers, Paestum (or Poseidonia as the city was originally called, in honour of Poseidon, the Greek god of the sea), was rediscovered in the late 18th century by road builders – who proceeded to plough their way right through the ruins.

To get there from Salerno, catch **CSTP** (☎ 089 48 70 01; www.cstp.it in Italian) bus 34 from Piazza della Concordia (€3.10, one hour 20 minutes, 12 daily).

Drivers can take the A3 from Salerno and exit for the SS18 at Battipaglia, or choose the more picturesque Litoranea, the minor road that hugs the coast.

this elegantly subdued restaurant serves a wonderful sliced octopus on green salad with olive oil and lemon, and an innovative chickpea and cod antipasto.

GETTING THERE & AWAY

SITA operates hourly buses from the eastern side of Piazza Flavio Gioia in Amalfi (€1.10, 25 minutes). By car, turn north about 2km east of Amalfi. Vehicles are not permitted in Ravello's town centre, but there's plenty of space in supervised car parks on the perimeter.

AMALFI TO SALERNO

Just beyond **Erchie** and its beautiful beach, **Cetara** is a picturesque tumble-down fishing village with a reputation as a gastronomic highlight. Tuna and ancho-vies are the local specialities, appearing in various guises at **Al Convento** (☎ 089 26 10 39; Piazza San Francesco 16; meals €20; ◷ closed Wed Oct–mid-May), a sterling seafood restaurant near the small harbour.

Shortly before Salerno, the road passes through **Vietri sul Mare**, the ceramics capital of Campania.

Salerno provides something of a reality check after the glut of postcard-pretty towns along the Amalfi Coast. As a major port and transport hub it's unlikely to detain you long, but if you do find yourself passing through en route to Paestum, don't despair. The *centro storico* is a vibrant area of medieval churches, neighbourhood trattorias and neon-lit wine bars, and the seafront is a fine place for an evening stroll.

SICILY & THE SOUTH

SICILY & THE SOUTH

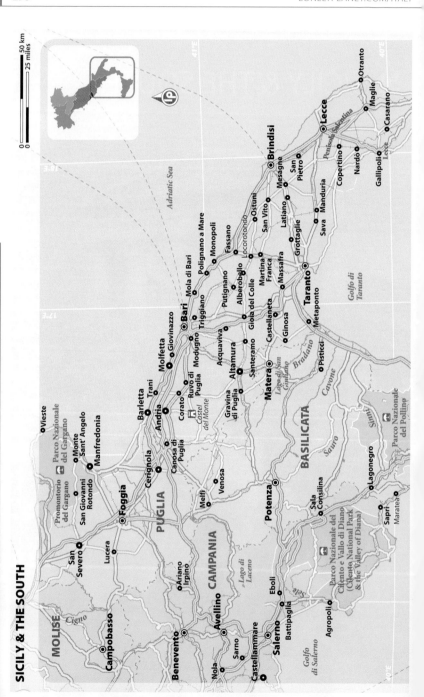

SICILY & THE SOUTH

MOLISE

Campobasso

Cigno

Benevento

CAMPANIA

Ariano
Irpino

Nola

Avellino

Sarno

Lago di
Laceno

Castellammare

Salerno

Battipaglia

Eboli

Golfo
di Salerno

Agropoli

Parco Nazionale del
Cilento e Vallo di Diano
(Cilento National Park
& the Valley of Diana)

MOLISE

San
Severo

Lucera

Foggia

Promontorio
del Gargano

Parco Nazionale
del Gargano

Vieste

**Monte
Sant' Angelo**

San Giovanni
Rotondo

Manfredonia

PUGLIA

Cerignola

Canosa di
Puglia

Melfi

Venosa

Barletta

Trani

Andria

Corato

Castel
del Monte

Ruvo di
Puglia

Gravina
di Puglia

Molfetta

Giovinazzo

Bari

Modugno

Triggiano

Acquaviva

Altamura

Santeramo

Potenza

Sala
Consilina

BASILICATA

Matera

Lago di San
Giuliano

Gioia del Colle

Castellaneta

Ginosa

Metaponto

Lagonegro

Sauro

Bradano

Cavone

Parco Nazionale
del Pollino

Sapri

Maratea

Putignano

Alberobello

Locorotondo

**Martina
Franca**

Massafra

Taranto

Golfo di
Taranto

Pisticci

Agri

Sinni

Polignano a Mare

Monopoli

Fassano

Ostuni

San Vito

Grottaglie

Sava

Mesagne

San
Pietro

Latiano

Manduria

Brindisi

Lecce

Penisola Salentina

Copertino

Nardò

Gallipoli

Lecce

Sava

Cavallino

Otranto

Maglie

Casarano

Adriatic Sea

50 km
25 miles

Parco Nazionale
del Pollino

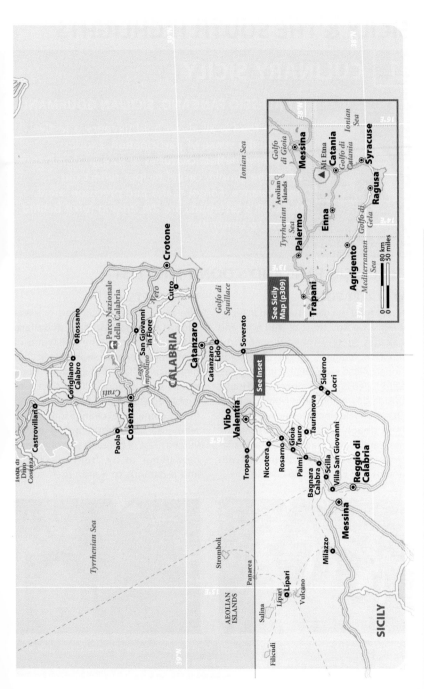

Crotone

Rossano

Parco Nazionale della Calabria

Corigliano Calabro

San Giovanni in Fiore

Cutro

Golfo di Squillace

CALABRIA

Catanzaro

Catanzaro Lido

Soverato

Lago Ampollino

Castrovillari

Cosenza

Crati

Paola

Vibo Valentia

See Inset

Siderno

Locri

Isola di Dino

Tyrrhenian Sea

Tropea

Nicotera

Rosarno

Gioia Tauro

Taurianova

Palmi

Bagnara Calabra

Scilla

Villa San Giovanni

Reggio di Calabria

Messina

Milazzo

Stromboli

Panarea

AEOLIAN ISLANDS

Salina

Lipari

Lipari

Vulcano

Filicudi

SICILY

Ionian Sea

See Sicily Map (p309)

Golfo di Gioia

Messina

Mt Etna

Catania

Golfo di Catania

Syracuse

Ionian Sea

Aeolian Islands

Tyrrhenian Sea

Palermo

Enna

Ragusa

Golfo di Gela

Trapani

Agrigento

Mediterranean Sea

0 — 80 km
0 — 50 miles

SICILY & THE SOUTH

SICILY & THE SOUTH HIGHLIGHTS

SICILY & THE SOUTH HIGHLIGHTS

1 CULINARY SICILY

BY ALESSIO FANGANO, SICILIAN GOURMAND

Sicilian food is all about bold flavours, a festive spirit and a sense of participation. Exotic ingredients reflect centuries of foreign domination, while the simple, casual recipes reflect our nonchalance. Forget scales and precision. Here, the cook's tastebuds are the driving force behind a meal to remember.

⬎ ALESSIO FANGANO'S DON'T MISS LIST

❶ STREET FOOD

Street food is a great tradition in Sicily, even if we buy most of it in bars and bakeries. King of the savouries is the *arancino,* a deep-fried rice cone traditionally filled with meat, tomato, peas, hardboiled egg and mozzarella. Hold it upside down and eat it from the base. Other snacks include *diavole* (deep-fried dough stuffed with prosciutto, mozzarella and black olives) and *sfincione* (a spongy, oily pizza topped with onions and caciocavallo cheese).

❷ MARKETS

The atmosphere at Sicilian markets such as Palermo's **Mercato di Ballarò** (p311) is electric – the bellowing of competing vendors shoots over your head like bullets in a crossfire. Here, rituals have changed little since our Arabic cousins ruled the island, and locals come to exchange gossip on who just died, got married or divorced. Best of all, each season brings new things to try, from wild herbs and asparagus to handpicked snails.

Clock-wise from top: Street-market stall, Lipari (p316); Gelati sign; Sicilian women preparing tomato sauce for bottling; Marsala wine barrels; Fruit at the Mercato di Ballarò (p311)

CLOCKWISE FROM TOP: IONAS KALTENBACH; DALLAS STRIBLEY; DALLAS STRIBLEY; BETHUNE CARMICHAEL; DALLAS STRIBLEY

Generally, the best periods are spring and autumn.

❸ SICILIAN WINES

Sicily is home to many interesting wines, amongst them the Nero d'Avola, a full-bodied, assertive red. For a fresh, sharp white, try Bianco d'Alcamo or Grecanico. Sweet Marsala wine is usually served after dessert or with *biscotti*. For something less sweet, try a *passito* (both the *passito di Pantelleria* and the Zibibbo are good bets). Indeed, a cold glass of a good *passito* is the perfect cap to the most Lucullan of meals.

❹ FESTIVE SPECIALITIES

During Carnevale, look out for *mpagnuccata* (unsweetened deep-fried dough tossed in soft caramel). The Festa di San Giuseppe on 19 March is famous for cigar-shaped *crispelle di riso* (citrus-scented rice fritters tossed in honey), and November's All Saints Day is time for *mostaccioli* and *moscardini* (spiced biscuits). One traditional type is called *ossa dei morti* (dead-people bones) because they're shaped like long thin logs and covered with dusting sugar.

⬊ THINGS YOU NEED TO KNOW

Best edible souvenirs Almonds *biscotti* and *pasta reale* (marzipan) fruits **Favourite summer treats** Almond granita, fruit-based gelato and Palermo watermelon jelly **Off the beaten track** Sicily's interior has some wonderful *agriturismi* serving simple dishes often made by the family's matriarch

SICILY & THE SOUTH HIGHLIGHTS

2

☑ ISLAND-HOP THE AEOLIANS

Easily accessible from the Sicilian mainland, the **Aeolian Islands** (p316) have all bases covered: nightly volcanic fireworks, therapeutic mud baths, vine-carpeted hillsides and whitewashed abodes owned by fashion royalty. A day in this sun-soaked wonderland might include snorkelling in turquoise seas, exploring secret grottoes and savouring regional treats like aubergine-stuffed fried ravioli.

3

☑ ROAM AROUND THE TEMPLES

Greek poet Pindar declared that the people of Akragas were 'built for eternity but feasted as if there were no tomorrow'. Centuries later, their once-glorious home-town makes up the **Valley of the Temples** (p329), one of Sicily's most celebrated ancient sites. Straddling a plateau overlooking the Mediterranean Sea, the ruins boast some of the largest, best-preserved Hellenic-era buildings outside Greece.

4

↘ GO GREEK IN SYRACUSE

In its Hellenic heyday, Syracuse (p324) was the West End or Broadway of Magna Graecia, pulling in top-billing playwrights like Aeschylus. Today it boasts the only school of classical Greek drama outside Athens, whose efforts are gloriously staged each May and June at the city's Teatro Greco (p326).

5

↘ SNOOZE IN A SASSI

It's a case of 'I don't think we're in Europe anymore, Toto' in the Basilicata's Matera (p338). The surreal, World Heritage–listed *sassi* (former cave dwellings) are the most extensive and complete troglodyte complex in the Mediterranean, not to mention one of the oldest human settlements on earth. They're also a fabulous place to slumber.

6

↘ LAP UP LECCE BAROQUE

There's baroque and then there's *barocco leccese,* the incredibly ornate, take-no-prisoners version that pimps the Puglian town of Lecce (p336). From crazy fruit-carved columns to grotesque frolicking gremlins, it's like one's wildest dreams carved into stone. Love it or loathe it, it's a jaw-dropping site and a hell of an urban show.

2 DALLAS STRIBLEY; 3 IONAS KALTENBACH; 4 CHRISTOPHER WOOD; 5 DOUGLAS SCOTT/ALAMY; 6 DAVID BORLAND

2 Harboured boats in the Aeolian Islands (p316); 3 Valley of the Temples (p329); 4 Syracuse's Teatro Greco (p326); 5 *Sassi* (p338) interior, Matera; 6 Facade detail, Basilica di Santa Croce (p336), Lecce

SICILY & THE SOUTH'S BEST...

SICILY & THE SOUTH

⬎ SPOTS FOR BEACHING AROUND

- **Vieste, Puglia** (p331) White sandy beaches and medieval side streets.
- **Maratea, Puglia** (p340) Basilicata's Amalfi Coast double.
- **Vulcano, Sicily** (p317) Dramatic black volcanic beaches.
- **Taormina, Sicily** (p319) A scenic summertime hotspot.

⬎ WORLD HERITAGE TREASURES

- **Matera, Basilicata** (p338) Surreal cave dwellings and an otherworldly vibe.
- **Aeolian Islands, Sicily** (p316) Lush hills, a glowing volcano and stunning turquoise waters.
- **Syracuse, Sicily** (p324) A city awash with Hellenic traces.
- **Castel del Monte, Puglia** (p332) An enigmatic castle with perfect dimensions.

⬎ WAYS TO GET A THRILL

- Taking a hike up grumpy **Mt Etna** (p323).
- Plunging into Palermo's exotic **Mercato di Ballarò** (p311).
- Watching Mother Nature's hissy fits on fiery **Stromboli** (p318).
- Hanging out with the well-dressed dead in Palermo's **Catacombe dei Cappuccini** (p311).

⬎ FOODIE EXPERIENCES

- Meeting your recommended (marzipan) fruit intake at Palermo's **Antico Caffè Spinnato** (p313).
- Dreaming of a seafood splurge at Catania's gut-rumbling fish market, **La Pescheria** (p322).
- Sampling salt-of-the earth Salentine dishes at Lecce's in-the-know **Cucina Casareccia** (p338).
- Devouring *cassata, torrone* (nougat) and lemon granita at Noto's **Caffè Sicilia** (p328).

SICILY & THE SOUTH

SICILY & THE SOUTH'S BEST...

LEFT: ANDREW BAIN; RIGHT: DALLAS STRIBLEY

Left: Gran Cratere, Vulcano (p317); Right: Beachside lounging at Taormina (p319)

THINGS YOU NEED TO KNOW

⤵ VITAL STATISTICS

- **Population** 12 million
- **Area codes** ☎ Palermo 091, Lecce 0832
- **Best time to visit** April to June, and September and October

⤵ LOCALITIES IN A NUTSHELL

- **Palermo** (p310) Mosaics and souklike markets.
- **Cefalù** (p314) Rugged slopes meet an Arab-Norman beach town.
- **Aeolian Islands** (p316) Volcanic activity and snorkel-friendly waters.
- **Ionian Coast** (p319) A cosmopolitan coast backed by a menacing volcano.
- **Southeastern Sicily** (p324) Magnificent ruins and baroque World Heritage towns.
- **Agrigento** (p328) Home to the Valley of the Temples.
- **Puglia** (p330) Topaz seas and sun-drenched rural landscapes.
- **Basilicata** (p338) Mountains, shadowy valleys and rock-hewn villages.

⤵ ADVANCE PLANNING

- **Three months before** Book accommodation, especially if travelling late June to mid-September.
- **One to two months before** Scan the Taormina Arte festival (p320) website for standout performances.
- **One week before** Make a reservation at Lecce's Cucina Casareccia (p338).

⤵ ONLINE RESOURCES

- **Sicilian Tourist Board** (www.regione.sicilia.it/turismo/web_turismo)
- **Best of Sicily** (www.bestofsicily.com)
- **Salentonet** (www.salentonet.it) Information on Puglia's Salento region (in Italian).
- **Ferula Viaggi** (www.materaturismo.it) Dedicated to Basilicata.

⤵ EMERGENCY NUMBERS

- **Fire** ☎ 115
- **Carabinieri/Police** ☎ 112/113
- **Ambulance** ☎ 118

⤵ GETTING AROUND

- **Air** European routes service Palermo, Catania and Bari.
- **Walk** In cities and towns, and up volcanoes.
- **Train** Efficient coastal Sicily service; slower to interior towns. Frequent connections between Bari and many Puglian towns.
- **Bus** Handy for towns not covered by trains.
- **Car** Outside the cities, an ideal way to explore.
- **Ferries & Hydrofoils** Regular summer services between Sicily and the Aeolian Islands. Reduced services rest of year. Frequent connections between Sicily and Calabria.

⤵ BE FOREWARNED

- **Museums** Many close Monday or Tuesday.
- **Pickpockets and bag snatchers** Particularly active in Palermo.

SICILY & THE SOUTH ITINERARIES

ARABESQUE SICILY Three Days

With its low domes and sweet-n-spicy flavours, Palermo's Arabic influence is as clear as Tunis is geographically close. The former jewel of the Arab-influenced Norman Empire, its halcyon days still shine through in Arab-Norman creations, both within and beyond its city limits.

Begin in raucous **(1) Palermo** (p310), its foreign flavours shining through in the Arabia-meets-Byzantine Cappella Palatina (p311). Arabesque tones also inform Palermo's whimsical cathedral (p311), the bijoux-domed Chiesa di San Cataldo (p310), and the souklike Mercato di Ballarò (p311). Start the next morning with *pane e pannelle* (chickpea fritters) – one of several Sicilian street foods – then bus it to Sicily's finest Arab-Norman creation, the mosaic-lined cathedral in **(2) Monreale** (p314).

Back in Palermo, catch an afternoon train to **(3) Cefalù** (p314), one of Sicily's favourite resort towns and home to the Arab-Norman beauty of Cefalù cathedral (p315).

SICILIAN DRAMA Five Days

Vicious volcanos, roaring markets and bombastically baroque buildings: Sicily is a tried-and-tested drama queen. Tension, passion and melodrama fuel the details, from the flourishing swirls of its buildings to the ominous threat of Mt Etna.

Plunge into pounding **(1) Catania** (p321), where black lava and white limestone contrast to bold effect on World Heritage–listed Piazza del Duomo (p321). Bolder still is La Pescheria (p322), Catania's hyper-theatrical fish market, though even it can't match the intensity of hiking up **(2) Mt Etna** (p323), your day-two day trip.

Spend days three and day four in civilised **(3) Syracuse** (p324), an easy train ride from Catania. Roam the ruins of the Parco Archaeologico della Neapolis (p326), whose Teatro Greco (Greek Theatre; p326) entertained ancient playwright Aeschylus. Tackle Sicily's finest archaeological collection at the Museo Archeologico Paolo Orsi (p326) and lose yourself in the tangled, atmospheric streets of Ortygia (p325).

On day five, catch a bus to World Heritage–listed **(4) Noto** (p327). Lauded as Sicily's top baroque town, its theatrical booty – which includes the wildly adorned Palazzo Villadorata (p328) – is deliciously paired with some of Italy's most celebrated ice cream.

ITALY'S AUTHENTIC SOUTHWEST Ten Days

Hotspots for savvy travellers, Puglia and Basilicata offer a refreshingly different take on Italy – one where topaz seas and sunburnt landscapes

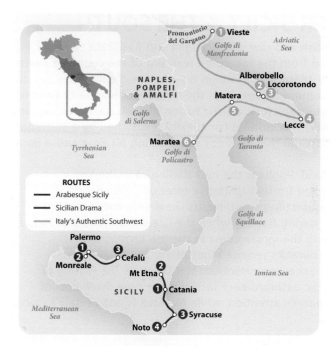

meet otherworldly abodes and paired-back Mediterranean flavours. Head in yourself and see why the southwest is quickly becoming Italy's worst-kept secret.

Consider a gentle start in laid-back (1) Vieste (p331), with its beautiful beaches, medieval backstreets and lush back garden of the Gargano National Park. Suitably relaxed, hit the road on day three to (2) Alberobello (p334), home to a dense neighbourhood of extraordinary cone-shaped *trulli* homes. Consider an overnight *trulli* stay before heading on to (3) Locorotondo (p335) to stroll (or cycle) around its gorgeous historic quarter. Pick up a few bottles of Puglian *vino* at Cantina del Cantina del Locorotondo (p335), then push on to dazzling (4) Lecce (p336), spending a couple of days soaking up the flamboyantly fronted baroque *palazzi* and churches, which include the Basilica di Santa Croce (p336).

Come day seven, nothing can prepare you for Basilicata's (5) Matera (p338) where the *sassi* (former cave dwellings) are a dramatic, albeit harrowing, reminder of the town's poverty-stricken past. Sample fried bread with local sweet peppers at Le Botteghe (p339) before tying up your road-trip adventure in refreshing (6) Maratea (p340), Basilicata's Amalfi Coast stand-in.

DISCOVER SICILY & THE SOUTH

Sun-soaked, raffish and raw, Sicily, Puglia and Basilicata serve a spicy Italy far removed from the measured restraint of the country's north.

After some 25 centuries of foreign domination, Sicilians are heir to an impressive cultural legacy, from the temples of Magna Graecia to a beguiling, if contradictory, artistic fusion of Arab craftsmanship and Norman austerity. This cultural complexity is matched by a startling diversity of landscape that includes smouldering Mt Etna and a tiara of island gems.

On the mainland, Puglia is the new darling of in-the-know travellers in. Famed for its superlative olive oil, idiosyncratic architecture and dazzling coastline, its Greek-influenced dialects reflect a legacy dating back to when the Greeks founded a string of settlements along the Ionian coast in the 8th century BC.

Next door, Basilicata's remote atmosphere and tremendous landscape is also drawing attention. Mel Gibson's *The Passion of Christ* brought the extraordinary *sassi* (former cave dwellings) of Matera to the world's attention, while Maratea is one of Italy's chicest seaside resorts.

SICILY

GETTING THERE & AWAY

AIR

An increasing number of airlines fly direct to Sicily – although most still require a transfer in Rome or Milan. Alitalia (www.alitalia.com) is the main carrier. See p313 for further details.

BOAT

Regular car and passenger ferries cross the strait between Villa San Giovanni (Calabria) and Messina. Hydrofoils connect Messina with Reggio di Calabria.

Sicily is also accessible by ferry from Naples, Genoa and Cagliari.

TRAIN

Direct trains run from Milan, Florence, Rome, Naples and Reggio di Calabria to Messina and on to Palermo, Catania and other provincial capitals – the trains are transported from the mainland by ferry from Villa San Giovanni.

GETTING AROUND

AIR

Palermo's Falcone-Borsellino is the hub airport for regular domestic flights to Pantelleria and Lampedusa. Local carriers Alitalia, Meridiana and Air One offer a good choice of flights.

BUS

Buses are usually faster if your destination involves travel through the island's interior; trains tend to be cheaper (and sometimes faster) on the major coastal routes.

CAR & MOTORCYCLE

There's no substitute for the freedom your own vehicle can give you, especially when getting to places not well served by public transport.

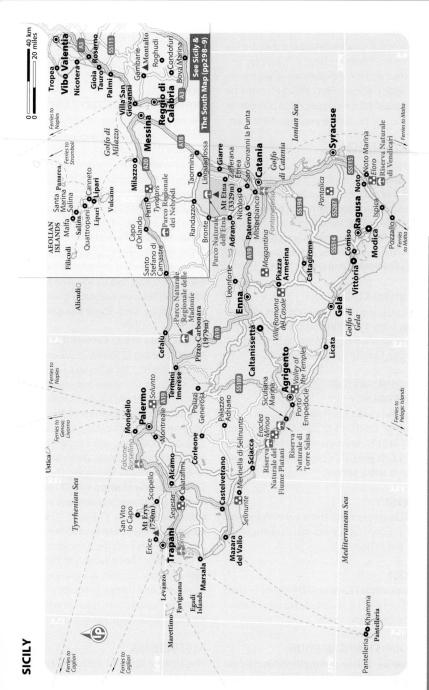

SICILY

SICILY & THE SOUTH

TRAIN

Trenitalia (www.trenitalia.com) is the partially privatised train system. IC trains are the fastest and most expensive, while the *regionale* is the slowest. All tickets must be validated via a machine on the platform or in the station before you board the train.

PALERMO

pop 663,200

Be prepared to explore: this giant treasure-trove of palaces, castles and churches has a unique architectural fusion of Byzantine, Arab, Norman, Renaissance and baroque gems. Palermitans themselves have inherited the intriguing looks and social rituals of their multicultural past.

ORIENTATION

Via Maqueda is the central street, extending from the train station in the south through Via Ruggero Settimo to the grand Piazza Castelnuovo in the north.

INFORMATION

EMERGENCY

Ambulance (☎ 091 30 66 41)
Police station (☎ theft & lost documents 091 21 01 11, foreigners office 091 656 91 11; Piazza della Vittoria) For reporting theft and other petty crimes.

MONEY

ATMs are plentiful. There are exchange offices open outside normal banking hours at the airport.

POST

Post office (Via Roma 322) Smaller branch offices can be found at the train station and on Piazza Verdi.

TOURIST INFORMATION

Tourist office (www.palermotourism.com) airport (☎ 091 59 16 98; ⏲ 8.30am-7.30pm Mon-Sat); city centre (☎ 091 605 83 51; Piazza Castelnuovo 34; ⏲ 8.30am-2pm & 2.30-6pm Mon-Fri)

SIGHTS

AROUND THE QUATTRO CANTI

The busy intersection of Corso Vittorio Emanuele and Via Maqueda marks the **Quattro Canti**, the centre of the oldest part of town, neatly dividing the historic nucleus into four manageable sectors.

Nearby Piazza Pretoria is the civic heart of Palermo, where a crowd of imposing churches and buildings surrounds the ornate **Fontana Pretoria**.

The twelfth-century **La Martorana** (Chiesa di Santa Maria dell'Ammiraglio; Piazza Bellini 3; ⏲ 8.30am-1pm & 3.30-5.30pm Mon-Sat, 8.30am-1pm Sun) was originally planned as a mosque by King Roger's Syrian Emir, George of Antioch.

The **Chiesa di San Cataldo** (Piazza Bellini 3; adult/concession €1.50/free; ⏲ 9.30am-1pm & 3.30-6pm Mon-Fri, 9.30am-1pm Sat & Sun) almost looks Eastern European but, disappointingly, is almost bare inside. Its main point of interest to visitors lies in the Arab-Norman style of its exterior: the dusky-pink bijoux domes, solid square shape, blind arcading and delicate tracery.

In nearby Piazza Sant'Anna, the **Civica Galleria d'Arte Moderna** (☎ 091 843 16 05; www.galleriadartemodernapalermo.it in Italian; adult/child/concession €7/free/5; ⏲ 9.30am-6.30pm Tue-Sun) is housed in a 15th-century *palazzo*, which became a convent in the 17th century. The collection of 19th- and 20th-century Sicilian art is beautifully displayed, and there's a regular program of modern exhibitions here, as well as an excellent bookshop and gift shop.

ALBERGHERIA

The austere fortified palace of **Palazzo dei Normanni** (Palazzo Reale; ☎ 091 705 70

Fontana Pretoria

RUSSELL MOUNTFORD

03; Piazza Indipendenza 1; adult/concession incl Cappella Palatina €7/5 Tue-Thu, €8.50/6.50 Fri-Mon; 8.30am-noon & 2-5pm Mon-Sat, 8.30am-12.30pm Sun) was once the centre of a magnificent medieval court.

On the middle level of the three-tiered loggia is Palermo's premier tourist attraction, the **Cappella Palatina** (☎ 091 705 47 49; 8.30am-noon & 2-5pm Mon-Sat, 8.30-9.45am & 11am-12.30pm Sun), designed by Roger II in 1130. Restoration work completed in July 2008 (after a small earthquake in 2002 damaged the structure) has returned the chapel to its original splendour, and the walls once again swarm with figures in glittering, dreamy gold.

Behind the splendours of the Palazzo dei Normanni lies the contrastingly shabby, run-down district of Albergheria, once inhabited by Norman court officials and now home to a growing number of immigrants who are attempting to revitalise its dusty backstreets. This is also the location of Palermo's busiest street market, the **Mercato di Ballarò**.

CAPO

Ambitious builders, the Normans gave birth to the extraordinary Arab-Norman style unique to Sicily. Chief among these is the **cathedral** (www.cattedrale.palermo.it; Corso Vittorio Emanuele; 7am-7pm), an extraordinary (and enormous) feast of geometric patterns, ziggurat crenulations, majolica cupolas and blind arches.

VUCCIRIA

North along Via Roma, the **Museo Archeologico Regionale** (☎ 091 611 68 05; Piazza Olivella 24; adult/concession €6/3; 8.30am-1.45pm & 3-6.45pm Tue-Fri, 8.30am-1.45pm Sat-Mon), in a Renaissance monastery, displays some of Sicily's most valuable Greek and Roman artefacts.

THE SUBURBS

The morbid **Catacombe dei Cappuccini** (☎ 091 652 41 56; Piazza Cappuccini; admission €3; 8.30am-1pm & 2.30-6pm) is home to the mummified bodies and skeletons of some 8000 Palermitans who died between the 17th and 19th centuries. From

PALERMO

0 _____ 500 m
0 _____ 0.25 miles

INFORMATION		Mercato di Ballarò................**11** B5	Trattoria Basile.......................**17** B4
British Consulate **1** B3		Museo	
Dutch Embassy **2** C3		Archeologico	**DRINKING**
Police Station.........................**3** B5		Regionale.........................**12** B4	Kursaal Kalhesa **18** D5
Post Office.............................**4** B4		Palazzo dei	
Tourist Office **5** A3		Normanni.........................**13** A5	**SHOPPING**
			Antico Caffè Spinnato...........**19** B3
SIGHTS & ACTIVITIES		**SLEEPING**	
Cappella Palatina.................(see 13)		Al Giardino	**TRANSPORT**
Cathedral................................**6** B5		dell'Alloro **14** C5	Auto Europa...........................**20** C3
Chiesa di San Cataldo **7** C5		Grand Hotel et des	Bus to Monreale.....................**21** A5
Civica Galleria d'Arte		Palmes **15** B3	Ferry Terminal **22** C3
Moderna **8** C5			Intercity Bus Station **23** C6
Fontana Pretoria.....................**9** B5		**EATING**	Main Bus Station....................**24** C5
La Martorana.........................**10** C5		Primavera..............................**16** B5	Rent a Scooter.......................**25** B3

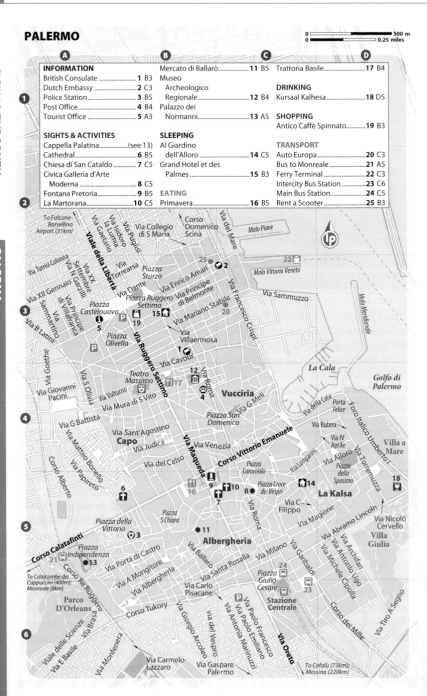

Piazza Independenza, it's a 15-minute walk; alternatively, catch any bus running along Via Cappuccini to the corner of Via Pindemonte, then walk one block to Piazza Cappuccini.

SLEEPING

Al Giardino dell'Alloro (☎ 091 617 69 04; www.giardinodellalloro.it; Vicolo San Carlo 8; s €40-45, d €80-90, tr €120; ❌ 💻 🛜) This bijou B&B with flat-screen TVs, free wi-fi and walls hung with artwork from the nearby academy is a very pleasant retreat.

Grand Hotel et des Palmes (☎ 091 602 81 11; www.hotel-despalmes.it; Via Roma 398; r €225-255; P ❌) The grand salons still impress with their chandeliers and gigantic mirrors, while the rooms are regally luxurious.

EATING & DRINKING

ourpick **Trattoria Basile** (☎ 091 33 56 28; Via Bara all'Olivella 76; meals €6-10; ⏲ noon-3.30pm Mon-Sat) This popular, unpretentious trattoria offers an unforgettable, authentic Palermitan eating experience.

Primavera (☎ 091 32 94 08; Piazza Bologni 4; meals €20-23; ⏲ closed Mon) This Slow Food-recommended spot doesn't look like much from the outside, but the kitchen prepares excellent, authentic Sicilian stalwarts at very reasonable prices, including *risotto funghi e noci* (mushroom-walnut risotto).

ourpick **Kursaal Kalhesa** (☎ 091 616 00 50; www.kursaalkalhesa.it in Italian; Foro Umberto I 21; ⏲ Tue-Sun noon-1.30am) Recline on plump sofas with silk cushions and sip a cocktail beneath the high vaulted ceilings.

SHOPPING

Palermo is famed for its elaborately sculptured marzipan sweets, the best of which are produced by **Antico Caffè Spinnato** (☎ 091 32 92 20; Via Principe di Belmonte 107-15; snacks €4-8).

RUSSELL MOUNTFORD

Cappella Palatina (p311)

GETTING THERE & AWAY

AIR

Falcone-Borsellino airport (PMO; ☎ 091 702 01 11; www.gesap.it) is at Punta Raisi, 31km west of Palermo.

BUS

The main intercity bus station is on Via Paolo Balsamo, one block east of the train station.

CAR & MOTORCYCLE

Car hire is not cheap in Sicily (a week can cost anything from €250 to €500). One dependable low-budget choice in downtown Palermo is **Auto Europa** (☎ 091 58 10 45; www.autoeuropa.it; Via Mariano Stabile 6a). Alternatively, the originally named **Rent a Scooter** (☎ 091 33 68 04; www.rentascooters.com; Via Amari 63) rents scooters starting at €27 per day.

Tiled pillar, Cattedrale di Monreale
BETHUNE CARMICHAEL

TRAIN

Regular trains leave for Messina (€11 to €24, 3½ hours), Agrigento (€7.60, 2¼ hours, 11 daily) and Cefalù (€4.70, one hour, 17 daily). There are also intercity trains to Reggio di Calabria, Naples and Rome.

GETTING AROUND

TO/FROM THE AIRPORT

Prestia e Comandè (☎ 091 58 63 51; www. prestiaecomande.it) runs a half-hourly bus service from the airport to the centre of town, with stops outside Teatro Politeama Garibaldi and at the train station. Tickets for the 50-minute journey cost €5.60 and are available on the bus.

There taxis outside the airport but the fare for the same trip is a crippling €50.

BUS

Tickets must be purchased before you get on the bus, available from *tabacchi* (tobacconists) or AMAT booths at major transfer points. They cost €1.20 for up to 90 minutes or €3.50 for a day.

MONREALE

Inspired by a vision of the Virgin and determined to outdo his grandfather Roger II, who was responsible for the cathedral in Cefalù and the Cappella Palatina in Palermo, William II set about building the **Cattedrale di Monreale** (☎ 091 640 44 03; Piazza del Duomo; ☸ cathedral 8am-6pm, treasury 9.30am-noon & 3.30-5.30pm), 8km southwest of Palermo. The resulting cathedral is considered the finest example of Norman architecture in Sicily, incorporating Norman, Arab, Byzantine and classical elements.

Outside the cathedral, the **cloister** (admission €6; ☸ 9am-7pm) is a tranquil courtyard with a tangible oriental feel.

To reach Monreale (€1.20, 35 minutes, half-hourly) take bus 389 from Piazza Indipendenza in Palermo.

CEFALÙ

pop 13,800

This popular holiday resort, wedged between a dramatic mountain peak and sweeping stretch of sand, comes with the lot: a great beach; a truly lovely historic centre with a grandiose cathedral; and winding medieval streets lined with restaurants, boutiques and small, intriguing shops.

INFORMATION

Police station (☎ 0921 42 11 04; Via Roma 15)
Tourist office (☎ 0921 42 10 50; strcefalu@ regione.sicilia.it; Corso Ruggero 77; ☸ 8am-8pm Mon-Sat)

SIGHTS

Looming over the town, the craggy mass of **La Rocca** appears a suitable home for the race of giants that are said to have been the first inhabitants of Sicily. An enormous staircase, the **Salita Saraceno**, winds up through three tiers of city walls, a 30-minute climb nearly to the summit.

Cefalù's **cathedral** (☎ 0921 92 20 21; Piazza del Duomo; ☼ 8am-5.30pm winter, to 7.30pm summer) is the final jewel in the Arab-Norman crown alongside the Cappella Palatina and Monreale.

SLEEPING

B&B Dolce Vita (☎ 0921 92 31 51; www.dolce vitabb.it; Via Bordonaro 8; r €60-120; ❌ ▣ ☍) This popular B&B has one of the loveliest terraces in town, complete with deck chairs overlooking the sea and a barbecue for those warm balmy evenings.

Hotel Kalura (☎ 0921 42 13 54; www.hotel -kalura.com; Via Vincenzo Cavallaro 13; d €90-150; P ❌ ☍) East of town on a rocky outcrop, this German-run, family-oriented hotel has its own pebbly beach, restaurant and fabulous pool.

EATING & DRINKING

Al Porticciolo (☎ 0921 92 19 81; Via Carlo Ortolani di Bordonaro 66; pizzas €5-11, meals €18-30; ☼ closed Wed Oct-Apr) If the indoor dining room looks empty, it's because everyone's piled out on the ample waterfront terrace, one of the prettiest in town.

Lo Scoglio Ubriaco (☎ 0921 42 33 70; Via Carlo Ortolani di Bordonaro 2; pizzas €5-10, meals €20-35; closed Tue) Dine in a five-star setting without shifting your credit card into overdrive at this elegant restaurant with its seaview terrace.

GETTING THERE & AWAY

The best way of getting to and from Cefalù is by train. The line links Cefalù with Palermo (€4.85, one hour, hourly) and virtually every other town on the coast.

From June to September, you can also get a hydrofoil from Cefalù to the Aeolian Islands with **Ustica Lines** (www.usticalines.it).

RUSSELL MOUNTFORD

Waterfront houses, Cefalù

AEOLIAN ISLANDS

Stunning cobalt sea, splendid beaches, some of Italy's best hiking, and an awe-inspiring volcanic landscape are just part of the appeal; the islands also have a fascinating human and mythological history that goes back several millennia.

GETTING THERE & AWAY

Siremar and NGI Traghetti (☎ 090 928 40 91; www.ngi-spa.it) both run car ferries from Milazzo to the islands; they're slightly cheaper, but slower and less regular than the summer hydrofoils.

Both Ustica Lines and Siremar run hydrofoils from Milazzo to Lipari (€15.80, one hour), and then on to the other islands.

In summer, Ustica Lines hydrofoils also connect Lipari with Messina (€22.90, 1½ to 3¾ hours, five daily), Reggio di Calabria (€23.90, two to three hours, five daily), Cefalù (€28.10, 3½ hours, one daily) and Palermo (€38.25, four hours, two daily).

LIPARI

pop 11,100 / elev 602m

Lipari is the best-equipped base for island-hopping, with plenty of places to stay, eat and drink.

INFORMATION

Corso Vittorio Emanuele is lined with ATMs. The other islands have fewer facilities so it's best to sort out your finances here before moving on.

Police (☎ 090 981 13 33; Via Guglielmo Marconi)
Siremar ticket office (Marina Lunga; per bag per 12/24 hrs €5/9; ⏱ 8am- 8pm) Left-luggage facilities.
Tourist office (☎ 090 988 00 95; www. aasteolie.191.it; Corso Vittorio Emanuele 202; ⏱ 9am-1pm & 4.30-7pm Mon-Fri year-round, 8.30am-1.30pm Sat & Sun Jul & Aug)

SIGHTS

After Barbarossa rampaged through the town in 1544, murdering most of the citizens, enslaving the women and desecrating the relics of St Bartholomew (charming fellow that he was), the Spaniards rebuilt and fortified Lipari with the citadel (⏱ 9am-7pm). Within these fortifications you will find the fabulous Museo Archeologico Eoliano (☎ 090 988 01 74; Castello di Lipari; admission €6; ⏱ 9am-1.30pm & 3-7pm), one of the very best museums in Sicily.

ACTIVITIES

Sunbathers and swimmers head for Canneto, a few kilometres north of Lipari town, to bask on the pebbly Spiaggia Bianca. Further north are the pumice mines of Pomiciazzo and Porticello, where there's another beach, Spiaggia della Papesca, dusted white by the fine pumice that gives the sea its limpid turquoise colour.

TOURS

You can take boat tours to the surrounding islands (€20 to €40), or arrange a day trip to hike up Stromboli with agencies throughout town, including Da Massimo/ Dolce Vita (☎ 090 981 30 86; www.damassimo.it; Via Maurolico 2) and Gruppo di Navigazione Regina (☎ 090 982 22 37; www.navigazionire gina.com; Via Maurolico).

SLEEPING

ourpick Diana Brown (☎ 090 981 25 84; www. dianabrown.it; Vico Himera 3; s €30-80, d €40-100; ✷) Tucked down a narrow alley, South African Diana has delightful rooms decorated in contemporary style with tile floors, abundant hot water, bright colours and welcome extras such as kettles and fridges. The optional breakfast costs €5 extra.

SICILY & THE SOUTH

SICILY

Bathers at Laghetto di Fanghi (p318)

HOLGER LEUE

Enzo Il Negro (☎ 090 981 31 63; www.enzoilnegro.altervista.org; Via Garibaldi 29; s €40-50, d €60-90; 🔀) This is a great low-season choice in the thick of the action.

EATING

La Cambusa (☎ 349 476 60 61; Via Garibaldi 72; meals €20; 🕑 lunch & dinner, closed Nov-Easter) This single-room, family-run place serves delicious, reasonably priced Aeolian food, from the *misto di capricci siciliani* (roast peppers, aubergine *caponata* and vegetables of the day) to the classic *fritto misto* (fried shrimp and squid).

Filippino (☎ 090 981 10 02; Piazza Municipio; meals €30-50; 🕑 closed Mon Oct-Mar) Celebrating its 100th anniversary in 2010, Filippino's is a mainstay of Lipari's culinary scene, its menu filled with traditional dishes named in Sicilian dialect such as *maccarruna i casa alla Filippino* (pasta with tomatoes, courgettes, basil, mint, mozzarella and ricotta) and close to 20 delectable desserts.

GETTING THERE & AROUND

Autobus Urso Guglielmo (☎ 090 981 12 62, 090 981 10 26; Via Cappuccini 9) runs frequent buses around the island from Marina Lunga (€1.50 to €1.90 depending on destination).

Roberto Foti (☎ 090 981 13 70; Via F Crispi 31) rents scooters (€20 to €35 per day) and cars (Fiat Uno €40 per day).

VULCANO

pop 720 / 500m

Vulcano is a memorable island, not least because of the vile smell of sulphurous gases. The island is worshipped by Italians for its therapeutic mud baths and hot springs, and its black beaches and weird steaming landscape make for an interesting day trip.

INFORMATION

Emergency doctor (☎ 090 985 22 20; Via Lentia)

Thermessa Turismo (☎ 090 985 22 30; Via Provinciale) Changes money and sells tickets for Ustica Lines hydrofoils.

ACTIVITIES

The top attraction is the trek up the **Fossa di Vulcano** (391m). Follow the signs south along Via Provinciale out of town.

If you want to hire a guide, contact **Gruppo Trekking Vulcano** (☎ 339 418 58 75). More sedentary volcano-watchers can visit the small museum administered by **Gruppo Nazionale Vulcanologia** (☎ 090 985 25 28; Porto Ponente; admission free; ⏰ 9.30am-12.30pm & 5-8pm Jun-Sep), which has displays about Vulcano and a video (in English, French and Italian) about Stromboli's last big eruption.

Mud-bath enthusiasts should head for the **Laghetto di Fanghi** (admission €2), a large mud pit of thick, smelly, sulphurous gloop that has long been considered an excellent treatment for arthritis, rheuma-tism and skin disorders. Afterwards you can hop into the water at the adjacent beach where *acquacalda* (hot springs) create a natural Jacuzzi effect.

SLEEPING

Vulcano is not a great place for an extended stay; the town is pretty soulless, the hotels are expensive and the mud baths really do smell.

La Giara (☎ 090 985 22 29; Via Provinciale 40; s €31-59, d €62-102; ⏰ Apr-Oct; ❄) A fine choice fronted by lemon trees in a quiet residential street.

Hotel Les Sables Noires (☎ 090 985 01 11; www.framon-hotels.com; Porto Ponente; s €95-170, d €150-250; ⏰ May-Sep; ❄ ▨) Vulcano's premier hotel has a fabulous pool backed by the volcano's looming presence, and a restaurant-bar with fine views of the island's best black-sand beach.

EATING

La Forgia Maurizio (☎ 339 137 91 07; Via Provinciale 45; meals €25-30) The owner of this devilishly good restaurant spent 20 winters in Goa, India; eastern influences sneak into a menu of Sicilian specialities, all prepared and presented with flair. The tasting menu is an excellent deal at €25 including wine and dessert.

GETTING THERE & AROUND

Vulcano is an intermediate stop between Milazzo and Lipari and a good number of vessels go both ways throughout the day.

Scooters (per day €15 to €45), bicycles (€5 to €8) and small motorised cars (€35 to €70) can be rented from **Sprint** (☎ 090 985 22 08) or **Da Paolo** (☎ 090 985 21 12), both well signposted near the hydrofoil dock.

STROMBOLI

pop 400 / elev 924m

Stromboli's perfect triangle of a volcano juts dramatically out of the sea. It's the

DALLAS STRIBLEY

Stromboli

only island whose smouldering cone is permanently active, thus attracting experts and amateurs alike, like moths to a massive flame. Boats arrive at Scari/San Vincenzo, downhill from the town.

INFORMATION

Emergency doctor (☎ 090 98 60 97; Via Vittorio Emanuele)

Police station (☎ 090 98 60 21; Via Roma) Just on the left as you walk up Via Roma.

Volcanological Information Centre (Porto Scari; ☻ 10.30am-1pm & 5-7.30pm Mon-Sat)

ACTIVITIES

Note that you're legally required to hire a guide if you're considering climbing the volcano.

The path to the summit (920m) is a demanding five- to six-hour trek (rest stops every 40 minutes), but the atmosphere is charged and you will be rewarded with tremendous views of the **Sciara del Fuoco** (Trail of Fire) and the constantly smoking crater.

Totem Trekking (☎ 090 986 57 52; Piazza San Vincenzo 4) hires out all the necessary equipment, including headlamps (€3), trekking boots (€6) and windbreakers (€5).

TOURS

Magmatrek (☎ 090 986 57 68; www.mag matrek.it; Via Vittorio Emanuele) has experienced, multilingual vulcanological guides that lead regular afternoon treks (maximum group size 20) up to the crater every afternoon (per person €28).

Società Navigazione Pippo (☎ 090 98 61 35) and **Antonio Caccetta** (☎ 090 98 60 23) are among the numerous boat companies at Porto Scari offering daytime circuits of the island (€20) and sunset excursions to watch the Sciara del Fuoco from the sea (€15 per person).

SLEEPING & EATING

Casa del Sole (☎ 090 98 63 00; casa-del-sole@ tiscali.it; Via Domenico Cincotta; dm €25-30, s €30-50, d €60-100) This wonderful Aeolian-style guesthouse, painted in warm colours, is only 100m from a sweet black-sand beach.

Locanda del Barbablù (☎ 090 98 61 18; www.barbablu.it; Via Vittorio Emanuele 17; d €110-240; ☻ Apr-Oct) Six sumptuous rooms each have private terrace, period furniture and the contemporary luxury of pure silk coverlets. The universally acclaimed restaurant is the island's classiest, serving a nightly four-course tasting menu of traditional Sicilian dishes for €50 (drinks excluded).

L'Osservatorio (☎ 090 98 63 60; pizzas €7-10; ☻ lunch & dinner) Sure, you could eat a pizza in town, but come on – you're on Stromboli! Make the long uphill trek to this pizzeria and you'll be rewarded with exceptional volcano views, best after sundown.

GETTING THERE & AWAY

It takes four hours to reach the island from Lipari by ferry, or 1½ to two hours by hydrofoil.

IONIAN COAST
TAORMINA

pop 11,000 / elev 204m

The capital of Byzantine Sicily in the 9th century, Taormina is an almost perfectly preserved medieval town, and if you can tear yourself away from the shopping and sunbathing, it has a wealth of small but perfect tourist sites.

ORIENTATION

The train station (Taormina-Giardini) is at the bottom of Monte Tauro. From there you'll need to hop on an Interbus coach (€1.50) to get to the bus station on Via Luigi Pirandello. A short walk uphill from the bus station brings you to Corso Umberto I, which traverses the length of the medieval town and connects its two historic town gates, Porta Messina and Porta Catania.

INFORMATION

Police station (☎ 0942 61 11 11; Corso Umberto I 219)
Post office (Piazza Sant'Antonio Abate)
Tourist office (☎ 0942 2 32 43; www.gate2taormina.com; Palazzo Corvaja, Corso Umberto I; ⏲ 8.30am-2pm Mon-Fri & 4-7pm Mon-Thu)

SIGHTS

One of the chief delights of Taormina is wandering along its medieval main avenue, and browsing among the antique and craft shops, delis and designer boutiques. If you're seeking more tranquillity, check out **Teatro Greco** (☎ 0942 2 32 20; Via Teatro Greco; adult/concession €6/3; ⏲ 9am-7pm Apr-Oct, 9am-4.30pm Nov-Mar), Taormina's premier attraction. This perfect horseshoe-shaped theatre, suspended between sea and sky, was built in the 3rd century BC and is the second largest in Sicily (after Syracuse), and the most dramatically situated Greek theatre in the world.

On the western side of Piazza IX Aprile is the 12th-century clock tower, **Torre dell'Orologio**, which leads you through into the Borgo Medievale, the oldest quarter of the town.

ACTIVITIES

Many visitors to Taormina come only for the beach scene. To reach **Lido Mazzarò**, directly beneath Taormina, take the **cable car** (Via Luigi Pirandello; one way/return €2/3.50; ⏲ 8am-8.15pm, to 1am in summer). To the west of the beach, past the Sant'Andrea hotel, is the minuscule **Isola Bella**, set in a stunning cove with fishing boats. You can walk here in a few minutes but it's more fun to rent a small boat from Mazzarò and paddle round Capo Sant'Andrea.

FESTIVALS & EVENTS

The **Taormina Arte festival** (☎ 0942 2 11 42; www.taormina-arte.com) from June to August includes films, theatrical events and music concerts from an impressive list of international names.

SLEEPING

Isoco Guest House (☎ 0942 2 36 79; www.isoco.it; Via Salita Branco 2; s €65-120, d €85-120; P ✕ ▣) Every room in this welcoming, gay-friendly B&B is dedicated to an artist – from Botticelli to the sculpted buttocks and pant-popping thighs on the walls of the Herb Ritts room. In summer, owner Michele serves multicourse dinners on the terrace for €25 (including drinks).

Hotel Villa Schuler (☎ 0942 2 34 81; www.hotelvillaschuler.com; Via Roma, Piazzetta Bastione; s €120, d €134-190; P ✕) Surrounded by shady terraced gardens and with views of Mt Etna, the rose-pink Villa Schuler is family-owned and preserves a homely atmosphere.

EATING & DRINKING

La Cisterna del Moro (☎ 0942 2 30 01; Via Bonifacio 1; sandwiches €5, pizzas €5.50-9.50) Affordability and aesthetics don't usually go hand in hand in Taormina, but this restaurant down an alley off Corso Umberto I is a welcome exception.

Tiramisù (☎ 0942 2 48 03; Via Cappuccini 1; pizzas €7-10, meals €30-40; ⏲ closed Tue) This stylish but unpretentious place hidden away just outside Porta Messina makes fabulous meals, from *linguine cozze, menta e zucchine* (pasta with mussels, mint and courgettes) to old favourites like *scaloppine al limone e panna* (veal escalope in lemon cream sauce).

OUR PICK **Bar Turrisi** (☎ 0942 2 81 81; Castelmola; ⏲ 9am-2am) A few kilometre outside Taormina, in the hilltop community of Castelmola, this whimsical bar is built on four levels overlooking the church square.

Couple shopping in Taormina

PHILIP & KAREN SMITH

Its decor is an eclectic tangle of Sicilian influences, with everything from painted carts to a giant stone *minchia* (you'll need no translation once you see it).

GETTING THERE & AROUND

The bus is the easiest way to reach Taormina. **Interbus** (☎ 0942 62 53 01; Via Luigi Pirandello) services leave daily for Messina (€3.70, 55 minutes to 1¾ hours, ten daily Monday to Saturday) and Catania (€5, 1¼ hours, six to nine daily).

California (☎ 0942 2 37 69; Via Bagnoli Croce 86; Vespa 125 per day/week €30/189, Fiat Punto per day/week €72/327) rents out cars and scooters at reasonable prices.

CATANIA
pop 299,000

Catania is a true city of the volcano. Much of it is constructed from the lava that poured down the mountain and engulfed the city in the 1669 eruption in which nearly 12,000 people lost their lives.

The main train station is near the port at Piazza Giovanni XXIII, and the intercity bus terminal is one block up at Via d'Amico.

INFORMATION

Municipal tourist office (☎ 095 742 55 73; bureau.turismo@comune.catania.it; Via Vittorio Emanuele 172; ⊗ 8.15am-7.15pm Mon-Fri, 8.15am-12.15pm Sat)

Police station (☎ 095 736 71 11; Piazza Santa Nicolella)

SIGHTS

Catania's central square, **Piazza del Duomo**, is a Unesco World Heritage site. It's a set piece of sinuous buildings and a grand cathedral, all built in Catania's own style of baroque, with its contrasting lava and limestone. In the centre of the piazza is Catania's most memorable monument, and a symbol of the city, the smiling **Fontana dell'Elefante** (built in 1736). The statue is crowned by a naive black-lava elephant, dating from the Roman period, surmounted by an improbable Egyptian obelisk.

Facing the statue is Catania's other defence against Mt Etna, St Agata's **cathedral** (☎ 095 32 00 44; Piazza del Duomo; ⊗ 8am-noon & 4-7pm), with its impressive marble facade. The saint's jewel-drenched effigy is

PHILIP & KAREN SMITH

Peak of Mt Etna

ecstatically venerated on 5 February in one of Sicily's largest *feste* (see below).

The best show in town, however, is the bustling **La Pescheria** (fish market; Via Pardo; ⏰ 5-11am) and adjoining **food market** (Via Naumachia; ⏰ 8-9am & 6-7pm) where carcasses of meat, silvery fish, skinned sheep's heads, strings of sausages, huge wheels of cheese and piles of luscious vegetables are all rolled together in a few noisy, jam-packed alleyways.

FESTIVALS & EVENTS

There are hysterical celebrations during **Festa di Sant'Agata** (3 to 5 February), where one million Catanians follow as the Fercolo (a silver reliquary bust of the saint) is carried along the main street of the city accompanied by spectacular fireworks.

SLEEPING

ourpick B&B Crociferi (☎ 095 715 22 66; www.bbcrociferi.it; Via Crociferi 81; s/d €65/90;) Affording easy access to the animated nightlife of Catania's historic centre, this B&B in a beautifully decorated family home is one of Catania's most delightful places to stay.

Il Principe (☎ 095 250 03 45; www.ilprincipe hotel.com; Via Alessi 24; s €89-114; d €124-159,) This boutique hotel in an 18th-century building features luxurious rooms on one of the liveliest streets in town (thank goodness for double glazing!).

EATING & DRINKING

Al Cortile Alessi (☎ 095 31 54 44; Via Alessi 28; pizzas €6-8; ⏰ 8pm-1am) Catanians of all ages flock here on weekend evenings, drawn by the excellent pizzas, draft beer and re-laxed atmosphere. The outdoor courtyard is especially fun, with its banana trees and overhanging silk tapestries.

Metrò (☎ 095 32 20 98; Via Crociferi 76; meals €25-35; ⏰ closed Sun) This Slow Food-recom-mended eatery prides itself on stylish presentation and innovative adaptations of traditional Sicilian specialities.

ourpick Agorá Bar (☎ 095 723 30 10; www.agorahostel.com; Piazza Currò 6) The super-atmospheric bar here is in a neon-lit cave 18m below ground, complete with its own subterranean river. The Romans used it as a spa and now a cosmopolitan crowd lingers over drinks in the cavern.

GETTING THERE & AWAY

Catania's airport, **Fontanarossa** (☎ 095 723 91 11; www.aeroporto.catania.it), is 7km southwest of the city centre. To get there, take the special Alibus 457 (€1, 30 minutes, every 20 minutes) from outside the train station. **Etna Transporti/Interbus** (☎ 095 53 03 96; www.interbus.it) also runs a regular shuttle from the airport to Taormina (€5.60, 1½ hours, six to nine daily).

Intercity buses terminate in the area around Piazza Giovanni XXIII, in front of the train station, and depart from Via d'Amico one block north. Catania's buses surpass the rather plodding train service.

Catania is easily reached from Messina on the A18 autostrada and from Palermo on the A19. From the autostrada, signs for the centre of Catania will bring you to Via Etnea.

Frequent trains connect Catania with Messina (€6.65, 1¾ hours, hourly) and Syracuse (€6, 1¼ hours, 11 daily).

GETTING AROUND

Many of the more useful **AMT city buses** (☎ 095 736 01 11) terminate in front of the train station.

For a taxi, call **CST** (☎ 095 33 09 66).

MT ETNA
elev 3329m

Dominating the landscape of eastern Sicily and visible from the moon (if you happen to be there), Mt Etna is Europe's largest volcano and one of the world's most active.

ORIENTATION & INFORMATION

The two main approaches to Etna are from Piano Provenzano on the northern flank and Rifugio Sapienza on the southern flank.

You can pick up information at a number of sources, the most convenient being the main tourist office in Catania (p321).

On Etna the office of the **Parco dell'Etna** (☎ 095 82 11 11; www.parcoetna.ct.it in Italian; Via del Convento 45; 🕑 9am-2pm & 4-7.30pm) is in Nicolosi on the southern side. Near the summit at Rifugio Sapienza, you will find the **Etna Sud Tourist Office** (☎ 095 91 63 56; 🕑 9am-4pm), plus souvenir shops, restaurants, a couple of *albergos* (hotels) and groups of shivering tourists wishing they had remembered to dress warmly.

On the northern side of the mountain, the local **tourist office** (☎ 095 64 73 52; www.prolocolinguaglossa.it; Piazza Annunziata 5; 🕑 9am-3pm) in Linguaglossa is the best source of information.

SIGHTS & ACTIVITIES

With a daily bus link from Catania via Nicolosi, the southern side of the volcano presents the easier ascent to the **craters**. The AST bus drops you off at the **Rifugio Sapienza** (1923m) from where **Funivia dell'Etna** (☎ 095 91 41 41; www.funiviaetna. com; cable car one way/return €14.50/27, incl bus & guide €60; 🕑 9am-4.30pm) runs a cable car up the mountain to 2500m (the ticket office accepts credit cards).

Once out of the cable car you can attempt the long walk (3½ to four hours return) up the winding track to the authorised crater zone (2920m). If you plan to do this, make sure you leave yourself enough time to get up *and* down before the last cable car leaves at 4.45pm.

TOURS

Siciltrek (☎ 095 96 88 82; www.sicilitrek.it; Via Marconi 27, Sant'Alfio) runs group tours up Etna, including the cable car and bus trip to 2900m. Andrea Ercolani of Siciltrek also organises and leads excellent private tours throughout the region.

SLEEPING & EATING

For information on local B&Bs, contact **EtnaTourism** (☎ 095 791 62 87; www.etna tourism.it), a consortium whose members will also grant you a 20% discount on the Mt Etna cable car.

Rifugio Sapienza (☎ 095 91 53 21; www.rifugiosapienza.com; Piazzale Funivia; per person B&B/half-board €55/75) As close to the summit as you can get, this place adjacent to the cable car offers comfortable accommodation with a good restaurant.

GETTING THERE & AWAY

AST (☎ 095 53 17 56) runs daily buses from Catania to Rifugio Sapienza (one way/return €3.40/5.60, one hour). Buses leave from the car park opposite Catania's train station at 8.15am, travelling via Nicolosi, and return at 4.45pm.

You can circle Etna on the private **Ferrovia Circumetnea** (FCE; ☎ 095 54 12 50; www.circumetnea.it; Via Caronda 352a, Catania) train line. Catch the metro from Catania's main train station to the FCE station at Via Caronda (metro stop Borgo) or take bus 429 or 432 going up Via Etnea and ask to be let off at the Borgo metro stop.

SOUTHEASTERN SICILY

SYRACUSE

pop 123,600

Settled by colonists from Corinth in 734 BC, Syracuse was considered to be the most beautiful city of the ancient world, rivalling Athens in power and prestige.

The main sights of Syracuse are in two areas: on the island of Ortygia and 2km across town in the Parco Archaeologico della Neapolis. The train station is located to the west of busy Corso Gelone.

INFORMATION

Tourist office (☎ 0931 46 42 55; Via Maestranza 33, Ortygia; ☾ 8am-2pm & 2.30-5.30pm Mon-Thu, 8am-2pm Fri)

Police station (☎ 0931 46 35 66; Piazza S Giuseppe)

Post office (Riva della Posta)

Syracuse's harbour

BETHUNE CARMICHAEL

SIGHTS
ORTYGIA

Despite Syracuse's baroque veneer, the Greek essence of this town is in evidence everywhere here, from the formal civility of the local people to the disguised architectural relics. The most obvious of these is the town's **cathedral** (Piazza del Duomo; ☻ 8am-noon & 4-7pm), which is, in fact, a Greek temple that was converted into a Christian church when the island was evangelised by St Paul.

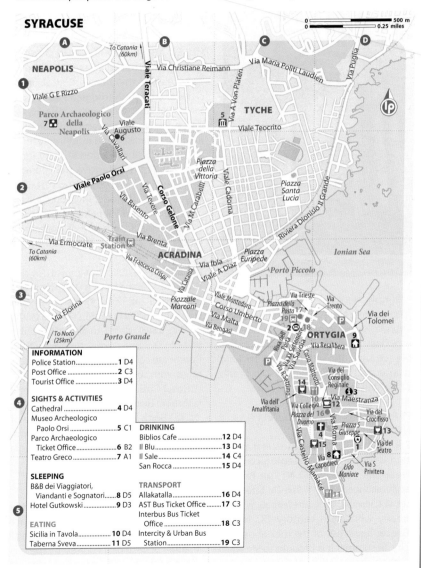

SYRACUSE

0 — 500 m
0 — 0.25 miles

INFORMATION	
Police Station	1 D4
Post Office	2 C3
Tourist Office	3 D4

SIGHTS & ACTIVITIES	
Cathedral	4 D4
Museo Archeologico Paolo Orsi	5 C1
Parco Archaeologico Ticket Office	6 B2
Teatro Greco	7 A1

SLEEPING	
B&B dei Viaggiatori, Viandanti e Sognatori	8 D5
Hotel Gutkowski	9 D3

EATING	
Sicilia in Tavola	10 D4
Taberna Sveva	11 D5

DRINKING	
Biblios Cafe	12 D4
Il Blu	13 D4
Il Sale	14 C4
San Rocca	15 D4

TRANSPORT	
Allakatalla	16 D4
AST Bus Ticket Office	17 C3
Interbus Bus Ticket Office	18 C3
Intercity & Urban Bus Station	19 C3

JOHN ELK III
Cathedral of Syracuse (p325)

Simply walking through the tangled maze of alleys that characterises Ortygia is an atmospheric experience, especially down the narrow lanes of **Via Maestranza**, the heart of the old guild quarter, and the crumbling Jewish ghetto of **Via della Giudecca**.

PARCO ARCHAEOLOGICO DELLA NEAPOLIS

For the classicist, Syracuse's real attraction is the **Parco Archaeologico della Neapolis** (☎ 0931 6 62 06; Viale Paradiso; adult/concession €8/4; ☺ 9am-2hr before sunset, to 4.30pm during theatre festival), with its pearly white, 5th century–BC **Teatro Greco**, hewn out of the rock above the city. In summer it is brought to life again with an annual season of classical theatre.

Check the www.apt-siracusa.it website for information.

To get to the park, take bus 4, 5, 6, 8, 11, 12 or 15 from Piazza della Posta to Corso Gelone/Viale Teracati. The walk from Ortygia will take about 30 minutes. If you have a car, you can park along Viale Augusto for €1 (for as long as you like).

MUSEO ARCHEOLOGICO PAOLO ORSI

In the grounds of Villa Landolina, about 500m east of the archaeological park, is the **Museo Archeologico Paolo Orsi** (☎ 0931 46 40 22; Viale Teocrito; admission €4; ☺ 9am-7pm Tue-Sat, 9am-2pm Sun). It contains the best organised and most interesting archaeological collection in Sicily (and one of the most extensive archaeological collections in Europe) and certainly merits a visit. The opening hours are all over the place and are often extended in summer; check with one of the tourist offices.

SLEEPING

B&B dei Viaggiatori, Viandanti e Sognatori (☎ 0931 2 47 81; www.bedand breakfastsicily.it; Via Roma 156; s €35-50, d €55-70, tr €75-85, q €100, ☒ ☜) An old palace at the end of Via Roma cradles this lovely B&B. Rooms are colourfully and stylishly decorated, with super-comfy beds.

Hotel Gutkowski (☎ 0931 46 58 61; www. guthotel.it; Lungomare Vittorini 26; s/d €80/110; ☒ ▣) Book well in advance for one of the seven seaview rooms at this charming and friendly hotel on the Ortygia waterfront.

EATING & DRINKING

Sicilia in Tavola (☎ 392 461 08 89; Via Cavour 28; meals €16-30; ☺ closed Mon) A tiny place with a dozen tables that specialises in all manner of fresh pasta dishes (try the speciality of the house, seafood ravioli).

Taberna Sveva (☎ 0931 2 46 63; Piazza Federico di Svevia; meals €23-30; ☺ closed Wed) Food is top-notch, all the way from *primi* like *gnocchi al pistacchio* (with olive oil, parmesan, pepper, garlic and grated pistachios) to a delicious tiramisu to wrap things up.

Four recommended drinking spots in Ortygia are the literary **Biblios Cafe** (Via del Consiglio Reginale 11; ☺ 10am-1.30pm & 5-9pm, closed Wed & Sun mornings), **Il Sale** (Via dell'Amalfitania 56/2), **Il Blu** (Via Nizza) and lovely **San Rocca** (Piazzetta San Rocca), the most popular of several bars with tables sprawled across bustling Piazzetta San Rocca.

GETTING THERE & AWAY
Long-distance buses operate from a strip along Corso Umberto, just east of Syracuse's train station.

There's a large underground car park on Via V Veneto on Ortygia where you can park for €1.

More than a dozen trains depart daily for Messina (Intercity/regional train €14.50/9.25, 2½ to 3¼ hours) via Catania (€7.50/6, 1¼ hours). For Palermo, the bus is a better option.

GETTING AROUND
AST city buses 1, 4 and 12 make the trip from Ortygia's Piazza della Posta to Parco Archeologico della Neapolis. A two-hour city bus ticket costs €1.

Allakatalla (☎ 0931 6 74 52; Via Roma 10; ☺ 9am-1pm & 4-8pm Mon-Fri, 9am-12.30pm Sat) hires out bicycles (€15 per day) and scooters (€35 per day).

NOTO
pop 23,500 / elev 160m
Flattened in 1693 by an earthquake, Noto was grandly rebuilt by its nobles. It is now the finest baroque town in Sicily, especially

appreciable at night when the illuminations introduced in 2006 accentuate its beauty and intricately carved facades.

INFORMATION
Ambulance (☎ 0931 89 02 35)
Police station (☎ 0931 83 52 02)
Tourist office (☎ 0931 57 37 79; www.comune.noto.sr.it; Piazza XVI Maggio; ☺ 9am-1pm & 4-8pm)

Ragusa street

◥ IF YOU LIKE...
If you like **Noto**, we think you'll like these other atmospheric Sicilian towns:

- **Modica** World Heritage–listed, Modica's ancient medieval buildings climb steeply up either side of a deep gorge that was cut in prehistoric times. Catch a train or bus from Syracuse.
- **Ragusa** Another Unesco-listed hotspot, where grand churches and *palazzi* line twisting, narrow streets interspersed with gelaterie and delightful piazzas sprinkled with wizened locals.
- **Erice** One of Italy's most spectacular hill towns, famed for its medieval lanes, local sweets and former role as a centre for the cult of Venus. Catch a bus from Palermo to Trapani, then a bus or funicular to Erice.

SICILY & THE SOUTH

SICILY

SIGHTS

The San Nicoló Cathedral stands in the centre of Noto's most graceful square, Piazza Municipio, and is surrounded by elegant town houses such as Palazzo Ducezio (Town Hall) and Palazzo Landolina, once home to Noto's oldest noble family. The only *palazzo* that has so far been restored to its former glory, however, is the Palazzo Villadorata (Palazzo Nicolaci; ☎ 0931 83 50 05; www.palazzonicolaci.it; Via Corrado Nicolaci; adult/concession €4/2; ☻ 9am-1pm & 3-7pm Tue-Sun), where wrought-iron balconies are supported by a swirling pantomime of grotesque figures.

For sweeping rooftop views of Noto's baroque splendour, climb the *campanile* (belltower) at Chiesa di San Carlo al Corso (admission €2; ☻ 9am-12.30pm & 4-7pm) or Chiesa di Santa Chiara (admission €1.50; ☻ 9.30am-1pm & 3-7pm).

SLEEPING & EATING

B&B Montandòn (☎ 0931 83 63 89; www.b-bmontandon.it; Via Sofia 50; s €40-55, d €65-80; P ☒) Accessed via imposing vaulted hallways, this B&B in a crumbling *palazzo* near the top of town has lovely, light rooms with elegant furnishings.

Hotel della Ferla (☎ 0931 57 60 07; www.hoteldellaferla.it; Via A Gramsci; s €48-78, d €84-120; P ☒ ☞) This small, friendly hotel is located in a residential area near the train station, around 10 minutes' walk downhill from the historic centre.

Trattoria Baglieri Crocifisso (☎ 0931 57 11 51; Via Principe Umberto 48; meals €25-30) This Slow Food-acclaimed trattoria is one of Noto's finest eateries. The list of bottled wines is extensive, but you can also get an excellent glass, starting at €3.50.

Caffè Sicilia (☎ 0931 83 50 13; Corso Vittorio Emanuele 125) Dating from 1892, this vies with Dolceria Corrado Costanzo for the honours of Noto's best dessert shop.

Dolceria Corrado Costanzo (☎ 0931 83 52 43; Via Silvio Spaventa 9) Just around the corner from Caffè Sicilia, Costanzo is famous for its gelati.

GETTING THERE & AROUND

Noto is easily accessible by AST and Interbus buses from Catania (€6.70, 1¾ hours, 12 daily Monday to Saturday, seven on Sunday) and Syracuse (€3, 50 minutes, 12 daily Monday to Saturday). Trains from Syracuse are frequent (€3.20, 30 minutes, 11 daily), but the station is located 1.5km south of the bus station area.

AGRIGENTO

pop 59,200 / elev 230m

Overshadowed by the new city on the hill above it, the splendid Valley of the Temples loses much of its immediate impact and it is only when you get down among the ruins that you can appreciate its true monumentality.

Intercity buses arrive on Piazza Rosselli; the train station is slightly south on Piazza Marconi. Frequent city buses run to the Valley of the Temples below the town (see opposite).

INFORMATION

Ambulance (☎ 0922 40 13 44)
Municipal tourist office (☎ 0922 59 61 68; hoteldoville@libero.it) Train Station (☻ 8am-8pm Mon-Fri, 8am-2pm Sat); Piazzale Aldo Moro (☻ 8am-2pm Mon-Fri, 3-6pm Tue & Thu) Provides maps of Agrigento & information about the archaeological park.
Police station (☎ 0922 59 63 22; Piazzale Aldo Moro 2)

TOURS

Michele Gallo (☎ 0922 40 22 57) is an excellent English-speaking guide who can organise individual and group itineraries (two to 3½ hours) according to travellers' specific interests.

SLEEPING & EATING

Atenea 191 B&B (☎ 349 59 55 94; www. atenea191.com; Via Atenea 191; s €35-55, d €50-85) The gregarious, multilingual and well-travelled Sonia runs this B&B, lo-cated on Agrigento's main shopping thoroughfare.

Camere a Sud (☎ 349 638 44 24; www. camereasud.it; Via Ficani 6; r €60-70) Run by a friendly Agrigentan couple, this extremely cute and well signposted B&B has cheer-ful rooms and a delightful roof terrace. Cash only.

STEPHEN SAKS

Ruins at the Valley of the Temples

⇲ VALLEY OF THE TEMPLES

Agrigento's Valley of the Temples is one of Sicily's premier attractions. A Unesco World Heritage site, it incorporates a complex of temples and old city walls from the ancient Greek city of Akragas.

The archaeological park is divided into two main sections. East of Via dei Templi are the most spectacular temples, the first of which is the **Tempio di Ercole** (Temple of Hercules), built towards the end of the 6th century BC and believed to be the oldest of the temples.

Across Via dei Templi, to the west, is what remains of the massive **Tempio di Giove** (Temple of Jupiter), never actually completed and now totally in ruins, allowing you to appreciate the sheer size of the rocks. It covered an area of 112m by 56m with columns 20m high.

The **Museo Archeologico**, north of the temples, has a huge collection of clearly labelled artefacts from the excavated site. It also has wheelchair access.

Things you need to know: Valley of the Tempes (☎ 0922 49 72 26; adult/conces-sion/child €8/4/free, incl archaeological museum €10/5/free; ⏲ 9am-11.30pm Jul-Aug; 9am-7pm Tue-Sat, 9am-1pm Sun & Mon Sep-Jun); Museo Archeologico (☎ 0922 4 01 11; Contrada San Nicola; adult/concession €6/3; ⏲ 9am-7pm Tue-Sat, 9am-1pm Sun & Mon)

Segesta's temple

DOUG MCKINLAY

➥ IF YOU LIKE...

If you like the **Valley of the Temples** (p329), we think you'll like these other ancient wonders:

- **Segesta** (☎ 0924 95 23 56; adult/concession €6/2.50; ⏲ 9am-4pm Nov-Mar, to 7pm Apr-Aug) A huge 5th-century BC temple set on the edge of a deep canyon, complete with an ancient amphitheatre. Catch a train from Palermo or Trapani to Segesta Tempio.
- **Selinunte** (☎ 0924 4 62 51; adult/concession/child €6/3/free; ⏲ 9am-1hr before sunset) The ruins of this 7th-century-BC coastal city are the most impressively sited in Sicily. Catch a bus from Agrigento to Castelvetrano, then an AST bus to Selinute.
- **Metaponto** (☎ 0835 74 53 27; Via Aristea 21; admission ruins free, archaeological museum €2.50; ⏲ 9am-8pm Tue-Sun, 2-8pm Mon) Metaponto's Greek ruins were once home to Pythagoras. Buses run to/from Matera.

Ristorante Per Bacco (☎ 0922 55 33 69; Vicolo Lo Presti 2; meals from €17; ⏲ dinner Tue-Sun) The set menus – including antipasto, *primo, secondo, contorno,* local wine, water and dessert for under €20 – are a great deal at this restaurant just above Via Atenea.

Leon d'Oro (☎ 0922 41 44 00; Viale Emporium 102; meals €30; ⏲ closed Mon) An excellent restaurant that warrants its high prices and perfectly mixes the fish and fowl that typify Agrigento cuisine.

GETTING THERE & AWAY
BUS
Autoservizi Camilleri (☎ 0922 59 64 90) runs buses to Palermo (€8.10, two hours, five daily Monday to Saturday, two on Sunday). **Lumia** (☎ 0922 2 91 36; www.auto lineelumia.it) has departures to Trapani (€11.10, three to four hours, three daily Monday to Saturday, one on Sunday) and **SAIS** (☎ 0922 2 93 24) runs buses to Catania (€12.20, three hours, hourly).

CAR & MOTORCYCLE
There's metered parking at the train station (Piazza Marconi) and free parking along Via Esseneto just below.

TRAIN
Trains run regularly to Palermo (€7.85, 2¼ hours, 11 daily). There's also one daily train to Catania (€10.95, 3¾ hours). Although trains serve other destinations as well, you're better off taking the bus.

GETTING AROUND
City buses (€1) run down to the Valley of the Temples from in front of the train station. Take bus 1, 2 or 3 and get off at either the museum or the Piazzale dei Templi.

PUGLIA
PROMONTORIO DEL GARGANO
The coast surrounding the promontory seems permanently bathed in a pink-hued, pearly light, providing a painterly contrast to the sea which softens from intense to powder blue as the evening draws in.

VIESTE

pop 13,600

Vieste is a small, steep, cobbled town, with a delightful *centro storico,* spilling down the hillside. It's the Gargano capital and sits above the area's most spectacular beach.

ORIENTATION & INFORMATION

From Piazzale Manzoni, where intercity buses terminate, a 10-minute walk east along Viale XXIV Maggio, which becomes Corso Fazzini, brings you into the old town and the Marina Piccola's attractive promenade.

Tourist office (☎ 0884 70 88 06; Piazza Kennedy; 8am-1.30pm Mon-Fri & 4-7pm Tue-Thu Oct-Apr, 8am-1.30pm & 3-9pm Mon-Sat May-Sep)

SIGHTS & ACTIVITIES

Vieste is all about beaches, eating and drinking; for the latter head for the seafront bars and clubs at Via Pola. The most gruesome of the handful of sights here is the **Chianca Amara** (Bitter Stone; Via Cimaglia), where thousands were beheaded when Turks sacked Vieste in the 16th century.

At the port, **Centro Ormeggi e Sub** (☎ 0884 70 79 83; May-Sep) offers diving courses and rents out sailing boats and motorboats. You can also visit nearby grottos with **Leonarda Motobarche** (☎ 0884 70 13 17; www.motobarcheleonarda.it; per person €13; Apr-Sep)

From May to September fast boats zoom to the Isole Tremiti.

Superb sandy beaches surround the town: in the south, Spiagga del Castello, Cala San Felice and Cala Sanguinaria and, due north head for the area known as La Salata.

Take a beach break and go walking or cycling with **Agenzia Sol** (☎ 0884 70 15 58; www.solvieste.it; Via Trepiccioni 5) in the Foresta Umbra.

SLEEPING

B&B Rocca sul Mare (☎ 0884 70 27 19; www.roccasulmare.it; Via Mafrolla 32; r incl breakfast €50-120) In a former convent in the old quarter, this place has charm, with large, plain, high-ceilinged rooms, some busy tilework and steep staircases.

Villa Scapone (☎ 0884 55 92 84; www.villascapone.it; Litoranea Mattinata–Vieste Km11.5; r €55-110; Apr-Oct; P X R) An attractive villa fantastically sited on the cliffs between Mattinata and Vieste. The hotel terraces, sundecks and elegant rooms all share stunning sea views.

EATING

our pick **Al Cantinone** (☎ 0884 70 77 53; Via Mafrolla 26; meals €20) Run by a charming Italian-Spanish couple who have a passion for cooking; the food is exceptional and exquisitely presented.

Enoteca Vesta (☎ 0884 70 64 11; Via Duomo 14; meals €25) Housed in a cool, vaulted cave, you can savour a magnificent selection of Puglian wines here to accompany innovative dishes like fried stuffed anchovies with cheese and eggs and baked grey mullet with wild fennel.

GETTING THERE & AROUND

Vieste's port is to the north, about a five-minute walk from the tourist office. In summer several companies, including **Navigazione Libera del Golfo** (☎ 0884 70 74 89; www.navlib.it), head to the Isole Tremiti. Tickets can be bought portside and there are several daily boats (€16.50, 1½ hours).

SITA (☎ 0881 35 20 11; www.sitabus.it in Italian) buses run between Vieste and Foggia (€5.70, 2¾ hours, four daily) via Manfredonia, and between Vieste and

Steps in the town centre of Vieste (p331)

PHILIP & KAREN SMITH

Monte Sant'Angelo (€4.40), while **Ferrovie del Gargano** (☎ 0881 58 72 11; www.ferroviedelgargano.com in Italian) services go to Peschici (€1.30, 35 minutes, 11 daily).

CASTEL DEL MONTE

You'll see **Castel del Monte** (☎ 0883 56 99 97; admission €3; ⏱ 9am-6.30pm Oct-Feb, 3pm-7.45pm Mar-Sep), an unearthly geometric shape on a hilltop, from miles away. Some theories claim that, according to mid-13th century beliefs in geometric symbolism, the octagon represented the union of the circle and square, of God-perfection (the infinite) and man-perfection (the finite).

You need your own wheels to get here, otherwise there is a sporadic daily service from nearby Andria.

BARI

pop 328,500

'Se Parigi avesse il mare, sarebbe una piccola Bari' (If Paris had the sea, it would be a little Bari). This popular saying tells you more about the local sense of humour than it does about the city, but Bari has a surprising amount of charm, particularly Bari Vecchia, its increasingly chic medieval old town.

Orient yourself from Piazza Aldo Moro in front of the main train station. Any of the streets heading north from Piazza Aldo Moro will take you to Corso Vittorio Emanuele II, which separates the old and new parts of the city, and further north to the ferry terminal.

INFORMATION

Police station (☎ 080 529 11 11; Via Murat 4)
Post office (Piazza Battisti; ⏱ 8am-6.30pm Mon-Fri, 8am-12.30pm Sat)
Tourist office (☎ 080 990 93 41; www.pugliaturismo.com; 1st fl, Piazza Moro 33a; ⏱ 10am-1pm & 3-6pm Mon-Fri, 10am-1pm Sat)

SIGHTS
BARI VECCHIA

Start your exploration with the chaotic **market** alongside Piazza del Ferrarese. Stumble out of there and walk north to the glorious medieval Piazza Mercantile, fronted by the **Sedile**, the headquarters of Bari's Council of Nobles. In the square's northeast corner is the **Colonna della Giustizia** (Column of Justice), where debtors were once tied and whipped.

Northwest past the small Chiesa di Santa Ana is the remarkable **Basilica di San Nicola** (Piazza San Nicola; ☉ 7am-1pm & 4-7pm Mon-Sat, 7am-1pm & 4-9pm Sun), one of the south's first Norman churches. A brief walk south along Via delle Crociate brings you to the 11th-century Romanesque **cathedral** (Piazza Odegitria; ☉ 8am-12.30pm & 4-7.30pm Mon-Fri, 8am-12.30pm & 5-8.30pm Sat & Sun).

CASTELLO SVEVO

The **Castello Svevo** (Swabian Castle; ☎ 083 184 00 09; Piazza Federico II di Svevia; admission €2; ☉ 8.30am-7.30pm Thu-Tue) broods on the edge of Bari Vecchia. The Normans originally built over the ruins of a Roman fort. Frederick II then built over the Norman castle, incorporating it into his design – the two towers of the Norman structure still stand.

SLEEPING & EATING

Hotel Adria (☎ 080 524 66 99; www.adria hotelbari.com; Via Zuppetta 10; s/d €70/110; P ☒ ☐) A dusky-pink building fronted by wrought-iron balconies, this is a great choice, with comfortable, good-value rooms that are bright and modern.

Domina Palace Hotel (☎ 080 521 65 51; www.dominahotels.com; Via Lombardi 13; s/d €195/260; P ☒ ☐ ☏) Look past the dated '60s style exterior and this is an oasis of luxury, with plush, elegant rooms and a renowned rooftop restaurant.

Maccheroni Pizzerie a Metro (☎ 080 521 33 56; Via Gimma 90; pizzas €7-9) The long and short of it is that the whole table's order is made into one continuous pizza, served by the metre and, most importantly, delicious.

Vini e Cucina (☎ 338 212 03 91; Strada Vallisa 23; meals €10; ☉ Mon-Sat) Run by the

same family for more than a century, this boisterous *osteria* (wine-bar serving some food) chalks up its daily specials of well-prepared and filling Pugliese dishes.

GETTING THERE & AWAY
AIR
Bari's Palese **airport** (BRI; ☎ 080 580 02 00; www.seap-puglia.it) is served by a host of international and budget airlines, including British Airways, Alitalia, Hapag-Lloyd Express and Ryanair.

BUS
From Via Capruzzi, south of the main train station, **SITA** (☎ 080 579 01 11; www.sitabus.it in Italian) covers local destinations. **Ferrovie Appulo-Lucane** (☎ 080 572 52 29; www.fal-srl.it in Italian) buses serving Matera also

PHILIP & KAREN SMITH

Vieste (p331)

depart from here, plus **Marozzi** (☎ 080 556 24 46; www.marozzivt.it) buses for Rome (€35, eight hours, 8.35 am, 1pm, 4pm, 5pm, 11.50pm – the overnight bus departs from Piazza Moro) and other long-distance destinations.

Piazza Eroi del Mare is the terminal for **STP** (☎ 080 505 82 80; www.stpspa.it) buses serving Trani (€2.95, 45 minutes, frequent).

Buses operated by **Ferrovie del Sud-Est** (FSE; ☎ 080 546 21 11; www.fseonline.it in Italian) leave from Largo Ciaia, south of Piazza Moro, for Brindisi (€6.60, 23 to 24 hours, four daily Monday to Saturday), Taranto (€5.30, 1¾ to 2¼ hours, frequent), Alberobello (€3.60, 1¼ hours) and on to Locorotondo (€2.60, one hour).

TRAIN

From the **main train station** (☎ 080 524 43 86) Eurostar trains go to Milan (from €68, eight to 9½ hours) and Rome (from €36, five hours). **Ferrovie Appulo-Lucane** (☎ 080 572 52 29; www.fal-srl.it) goes to Matera (€4.35, 1½ hours, 12 daily).

GETTING AROUND

Central Bari is compact – a 15-minute walk will take you from Piazza Moro to the old town.

TO/FROM THE AIRPORT

To get to the airport, take the Cotrap bus (€4.50) which leaves regularly from the main train station. A taxi trip from the airport to town costs around €24.

MURGIA PLATEAU & TRULLI COUNTRY

At the heart of the Murgia lies the idyllic Valle d'Itria. Here you will begin to spot curious circular stone-built houses dotting the countryside, their roofs tapering up to a stubby and endearing point. These are *trulli*, Puglia's unique rural architecture.

ALBEROBELLO

pop 10,930

Unesco World Heritage Site Alberobello resembles a mini urban sprawl – for gnomes. The Zona dei Trulli on the western hill of town is a dense mass of 1500 beehive-shaped houses, white-tipped as if dusted by snow.

The new town is perched on the eastern hilltop, while the Zona dei Trulli lies on the western hill, and consists of two adjacent neighbourhoods, the Rione Monti and the Rione Aia Piccola.

There's a local **tourist information office** (☎ 080 432 28 22; www.prolocoalberobello.it; Monte Nero 1; ☺ 9am-7.30pm) in the Zona dei Trulli.

SIGHTS

Within the old town quarter of **Rione Monti** over 1000 *trulli* cascade down the hillside, most of which are now souvenir shops. To its east, on the other side of Via Indipendenza, is **Rione Aia Piccola**. This neighbourhood is much less commercialised, with 400 *trulli,* many still used as family dwellings.

In the modern part of town, the 18th-century **Trullo Sovrano** (☎ 080 432 60 30; www.trullosovrano.it; Piazza Sacramento; admission €1.50; ☺ 10am-6pm) is the only two-floor *trullo,* built by a wealthy priest's family. It's a small museum giving something of the atmosphere of *trullo* life, with sweet, rounded rooms which include a re-created bakery, bedroom and kitchen.

SLEEPING & EATING

Trullidea (☎ 080 432 38 60; www.trullidea.it; Via Monte San Gabriele 1; 2 person trulli from €63-149) A series of 20 renovated *trulli* in Alberobello's Trulli Zone, these are snug but can feel a bit dark as you're hemmed in by the other *trulli.* They're available on a self-catering, B&B, or half- or full-board basis.

Trulli houses, Alberobello

OLIVER STREWE

ourpick **Trattoria Amatulli** (☎ 080 432 29 79; Via Garibaldi 13; meals €15; ✆ Tue-Sun) Excellent trattoria with a cheerily cluttered interior papered with photos of smiley diners, plus superb down-to-earth dishes like *orecchietta al ragù con carne* ('little ears' pasta in a meat-and-tomato based sauce).

La Cantina (☎ 080 432 34 73; Vico Lippolis 8; meals €20; ✆ Wed-Mon Jul-Sep) There are just seven tables and one frenetic waiter, who serves dishes like *tagliolina* (fettuccine-style pasta) with porcini mushrooms and chestnuts, grilled meats and superb seasonal vegetables.

GETTING THERE & AWAY

Alberobello is easily accessible from Bari (€4.10, 1½ hours, hourly) on the FSE Bari–Taranto train line.

LOCOROTONDO

pop 14,000

Locorotondo (circular place) has an extraordinarily beautiful and whisper-quiet *centro storico,* where everything is shimmering white aside from the blood-red geraniums that tumble from the window boxes.

The **tourist office** (☎ 080 431 30 99; www.prolocolocorotondo.it; Piazza Vittorio Emanuele 27; ✆ 10am-1pm & 3-6pm Mon-Fri, 10am-1pm Sat) is also in this part of town and offers free internet access.

You simply cannot come to Locorotondo without sampling some of the local Spumante. You can do this at the local winery, **Cantina del Locorotondo** (☎ 080 431 16 44; www.locorotondodoc.com; Via Madonna della Catena 99) run by congenial Oronzo Mastro.

Charming trattoria **U'Curdunn** (☎ 080 431 70 70; Via Dura 19; meals €25; ✆ 9am-1am Sep-May, to 2am Wed-Mon Jun-Aug) is well signposted in the midst of the historic centre. All produce here is organic and you can expect good service and a buzzing atmosphere.

Locorotondo is easily accessible by frequent trains from Bari (€4, 1½ to two hours) on the FSE Bari–Taranto train line.

LECCE

pop 91,600

Central, historic Lecce is a beautiful baroque town; a glorious architectural confection of palaces and churches intricately sculpted from the soft local sandstone.

The train station is 1km southwest of Lecce's historic centre.

INFORMATION

Police station (☎ 0832 69 11 11; Viale Otranto 1)

Salento Time (☎ 0832 30 36 86; www.salentotime.it; Via Revina Isabella 22; ☻ 9am-2pm & 4-7pm Mon-Sat)

Tourist office (☎ 0832 24 80 92; Corso Vittorio Emanuele 24; ☻ 9am-1pm & 4.30-9pm Mon-Sat)

SIGHTS

BASILICA DI SANTA CROCE

It seems that hallucinating stonemasons have been at work on the **Basilica di Santa Croce** (☎ 0832 24 19 57; Via Umberto I; ☻ 9am-12.30pm & 5-9pm). Sheep, dodos, cherubs and beasties writhe across the facade, a swirling magnificent allegorical feast. Throughout the 16th and 17th centuries a team of artists – under Giuseppe Zimbalo – laboured to work the building up to this pitch.

PIAZZA DEL DUOMO

The 12th-century **cathedral** (☻ 6.30am-noon & 4-6.30pm) is one of Giuseppe Zimbalo's finest works – he was also responsible for the towering, 68m-high **bell tower**. The cathedral is unusual in that it has two facades, one on the western end and the other, more ornate, facing the piazza. It's framed by the 15th-century **Palazzo Vescovile** (Episcopal Palace) and the 18th-century **Seminario** (☻ exhibitions only), designed by Giuseppe Cino.

ROMAN REMAINS

Below the ground level of Piazza Sant'-Oronzo is the restored 2nd-century-AD **Roman amphitheatre,** (€2; ☻ 10am-noon & 4-6pm) discovered in 1901 by construction workers.

GREG ELMS

Facade detail, Basilica di Santa Croce

The small Roman theatre near here was also uncovered in the 1930s – a neat little arc hemmed between buildings. It contains the **Museo Teatro Romano** (☎ 0832 27 91 96; Via Ammirati; admission €2.60; ⏱ 9.30am-1pm Mon-Sat), with well-preserved russet-coloured Roman mosaics and frescoes.

OTHER SIGHTS

The **Museo Provinciale** (☎ 0832 68 35 03; Via Gallipoli 28; admission free; ⏱ 9am-1.30pm & 2.30-7.30pm Mon-Sat, 9am-1.30pm Sun) stylishly covers 10,000 years of history, from Palaeolithic and Neolithic bits and bobs to a handsome display of Greek and Roman jewels, weaponry and ornaments.

Lecce's 16th-century **Castello di Carlo V** (admission free; ⏱ 9am-1pm & 4-8.30pm) was built around a 12th-century Norman tower to the orders of Charles V.

SLEEPING & EATING

B&B Centro Storico Prestige (☎ 0832 24 33 53; www.bbprestige-lecce.it; Via Santa Maria del Paradiso 4; s €60-70, d €70-90; P 🖳) Rooms are light, airy and beautifully finished, with traditional furnishings and small balconies.

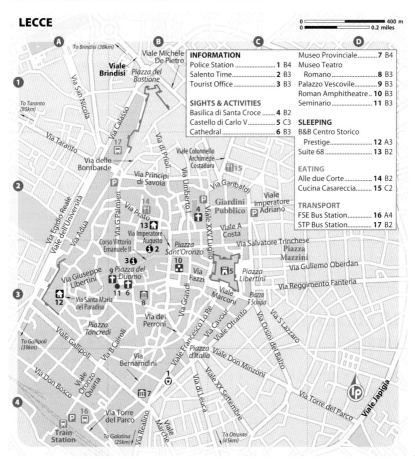

LECCE

INFORMATION	
Police Station	1 B4
Salento Time	2 B3
Tourist Office	3 B3

SIGHTS & ACTIVITIES	
Basilica di Santa Croce	4 B2
Castello di Carlo V	5 C3
Cathedral	6 B3

Museo Provinciale	7 B4
Museo Teatro Romano	8 B3
Palazzo Vescovile	9 B3
Roman Amphitheatre	10 B3
Seminario	11 B3

SLEEPING	
B&B Centro Storico Prestige	12 A3
Suite 68	13 B2

EATING	
Alle due Corte	14 B2
Cucina Casareccia	15 C2

TRANSPORT	
FSE Bus Station	16 A4
STP Bus Station	17 B2

ourpick Suite 68 (☎ 0832 30 35 06; www.kalekora.it; Via Prato; r €80-120; ✖) This place has a North African feel with light streaming in the large bright rooms, painted in desert hues and decorated with vividly coloured rugs.

Alle due Corti (☎ 0832 24 22 23; www.alleduecorti.com; Corte dei Giugni 1; meals €15-20) The seasonal menu is classic Pugliese, written in a dialect that even some Italians struggle with. Go for the real deal with a dish of *tajeddha* (layered potatoes, rice and mussels) or *ciceri e tria* (crisply fried pasta with chickpeas).

Cucina Casareccia (☎ 0832 24 51 78; Viale Costadura 19; meals €40; ✖ lunch Tue-Sun, dinner Tue-Sat) Ring the bell to gain entry here. This place feels more like a private home, with its patterned cement floor tiles, desk piled high with papers and charming owner Carmela Perrone. She'll whisk you through a dazzling array of Salentine dishes from the true *cucina povera* (cooking of the poor), including horsemeat done here in a *salsa piccante* (spicy sauce). Booking is a must.

GETTING THERE & AWAY

There are frequent trains to Bari (from €13.80, 1½ to two hours), to Brindisi (from €8.10, 30 minutes), to Rome (from €62, 5½ to nine hours) and Bologna (from €66, 8½ to 9½ hours). For Naples (from €44, 5½ hours), change in Caserta.

BASILICATA

MATERA

pop 59,144 / elev 405m

Approach Matera from virtually any direction and your first glimpse of its famous *sassi* (stone houses carved out of the caves and cliffs) is sure to be etched in your memory forever.

ORIENTATION

A short walk down Via Roma from the train and bus stations off Piazza Matteotti brings you to the Piazza Vittorio Veneto, the town's pedestrianised heart. The two *sassi* ravines open up to its east and southeast.

INFORMATION

Police station (☎ 0835 37 81; Piazza Vittorio Veneto)

Sassi Tourism (☎ 0835 31 94 58; www.sassitourism.it; Via Buozzi 141) Tourism organisation offering tours around Matera as well as entry into sites.

Tourist office (☎ 0835 33 19 83; www.materaturismo.it; Via Spine Bianche; ✖ 9am-1pm & 4-6.30pm Mon-Sat)

SIGHTS & ACTIVITIES

THE SASSI

There are two *sasso* districts: the more restored, northwest-facing Sasso Barisano and the more impoverished, northeast-facing Sasso Caveoso. Both are extraordinary, riddled with serpentine alleyways and staircases, and dotted with frescoed *chiese rupestri* (cave churches) created between the 8th and 13th centuries. Matera contains some 3000 habitable caves.

Sasso Caveoso includes the highlights of Chiesa di San Pietro Caveoso (Piazza San Pietro Caveoso) and the richly frescoed rock churches Santa Maria d'Idris (Piazza San Pietro Caveoso) and Santa Lucia alle Malve (Via la Vista). A couple of *sassi* have been refurbished as they were when inhabited. The most interesting is the Casa-Grotta di Vico Solitario (admission €1.50), off Via Buozzi.

The Museo della Scultura Contemporanea (Musma; www.musma.it; ✖ 10am-2pm & 4-8pm Apr-Oct, 10am-2pm Nov-Mar; adult/concession €5/3.50) is a fabulous contemporary sculpture museum, housed in Palazzo Pomarici.

TOWN CENTRE

The **Museo Nazionale Ridola** (☎ 0835 31 00 58; Via Ridola 24; adult/concession €2.50/1.25; 9am-8pm Tue-Sun & 2-8pm Mon) occupies the 17th-century convent of Santa Chiara. The impressive collection includes some remarkable Greek pottery, such as the *Craterea Mascheroni*, a huge urn over 1m high. A little south, on Piazzetta Pascoli, is the **Museo Nazionale d'Arte Medievale e Moderna della Basilicata** (☎ 0835 31 42 35; Palazzo Lanfranchi; adult/concession €2/1; 9am-1pm & 3.30-7pm Tue-Sun). The stars of the show are Levi's paintings, including the enormous mural, *Lucania '61,* depicting peasant life in biblical Technicolour.

SLEEPING

La Dolce Vita (☎ 0835 31 03 24; Rione Malve 51; s €40-60, d €50-80) Owner Vincenzo Altieri (ex-manager of Hotel Sant'Angelo) has created a delightful eco-friendly B&B in Sasso Caveoso, with solar panels and recycled rain water for plumbing. The rooms are cool and simply furnished with cream paintwork, dark-wood furniture and the occasional religious picture.

ourpick Hotel in Pietra (☎ 0835 31 40 10; www.hotelinpietra.it; Via San Giovanni Vecchio 22; Barisano; s €70 d €110-150;) The lobby is set in a former 13th-century chapel complete with soaring arches, while the eight rooms combine soft golden stone with the natural cave interior.

EATING

ourpick La Talpa (☎ 0835 33 50 86; Via Fiorentini 168; meals €15; Wed-Mon) A popular spot for romancing couples, the standard is very high, both for pizzas and specialities like *capuntí con purea dí cicerchié, funghi e rucola* (pasta with a bean, mushrooms and rocket sauce).

Le Botteghe (☎ 0835 34 40 72; Piazza San Pietro Barisano; meals €40; lunch & dinner Mon-Sat, lunch Sun) Try delicious local specialities like *fusilli mollica e crusco* (pasta and fried

Sasso Caveoso, Matera

GUIDO BAVIERA/GRAND TOUR/CORBIS

SIME/KAOS03/4CORNERS

Maratea coastline

bread with local sweet peppers) followed by the *strascinate salsiccia e funghi* (pasta with sausage and mushrooms).

GETTING THERE & AWAY
SITA (☎ 0835 38 50 07; www.sitabus.it in Italian) goes to Taranto (€4.60, two hours, one daily) and Metaponto (€3.20, one hour, up to five daily) and many small towns in the province.

Marozzi (☎ 06 225 21 47; www.marozzivt.it) runs three daily buses to Rome (€32.50, 6½ hours). A joint SITA and Marozzi service leaves daily for Siena, Florence and Pisa, via Potenza. Advance booking is essential.

Ferrovie Appulo-Lucane (FAL; ☎ 0835 33 28 61; www.fal-srl.it) runs regular trains

(€4.35, 1½ hours, 12 daily) and buses to Bari.

MARATEA
pop 5300

Maratea is a charming, if confusing, place at first, being comprised of several distinct localities ranging from a medieval village to a stylish harbour. The setting is lush and dramatic, with a coastal road (narrower even than the infamous Amalfi Coast road!) that dips and winds past the cliffs and pocket-size beaches that line the sparkling Golfo di Policastro.

SIGHTS & ACTIVITIES
Your first port of call should be the pretty **Porto di Maratea**, a harbour where sleek yachts and bright-blue fishing boats bob in the water, overlooked by bars and restaurants. Then there's the enchanting 13th-century medieval *borgo* (small town) of **Maratea Inferiore**, with pint-sized piazzas, wriggling alleys and interlocking houses, offering startling coastal views. It's all overlooked by a 21m-high, gleaming white statue of Christ the Redeemer – if you have your own transport, don't miss the rollercoaster road and stupendous views from the statue-mounted summit – below which lie the ruins of **Maratea Superiore**, all that remains of the original 8th-century-BC Greek colony.

The deep green hillsides that encircle this tumbling conurbation offer excellent walking trails and there are a number of easy day trips to the surrounding hamlets of **Acquafredda di Maratea** and **Fiumicello**, with its small sandy beach. You will find the **tourist office** (☎ 0973 87 69 08; Piazza Gesù 40; ⏱ 8am-2pm & 4-6pm Mon-Fri, 9am-1pm & 5-8pm Sun Jul & Aug, shorter hr Sep-Jun) in Fiumicello.

Centro Sub Maratea (☎ 0973 87 00 13; www.csmaratea.it; Via Santa Caterina 28, Maratea) offers diving courses and boat tours that include visits to surrounding grottoes and coves. Also rent boats.

A worthwhile day trip via car is to pretty **Rivello** (elevation 479m). Perched on a ridge, framed by the southern Apennines, these days it is a centre for arts and crafts and has long been known for its exquisite working of gold and copper.

SLEEPING

B&B Nefer (☎ 0973 87 18 28; www.bbnefer.it; Via Cersuta; s €50-60, d €65-80; ℗) A B&B set in a small hamlet (Via Cersuta), 5km northwest of Maratea. It has three rooms decorated in sea greens and blues that open onto a lush green lawn complete with deckcairs for contemplating the distant sea view.

Hotel Villa Cheta Elite (☎ 0973 87 81 34; www.villacheta.it; Via Timpone 46; d €90-125; ☯ May-Oct; ℗ ✹) A charming art nouveau villa at the entrance to the hamlet of Acquafredda.

EATING

Lanterna Rossa (☎ 0973 87 63 52; Maratea Porto; meals €30; ☯ Apr-Sep) Head for the terrace overlooking the port to dine on exquisite seafood dishes, like marinated anchovies with chilli red peppers, or a sumptuous antipasto.

Taverna Rovita (☎ 0973 87 65 88; Via Rovita 13; meals €35; ☯ Wed-Mon mid–Mar-Dec) Rovita is excellent value and specialises in hearty local fare, with Lucanian specialities involving stuffed peppers, game birds, local salami and fine seafood.

GETTING THERE & AWAY

SITA (☎ 0971 50 68 11; www.sitabus.it in Italian) operates a comprehensive network of routes including up the coast to Sapri in Campania (€1.60, 50 minutes, six daily). Local buses (€1) connect the coastal towns and Maratea train station with Maratea Inferiore, running frequently in summer. Intercity and regional trains on the Rome–Reggio line stop at Maratea train station, below the town.

SICILY & THE SOUTH

BASILICATA

↘ITALY IN FOCUS

ART & ARCHITECTURE

SHANIA SHEGEDYN

Temple ruins, Paestum (p296)

From Da Vinci and Michelangelo to Bernini and Canova, Italy's artistic roll call is unparalleled. Birthplace of the Renaissance, the country boasts more World Heritage–listed sites than any other country on earth. And of its 44 World Heritage treasures, many are there in their guise as repositories of great art.

The history of Italian art is in many ways also the history of European art. A browse through any text on the subject brings up the names of seminal movements and periods including classical, Renaissance, baroque, futurist and metaphysical.

Its booty of *palazzi* and churches includes some of the world's architectural highlights, from engineering show-off the Pantheon (p73) to no-holds-barred St Peter's Basilica (p85).

The bad news is that even the most determined culture vulture cannot expect to see it all. The good news is that with so much creative brilliance on show, an artistic epiphany is always just around the corner.

CLASSICAL TIMES

In art and architecture, as in so many other areas, the ancient Romans looked up to the Greeks. They didn't have to look far. The Greeks had settled parts of Sicily and southern Italy as early as the 8th century BC, and their magnificent temples sparkled with sculptures inspired by the works of Praxiteles, Lysippos and Phidias. A trip to the archaeological museums in Naples (p274), Palermo (p310) and Syracuse (p324) gives a taste of the Hellenic aesthetic.

Roman sculpture focussed less on harmony and form and more on accurate representation, as seen in the brutally honest busts in Rome's Museo Nazionale Romano: Palazzo Massimo alle Terme (p81).

For Rome's emperors, art was the perfect PR tool, propagating messages from battlefield victories (see Rome's Colonna di Traiano, p71) to harmony (see Rome's Ara Pacis Augustae, p78). For cashed-up Roman citizens, sculpture was the perfect villa accessory, whether looted Greek pieces or locally made copies. Amongst the finest survivors is the extraordinary *Laocoön and His Sons* (c 160–140 BC), on show in the Vatican Museums (p88).

And though the Greeks invented the architectural orders (Doric, Ionic and Corinthian), it was the Romans who mixed-and-matched with bold bravura; consider the Colosseum (p66), with its ground tier of Doric, middle tier of Ionic and penultimate tier of Corinthian columns.

THE BYZANTINE & THE ROMANESQUE

After Constantine became Christianity's star convert, the empire's architects turned their talents to church design. His successors in Constantinople, most notably Justinian and his wife, Theodora, heralded the Byzantine 'look', its penchant for glittering handcut mosaics now best viewed in Ravenna's astounding basilicas (p204).

Ideas of clarity and simplicity of religious message began to outweigh ideals of faithful representation during the Italian Middle Ages. Painting and sculpture of this period played second fiddle to its architecture, commonly dubbed 'Romanesque'.

Italian Romanesque came in four regional forms: the Lombard, Pisan, Florentine and Sicilian Norman. While all four focussed on width and horizontal lines, as well as detached campaniles and baptisteries, the Florentine and Pisan styles had a soft spot for striped, green-and-white marble facades. The Lombard style featured elaborately carved facades and exterior bands and arches, while the Sicilian Norman version fused Saracen and Norman influences. Among Italy's Romanesque pin-ups are Sicily's Cattedrale di Monreale (p314) and Pisa's magnificent cathedral group (p236).

BETHUNE CARMICHAEL

Mosaic at Cattedrale di Monreale, Monreale (p314)

ITALY IN FOCUS

ART & ARCHITECTURE

GOTHIC TOUCHES & THE 'REBIRTH' OF ITALIAN ART

While the classical-loving Italians didn't embrace the Gothic's wild flying buttresses and grotesque gargoyles as much as the French, Spanish and Germans, the Venetians embraced the style in grand *palazzi*, among them Palazzo Ducale (p173). Further west, the fashion-victim Milanese went to extremes with their outrageous Duomo (p117).

In the art world, the Gothic style marked the transition from medieval to Renaissance art. One of its leading lights was Florentine painter Giotto di Bondone (c 1266–1337), who broke the spell of Byzantine conservatism and ventured into a new world of naturalistic painting and dramatic narrative.

Giotto's most famous works are his frescoes, and his supreme achievement is the cycle gracing the walls of Padua's Cappella degli Scrovegni (p189), southwest of Venice. Amongst his admirers was pioneering art historian Giorgio Vasari, who proclaimed that Giotto initiated the 'rebirth' *(rinascità* or *renaissance)* in art in his book *Lives of the Artists* (1550).

THE EARLY RENAISSANCE

During the 15th century (Quattrocento), painting upstaged sculpture and architecture, becoming the pre-eminent art form for the first time in European art's history. At its core were the exploration of perspective and proportion, a new interest in realistic portraiture and the beginnings of a new tradition of landscape painting. At the start of the Quattrocento, most of these were explored and refined in one city: Florence.

The first innovations of this period were in sculpture and architecture. Sculptors Lorenzo Ghiberti (1378–1455) and Donatello (c 1386–1466) replaced the stiff, drapery-clad statues of the Middle Ages with dynamic and anatomically accurate figures reminiscent of classical art.

Architect Filippo Brunelleschi (1377–1446) was also heavily influenced by the classical masters, his dome for Florence's Duomo as innovative in engineering terms as the Pantheon's dome had been 1300 years before. But Brunelleschi was able to do

LEFT: HANNAH LEVY; RIGHT: ROBERTO GEROMETTA

Left: Fresco detail, Santa Maria Novella (p227), Florence; **Right:** Scrovegni Chapel (p189), Padua

something that the ancients hadn't – discover the mathematical rules by which objects appear to diminish as they recede from us.

One of the first artworks created according to these rules was Masaccio's (1401–28) *The Holy Trinity, the Virgin, St John and Donors*, a wall painting in Florence's Basilica di Santa Maria Novella (p227). One of Masaccio's fans, Leonardo da Vinci, adopted a similar mathematical 'stage management' in his famous *Last Supper* fresco, found in the refectory of Milan's Chiesa di Santa Maria delle Grazie (p121).

Ironically, the rigid new formulas of the Quattrocento often made harmonious arrangements of figures in a painting difficult, resulting in groups that appeared artificial. Artists like Sandro Botticelli (c 1444–1510) led the way in seeking a solution, aiming for both accurate perspective and harmonious composition. His *Birth of Venus* (1485), now hung in the Uffizi, was one of his most successful attempts. It's not perfect – note Venus' unnaturally elongated neck – but it was certainly a breathtaking attempt.

THE BEST

SEAN CAFFREY

Florence's Duomo (p221)

RENAISSANCE ARCHITECTURE

- **Duomo, Florence** (p221)
- **Tempietto, Rome** (p84)
- **Basilica di San Lorenzo, Florence** (p227)
- **La Rotonda, Vicenza** (p190)
- **Palazzo Farnese, Rome** (p76)

THE HIGH RENAISSANCE

A golden age for Italian creativity, the 16th century (Cinquecento) launched the multi-talented Leonardo da Vinci (1452–1519), Michelangelo Buonarotti (1475–1564) and Raphael Santi (1483–1520) – all three painters and architects of genius.

While Leonardo took the radical step of modulating his contours using colour (a technique called *sfumato*), Michelangelo's representations of the human body radically captured the essence of the human experience itself. One look at his chiselled *David* in the Galleria dell'Accademia (p228) or at the painted ceiling of the Sistine Chapel (p88) and you'll understand.

Raphael's forte was in rising to the Quattrocento challenge of achieving harmonious, perspectively accurate arrangement of figures. A superlative example of this is his painting *La Scuola d'Atene* (The School of Athens) in the Stanza della Segnatura in the Vatican Museums (p88).

This sense of evolution flavoured architecture as well. While Florentine masterpieces like the Duomo and Cappella de' Pazzi epitomised the Early Renaissance's architectural essence – a classical-inspired elegance of line and innovation that celebrated man's centrality in the universe – its refinements mainly occurred in 16th-century Rome, where a progression of popes enticed architects and artists to build bigger, ever more beautiful buildings.

A number of these were designed by the great Donato Bramante (1444–1514), a devotee of pure classicism and the mind behind Rome's Tempietto (p84), often described as the pinnacle of High Renaissance architecture. Equally fascinated with the architecture of ancient Rome was Veneto-based architect Andrea Palladio (1508–1580), whose elegantly symmetrical Villa Capra (aka La Rotonda, p190) was strongly influenced by Bramante's Tempietto.

While Palladio found inspiration in central Italian trends, Venetian painters Giorgione (c 1477–1510) and Titian (c 1490–1576) took a different path, snubbing the figure arrangement and form of their contemporaries for compositions unified through light and shade. The finest example of this is Giorgione's enigmatic *La Tempesta* (The Storm) in Venice's Gallerie dell'Accademia (p228).

BOMBASTIC BAROQUE

Predictably, all that Renaissance restraint would ultimately lead to a backlash. Ready to spice things up was the baroque. Ditching classical rules for a dramatic, curvaceous and downright sexy impact, its booty of masterpieces include Andrea Palma's facade of Syracuse Cathedral (p325) and master sculptor Gian Lorenzo Bernini's (1598–1680) baldachin in St Peter's (p85).

For the Catholic Church, baroque's spectacular, seductive qualities were a nifty weapon against the spread of no-nonsense Protestant Reformation. One look at Bernini's suggestive sculpture *Vision of Saint Theresa* in Rome's Chiesa della Santa Maria della Vittoria and it's hard not to think of the modern term 'sex sells'.

A generation before Bernini, artists Michelangelo Merisi da Caravaggio (1573–1610) and Annibale Caracci (1560–1609) had played a vital role in pushing art towards the baroque. Bored with the polite, heightened expression of mannerism – a style which grew out of the Renaissance and dominated the Italian scene from the 1520s to the 1580s – *enfant terrible* Caravaggio shocked his contemporaries with faithful depictions of nature in all its beauty and ugliness. Yet even critics of his visual 'brutality' were forced to admire his trademark chiaroscuro (the bold contrast of light and dark), dramatically exemplified in his painting *Flagellazione* in Naples' Museo di Capodimonte (p280).

Caracci, considered the major artist of the baroque Bolognese school, would inspire later baroque painters like Cortona, Pozzo and Gaulli with his innovative illusionistic elements, clearly seen in his frescoes in Rome's Palazzo Farnese (p76).

NEOCLASSICAL RESTRAINT

While Italy's 18th-century art scene was dominated by the painting and engraving of views for souvenir-hungry Grand Tour travellers, neoclassicism was the following century's buzzword. Its greatest local exponent was sculptor Antonio Canova (1757–1822), who renounced movement

THE BEST

Palace facade, Catania (p321)

BETHUNE CARMICHAEL

BAROQUE CITIES & TOWNS

- Rome (p50)
- Naples (p274)
- Lecce (p336)
- Noto (p327)
- Catania (p321)

Galleria Vittorio Emanuele II (p120), Milan

PAOLO CORDELLI

in favour of stillness, emotion in favour of restraint and illusion in favour of simplicity. His most famous work is a daring sculpture of Pauline Bonaparte Borghese as a reclining *Venere Vincitrice* (Conquering Venus), in Rome's Museo e Galleria Borghese (p79).

Italian architecture, sculpture and painting had played a dominant role in the cultural life of Europe for some 400 years, but with Canova's death in 1822, this supremacy came to an end.

Architecturally, the 19th century brought few moments of note. One of these stemmed directly from the Industrial Revolution, and saw the application of industrial innovations in glass and metal to building design. Its most iconic example is Milan's Galleria Vittorio Emanuele II (p120), designed in 1865 by Giuseppe Mengoni.

THE 20TH CENTURY

Debuting with 'Stile Floreale' (Italy's extravagant version of art nouveau), early 20th-century Italian architecture soon moved onto modernism. While the first of its two forms was purely theoretical, the second form was rationalism, promoted in Italy by two groups: the Bauhaus-inspired Gruppo Sette and its rival group, MIAR (Movimento Italiano per l'Architettura Razionale; the Italian Movement for Rational Architecture). The groups' leading architects were Giuseppe Terragni (1904–943) and Adalberto Libera (1903–63) respectively, whose uncompromisingly modernist structures for Mussolini's regime led to the label 'fascist architecture'.

While futurism and metaphysical painting *(Pittura Metafisica)* defined the art surrounding WWI, it was the 1950s that brought new spark to the Italian art scene and saw artists like Alberto Burri (1915–95) and Lucio Fontana (1899–1968) experiment with abstract art. While Fontana's punctured canvases were characterised by *spazialismo* (spatialism), Burri provoked with avowedly anti-traditional assemblages made of burlap, wood, iron and plastic. Now housed in Rome's Galleria Nazionale d'Arte Moderna e Contemporanea (p79), Burri's

THE BEST

OLIVIER CIRENDINI

Mosaic, Basilica di San Marco (p172)

MOSAIC INTERIORS

- **Basilica di San Vitale, Ravenna** (p204)
- **Basilica di Sant'Apollinare Nuovo, Ravenna** (p205)
- **Basilica di San Marco, Venice** (p172)
- **Cattedrale di Monreale, Monreale** (p314)
- **Battistero Neoniano, Ravenna** (p204)

Grande Sacco (Large Sack) caused major controversy when first unveiled in 1952.

In the swinging 1960s, the radical *Arte Povera* (Poor Art) movement took off, its followers using simple materials to trigger memories and associations. Major exponents included Mario Merz (1925–2003), Giovanni Anselmo (b 1934), Luciano Fabro (1936–2007), Giulio Paolini (b 1940) and Greek-born Jannis Kounellis (b 1936), all of whom experimented with sculpture and installations.

By the 1980s, everything old was new again as artists like Sandro Chia (b 1946), Mimmo Paladino (b 1948) and Francesco Clemente (b 1952) heralded a return to painting and sculpture in a traditional, primarily figurative sense. Dubbed 'Transavanguardia', this movement broke with the prevailing international focus on conceptual art and was thought by some critics to signal the death of avant-garde.

By the end of the century, Italy's art-world darlings would include mixed-media artist Stefano Arienti (b 1961), installation artist Mario Airò (b 1961), video artist Grazia Toderi (b 1963) and photographer Luisa Lambri (b 1969).

NEW MILLENNIUM LANDMARKS

In the second half of the 20th-century, Italy reinvented itself as a hub of cutting-edge fashion and design. The same couldn't be said for its architecture. One of the few high points include Gio Ponti's 1956 Pirelli Tower in Milan. But the architecture scene is hotting up again, with names like Massimiliano Fuksas; King, Roselli & Ricci; and Cino Zucchi turning heads with their innovative building designs.

Cream of the current crop is Renzo Piano (b 1937), whose 2002 Auditorium Parco della Musica (p99) dragged Rome into the 21st century and injected some much needed verve into the city's cultural life.

Lending a hand is a swathe of projects by foreign architects, from Richard Meier's controversial Ara Pacis pavilion (p78) and Zaha Hadid's MAXXI art gallery in Rome to Arato Isozaki's Uffizi extensions (p226) and Tadao Ando's acclaimed Punta della Dogana and Palazzo Grassi renovation (p174) in Venice.

The most exciting building project since the Renaissance is under way at Milan's former trade fairground. Dubbed 'CityLife', its star turn will be a trio of striking skyscrapers – one straight, one twisting and one curving – by Zaha Hadid, Arata Isozaki and Daniel Liebeskind.

FAMILY TRAVEL

WAYNE WALTON

Family taking photographs at Pisa's Leaning Tower (p237)

In the land of doting *mamme* (mums) and indulgent *nonni* (grandparents), children are adored and welcomed almost everywhere. Italy's battalion of ancient sites and colourful festivals should pique the interest of most young minds, though it's worth investing in a few good children's history books to help their imagination along. On the downside, Italy offers few special amenities for little ones: preparation is the key to success.

INSPIRATION

As tempting as it may be on a short trip, don't try to overdo things, and make sure activities include the kids – older children could help in the planning of these. Think of things that might capture their imagination, like Rome's gladiatorial Colosseum (p66) and the Roman Forum (p70), the ruins at Pompeii (p288), Sicily's Valley of the Temples (p329), and the gondolas of Venice (p178). Another good bet is the volcanoes in the south, as well as water activities, from lolling on a beach to snorkelling.

For colour, spectacle and scrumptious food, consider attending one of Italy's historic festivals, such as Venice's Carnevale and Festa del Redentore (p179), and Siena's flag-twirling, horse-racing Palio (boxed text, p243).

When choosing museums, throw in the odd curio that may be more likely to stir a young child's fascination than yet another worthy art gallery. Options include Venice's Museo Storico Navale (p177), a little fashion therapy in Milan's Quadrilatero d'Oro (boxed text, p125) district and a guided tour of Naples' atmospheric aqueducts (p281).

Lastly, allow time for kids to play, and make sure treats such as a whopping gelato or slice of their favourite pizza are included in the bag of tricks.

↘ THE NITTY GRITTY

- **Baby formula & sterilising solution** Available at pharmacies
- **Car safety seats** Book ahead from car hire company
- **Change facilities** Rare beyond airports, malls and McDonald's
- **Cots** Request ahead at hotels
- **Highchairs** Request ahead at hotels and restaurants
- **Nappies** Available at supermarkets and pharmacies
- **Strollers** Bring your own umbrella-style stroller
- **Transport** Reserve train seats where possible to avoid standing

PRACTICALITIES

Always make a point of asking staff members at tourist offices if they know of any special family activities or have suggestions on hotels that cater for kids, and always book accommodation in advance to avoid any inconvenience.

Be aware that discounts are available for children (usually aged under 12 but sometimes based on the child's height) on public transport and for admission to sites.

For more tips on the art of travelling with kids, see Lonely Planet's *Travel with Children* or click onto www.travelwithyourkids.com and www.familytravelnetwork.com.

HISTORY

Rome's Imperial Forums (p70)

PAOLO CORDELLI

Anyone who says history is boring has never known Italy. Like a soap opera on speed, this knee-high boot has seen it all: imperial domination, humiliating poverty and postwar boom. Its backstory has all the prime-time essentials: perverted emperors, ambitious invaders and philandering politicians. Never buried, it's a past that vividly colours the present, from ancient ruins in designer bars to papal power in politics.

ETRUSCANS, GREEKS & THE BIRTH OF ROME

Long before the Renaissance *palazzi* and cypress-fringed landscapes, the area between the Arno and Tiber rivers was known as Etruria. Based on a number of city-states, it was the domain of the Etruscans, who dominated the peninsula by the 7th century BC. Though redoubtable warriors and seafarers, the Etruscans lacked cohesion.

More disciplined were Greek traders, who had set up independent city-states along Italy's southern coast and in Sicily in the 8th century BC. Collectively known as Magna

474 BC	396 BC	264–241 BC
Etruscan power is eclipsed after Greek forces win the naval Battle of Cumae.	Romans conquer the key Etruscan town of Veio, north of Rome, after an 11-year siege.	War breaks out between Rome and the empire of Carthage, which stretches into Sicily and Sardinia.

Ruins at the Valley of the Temples (p329)
IONAS KALTENBACH

Graecia, the Hellenic settlements flourished until the 3rd century BC. Even today, the magnificent Doric ruins at Paestum and on Sicily (at Agrigento, Selinunte and Segesta) lie testament to the Greeks' colonial splendour.

While the Greeks survived Etruscan attacks, the death knell for both would come from the same, unexpected source – the grubby but growing Latin town of Rome.

According to legend, Italy's future capital was founded by twins Romulus and Remus on 21 April 753 BC, on the site where they had been suckled by a she-wolf as orphan infants. The twins fought over the city walls. In a fit of rage, Romulus killed his brother, continued building the walls as he wished and named the city in his own honour. Over the following centuries, this town would grow to become Italy's major power, sweeping aside the Etruscans, whose language and culture vanished by the 2nd century AD.

THE ROMAN REPUBLIC

Although monuments were emblazoned with the initials SPQR (Senatus Populusque Romanus, or the Senate and People of Rome) from the beginning of the republic, the 'people' initially had precious little say in the city's affairs. (Many Romans would argue that little has changed.) Known as plebeians (literally 'the many'), the disenfranchised majority slowly wrested concessions from the patrician class in the more than two centuries that followed the founding of the republic.

Slowly at first, then with gathering pace, Roman armies conquered the Italian peninsula. Defeated city-states were not taken over directly; rather they were cleverly obliged to become allies. They retained their government and lands but had to provide troops on demand to serve in the Roman army. Under this tactic, wars with Carthage and in

AD 79	476	568
A massive eruption of Mt Vesuvius showers molten rock and ash upon Pompeii and Herculaneum.	German tribal leader Odovacar proclaims himself king in Rome.	Lombards occupy northern Italy, leaving just Ravenna, Rome and southern Italy in the Empire's hands.

the East led Rome to take control of Sardinia, Sicily, Corsica, mainland Greece, Spain, most of northern Africa and part of Asia Minor by 133 BC.

By then, Rome was the Mediterranean's most important city.

BEWARE THE IDES OF MARCH

One of Rome's most important figures would be Gaius Julius Caesar (100-44 BC). After a successful stint governing the province of Gallia Narbonensis (a southern swathe of modern France), Caesar raised troops and in 60 BC entered Gaul proper to head off Helvetic tribes invading from Switzerland. What started as an essentially defensive effort soon became a full-blown campaign of conquest. In the next five years, he subdued Gaul and made forays into Britain and across the Rhine. In 52–1 BC he stamped out the last great revolt in Gaul, led by Vercingetorix.

Pompey the Great, a powerful leader in the Republic, severed his political alliance with Caesar and joined like-minded factions in the Senate to outlaw Caesar in 49 BC. Caesar and his devoted army crossed the Rubicon river into Italy on 7 January, sparking a civil war. His three-year campaign in Italy, Spain and the Eastern Mediterranean proved a crushing victory. Upon his return to Rome in 46 BC, Caesar assumed dictatorial powers.

Though he launched reforms and commissioned impressive buildings (including the surviving Curia and Basilica Giulia at the Roman Forum, p70), by 44 BC it was clear that this high-achieving ruler had no plans to restore the Republic. Dissent grew in the Senate and on the Ides of March (15 March) that very year, a small band of conspirators led by former supporter Marcus Junius Brutus stabbed the dictator to death.

In the years following Caesar's death, his lieutenant, Mark Antony (Marcus Antonius), and nominated heir, great-nephew Octavian, plunged into civil war against Caesar's assassins. Octavian took control of the empire's western half and Antony headed to the east. But when Antony fell head over heels for Cleopatra VII in 31 BC, Octavian went to war, eventually claiming victory over Antony and Cleopatra at Actium, in Greece. The next year Antony and Cleopatra committed suicide and Egypt was added to Rome's property portfolio.

AUGUSTUS & THE GOLDEN YEARS

By 27 BC, Octavian had been acclaimed Augustus (Your Eminence) and conceded virtually unlimited power by the Senate. In effect, he had become emperor. Under him, the arts flourished, old buildings were restored and new buildings constructed, among them the Pantheon (p73).

By AD 100, Rome was the New York of the ancient world; a dazzling spectacle of marble temples, theatres, libraries and a multicultural population exceeding 1.5 million.

754–56	902	962
Frankish king Pepin the Short defeats the Lombards and declares the creation of the Papal States.	Muslims from northern Africa complete the occupation of Sicily, installing an enlightened regime.	Otto I is crowned Holy Roman Emperor, the first in a long line of Germanic rulers.

LOOPY ROMAN LEADERS

Tiberius (AD 14–37) Prone to depression, Tiberius withdrew in his latter years to Capri (p284), where he apparently devoted himself to drink and orgies.

Gaius (Caligula; 37–41) Tiberius' grand-nephew counted sex, including with his sisters, and gratuitous violence among his hobbies. He suggested making a horse consul before being assassinated.

Claudius (41–54) Apparently timid as a child, he proved ruthless with his enemies (among them 35 senators), whose executions he greatly enjoyed watching.

Nero (54–68) Accused of playing his fiddle while Rome burned in 64, Nero executed the evangelists Peter and Paul and had other Christians thrown to wild beasts.

Yet poverty was rife among an often disgruntled lower class – Augustus created Rome's first police force under a city prefect *(praefectus urbi)* to curb mob violence.

While the Empire reached its greatest extent under Hadrian (76–138), by the time Diocletian (245–305) took charge attacks from without and revolts within had become part and parcel of imperial existence. Christianity was gaining popularity and under Diocletian persecution of Christians became common, a policy ended in 313 under the Christian Constantine I.

The Empire was later divided in two, with the second capital in Constantinople (modern-day Istanbul) founded by Constantine in 330. It was this, the eastern Empire, which survived as Italy and Rome were overrun.

POPES & EMPERORS

In an odd twist, the minority religion that Emperor Diocletian had tried so hard to stamp out saved the glory of the city of Rome. Through the chaos of invasion and counter-invasion that saw Italy succumb to Germanic tribes, the Byzantine reconquest and the Lombard occupation in the north, the papacy established itself in Rome as a spiritual and secular force.

In return for formal recognition of the pope's control of Rome and surrounding Byzantine-held territories (henceforth to be known as the Papal States), the Carolingian Franks were granted a leading, if ill-defined, role in Italy and their king, Charlemagne, the title of Holy Roman Emperor. He was crowned by Pope Saint Leo III on Christmas Day 800. The bond between the papacy and the Byzantine Empire was thus broken and political power in what had been the Western Roman Empire shifted north of the

1130	1348	1506
Roger II is crowned king of Sicily. Norman architecture fuses with Byzantine and Muslim styles.	The Black Death (bubonic plague) wreaks havoc across Italy and much of western Europe.	Work starts on the new St Peter's Basilica to a design by Donato Bramante.

Alps, where it would remain for more than 1000 years.

The stage was set for a future of seemingly endless struggles. Similarly, Rome's aristocratic families engaged in battle for the papacy, creating centuries of ruthless fighting for the imperial crown. The clash between Pope Gregory VII and Emperor Henry IV over who had the right to appoint the politically powerful bishops in the last quarter of the 11th century showed just how bitter these struggles could become. Resentful of Pope Gregory's deposition of Henry as king of Germany in 1076 (which removed the king from the church), Henry IV invaded Rome in 1081 in order to remove the 'unfriendly' pope. Three attempts later, in 1084, Henry succeeded. Pope Gregory was declared deposed and on 31 March of that year, Henry was crowned Holy Roman Emperor. Such skirmishes became a focal point of Italian politics in the late Middle Ages and across the cities and regions of the peninsula two camps emerged: Guelphs (Guelfi, who backed the pope) and Ghibellines (Ghibellini, in support of the emperor).

GREG ELMS

Bust of Constantine I, Capitoline Museums (p72)

THE WONDER OF THE WORLD

The Holy Roman Empire had barely touched southern Italy until Henry VI, son of the Holy Roman Emperor Frederick I (Barbarossa), married Constance de Hauteville, heir to the Norman throne in Sicily. Of this match was born one of the most colourful figures of medieval Europe: Frederick II (1194–1250).

Crowned Holy Roman Emperor in 1220, Frederick was a German with a difference. Having grown up in southern Italy, he considered Sicily his natural base and left the German states largely to their own devices. A poet, linguist, mathematician and philosopher (his nickname was 'Stupor Mundi' – Wonder of the World), Frederick was

1508–12	1582	1600
Pope Julius II commissions Michelangelo to paint the ceiling frescoes in the restored Sistine Chapel.	Pope Gregory XIII replaces the Julian calendar with the modern-day Gregorian calendar.	Giordano Bruno, Dominican monk, rebellious intellectual and heretic, is burned alive at the stake in Rome.

JEAN-PIERRE LESCOURRET

Galleria Palatina in Palazzo Pitti (p229), originally built for the Pitti family, rivals of the Medici dynasty

also an enlightened ruler who allowed freedom of worship to Muslims and Jews. He also founded a university in Naples.

Having reluctantly carried out a crusade (marked more by negotiation than the clash of arms) in the Holy Land in 1228–29 on pain of excommunication, Frederick returned to Italy to find Papal troops invading Neapolitan territory. Frederick soon had them on the run and turned his attention to gaining control of the complex web of city-states in central and northern Italy, where he found allies and many enemies, in particular the Lombard league. Years of inconclusive battles ensued, which even Frederick's death did not end.

FLOURISHING CITY-STATES

While the south of Italy tended to centralised rule, the north did not. Port cities such as Genoa, Pisa and especially Venice, along with internal centres such as Florence, Milan, Parma, Bologna and Padua, became increasingly insolent towards attempts by the Holy Roman Emperors to meddle in their affairs.

Between the 12th and 14th centuries, these cities developed new forms of government. Venice adopted an oligarchic 'parliamentary' system in an attempt at limited democracy. More commonly, the city-state created a *comune* (town council), a form

1714	1805	1848
The Spanish Bourbon family establishes an independent Kingdom of the Two Sicilies.	Napoleon is proclaimed king of the newly constituted Kingdom of Italy.	Revolts across Europe spark rebellion in Italy, especially in Austrian-occupied Milan and Venice.

ITALY IN FOCUS

◥ HELLFIRE HERETIC

Since 1481, Dominican friar Girolamo Savonarola had been in Florence preaching repentance. His bloodcurdling warnings of horrors to come if Florentines did not renounce their vices captured everyone's imagination, and soon books, jewellery, fancy furnishings and art were burned on 'bonfires of the vanities'. But pleasure-loving Florentines soon began to tire of this fundamentalism, as did Pope Alexander VI, and finally the city government, or *signoria,* had the fiery friar arrested. In 1498, after weeks at the hands of the city rackmaster, Savonarola was hanged and burned at the stake as a heretic, along with two supporters.

HISTORY

of republican government dominated at first by aristocrats but then increasingly by the wealthy middle classes.

In some cities, great dynasties, such as the Medici in Florence and the Visconti and Sforza in Milan, came to dominate their respective stages.

War between the city-states was a constant. Eventually a few, notably Florence, Milan and Venice, emerged as regional powers and absorbed their neighbours.

These independent-minded cities proved fertile ground for the intellectual and artistic explosion that would take place across northern Italy in the 14th and 15th centuries. After centuries of Church-dominated obscurantism, the arrival of eastern scholars fleeing Constantinople in the wake of its fall to the Ottoman Turkish Muslims in 1453 prompted a renewed interest in classical learning. This coincided with a burst of new and original artistic activity that would snowball into the wonders of the Renaissance. Of them all, Florence was the launch pad for this fevered activity, in no small measure due to the generous patronage of the long-ruling house of Medici.

CAVOUR & THE BIRTH OF ITALY

By the late 18th century, Italy's divided mini-states had lost power and the peninsula had become little more than a backward playground for Europe's main players.

Napoleon finished off the Venetian republic in 1797 (ending 1000 years of Venetian independence) and created the so-called Kingdom of Italy in 1804. Though the kingdom was hardly independent, the Napoleonic earthquake spurred many Italians to believe that a single Italian state could be created after the emperor's demise.

It was not to be so easy. The reactionary 1814–15 Congress of Vienna returned regional control of Italy to a collection of foreign rulers.

1860	1861	1915
Giuseppe Garibaldi arrives with a thousand men and takes Sicily and parts of mainland southern Italy.	Vittorio Emanuele II is proclaimed king of a newly united Italy.	Italy enters WWI on the side of the Allies to win Italian territories still in Austrian hands.

THE BEST

WILL SALTER

The Palatine (p67), Rome

PLACES TO TIME TRAVEL

- **Herculaneum & Pompeii** (p289 and p288)
- **Colosseum & Palatine, Rome** (p66 and p67)
- **Paestum** (p296)
- **Via Appia Antica, Rome** (p87)
- **Assisi** (p253)

Count Camillo Benso di Cavour (1810–61) of Turin, prime minister of the Savoy monarchy, became the diplomatic brains behind the Italian unity movement. He conspired with the French and won British support for the creation of an independent Italian state. His 1858 treaty with France's Napoleon III foresaw French aid in the event of a war with Austria and the creation of a northern Italian kingdom, in exchange for parts of Savoy and Nice.

The bloody Franco–Austrian War (also known as the war for Italian independence; 1859–61), unleashed in northern Italy, led to the occupation of Lombardy and the retreat of the Austrians to their eastern possessions in the Veneto. Revolutionary Giuseppe Garibaldi took Sicily and southern Italy in a military blitz in the name of Savoy king Vittorio Emanuele II in 1860. Spotting the chance, Cavour and the king moved to take parts of central Italy, proclaiming the creation of a single Italian state in 1861.

Unity was complete and parliament was established in Rome in 1871.

FROM THE TRENCHES TO FASCISM

Although a member of the Triple Alliance with Austria and Germany, Italy remained neutral when war broke out in 1914. That changed with Austria's intransigence in handing over territory claimed by Italy – including Trento (Trentino and Trieste) – leading Italy to declare war on Austria and plunging it into a 3½-year nightmare.

Despite Italy's managing to claim Trieste and Trento, the postwar Treaty of Versailles failed to award Rome the remaining territories it had sought.

This humiliation, combined with a loss of 600,000 Italians and rampant unemployment and poverty created an ideal political climate for young socialist newspaper editor and one-time draft dodger, Benito Mussolini (1883–1945). Giving his political leanings an extreme makeover, he formed a militant right-wing political group that by 1921 had become the Fascist Party, famed for its black-shirted street brawlers and Roman

1922	1929	1940
A fearful King Vittorio Emanuele III entrusts Mussolini with the formation of a government.	Catholicism is declared Italy's sole religion; the Vatican is recognised as a separate state.	Italy enters WWII on Nazi Germany's side and invades Greece.

salute. After his march on Rome in 1922 and victory in the 1924 elections, Mussolini (who called himself the Duce, or Leader) took full control of Italy by 1926.

While Mussolini at first showed a cautious, cooperative hand on the international front, his invasion of Abyssinia (Ethiopia) in 1935–6 revealed his dream for a 'new Roman empire'. Condemned by the League of Nations and impressed by Hitler's own territorial expansion, 'Il Duce' led Italy into WWII on Germany's side in 1940.

By the time the Allies landed in Sicily in 1943, the Italians – including Mussolini's own government – had had enough of the dictator and his war, and so the king (whose full powers had been returned via parliamentary vote) had him arrested. In September, however, Italy surrendered and the Germans, who had rescued Mussolini, occupied the bulk northern two-thirds of the country and reinstalled the dictator. Yet, Mussolini's luck was about to run out. The painfully slow Allied campaign up the peninsula and German repression led to the formation of the Resistance, which played a growing role in harassing German forces. Northern Italy was finally liberated in April 1945. Resistance fighters caught a Switzerland-bound Mussolini, shooting him and his lover, Clara Petacci, and stringing up their corpses in Milan's Piazzale Lotto.

REDS, CONSPIRACY & TERROR

In the aftermath of the war, the left-wing Resistance was disarmed and Italy's political forces scrambled to regroup. The USA, through the economic largesse of the Marshall Plan, wielded considerable political influence and used this to keep the left in check.

Immediately after the war, three coalition governments succeeded one another. The third, which came to power in December 1945, was dominated by the newly formed right-wing Democrazia Cristiana (DC; Christian Democrats), led by Alcide de Gasperi, who remained prime minister until 1953. Italy became a republic in 1946 and De Gasperi's DC won the first elections under the new constitution in 1948.

Until the 1980s, the Partito Comunista Italiano (PCI; Communist Party), at first under Palmiro Togliatti and later the charismatic Enrico Berlinguer, played a crucial role in Italy's social and political development, in spite of being systematically kept out of government.

The very popularity of the party led to a grey period in the country's history, the *anni di piombo* (years of lead) in the 1970s. Just as the Italian economy was booming, Europe-wide paranoia about the power of the communists in Italy fuelled a secretive reaction that, it is said, was largely directed by the CIA and NATO. Even today, little is known about Operation Gladio, an underground paramilitary organisation supposedly behind various unexplained terror attacks in the country.

1943	1946	1957
King Vittorio Emanuele III sacks Mussolini. German forces free Mussolini and occupy most of Italy.	Italians vote to abolish the monarchy and create a republic.	Italy joins France, West Germany and the Benelux countries to sign the Treaty of Rome.

LEFT: MARTIN MOOS; RIGHT: MARTIN LLADO

Left: Italy gave up the lira for the euro in 2001; Right: Political poster for Silvio Berlosconi

The 1970s were thus dominated by the spectre of terrorism, which included both right- and left-wing bombings and the shock 1978 kidnapping and assassination of former DC prime minister Aldo Moro by leftist militant group Brigate Rosse (Red Brigades).

Despite the disquiet, the 1970s was also a time of positive change, with the legalisation of divorce and the introduction of anti-sexism legislation.

MODERN ITALY: EUROS, KICKBACKS AND SCANDALOUS CLAIMS

A growth spurt in the 1980s saw Italy become one of the world's leading economies, but by the mid-1990s a new and prolonged period of crisis had set in. High unemployment and inflation, combined with a huge national debt and mercurial currency (the lira), led the government to introduce draconian measures to cut public spending, allowing Italy to join the single currency (euro) in 2001.

The Italian political scene was rocked by the Tangentopoli ('kickback city') scandal, which broke in Milan in 1992. Led by a pool of Milanese magistrates, including the tough Antonio di Pietro, investigations known as Mani Pulite (Clean Hands) implicated thousands of politicians, public officials and businesspeople in scandals ranging from bribery to blatant theft.

1970	1980	1999
Parliament approves the country's first ever divorce legislation, vociferously opposed by the Church.	A terrorist bomb in Bologna kills 85 and injures hundreds more.	Italy becomes a primary base in NATO's air war on Yugoslavia.

The old centre-right political parties collapsed in the wake of these trials and from the ashes rose what many Italians hoped might be a breath of fresh political air. Media magnate Silvio Berlusconi's Forza Italia (Go Italy) party swept to power in 2001 and, after an inconclusive two-year interlude of centre-left government under former European Commission head Romano Prodi from 2006, again in April 2008.

From 2001 to 2006, Berlusconi's rule was marked by the introduction of laws which seemed aimed principally at protecting his extensive business interests (he controls as much as 90% of the country's free TV channels). He also spent considerable time haranguing what he claimed to be the country's 'politicised' judges. The latter have been looking into his myriad business affairs since the beginning of the 1990s, but one trial after another has collapsed.

Controversies of a sexual kind plagued the prime minister in 2009, with questions concerning 'Papi' Berlusconi's friendship

⬊ DRAG, DRUGS & THE CAMORRA

While Mafia arrests are common in Italy, the February 2009 arrest of Ugo Gabriele in Naples broke the mould like no other. Beefy and ruthless, the 27-year-old would go down in history as Italy's first cross-dressing mobster. In between managing lucrative prostitution and drug rackets for the city's Scissionisti clan, 'Kitty' (as Gabriele demanded to be addressed) found time to shape his eyebrows and dye his hair platinum blonde.

Naples' homegrown Mafia, the Camorra, has its tentacles on everything from drugs, arms and counterfeit smuggling to construction, transport and waste disposal contracts. Its estimated annual turnover exceeds €30 million.

with a teenage starlet soon overshadowed by prostitute Patrizia D'Addario's claims that she had spent several evenings with Berlusconi at his official Rome residence. According to the former actress, the prime minister had even offered her a seat in the European Parliament. At the time of writing, the heat is only set to increase for Berlusconi. On 7 October 2009, Italy's constitutional court declared that a controversial law protecting the Prime Minister from prosecution, was unconstitutional. As a result, the media mogul may soon have little choice but to face the string of charges against him, from bribery and corruption to tax fraud.

2005	2007	2009
Pope John Paul II dies aged 84. Grieving crowds in Rome chant *santo subito* (sainthood now).	Former heir to the Italian throne, Vittorio Emanuele di Savoia, is cleared of corruption and fraud charges.	A sex scandal embroils Prime Minister Silvio Berlusconi. His wife, Veronica Lario, denounces him publicly.

THE ITALIAN TABLE

Variety of Italian cheeses for sale

WILL SALTER

'Tutti a tavola!' ('Everyone to the table!'). While traffic lights are merely suggestions and queues fine ideas in theory, this is one command every Italian heeds without question. To disobey would be unthinkable – what, you're going to eat your pasta cold? And insult the cook? Even anarchists wouldn't dream of it.

Eating is a national obsession in Italy, where plump produce, venerated traditions and picky palates have carved out a culinary nirvana. Each ingredient must be chosen for its scent, texture, ripeness and ability to play well with others. This means getting to the right market early and often, and remaining open to seasonal inspiration. To balance the right ingredients in exactly the right proportions, Italian cooks apply an intuitive Pythagorean theorem of flavours you won't find spelt out in any recipe – but you'll surely know a winning formula when you taste it.

REGIONAL FLAVOURS

The word for Italian pride of place might be *campanilismo*, but a more accurate term would be *formaggismo*: loyalty to the local cheese. Clashes among medieval city-states involving boiling oil have been replaced by competition in speciality foods and wines. Regional variations in climate, geography and foreign influences have created a richly diverse culinary landscape far removed from the 'one size fits all' Italian culinary clichés often served up beyond the country's borders. Below is a bite-size regional rundown.

ROME

Italy's capital is more than just Viagra-strength espresso at Caffè Tazza d'Oro (p97) and glorious gelato (p93). It's about thin-crust pizza, Italo-Jewish *carciofi fritti* (fried artichokes), *saltimbocca* (veal sautéed with prosciutto and sage) and the calorific pasta classics spaghetti carbonara (with bacon, egg and cheese) and *bucatini all'amatriciana* (tube pasta with tomato, pecorino romano and *guanciale*, or pigs' cheeks). Rome's Testaccio district is the spiritual home of nose-to-tail noshing, where staples like *trippa alla Romana* (tripe with tomato and mint) and *pajata* (a pasta dish of milk-fed calf's intestines in tomato sauce) beckon brave gourmands.

THE NORTHWEST

Cooler weather and Gallic neighbours underscore the northwest's flavours, especially in classic Piedmontese creations like risotto made with frog meat and local Carnaroli rice. Frigid winters are compensated with irresistible gorgonzola and *castelmagno* blue cheeses, white truffles from Alba and chocolate from Turin.

While coastal Liguria is famed for its pesto, focaccia and *burrida* (seafood simmered in white wine, parsley, garlic, onions and oregano), Lombardy keeps it meaty with *risotto milanese con ossobucco* (veal shank and marrow with saffron rice) and *bresaola* (air-dried salted beef). The latest culinary comeback in trend-obsessed Milan is *latterie* ('milk bars'); comfort-food restaurants where heavy dishes are ditched for cheese, vegetables and simple homemade pasta.

THE NORTHEAST

Warming soul food is equally at home in Italy's northeast, from *speckknödelsuppe* (bacon-dumpling soup) in the Teutonic Alto-Adige to *polenta con quaglie* (polenta with roasted quails) in the Veneto. While the Veneto's inland staples include spiced calf liver (echoing the region's spice-trade past), its coastal areas celebrate the Adriatic in dishes like squid-ink risotto and *granseole* (spider-crab). Sweet tooths in Venice should head straight to kiosks selling *fritole* (doughnuts) and to Caffè Florian (p183), whose decadent cocoa is criminally dense.

Across the Po, culinary mecca Emilia-Romagna claims two of Italy's best-known exports: *parmigiano reggiano* (Parmesan) and Modena aged balsamic vinegar. And while bloodlust isn't strictly required to appreciate Emilia-Romagna's lauded

Pistachio *cannoli*
ALAN BENSON

Prosciutto being carved
ALAN BENSON

ITALY IN FOCUS

THE ITALIAN TABLE

cuisine, it doesn't hurt. Cold-cut platters feature *prosciutto di Parma*, salami, mortadella, *zampone* (trotters) and *coppa*, a surprisingly tasty combo of neck meat and lard cured in brine. Sharing the local limelight are meat-stuffed tortellini and *pasta alla Bolognese* with white wine, tomato, oregano, beef and belly pork. No wonder Bologna is dubbed *La Grassa* (the fat one).

CENTRAL ITALY

The Tuscans have a way with meat, herbs and olive oil that sometimes verges on pornographic. A whole boar, pheasant, or rabbit on a spit basted with a sprig of rosemary is a low-key revelation here, while pampered Maremma beef makes a splendid *spiedino toscano* (mixed grill with rosemary). Another must for carnivores is the tender, hulking *bistecca alla fiorentina,* the bone-in steak that locals insist should be 'three fingers thick'.

Even peasant soup becomes a royal feast in Tuscany, with the addition of farm-fresh eggs, local pecorino, toasted bread and a drizzle of Tuscany's prized golden olive oil: all hail the *acquacotta* (literally 'cooked water', or soup). To top that, try anything featuring fungi, especially wild mushrooms or suave, smoky porcini.

In neighbouring Umbria, locals can be found foraging alongside the local boars for wild asparagus, mushrooms and the legendary black Norcia truffles. White truffles are more rare and subtle in flavour, but grate a pungent Umbrian black truffle atop fresh *tagliatelle* egg pasta and you'll discover one of the most instantly addictive flavours on the planet. Add the prospect of Perugian desserts from Sandri (p252) and you'll understand why Umbria is a culinary must.

NAPLES & THE AMALFI COAST

Sun-soaked Mediterranean flavours sparkle in Naples and its surrounds, where hot capsicums (peppers), citruses and prized San Marzano tomatoes thrive in the volcanic soils that buried Pompeii. Team local buffalo-milk mozzarella with basil and tomato sauce on pizza dough for Naples' most famous export: *pizza margherita*.

Equally moreish is pasta *cacio e pepe* (with zesty *caciocavallo* cheese and pepper) and Naples' cheap, golden *fritture* (deep-fried snacks). Spanning *arancini* (mozzarella-filled rice balls) to tempura-style zucchini (courgettes) and egg-

TOP LOCAL DROPS

- **Sparkling wines** Prosecco (Veneto), Asti (aka Asti Spumante; Piedmont), Lambrusco (Emilia-Romagna)
- **Citrusy whites with grassy or floral notes** Orvieto (Umbria), Soave (Veneto), Tocai (Friuli)
- **Dry whites with aromatic herbal or mineral aspect** Cinque Terre (Liguria), Gavi (Piedmont), Falanghina (Campania)
- **Versatile, food-friendly reds with pleasant acidity** Barbera d'Alba (Piedmont), Valpolicella (Veneto), Chianti Classico (Tuscany)
- **Big, structured reds with velvety tannins** Amarone (Veneto), Barolo (Piedmont), Sagrantino di Montefalco secco (Umbria)
- **Fortified and dessert wines** Sciacchetrá (Liguria), Moscato d'Asti (Piedmont)

plant, you can grab a bag at old-school Neapolitan *friggitorie* (fast-food kiosks) like Friggitoria Fiorenzano (p281).

But the gut-busting fun doesn't stop there: local *pasticcerie* (patisseries) sell everything from *sfogliatelle* (pastries filled with cinnamon-laced ricotta) to *rum baba* (a rich rum cake brought from France and made Neapolitan with sinful eruptions of cream).

SICILY & SOUTHERN ITALY

Fresh seafood and vegetables shape Italy's southernmost staples. While past poverty lingers in rustic Puglian fare like *strascinati con la mollica* (pasta with breadcrumbs and anchovies) and *tiella di verdure* (baked vegetable casserole), Sicily's ancient Arab influences make pasta dishes velvety and complex, and sweets nothing short of spectacular. Plan your meals around Sicilian *dolci*

WILL SALTER

Campo de' Fiori (p97), Rome

THE BEST

PRODUCE MARKETS

- La Pescheria, Catania (p322)
- Mercato di Ballarò, Palermo (p311)
- Porta Palazzo, Turin (p147)
- Mercato di Porta Nolana, Naples (p279)
- Campo de' Fiori, Rome (p97)

(sweets), from *cannoli* (pastry shells stuffed with sweet ricotta) to meticulously detailed fruit-shaped marzipan. Wild-caught tuna and sardines shine in mains like tuna baked in a sea-salt crust, while prime *primi* (first courses) include *fiori di zucca ripieni* (cheese-stuffed squash blossoms) and *arancini siciliani* (risotto balls).

EAT LIKE A LOCAL

Forget toast and OJ. Breakfast in Italy is usually a wham-bam espresso, cappuccino or *caffè latte* at the local bar, paired with a *cornetto* (jam, chocolate or custard-filled Italian croissant), *crostata* (buttery, jam-laced breakfast tart) or *ciambella* (Italian doughnut).

While many shops and businesses still close for *la pausa* (literally, 'pause') a two- to three-hour midday break, harried city commuters increasingly opt for a quick lunch on the go, from prosciutto-filled *panini* to *supplì* (fried risotto balls stuffed with molten mozzarella). One bite of *pizza al taglio* (pizza by the slice) from Rome's Pizzeria Sisini (p95) and it's clear that even Italy's fast food retains a gastronomic dignity.

Seated lunch or dinner options range from family-run trattorias serving low-fuss classics to vino-versed *osterie* (wine-focussed bars with grazing options) or crisp-linen *ristoranti* (restaurants) with bow-tied waiters, fine-dining degustation menus and a heftier cheque. Yet even in the latter, opting for just a *primo* (first course) won't raise eyebrows, making a luxe nosh viable for budget-conscious foodies.

'But what is a *primo*?', you ask. Read on for a crash course in courses.

ANTIPASTI (APPETIZER)

Pique the appetite with olives or *sott'aceti* (pickled vegetables), *grissini* (Turin-style breadsticks) or a serve of rustic cured meats. Scour the menu for house *bruschetta*

LEFT: ALAN BENSON; RIGHT: ALAN BENSON

Italian espresso *caffe;* Black-truffle appetiser

(grilled bread with a variety of toppings, from chopped tomato and garlic to black truffle spread) and seasonal treats like *insalata caprese* (fresh mozzarella with ripe tomatoes and basil leaves).

PRIMO (FIRST COURSE)

Starch is the staple of the *primi*, with pasta, risotto, gnocchi and polenta standard options.

While vegetarians and vegans are often well-catered for with dishes like pasta *alla norma* (with eggplant and tomato, Sicilian style) or *risotto ai porcini* (risotto with pungent porcini mushrooms), it's worth asking about the stock used in that risotto or polenta, or the ingredients in that suspiciously rich tomato sauce – beef, ham or ground anchovies may lurk in the mix.

Carnivores will rejoice in gems like *pappardelle alle cinghiale* (ribbon pasta with wild boar sauce – a Tuscan speciality) and *polenta col ragú* (polenta with meat sauce – a

APERITIVI: CHEAP FEASTS

The hottest recession trend in Italy is *aperitivi,* often described as a 'pre-meal drink and light snack'. Don't be fooled. Italian 'happy hour' is dinner disguised as a casual swill, accompanied by heaving buffets of antipasti, pasta salads, cold cuts and the random hot dish (this may include your fellow diners: *apertivi* is prime time for hungry singles). You can pillage buffets in Rome, Milan and Turin from about 5pm to 8pm for the price of a single drink – which crafty diners nurse for the duration – or join the Venetians for *ombre* (wine by the glass) and bargain seafood *cicheti* (Venetian tapas).

northern favourite). Near the coasts, look for seafood variations like *pasta ai frutti di mare* (pasta with seafood).

Portions can be generous, so consider a *mezzo piatto* (half-portion) for kids.

SECONDO (SECOND COURSE)

Light lunchers usually call it a day after the *primo,* but foodies pace themselves for meat, fish or *contorni* (side dishes, such as cooked vegetables) in the second course. These options may range from the outrageously thick *bistecca alla fiorentina* to *carciofi alla romana* (Roman artichokes stuffed with mint and garlic).

A less inspiring option is *insalata mista* (mixed green salad), typically unadorned greens with vinegar and oil on the side – croutons, crumbled cheeses, nuts and other froufrou ingredients have no business in a classic Italian salad.

FRUTTI E DOLCI

'*Siamo arrivati alla frutta*' ('we've arrived at the fruit') is an idiom roughly meaning 'we've hit rock bottom' – but hey, not until you've had one last tasty morsel. Ditch the imported pineapple for local and seasonal fruits. *Formaggi* (cheeses) are another option, but only diabetics or the French would go that route when there's room for *dolci* (sweets) – think *zabaglione* (egg and marsala custard), cream-stuffed profiteroles or Sicilian *cannoli,* the cream-stuffed shell pastry immortalised thus in *The Godfather:* 'Leave the gun. Take the *cannoli.*'

CAFFÈ (COFFEE) & DIGESTIVI (DIGESTIVES)

No amount of willpower is going to move your feet into a museum after a three-course Italian lunch, so administer espresso immediately. Your barista may take pity and deliver your cappuccino with a *cioccolatino* (a square of chocolate) or grant you a tiny stain of milk in a *caffè macchiato,* but usually you'll be expected to take espresso as it comes, with scant sweetness and no apology.

While failure to order a postprandial *caffè* may shock your server, you may yet save face by ordering a digestive, such as a *grappa* (a potent grape-derived alcohol), *amaro* (herbal bitters) or *limoncello* (sweet lemon-scented liqueur). Fair warning though: Italian digestives can pack a serious punch.

ALAN BENSON

Gelato

ITALY IN FOCUS

LIFESTYLE

LIFESTYLE

Customers enjoying a standing coffee

JULIET COOMBE

Imagine your own *Freaky Friday* moment. You wake up and discover you're Italian. Your suits are better tailored, your socks longer (shin skin is *così vulgare*) and your mother's *pasta al forno* is unbeatable. But how else would life be different, and what could you discover about Italy in just one day as a local?

A DAY IN THE LIFE OF ITALY

Sveglia! You're woken not by an alarm but by the burble and clatter of the *caffettiera,* the ubiquitous stovetop espresso maker. If you're between the ages of 18 and 34, there's a 60% chance that's not a roommate in the kitchen making your morning coffee: it's mum or dad. This is not because Italy is a nation of pampered *mammoni* (mama's boys) and spoilt *figlie di papà* (daddy's girls) – at least, not entirely. Scandalous rents make independent living a prohibitive dream for many young Italians.

Running late, you bolt down your *caffè* scalding hot (an acquired Italian skill) and walk blocks out of your way to buy your morning paper from Eduardo, your favourite news vendor, and chat briefly about his new baby – you may be late but at least you're not rude.

On your way to work you scan the headlines: a rebuttal of the pope's latest proclamation, yesterday's football results and today's match-fixing scandal, and an announcement of new EU regulations on cheese. Outrageous! The cheese regulations, that is; the rest is to be expected. At work, you're buried in paperwork until noon, when it's a relief to join friends for lunch and a glass of wine. Afterwards you toss

MEDIA INTERESTS

According to a 2008 poll, only 24% of Italians trust television as a reliable source. Italians are more likely to trust online news sites like Corriere della Sera (www.corriere.it/english/), La Repubblica (www.repubblica.it, in Italian), Il Manifesto (www.ilmanifesto.it, in Italian) or L'Unitá (www.unita.it, in Italian), perhaps with good reason: in 2008, Reporters Without Borders ranked Italy below Taiwan, Mali and Bosnia in freedom of the press, calling Prime Minister Silvio Berlusconi's television empire a 'conflict of interest' that threatens democracy. Yet 80% of Italy's population relies on TV news as its prime information source, including three main channels run by the Berlusconi-backed Mediaset company.

back another scorching espresso at your favourite bar, and find out how your barista's latest audition went – turns out you went to school with the sister of the director of the play, so you promise to put in a good word. Putting in a good word isn't just a nice gesture, but an essential career boost. In Europe's most ancient, entrenched bureaucracy, social networks are essential to get things done.

Back at work by 2pm, you multitask Italian-style, chatting with co-workers as you dash off work emails, text your schoolmate about the barista on your *telefonino* (mobile phone), and surreptitiously check *l'Internet* for employment listings – your contract is due to expire soon. After a busy day like this, *aperitivi* are definitely in order, so at 6.30 you head directly to the latest happy-hour hot spot. The decor is *molto design,* the vibe *molto cool* and the DJ *abbastanza hot,* but suddenly it's time for your English class – everyone's learning it these days, if only for the slang.

LA BELLA FIGURA

Translating as 'making a good impression', *la bella figura* encapsulates the Italians' obsession with beauty, gallantry and looking good in the eyes of the world.

Italians have strong opinions about aesthetics and aren't afraid to share them. A common refrain is *Che brutta!* (How hideous!), which may strike visitors as tactless. But consider it from an Italian point

Fashion on display in Florence (p220)

JULIET COOMBE

GIORGIO COSULICH

Diners in a Florence cafe

of view – everyone is rooting for you to look good, and who are you to disappoint? The shop assistant who tells you with brutal honesty that yellow is not your colour is doing a public service, and will consider it a personal triumph to see you outfitted in orange instead.

If it's a gift, though, you must allow 10 minutes for the sales clerk to *fa un bel pacchetto,* wrapping your purchase with string and an artfully placed sticker. This is the epitome of *la bella figura* – the sales clerk wants you to look good by giving a good gift. When you do, everyone basks in the glow of *la bella figura:* you as the gracious gift-giver and the sales clerk as savvy gift consultant, not to mention the flushed and duly honoured recipient.

As a national obsession, *la bella figura* gives Italy its undeniable edge in design, cuisine, art and architecture. Though the country could get by on its striking good looks, Italy is ever mindful of delightful details. They are everywhere you look, and many places you don't: the intricately carved cathedral spire only the bell-ringer could fully appreciate or the absinthe-green silk lining inside a sober grey suit sleeve.

THE PEOPLE

Who are the people you'd encounter in your day as an Italian? On average, about half your co-workers will be women – quite a change from 10 years ago, when women represented just a quarter of the workforce. But a growing proportion of the people you'll meet are already retired. One out of five Italians is over 65.

You might also notice a striking absence of children. Italy's birth rate is the lowest in Europe, at just under one child per woman. Dismayed by such incontrovertible evidence of contraception in an ostensibly Catholic culture, the pope recently called on Italian women to return to traditional roles as wives and mothers. The state is also concerned that a shrinking Italian workforce will mean fewer taxes to fund services for growing numbers of pensioners, and instituted an incentive of €1000 for any Italian woman to give birth. But neither Church nor State can cajole Italian women into motherhood, and Italy's birth rate remains below replacement level.

MULTICULTURALISM & NATIONAL IDENTITY

But wait, you say: you chatted with Eduardo the news vendor about his baby. Like a growing percentage of Italy's population, Eduardo is an immigrant. (His Spanish name would be spelt Edouardo in Italian.) Eduardo probably lives and works in a northern Italian city, like three-fifths of Italy's immigrants. But as a Peruvian, Eduardo is not representative of Italy's immigrants, the majority of whom are European – primarily Albanian, Ukrainian and especially Romanian.

FROM EMIGRANTS TO IMMIGRANTS

Immigration is the newest development in the century-old debate over Italian identity. From the Industrial Revolution through to the 1960s, cultural frictions focused on internal migrants from Italy's largely rural southern 'Mezzogiorno' region (from Calabria to Abruzzo, plus Sicily) arriving in industrialised northern cities for factory jobs. Just as northern Italy was adjusting to these 'foreign' southerners, political and economic upheavals in the 1980s brought new arrivals from central Europe, Latin America and northern Africa, including Italy's former colonies in Tunisia, Somalia and Ethiopia.

To some, the anti-immigration rhetoric of politicians like Berlusconi seems somewhat ironic. From 1876 to 1976, Italy was a country of net emigration. With some 30 million Italian emigrants dispersed throughout Europe, the Americas and Australia, remittances from Italians abroad helped keep Italy's economy afloat during economic crises after independence and World War II. Today, people of Italian origin account for more than 40% of the population in Argentina and Uruguay, more than 10% in Brazil, more than 5% in Switzerland and the US, and more than 4% in Australia, Venezuela and Canada.

Immigrants account for just 6.3% of Italy's own population today, though according to the Catholic agency Caritas, the rate of immigration is growing faster in Italy than other European nations. And as fewer Italians enter blue-collar agricultural and industrial fields, immigrant workers play an integral part in filling the gaps. Indeed, without their

ITALY IN FOCUS

LIFESTYLE

SISTERS ARE (ALMOST) DOIN' IT FOR THEMSELVES

According to a recent census, Italian women represent 65% of college graduates, are more likely than men to pursue higher education (53% to 45%), and twice as likely to land responsible positions in public service – though Italy still has fewer women in parliament than other western European nations, and Italian men enjoy 80 more minutes of leisure time daily than Italian women. Adding insult to injury are Prime Minister Berlusconi's infamous gaffes, which included telling prospective US investors that Italy has beautiful secretaries.

labour, Italy would be sorely lacking in tomato sauce and shoes. Visitors may glimpse immigrant workers in low-paid service jobs that keep Italy's tourism economy afloat.

ITALY'S IDENTITY CRISIS

As a founding member of the European Union, Italy became subject to EU regulations on everything from immigration to cheese making, raising concerns that Italian identity would be lost. Many feared immigration would dilute the culture, and promises of immigration crackdowns helped Silvio Berlusconi win elections in 1994 and 2008. In 2002 right-wing group Lega Nord introduced 'security laws' mandating detention and expulsion for immigrants suspected of crimes or lacking papers, raising Amnesty International's concern for asylum seekers and law-abiding immigrants.

However, Italy's immigration policy also created an unlikely coalition among Catholics, leftists and capitalists. Catholic charities and leftist groups established centres across Italy to help immigrants acclimate and seek citizenship. Supporters of this integrationist approach point out that foreigners aren't the source of all Italy's crime and terrorism – the Camorra, Brigate Rosse (Red Brigades) and other underground Italian organisations terrorised the country for decades. Meanwhile, free-market economists emphasise that more taxpayers mean more funds for Italian social services, and immigrants are statistically more likely to start small businesses needed for Italy's economic recovery.

RELIGION, LOOSELY SPEAKING

Although you read about the Church in the headlines on your day as an Italian, you don't actually attend mass. While the Church remains highly influential in Italy – *La Famiglia Cristiana* (the Christian Family) is Italy's most popular weekly magazine – you'll notice that except for tourists, Italian churches are often empty: according to a 2007 study,

St Peter's Sq (p85), Vatican City

PAOLO CORDELLI

only 15% of the population regularly attends Sunday mass.

Church doctrine is often the subject of popular debate. An Umbrian teacher's suspension for removing the crucifix from his public classroom in 2009 sparked arguments over Church symbols in public buildings, and fuelled ongoing debates over the appropriate division of Church and state in Italy. The pope's latest book shot to the top of Italian bestseller lists in 2007, as did the anticlerical tract *Perché non possiamo essere cristiani (e meno che mai cattolici)* (Why We Can't Be Christian (And Even Less, Catholics)) by mathematician Piergiorgio Odifreddi, who examines apparent contradictions in Church doctrine and posits an inverse relationship to the development of civil society.

If the Church hasn't always been entirely consistent, neither have its critics. Many Italians who fiercely debate the Vatican's right to interfere in policy decisions regarding divorce, abortion, civil unions and condom use to prevent AIDS have welcomed the pope's foreign policy interventions and personal appeals to end war in the Middle East. The Vatican's move to initiate dialogue with Muslim leaders has been widely credited with easing social tensions for Italy's 1.2 million Muslims, and the Church's many charitable organisations lauded for providing essential support to those in need where the state leaves off.

FOR THE LOVE OF CALCIO (FOOTBALL)

Yes, Italy's best players frequently trade teams for the right price. Yes, match-fixing 'Calciopoli' scandals resulted in demotion of Serie A (top-tier national) teams, including the mighty Juventus. Yes, Italian defender Marco Materazzi probably did whisper something impolite about the womenfolk of Zinedine Zidane's family, earning himself a headbutt from the French midfielder.

Yet when Italian footballers are in top form and the ball ricochets off the post and slips through the goalie's hands, all is forgiven and the moment savoured in true Italian style. Nine months after Italy won the 2006 World Cup, northern Italian hospitals reported a baby boom.

ITALY IN FOCUS

THE OUTDOORS

THE OUTDOORS

WAYNE WALTON

Vulcano (p317), Sicily

As if its cultural bite wasn't fierce enough, Italy boasts some of the planet's most spectacular scenery, from icy Alps and epic lakes to vine-laced hills and sunburnt coasts. One day you're cycling through an Alpine national park, the next you're sunning it up on a sizzling volcanic beach. Not bad for a country smaller than New Mexico.

Outdoor aficionados are spoilt rotten for choice, with active options spanning high-octane trekking and skiing to diving excursions and lazy coastal meanders. Not that we suggest you snub life's more decadent pleasures: Chianti wine trails make for tasty cycling trips, while Piedmont truffle hunts turn a walk in the woods into a gourmet adventure. So strap up, hit the track or make a splash in one of Europe's best alfresco playgrounds.

HIKING & WALKING

Thousands of kilometres of *sentieri* (marked trails) crisscross Italy, ranging from mountain treks to gentle lakeside *passeggiate* (strolls). In season (the end of June to September), northern Italy's sweeping Alps provide superb walking with breathtaking backdrops. Some of the best trails traverse the high passes and stunning valleys of the Parco Nazionale del Gran Paradiso (p153) in Valle d'Aosta. This national park is well-known for its wildlife, which includes marmots, bearded vultures and once-threatened ibex.

South of the Valle d'Aosta in Piedmont, delicious rambles lace the truffle- and vine-laden countryside of Alba (p148), while further south on the coast, Liguria's Cinque Terre (p137) lets you village-hop along terraced hills choked with olive groves and dry-stone-walled vineyards.

More vino-centric strolls await in Tuscany's Chianti region (drop into Radda in Chianti's Ufficio Pro, p242, for walking itineraries), while further east in Assisi, you can walk in the footsteps of St Francis on the wooded Monte Subasio (p255).

On the trails above the Amalfi Coast (p294), age-old paths disappear into wooded mountains and ancient olive groves, skirt plunging cliffs, and offer the finest coastal views this side of heaven.

Even closer to Naples, Mt Vesuvius (p288) offers a relatively easy walk up to its ashen crater, from where the views across Naples, the bay islands and the Apennines strangely redeem this slumbering menace.

For more peering into craters, consider the more challenging climb up Sicily's Mt Etna (p323) or a trek up the Fossa di Vulcano (p318) on the island of Vulcano. It's about an hour's scramble to the lowest point of the crater's edge (290m), but once you reach the top, the sight of the steaming crater encrusted with red and yellow crystals is reward enough. The bottom is clearly visible from the rim and you can even take a steep trail down to walk along the crater floor. Even more dramatic (and challenging) is an organised trek up Stromboli's (p318) hyperactive crater.

Back on the mainland, the regions of Puglia and Basilicata also serve up some blissful walking opportunities, with top choices including gorge tours in Matera (p338), hikes through rugged hills in seaside Maratea (p340) and wanderings in the wildlife-loaded Foresta Umbra ('Forest of Shadows') near Vieste (p331).

Tourist offices can generally provide walking information and basic maps.

CYCLING

Whether you want a gentle ride between trattorias or a 100km road-race, you'll find a route to suit in Italy, with tourist offices usually providing details on trails and guided rides.

Cyclists adore Tuscany's famously rolling countryside, particularly the Chianti area south of Florence. Foodies can combine exercise and feasting on a guided, day-long bike tour (p240) of the region. Neighbouring Umbria (p249) is also a great place to pedal, with an abundance of beautiful landscapes and quiet country roads.

Further north, the flatlands of Emilia-Romagna make bike touring a relative breeze. Add to this some of Italy's most celebrated culinary towns, and you could easily spend a week cycling from one producer to the next, with pit stops at Michelin-star restaurants and rustic *osterie*.

Down south in Puglia, the countryside surrounding Lecce (p336) is perfect for cycling, and several companies organise cycling tours across the region and rugged neighbour Basilicata.

↘**THE BEST**

GLENN VAN DER KNIJFF

Vernazza (p139), Cinque Terre

WORLD HERITAGE-LISTED LANDSCAPES

- **Amalfi Coast** (p293)
- **Cinque Terre** (p137)
- **Aeolian Islands** (p316)
- **Venice** (p168)
- **Matera** (p338)

ITALY IN FOCUS

THE OUTDOORS

NATIONAL PARKS

Italy has 24 national parks and well over 400 nature reserves, natural parks and wetlands. Covering approximately 13,000 sq km (nearly 5% of the country), the national parks play a crucial part in the protection of the country's flora and fauna, including the Marsican brown bears that prowl the Parco Nazionale d'Abruzzo, Lazio e Molise.

For more on Italy's national and regional parks, marine reserves and designated wetlands, hit the official parks website (www.parks.it).

In summer, northern Italy's Alpine regions are a big hit with mountain bikers, with several outstanding trails cutting through the majestic Dolomites and, further west, the Parco Nazionale del Gran Paradiso (p153).

For the ultimate Italian cycling experience, hit the saddle in spring, when it's not too hot and the countryside is ablaze with wildflowers.

HORSE RIDING

Horse riding is another popular, relaxing way to explore Italy's great outdoors.

Go galloping in the mountain valleys of the Parco Nazionale del Gran Paradiso (p153) or through the Langhe countryside outside Alba (p148). Summertime horse riding is plentiful in Piedmont, and **Agriturismo Piedmont** (www.agriturismopiemonte.it, in Italian) can give you a list of farms that offer a range of activities, including riding, as well as accommodation and dining. The Veneto, Tuscany, Umbria and Le Marche are also well-known for their agriturismi, several of which offer rural gallops for guests.

Tourist offices should be able to provide details of local riding facilities.

DIVING

Diving is one of Italy's favourite summer pastimes, with hundreds of schools offering courses, equipment and dives for all levels.

Just off the Sorrentine peninsula in Campania, the Punta Campanella Marine Reserve supports a healthy marine ecosystem with flora and fauna flourishing among underwater grottoes and ancient ruins. Dives are run out of the small village of Marina del Cantone, a stone's throw from the Amalfi Coast. Diving courses are also available in Positano (p291), as well as on Capri (p284). For a plunge into grottoes, hit the waters of beautiful Maratea (p340) in Basilicata.

The Aeolian Islands (p316) also offer fabulous crystal clear waters for underwater adventures. Further west, just off Palermo's coast, the small volcanic island of Ustica serves up a feast of coral and technicolour fauna in shimmering seas. Regular ferries between Ustica and Palermo make the island an easy overnight trip.

Most diving schools open seasonally, typically from about June to October. If possible, avoid August, when the Italian coast is besieged by holidaymakers and prices peak.

Information is available from local tourist offices and online at www.diveitaly.com (in Italian).

⇘ DIRECTORY & TRANSPORT

DIRECTORY

ACCOMMODATION

Accommodation in Italy can range from the sublime to the ridiculous with prices to match. Hotels and *pensioni* (guesthouses) make up the bulk of the offerings, while other options include charming B&B-style places, villa and apartment rentals, and *agriturismi* (farm stays). Some of the latter are working farms, others converted farmhouses (often with pool). Mountain walkers will find *rifugi* (alpine huts) handy. Capturing the imagination still more are the options to stay in anything from castles to convents and monasteries.

An original option born in the Friuli-Venezia Giulia region is the **albergo diffuso** (www.albergodiffuso.com). In several villages, various apartments and houses are rented to guests through a centralised hotel-style reception in the village.

In this book a range of prices is quoted from low to high season; these are intended as a guide only. Hotels are listed according to three categories (budget, midrange and top end). Half-board equals breakfast and either lunch or dinner; full board includes breakfast, lunch and dinner.

Prices can fluctuate enormously depending on the season, with Easter, summer and the Christmas–New Year period being the typical peak tourist times. There are many variables. Expect to pay top prices in the mountains during the ski season (December to March). Summer is high season on the coast, but in the parched cities can equal low season. In August especially, many city hotels charge as little as half price. It is always worth considering booking ahead in high season (although in the urban centres you can usually find something if you trust to luck).

As an average guide, a budget double room can cost up to €80, a midrange one from €80 to €200 and top-end anything from there to thousands of euros for a suite in one of the country's premier establishments. Price depends greatly on where you're looking. A bottom-end budget choice in Venice or Milan will set you back the price of a decent midrange option in, say, rural Campania. Where possible and appropriate, we have presented prices with the maximum low- and high-season rates thus: s €40–60, d €80–130, meaning that a single might cost €40 at most in low season and a double €130 at most in high season.

Some hotels barely alter their prices throughout the year. This is especially true of the lower-end places, although in low season there is no harm in trying to bargain for a discount. You may find hoteliers especially receptive if you intend to stay for several days.

To make a reservation, hotels usually require confirmation by fax or, more commonly, a credit-card number. In the latter case, if you don't show up you will be docked a night's accommodation.

AGRITURISMI & B&BS

Holidays on working farms, or *agriturismi*, are popular with travellers and property owners looking for extra revenue.

⟱ BOOK YOUR STAY ONLINE

For more accommodation reviews and recommendations by Lonely Planet authors, check out the online booking service at www.lonelyplanet.com. You'll find the true, insider lowdown on the best places to stay. Reviews are thorough and independent. Best of all, you can book online.

PRACTICALITIES

- Use the metric system for weights and measures.
- If your Italian's up to it, try the following newspapers: *Corriere della Sera*, the country's leading daily; *Il Messaggero*, a popular Rome-based broadsheet; or *La Repubblica*, a centre-left daily with a flow of Mafia conspiracies and Vatican scoops. For the Church's view, try the *Osservatore Romano*.
- Tune into Vatican Radio (www.radiovaticana.org; 93.3 FM and 105 FM in the Rome area) for a run-down on what the pope is up to (in Italian, English and other languages); or state-owned Italian RAI-1, RAI-2 and RAI-3 (www.rai.it), which broadcast all over the country and abroad. Commercial stations such as Rome's Radio Centro Suono (www.radiocentrosuono.it) and Radio Città Futura (www.radiocittafutura.it), Naples' Radio Kiss Kiss (www.kisskissnapoli.it) and Milan-based leftwing Radio Popolare (www.radiopopolare.it) are all good for contemporary music.
- Switch on the box to watch the state-run RAI-1, RAI-2 and RAI-3 (www.rai.it) and the main commercial stations (mostly run by Silvio Berlusconi's Mediaset company): Canale 5 (www.canale5.mediaset.it), Italia 1 (www.italia1.mediaset.it), Rete 4 (www.rete4.mediaset.it) and La 7 (www.la7.it).

Accommodation can range from simple, rustic affairs to luxury locations where little actual farming is done and the swimming pool sparkles. *Agriturismo* business has long boomed in Tuscany and Umbria, but is also steadily gaining ground in other regions.

Local tourist offices can usually supply lists of operators. For detailed information on *agriturismo* facilities throughout Italy check out Agriturist (www.agriturist.com) and Agriturismo.com (www.agriturismo.com). Other sites include Network Agriturismo Italia 2005 (www.agriturismo-italia2005.com), which in spite of its name is updated annually, Agriturismo-Italia.Net (www.agriturismo-italia.net), Agriturismoitalia.com (www.agriturismoitalia.com) and Agriturismo Vero (www.agriturismovero.com).

B&B options include everything from restored farmhouses, city *palazzi* and seaside bungalows to rooms in family houses. Tariffs per person cover a wide range from around €25 to €75. For more information, contact Bed & Breakfast Italia (Map pp74-5; ☎ 06 687 86 18; www.bbitalia.it; Corso Vittorio Emanuele II 282, 00186).

CONVENTS & MONASTERIES

Some convents and monasteries let out cells or rooms as a modest revenue-making exercise and happily take in tourists, while others are single sex and only take in pilgrims or people who are on a spiritual retreat. Many do not take in guests at all. Convents and monasteries generally impose a fairly early curfew. Charges hover around €40/75/100 for a single/double/triple, although some charge more like €65/100 for singles/doubles.

As a starting point, take a look at the website of the Chiesa di Santa Susana (www.santasusanna.org/comingToRome/convents.html), an American Catholic church in Rome. On this site, it has searched out convent and monastery accommodation options around the country. Don't ask the church to set things up for you – staff has simply put together the information.

It was probably just a matter of time before someone set up a central booking centre for monasteries – check out www.monasterystays.com. Note that some places are just residential accommodation run by religious orders and not necessarily big on monastic atmosphere.

HOTELS & PENSIONI

There is often little difference between a *pensione* and an *albergo* (hotel). However, a *pensione* will generally be of one- to three-star quality and traditionally it has been a family-run operation, while an *albergo* can be awarded up to five stars. *Locande* (inns) long fell into much the same category as *pensioni,* but the term has become a trendy one in some parts and reveals little about the quality of a place. *Affittacamere* are rooms for rent in private houses. They are generally simple affairs.

One-star hotels/*pensioni* tend to be basic and usually do not offer private bathrooms. Two-star places are similar but rooms will generally have a private bathroom. At three-star joints you can usually assume reasonable standards. Four- and five-star hotels offer facilities such as room service, laundry and dry-cleaning.

Prices are highest in major tourist destinations. They also tend to be higher in northern Italy. A *camera singola* (single room) costs from €25. A *camera doppia* (twin beds) or *camera matrimoniale* (double room with a double bed) will cost from around €40.

Tourist offices usually have booklets with local accommodation listings. Many hotels are also signing up with (steadily proliferating) online accommodation-booking services. You could start your search here:

Alberghi in Italia (www.alberghi-in-italia.it)
All Hotels in Italy (www.hotelsitalyonline.com)
Hotels web.it (www.hotelsweb.it)
In Italia (www.initalia.it)
Travel to Italy (www.travel-to-italy.com)

MOUNTAIN HUTS

The network of *rifugi* in the Alps, Apennines and other mountains in Italy is usually only open from July to September. Accommodation is generally in dormitories but some of the larger refuges have doubles. The price per person (which usually includes breakfast) ranges from €17 to €26 depending on the quality of the refuge (it's more for a double room). A hearty postwalk single-dish dinner will set you back another €11.50.

Rifugi are marked on good walking maps. Some are close to chair lifts and cable-car stations, which means they are usually expensive and crowded. Others are at high altitude and involve hours of hard walking. It is important to book in advance. Additional information can be obtained from the local tourist offices.

The **Club Alpino Italiano** (CAI; www.cai.it, in Italian) owns and runs many of the mountain huts. Members of organisations such as the Australian Alpine Club and British Mountaineering Council can enjoy discounted rates for accommodation and meals by obtaining a reciprocal rights card (for a fee).

VILLA RENTALS

Long the preserve of the Tuscan sun, the villa-rental scene in Italy has taken off in recent years, with agencies offering villa accommodation – often in splendid rural locations not far from enchanting medieval towns or Mediterranean beaches – up and down the country. More eccentric options include renting *trulli,* the conical traditional houses of southern Puglia. You can start your search with the following agencies but there are dozens of operators.

Cuendet (www5.cuendet.com) One of the old hands in this business; operates from the heart of Siena province in Tuscany.

Ilios Travel (www.iliostravel.com) UK-based company with villas, apartments and castles in Venice, Tuscany, Umbria, Lazio, Le Marche, Abruzzo and Sardinia.

Invitation to Tuscany (www.invitationto tuscany.com) A wide range of properties across Tuscany, Umbria & Liguria.

Long Travel (www.long-travel.co.uk) From Lazio and Abruzzo south, including Sardinia and Sicily.

Simpson (www.simpson-travel.com) Concentrates on Tuscany, Umbria, the Amalfi coast and Sicily. They also have properties in Rome, Florence and Venice.

Think Sicily (www.thinksicily.com) Strictly Sicilian properties.

CHILDREN

See Family Travel, p351, for suggestions and practical information.

CLIMATE CHARTS

In the Alps, temperatures are lower and winters can be long and severe. Generally the weather is warm from July to September, although rainfall can be high in September. While the first snowfall is usually in November, light snow sometimes falls in mid-September and heavy falls can occur in early October. Freak snowfalls in June are not unknown at high altitudes. Mind you, with climate change, many ski resorts can remain

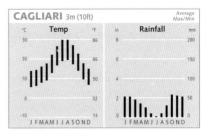

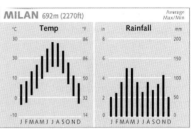

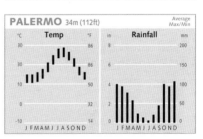

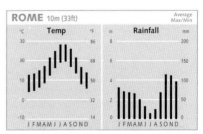

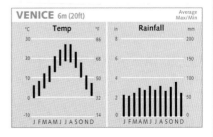

DIRECTORY

CHILDREN

distressingly snow-free until early January (the exceptionally snowy winter of 2008–09 notwithstanding!).

The Alps shield northern Lombardy and the Lakes area, including Milan, from the extremes of the northern European winter, and Liguria enjoys a mild, Mediterranean climate similar to that in southern Italy because it is protected by the Alps and Apennine range.

Venice can be hot and humid in summer and, although not too cold in winter, it can be unpleasant if wet or when the sea level rises and acque alte (literally 'high waters') inundate the city. This is most likely in November and December. Along the Po valley, and in Venice especially, January and February can be surprisingly crisp and stunning.

In Florence, encircled by hills, the weather can be quite extreme but, as you travel towards the tip of the boot, temperatures and weather conditions become milder. Rome, for instance, has an average July and August temperature in the mid-20s (Celsius), although the impact of the sirocco (a hot, humid wind blowing from Africa) can produce stiflingly hot weather in August, with temperatures in the high 30s for days on end. Winters are moderate and snow is rare in Rome, although winter clothing (or at least a heavy overcoat) is still a requirement.

The south of Italy and the islands of Sicily and Sardinia have a Mediterranean climate. Summers are long, hot and dry, and winter temperatures tend to be relatively moderate, with daytime averages not too far below 10°C.

CUSTOMS REGULATIONS

Duty-free sales within the EU no longer exist (but goods are sold tax-free in European airports). Visitors coming into Italy from non-EU countries can import,

duty free: 1L of spirits (or 2L wine), 50g perfume, 250mL eau de toilette, 200 cigarettes and other goods up to a total of €175; anything over this limit must be declared on arrival and the appropriate duty paid. On leaving the EU, non-EU citizens can reclaim any Value Added Tax (VAT) on expensive purchases (see p391).

DANGERS & ANNOYANCES

It sometimes requires patience to deal with the Italian concept of service, which does not always seem to follow the maxim that the customer is always right. While often courteous and friendly, some people in uniform or behind a counter (including police officers, waiters and shop assistants) may regard you with supreme indifference.

POLLUTION

In summer (and occasionally other seasons) pollution alerts come as a wake-up call in cities like Rome, Milan, Naples and Florence. The elderly, children and people with respiratory problems are warned to stay indoors. If you fit into one of these categories, keep yourself informed through the tourist office or your hotel. Often traffic is cut by half during these alerts by obliging drivers with odd and even number plates to drive on alternate days.

Italy's beaches can be polluted by industrial waste, sewage and oil spills from the Mediterranean's considerable sea traffic. The best and cleanest beaches are on Sardinia, Sicily, less-populated southern areas of the mainland and Elba.

SMOKING

Since early 2005, smoking in all closed public spaces (from bars to elevators, offices to trains) has been banned.

THEFT

Pickpockets and bag-snatchers operate in most cities, especially Naples and Rome. Reduce the chances of such petty theft by wearing a money belt (with money, passport, credit cards and important documents) *under* your clothing. Wear bags or cameras slung across the body to make it harder to snatch them. If your hotel has a safe, use it.

Watch for groups of dishevelled-looking women and children asking you for money. Their favourite haunts are train stations, tourist sights and shopping areas. If you've been targeted by a group take evasive action (such as crossing the street) or shout '*Va via!*' (Go away!).

Parked cars, particularly those with foreign number plates or rental-company stickers, are prime targets. Try not to leave anything in the car and certainly not overnight. Car theft is a problem in Rome, Campania and Puglia.

In case of theft or loss, always report the incident to police within 24 hours and ask for a statement, otherwise your travel-insurance company won't pay out.

TRAFFIC

Italian traffic can seem chaotic, although it has improved a trifle now that Italian drivers have point-system licences. Drivers are not keen to stop for pedestrians, even at pedestrian crossings, and are more likely to swerve. Where this is the case, follow the locals (even if they seem bent on suicide) by marching out into the (swerving) traffic.

Confusingly, in some cities, roads that appear to be only for one-way traffic have lanes for buses travelling in the opposite direction – always look both ways before stepping onto the road.

Signposting is often confusing. It is not uncommon to see signs to the same place pointing in two opposing directions at once. This can be especially unnerving for drivers navigating their way out of a city for the first time (although one becomes accustomed to these 'options' after a while).

Motorcyclists should be prepared for anything in the cities. Once you get the hang of Italian-style urban driving, though, you might come to like it!

DISCOUNT CARDS

At museums and galleries, never hesitate to enquire after discounts for students, young people, children, families or the elderly. When sightseeing and wherever possible buy a *biglietto cumulativo,* a ticket that allows admission to a number of associated sights for less than the combined cost of separate admission fees.

SENIOR CARDS

Senior citizens are often entitled to public-transport discounts but usually only for monthly passes (not daily or weekly tickets); the minimum qualifying age is 65 years.

Seniors (over 60) travelling extensively by rail should consider the one-year Carta d'Argento.

Admission to most museums in Rome is free for over-60s but in other cities (such as Florence) often no concessions are made for nonresidents. In numerous places, EU seniors have free entry to sights, sometimes only on certain days. Always ask.

STUDENT & YOUTH CARDS

Free admission to some galleries and sites is available to under-18s. Discounts (usually half the normal fee) are available for some sights to EU citizens aged between 18 and 25. An **International Student Identity Card** (ISIC; www.isic.org) is no longer sufficient at many tourist sites as prices are usually based on age so a passport, driver's licence or **Euro<26** (www.euro26. org) card is preferable.

An ISIC card may still, however, prove useful for cheap transport, theatre and cinema discounts, as well as occasional discounts in some hotels and restaurants (check the lists on the ISIC website); similar cards are available to teachers (International Teacher Identity Card, or ITIC). For nonstudent travellers under 25, the International Youth Travel Card (IYTC) offers the same benefits.

Student cards are issued by student unions and hostelling organisations as well as some youth travel agencies. In Italy, the **Centro Turistico Studentesco e Giovanile** (CTS; www.cts.it) youth travel agency can issue ISIC, ITIC and Euro<26 cards.

EMBASSIES & CONSULATES

For foreign embassies and consulates in Italy not listed here, look under 'Ambasciate' or 'Consolati' in the telephone directory. In addition to the following, some countries run honorary consulates in other cities.

Australia Rome (Map p53; ☎ 06 85 27 21, emergencies 800 877 790; www.italy.embassy. gov.au; Via Antonio Bosio 5, 00161); Milan (Map pp118-19; ☎ 02 7770 4217; www.austrade.it; Via Borgogna 2, 20122)

Canada (Map p53; ☎ 06 85 44 41; www.dfait -maeci.gc.ca/canadaeuropa/italy; Via Zara 30, Rome, 00198)

France Rome (Map pp74-5; ☎ 06 68 60 11; www.france-italia.it; Piazza Farnese 67, 00186); Milan (Map pp118-19; ☎ 02 655 91 41; Via della Moscova 12, 20121); Naples (Map pp276-7; ☎ 081 598 07 11; Via Francesco Crispi 86, 80121); Turin (☎ 011 573 23 11; Via Roma 366, 10121); Venice (Map pp180-1; ☎ 041 522 43 19; Palazzo Morosini, Castello 6140, 30123)

Germany Rome (Map p80; ☎ 06 49 21 31; www.rom.diplo.de; Via San Martino della Battaglia 4, 00185); Milan (Map pp118-19; ☎ 02 623 11 01; www.mailand.diplo.de; Via Solferino 40, 20121); Naples (Map pp276-7; ☎ 081 248 85 11; www.neapel.diplo.de; Via Francesco Crispi 69, 80121)

Ireland (Map p84; ☎ 06 697 91 21; www. ambasciata-irlanda.it; Piazza Campitelli 3, Rome, 00186)

Japan Rome (Map p80; ☎ 06 48 79 91; www. it.emb-japan.go.jp; Via Quintino Sella 60, 00187); Milan (Map pp118-19; ☎ 02 624 11 41; Via Cesare Mangili 2/4, 20121)

Netherlands Rome (Map p53; ☎ 06 3228 6001; www.olanda.it; Via Michele Mercati 8, 00197); Milan (Map pp118-19; ☎ 02 485 58 41; Via San Vittore 45, 20123); Naples (Map pp276-7; ☎ 081 551 30 03; Via Agostino Depretis 114, 80133); Palermo (Map p532; ☎ 091 58 15 21; Via Enrico Amari 8, 90139)

New Zealand Rome (Map p53; ☎ 06 853 75 01; www.nzembassy.com; Via Clitunno 44, 00198); Milan (Map pp118-19; ☎ 02 7217 0001; Via Terraggio 17, 20123)

UK Rome (Map p53; ☎ 06 4220 0001; www. britishembassy.gov.uk; Via XX Settembre 80a, 00187); Florence (Map pp222-3; ☎ 055 28 41 33; Lungarno Corsini 2, 50123); Milan (Map pp118-19; ☎ 02 72 30 01; Via San Paolo 7, 20121); Naples (Map pp276-7; ☎ 081 423 89 11; Via dei Mille 40, 80121)

USA Rome (Map p80; ☎ 06 4 67 41; www. usis.it; Via Vittorio Veneto 119a, 00187); Florence (Map pp222-3; ☎ 055 26 69 51; Lungarno Amerigo Vespucci 38, 50123); Milan (Map pp118-19; ☎ 02 29 03 51; Via Principe Amedeo 2/10, 20121); Naples (Map pp276-7; ☎ 081 583 81 11; Piazza della Repubblica, 80122)

FOOD & DRINK

Restaurant listings in this book are given in order of cheapest to most expensive, going by the price of a meal, unless otherwise stated. A meal in this guide consists of a *primo* (first course), a *secondo* (second course) and a dessert. Drinks are not included. The budget category is for meals costing up to €20, midrange is €20 to €45 and top end is anything over €45. These figures represent a halfway point between the expensive cities such as Milan and Venice and the considerably cheaper towns across the south. Indeed, a restaurant rated as midrange in one place might be considered cheap as chips in Milan. It is best to check the menu, usually posted by the entrance, for prices. Most eating establishments have a cover charge (called *coperto;* usually around €1 to €2) and *servizio* (service charge) of 10% to 15%.

GAY & LESBIAN TRAVELLERS

Homosexuality is legal in Italy and well tolerated in the major cities. However, overt displays of affection by homosexual couples could attract a negative response in the more conservative south, and smaller towns. The legal age of consent is generally 16 (there are some exceptions where people below that age are concerned, in which case it can drop to as low as 13).

The useful website **Gay.it** (www.gay.it, in Italian) lists gay bars and hotels across the country. **Arcigay & Arcilesbica** (☎ 051 649 30 55; www.arcigay.it; Via Don Minzoni 18, Bologna), is a worthy national organisation for gay men and lesbians.

Check out the English-language **GayFriendlyItalia.com** (www.gayfriendly italy.com), which is produced by Gay.it. It has information on everything from hotels to homophobia issues and the law.

HEALTH
BEFORE YOU GO
While Italy has reasonable health care (although public hospitals tend to be less impressive the further south you travel),

prevention is the key to staying healthy while abroad. Bring medications in their original, clearly labelled containers. A signed and dated letter from your physician describing your medical conditions and medication, including generic names, is also a good idea. If carrying syringes or needles, be sure to have a physician's letter documenting their medical necessity. If you are embarking on a long trip, make sure your teeth are OK (dental treatment is expensive in Italy) and take your optical prescription with you.

INSURANCE
If you're an EU citizen (or from Switzerland, Norway or Iceland), a European Health Insurance Card (EHIC) covers you for most medical care in public hospitals free of charge, but not for emergency repatriation home or non-emergencies. Citizens from other countries should find out if there is a reciprocal arrangement for free medical care between their country and Italy (Australia, for instance, has such an agreement; carry your Medicare card). If you do need health insurance, make sure you get a policy that covers you for the worst possible scenario, such as an accident requiring an emergency flight home.

RECOMMENDED VACCINATIONS
No jabs are required to travel to Italy. The World Health Organization (WHO), however, recommends that all travellers should be covered for diphtheria, tetanus, the measles, mumps, rubella and polio, as well as hepatitis B.

Make sure children are up to date with routine vaccinations and discuss possible travel vaccines well before your departure as some vaccines are not suitable for children under a year. Lonely Planet's *Travel with Children* includes travel health advice for younger children.

IN ITALY

AVAILABILITY OF HEALTH CARE

If you need an ambulance anywhere in Italy, call ☎ 118. For emergency treatment, head straight to the *pronto soccorso* (casualty) section of a public hospital, where you can also get emergency dental treatment.

Pharmacists can give you valuable advice and sell over-the-counter medication for minor illnesses. They can also advise you when more specialised help is required and point you in the right direction.

ENVIRONMENTAL HAZARDS

BITES, STINGS & INSECT-BORNE DISEASES

Italian beaches are occasionally inundated with jellyfish. Their stings are painful but not dangerous. Dousing in vinegar will deactivate any stingers that have not fired. Calamine lotion, antihistamines and analgesics may reduce the reaction and relieve pain.

Italy's only dangerous snake, the viper, is found throughout the country except on Sardinia. To minimise the possibilities of being bitten, always wear boots, socks and long trousers when walking through undergrowth where snakes may be present. Don't put your hands into holes or crevices, and be careful when collecting firewood. Viper bites do not cause instantaneous death, and an antivenin is widely available in pharmacies. Keep the victim calm and still, wrap the bitten limb tightly, as you would for a sprained ankle, and attach a splint to immobilise it. Seek medical help, if possible with the dead snake for identification. Don't attempt to catch the snake if there is a possibility of being bitten again. Tourniquets and sucking out the poison are now comprehensively discredited.

Always check all over your body if you have been walking through a potentially tick-infested area, as ticks can cause skin infections and other more serious diseases such as Lyme disease and tick-borne encephalitis. If a tick is found attached, press down around the tick's head with tweezers, grab the head and gently pull upwards. Avoid pulling the rear of the body as this may squeeze the tick's gut contents through the attached mouth parts into the skin, increasing the risk of infection and disease. Lyme disease begins with the spreading of a rash at the site of the bite, accompanied by fever, headache, extreme fatigue, aching joints and muscles, and severe neck stiffness. If untreated, symptoms usually disappear, but disorders of the nervous system, heart and joints can develop later. Treatment works best early in the illness – medical help should be sought. Symptoms of tick-borne encephalitis include blotches around the bite, which is sometimes pale in the middle, and headaches, stiffness and other flu-like symptoms (as well as extreme tiredness) appearing a week or two after the bite. Again, medical help must be sought.

Rabies is still found in Italy but only in isolated areas of the Alps. Any bite, scratch or even lick from a mammal in an area where rabies does exist should be scrubbed with soap and running water immediately and then cleaned thoroughly with an alcohol solution. Medical help should be sought.

Leishmaniasis is a group of parasitic diseases transmitted by sandflies and found in coastal parts of Italy. Cutaneous leishmaniasis affects the skin tissue and causes ulceration and disfigurement; visceral leishmaniasis affects the internal organs. Avoiding sandfly bites by covering up and using repellent is the best precaution against this disease.

SEXUAL HEALTH

Condoms are readily available but emergency contraception is not, so take the necessary precautions.

HOLIDAYS

Most Italians take their annual holiday in August. This means that many businesses and shops close for at least a part of that month. The *Settimana Santa* (Easter week) is another busy holiday period for Italians.

Individual towns have public holidays to celebrate the feasts of their patron saints. National public holidays include the following:

New Year's Day (Capodanno or Anno Nuovo) 1 January

Epiphany (Epifania or Befana) 6 January

Easter Monday (Pasquetta or Lunedì dell'Angelo) March/April

Liberation Day (Giorno della Liberazione) On 25 April – marks the Allied Victory in Italy, and the end of the German presence and Mussolini, in 1945.

Labour Day (Festa del Lavoro) 1 May

Republic Day (Festa della Repubblica) 2 June

Feast of the Assumption (Assunzione or Ferragosto) 15 August

All Saints' Day (Ognissanti) 1 November

Feast of the Immaculate Conception (Immaculata Concezione) 8 December

Christmas Day (Natale) 25 December

Boxing Day (Festa di Santo Stefano) 26 December

INSURANCE

A travel-insurance policy to cover theft, loss and medical problems is a good idea. It may also cover you for cancellation or delays to your travel arrangements. Paying for your ticket with a credit card can often provide limited travel accident insurance and you may be able to reclaim the payment if the operator doesn't deliver. Ask your credit-card company what it will cover.

For information on health insurance, see p387.

INTERNET ACCESS

If you plan to carry your notebook or palmtop computer with you, carry a universal AC adaptor for your appliance (most are sold with these). Do not rely on finding wi-fi whenever you want it, as hot spots remain few and far between and often require payment. Another option is to buy a card pack with one of the Italian mobile-phone operators, which gives wireless access through the mobile telephone network. These are usually prepay services that you can top up as you go.

Most travellers make constant use of internet cafes and free web-based email such as Yahoo, Hotmail or Gmail. Internet cafes and centres are present, if not always abundant, in all cities and most main towns (don't forget your incoming mail server name, account name and password). Prices hover at around the €5 to €8 mark per hour. For some useful internet addresses, see p43. By law, you must present photo ID (such as passport or drivers licence) to use internet points in Italy.

LEGAL MATTERS

The average tourist will only have a brush with the law if robbed by a bag-snatcher or pickpocket.

ALCOHOL & DRUGS

Those caught in possession of 5g of cannabis can be considered traffickers and prosecuted as such. The same applies to tiny amounts of other drugs. Those caught with amounts below this threshold can be subject to minor penalties.

The legal limit for blood-alcohol level is 0.05% and random breath tests do occur.

POLICE

If you run into trouble in Italy, you are likely to end up dealing with the *polizia statale* (state police) or the *carabinieri* (military police).

The *polizia* deal with thefts, visa extensions and permits (among other things). They wear powder blue trousers with a fuchsia stripe and a navy blue jacket. Details of police stations, or *questure,* are given throughout this book.

The *carabinieri* deal with general crime, public order and drug enforcement (often overlapping with the *polizia*). They wear a black uniform with a red stripe and drive night blue cars with a red stripe.

One of the big differences between the police and *carabinieri* is the latter's reach – even many villages have a *carabinieri* post.

Other police include the *vigili urbani,* basically local traffic police. You will have to deal with them if you get a parking ticket or your car is towed away. The *guardia di finanza* are responsible for fighting tax evasion and drug smuggling.

For national emergency numbers, see the inside front cover.

YOUR RIGHTS

Italy still has antiterrorism laws on its books that could make life difficult if you are detained. You should be given verbal and written notice of the charges laid against you within 24 hours by arresting officers. You have no right to a phone call upon arrest. The prosecutor must apply to a magistrate for you to be held in preventive custody awaiting trial (depending on the seriousness of the offence) within 48 hours of arrest. You have the right not to

respond to questions without the presence of a lawyer. If the magistrate orders preventive custody, you have the right to then contest this within the following 10 days.

MAPS
ROAD ATLASES

If you are driving around Italy, the Automobile Association's (AA) *Road Atlas Italy,* available in the UK, is scaled at 1:250,000 and includes 31 town maps. Just as good is Michelin's *Tourist and Motoring Atlas Italy,* scaled at 1:300,000, with 74 town maps.

In Italy, De Agostini publishes a comprehensive *Atlante Turistico Stradale d'Italia* (1:250,000), which includes 140 city maps (the AA Road Atlas is based on this). TCI publishes an *Atlante Stradale d'Italia* (1:200,000) divided into three parts – Nord, Centro and Sud (€45 for the lot at www.touringclub.com). They contain a total of 147 city maps.

Check out TrekTools.com (www.trektools.com).

SMALL-SCALE MAPS

Michelin has a series of good foldout country maps. No 735 covers the whole country on a scale of 1:1,000,000. You could also consider the series of six area maps at 1:400,000. TCI publishes a decent map of Italy at 1:800,000, as well as a series of 15 regional maps at 1:200,000 (costing €7 each).

WALKING MAPS

Maps of walking trails in the Alps and Apennines are available at all major bookshops in Italy, but the best are the TCI bookshops.

The best walking maps are the 1:25,000 scale series published by **Tabacco** (www.tabaccoeditrice.com), covering an area from Bormio in the west to the Slovene border in the east. **Kompass** (**www.kompass -italia.it**) also publishes 1:25,000 scale maps of various parts of Italy, as well as a 1:50,000 series and several in other scales (including one at 1:7500 of Capri). The Club Alpino Italiano (CAI) produces many hiking maps too, and Edizioni Multigraphic Florence produces a series of walking maps concentrating mainly on the Apennines.

MONEY

The euro is Italy's currency. The seven euro notes come in denominations of €500, €200, €100, €50, €20, €10 and €5. The eight euro coins are in denominations of €2 and €1, and 50, 20, 10, five, two and one cents.

Exchange rates are given on the inside front cover of this book. For the latest rates, check out www.xe.com.

CASH

There is little advantage in bringing foreign cash into Italy. True, exchange commissions are often lower than for travellers cheques, but the danger of losing the lot far outweighs such gains.

CREDIT & DEBIT CARDS

Credit and debit cards can be used in a *bancomat* (ATM) displaying the appropriate sign. Visa and MasterCard are among the most widely recognised, but others like Cirrus and Maestro are also well covered. Only some banks give cash advances over the counter, so you're better off using ATMs. Cards are also good for payment in most hotels, restaurants, shops, supermarkets and tollbooths.

Check any charges with your bank. Most banks now build a fee of around 2.75% into every foreign transaction. In addition, ATM withdrawals can attract a further fee, usually around 1.5%.

If your card is lost, stolen or swallowed by an ATM, you can telephone toll free to have an immediate stop put on its use: **Amex** (☎ 06 7290 0347 or your national call number) **Diners Club** (☎ 800 864064) **MasterCard** (☎ 800 870866) **Visa** (☎ 800 819014)

MONEYCHANGERS

You can change money in banks, at the post office or in a *cambio* (exchange office). Post offices and most banks are reliable and tend to offer the best rates.

TAXES & REFUNDS

A value-added tax of around 20%, known as IVA (Imposta di Valore Aggiunto), is slapped onto just about everything in Italy. If you are a non-EU resident and spend more than €155 (€154.94 to be more precise!) on a purchase, you can claim a refund when you leave. The refund only applies to purchases from affiliated retail outlets that display a 'tax free for tourists' (or similar) sign. You have to complete a form at the point of sale, then have it stamped by Italian customs as you leave. At major airports you can then get an immediate cash refund; otherwise it will be refunded to your credit card.

TIPPING

If there is no service charge, the customer should consider leaving a 10% tip, but this is not obligatory. In bars, Italians often leave small change as a tip, maybe only €0.10. Tipping taxi drivers is not common practice, but you are expected to tip the porter at top-end hotels.

TRAVELLERS CHEQUES

Various readers have reported having trouble changing travellers cheques in

Italy and it seems most banks apply hefty commissions, even on cheques denominated in euros.

Visa, Travelex and Amex are widely accepted brands. Get most of your cheques in fairly large denominations to save on per-cheque commission charges. Amex exchange offices do not charge commission to exchange travellers cheques.

Take along your passport as identification when you go to cash travellers cheques.

Phone numbers to report lost or stolen cheques:

Amex (☎ 800 914912)
MasterCard (☎ 800 872050)
Visa (☎ 800 874155)

SHOPPING

Italy is a shopper's paradise, so bring your plastic well charged up and even an empty bag for your purchases (or buy a new one while in Italy).

The big cities and tourist centres, especially Milan, Rome and Florence, are home to countless designer boutiques spilling over with clothes, shoes and accessories by all the great Italian names, and many equally enticing unknowns.

Foodies and wine lovers will want to bring home some souvenirs for the kitchen, ranging from fine Parma ham to aromatic cheeses, from class wines (especially from Tuscany, Piedmont and the Veneto) to local tipples (such as Benevento's La Strega, grappa from Bassano del Grappa, the almond-based Amaretto, and *limoncello,* the lemon-based liqueur common in Naples and Sicily as well as other parts of the south).

Many cities and provinces offer specialised products.

TELEPHONE
DOMESTIC CALLS

A local call from a public phone costs €0.10 every minute and 10 seconds. For a long-distance call within Italy you pay €0.10 when the call is answered and then €0.10 every 57 seconds. Calling from a private phone is cheaper.

Telephone area codes all begin with 0 and consist of up to four digits. The area code is followed by a number of anything from four to eight digits. The area code is an integral part of the telephone number and must always be dialled, even when calling from next door. Mobile-phone numbers begin with a three-digit prefix such as 330. Toll-free (free-phone) numbers are known as *numeri verdi* and usually start with 800.

INTERNATIONAL CALLS

Direct international calls can easily be made from public telephones by using a phonecard. Dial ☎ 00 to get out of Italy, then the relevant country and area codes, followed by the telephone number.

To call home, use your country's direct-dialling services paid for at home-country rates (such as AT&T in the USA and Telstra in Australia). Get their access numbers before you leave home. Alternatively, try making calls from cheap-rate call centres or using international call cards, which are often on sale at newspaper stands.

To call Italy from abroad, call the international access number (usually 00), Italy's country code (☎ 39) and then the area code of the location you want, including the leading 0.

DIRECTORY ENQUIRIES

National and international phone numbers can be requested at ☎ 1254 (or online at http://1254.alice.it). Another handy number, where operators will respond in several languages, is ☎ 89 24 12.

MOBILE PHONES

Italy uses GSM 900/1800, which is compatible with the rest of Europe and Australia but not with North American GSM 1900 or the totally different Japanese system (though some GSM 1900/900 phones do work here). If you have a GSM phone, check with your service provider about using it in Italy and beware of calls being routed internationally (very expensive for a 'local' call).

Italy has one of the highest levels of mobile-phone penetration in Europe, and you can get a temporary or prepaid account from several companies if you already own a GSM, dual- or tri-band cellular phone. You will usually need your passport to open an account.

Of the four main mobile phone companies, TIM (Telecom Italia Mobile) and Vodafone have the densest networks of outlets across the country.

PAYPHONES & PHONECARDS

Partly privatised Telecom Italia is the largest telecommunications organisation in Italy and its orange public payphones are liberally scattered about the country. The most common accept only *carte/schede telefoniche* (phonecards), although you'll still find some that take cards and coins. Some card phones accept credit cards.

You can buy phonecards (most commonly €2.50 or €5) at post offices, tobacconists and newsstands. You must break off the top left-hand corner of the card before you can use it. Phonecards have an expiry date.

TIME

Italy is one hour ahead of GMT. Daylight-saving time, when clocks are moved forward one hour, starts on the last Sunday in March. Clocks are put back an hour on the last Sunday in October. Italy operates on a 24-hour clock.

TOURIST INFORMATION

The quality of tourist offices in Italy varies dramatically. Three tiers of tourist office exist: regional, provincial and local. They have different names, but roughly offer the same services, with the exception of regional offices, which are generally concerned with promotion, planning and budgeting.

LOCAL & PROVINCIAL TOURIST OFFICES

Throughout this book, offices are referred to as tourist offices rather than by their more elaborate titles. The Azienda Autonoma di Soggiorno e Turismo (AAST) is the local tourist office in many towns and cities of the south. AASTs have town-specific information and should also know about bus routes and museum opening times. The Azienda di Promozione Turistica (APT) is the provincial (ie main) tourist office, which should have information on the town you are in and the surrounding province. Informazione e Assistenza ai Turisti (IAT) has local tourist office branches in towns and cities, mostly in the northern half of Italy. Pro Loco is the local office in small towns and villages and is similar to the AAST office. Most tourist offices will respond to written and telephone requests for information.

Tourist offices are generally open from 8.30am to 12.30pm or 1pm and 3pm to 7pm Monday to Friday. Hours are usually extended in summer, when some offices also open on Saturday or Sunday.

Information booths at most major train stations tend to keep similar hours but in some cases operate only in summer. Staff can usually provide a city map, list of hotels and information on the major sights.

English, and sometimes French or German, is spoken at tourist offices in larger towns and major tourist areas. German is spoken in Alto Adige and French in much of the Valle d'Aosta.

REGIONAL TOURIST AUTHORITIES

Regional tourist authorities tend to be more concerned with planning and marketing than offering public information; that work's done at a provincial and local level. Local tourist office addresses appear throughout the guide. Following are some useful regional websites. In some cases you'll need to look for the Tourism or Turismo link. At the website of the **Italian National Tourist Office** (www.enit.it) you can find details of all provincial and local tourist offices across the country.

Abruzzo (www.abruzzoturismo.it)
Basilicata (www.aptbasilicata.it)
Calabria (www.turiscalabria.it)
Campania (www.in-campania.com)
Emilia-Romagna (www.emiliaromagna turismo.it)
Friuli-Venezia Giulia (www.turismo.fvg.it)
Lazio (www.turislazio.it)
Le Marche (www.le-marche.com)
Liguria (www.turismoinliguria.it)
Lombardy (www.turismo.regione.lombardia.it)
Molise (www.regione.molise.it/turismo, in Italian)
Piedmont (www.regione.piemonte.it/turismo, in Italian)
Puglia (www.pugliaturismo.com)
Sardinia (www.sardegnaturismo.it)
Sicily (www.regione.sicilia.it/turismo)
Trentino-Alto Adige (www.trentino.to, www.provincia.bz.it)
Tuscany (www.turismo.toscana.it)
Umbria (www.umbria.org)
Valle d'Aosta (www.regione.vda.it/turismo)
Veneto (www.veneto.to)

TOURIST OFFICES ABROAD

Information on Italy is available from the Italian National Tourist Office (ENIT; ☎ 06 4 97 11; www.enit.it; Via Marghera 2, Rome, 00185) in the following countries:

Australia (☎ 02 9262 1666; italia@italiantour ism.com.au; Level 4, 46 Market St, Sydney, NSW 2000)
Austria (☎ 01 505 16 39; delegation.wien@ enit.at; Kärntnerring 4, Vienna, A-1010)
Canada (☎ 416 925 4882; www.italiantour ism.com; Suite 907, South Tower, 175 Bloor St East, Toronto, M4W 3R8)
France (☎ 01 42 66 03 96; enit.direction@wana doo.fr; 23 rue de la Paix, Paris, 75002)
Germany Berlin (☎ 030 247 8398; enit. berlin@t-online.de; Kontorhaus Mitte, Friedrich-strasse 187, 10117); Frankfurt (☎ 069 237 069; enit.ffm@t-online.de; Neue Mainzerstrasse 26, 60311); Munich (☎ 089-531 317; enit. muenchen@t-online.de; Prinzregentenstrasse 22, 80333)
Japan (☎ 03 3478 2051; enittky@dream.com; 2-7-14 Minami Aoyama, Minato-ku, Tokyo, 107-0062)
Netherlands (☎ 020 616 82 46; amsterdam@ enit.it; Stadhouderskade 2, 1054 ES Amsterdam)
Switzerland (☎ 043 466 40 40; info@enit.ch; Uraniastrasse 32, Zurich, 8001)
UK (☎ 020 7399 3562; italy@italiantourist board.co.uk; 1 Princes St, London W1B 2AY)
USA Chicago (☎ 312 644 09 96; enitch@ italiantourism.com; www.italiantourism.com; 500 North Michigan Ave, Suite 2240, IL 60611); Los Angeles (☎ 310 820 1898; enitla@italian-tourism.com; 12400 Wilshire Blvd, Suite 550, CA 90025); New York (☎ 212 245 5618; enitny@ italiantourism.com; 630 Fifth Ave, Suite 1565, NY 10111)

TRAVELLERS WITH DISABILITIES

Italy is not an easy country for disabled travellers and getting around can be a problem for wheelchair users.

The Italian National Tourist Office (opposite) in your country may be able to provide advice on Italian associations for the disabled and information on what help is available. It may also carry a small brochure, *Services for Disabled Passengers,* published by Italian railways, which details facilities at stations and on trains. It also has a national helpline at ☎ 199 303060.

A handful of cities also publish general guides on accessibility, among them Bologna, Milan, Padua, Reggio Emilia, Turin, Venice and Verona.

Some organisations that may help:

Accessible Italy (☎ +378 94 11 11; www. accessibleitaly.com) A San Marino–based company that specialises in holiday services for the disabled, ranging from tours to the hiring of adapted transport. It can even arrange romantic Italian weddings. This is the best first port of call.

Consorzio Cooperative Integrate (COIN; ☎ within Italy 800 271027; www.coinso ciale.it) Based in Rome, COIN is the best reference point for disabled travellers. It provides information on the capital (including transport and access) and is happy to share its contacts throughout Italy.

Holiday Care (☎ 0845 124 9971; www. holidaycare.org.uk) Has information on hotels with disabled access, where to hire equipment and tour operators dealing with the disabled.

You can also check out **Tour in Umbria** (www.tourinumbria.org) and **Milano per Tutti** (www.milanopertutti.it) for information on getting around those destinations.

VISAS

Italy is one of 25 member countries of the Schengen Convention, under which 22 EU countries (all but Bulgaria, Cyprus, Ireland, Romania and the UK) plus Iceland, Norway and Switzerland have abolished permanent checks at common borders.

Legal residents of one Schengen country do not require a visa for another. Residents of 28 non-EU countries, including Australia, Brazil, Canada, Israel, Japan, New Zealand and the USA, do not require visas for tourist visits of up to 90 days (this list varies for those wanting to travel to the UK and Ireland).

The standard tourist visa is valid for up to 90 days. You must apply for a Schengen visa in your country of residence. A Schengen visa issued by one Schengen country is generally valid for travel in other Schengen countries. It is worth checking visa regulations with the consulate of each country you plan to visit.

PERMESSO DI SOGGIORNO

Non-EU citizens planning to stay at the same address for more than one week are supposed to report to the police station to receive a *permesso di soggiorno* (a permit to remain in the country). Tourists staying in hotels are not required to do this.

A *permesso di soggiorno* only really becomes a necessity if you plan to study, work (legally) or live in Italy.

WOMEN TRAVELLERS

As with anywhere in the world, women travelling alone need to take certain precautions and, in some parts of the country, be prepared for more than their fair share of unwanted attention.

Foreign women are particular objects of male attention in tourist towns like Florence and more generally in the south. Usually the best response to undesired advances is to ignore them. If that doesn't work, politely tell your interlocutors you're waiting for your *marito* (husband) or *fidanzato* (boyfriend) and, if necessary, walk away. Avoid becoming aggressive as this may result in an unpleasant confrontation. If all else fails, approach the nearest member of the police.

Watch out for men with wandering hands on crowded buses. Either keep your back to the wall or make a loud fuss if someone starts fondling your behind. A loud '*Che schifo!*' (How disgusting!) will usually do the trick. If a more serious incident occurs, report it to the police, who are then required to press charges.

Avoid walking alone in dark streets, and look for hotels that are central (unsafe areas are noted in this book). Women should avoid hitchhiking alone.

TRANSPORT

GETTING THERE & AWAY

Competition between airlines means you should be able to pick up a reasonably priced fare to Italy, even from as far away as Australia. There are plenty of rail and bus connections, especially with northern Italy. Car and passenger ferries operate to ports in Albania, Corsica, Croatia, Greece, Malta, Spain, Tunisia & Turkey.

THINGS CHANGE

The information in this chapter is particularly vulnerable to change. Check directly with the airline or a travel agent to make sure you understand how a fare (and ticket you may buy) works and be aware of the security requirements for international travel. Shop carefully. The details given in this chapter should be regarded as pointers and are not a substitute for your own careful, up-to-date research.

Flights, tours and rail tickets can be booked online at www.lonelyplanet.com/travel_services.

ENTERING THE COUNTRY

Citizens of the 27 European Union (EU) member states and Switzerland can travel to Italy with their national identity card alone. If such countries do not issue ID cards – as in the UK – travellers must carry a full valid passport. All other nationalities must have a valid passport.

If applying for a visa (see p395), check that your passport's expiry date is at least six months away).

By law you are supposed to have your passport or ID card with you at all times.

AIR

High seasons are generally June to September, Christmas and Easter, although it depends in part on your destination. Shoulder season is often from mid-September to the end of October and again in April. Low season is generally November to March.

AIRPORTS & AIRLINES

Italy's main intercontinental gateway is the **Leonardo da Vinci Airport** (Fiumicino; ☎ 06 6 59 51; www.adr.it) in Rome, but many low-cost carriers land at Rome's **Ciampino Airport** (☎ 06 6 59 51; www.adr.it) – see p100 for more details. Regular intercontinental flights also serve Milan's **Malpensa Airport** (☎ 02 7485 2200; www.sea-aeroportimilano.it), 50km from the city. Plenty of flights from other European cities fly to regional capitals.

Many European and international airlines compete with the country's national carrier, Alitalia.

TICKETS

The internet is increasingly becoming the easiest way of locating and book-

↘ CLIMATE CHANGE & TRAVEL

Travel – especially air travel – is a significant contributor to global climate change. At Lonely Planet, we believe that all who travel have a responsibility to limit their personal impact. As a result, we have teamed with Rough Guides and other concerned industry partners to support Climate Care, which allows people to offset the greenhouse gases they are responsible for with contributions to energy-saving projects and other climate-friendly initiatives in the developing world. Lonely Planet offsets all staff and author travel.

For more information, turn to the responsible travel pages on www.lonelyplanet.com. For details on offsetting your carbon emissions and a carbon calculator, go to www.climatecare.org.

ing reasonably priced seats. Full-time students and those under 26 sometimes have access to discounted fares, especially on longer-haul flights from beyond Europe.

There is no shortage of online agents:
www.cheapflights.com
www.cheaptickets.com
www.discount-tickets.com
www.ebookers.com
www.expedia.com
www.kayak.com
www.lastminute.com
www.opodo.com
www.orbitz.com
www.skyscanner.net
www.tripadvisor.com

LAND

There are plenty of options for entering Italy by train, bus or private vehicle. Bus is the cheapest option, but services are less frequent, less comfortable and significantly longer than the train.

BORDER CROSSINGS

The main points of entry to Italy from France are the coast road from Nice, which becomes the A10 motorway along the Ligurian coast, and the Mont Blanc Tunnel near Chamonix, which connects with the A5 for Turin and Milan. From Switzerland, the Grand St Bernard tunnel also connects with the A5 and the Simplon tunnel connects with the SS33 road that leads to Lago Maggiore. From Austria, the Brenner Pass connects with the A22 to Bologna. The Gotthard tunnel (which will have a new parallel railway tunnel, the Gotthard Base Tunnel, possibly by 2015) in Switzerland crosses the Swiss Alps into the Swiss canton of Ticino, from where the N2 highway heads south into Italy via Lugano.

Regular trains on two lines connect Italy with France in the west (one along the coast and the other via the French Alps to Turin). Trains from Milan head for Switzerland and on into France and the Netherlands. Two main lines head for the main cities in Austria and on into Germany, France or Eastern Europe.

BUS

Eurolines (www.eurolines.com) is a consortium of European coach companies that operates across Europe with offices in all major European cities. Italy-bound buses head to Milan, Rome, Florence, Siena, Venice and other Italian cities and all come equipped with on-board toilet facilities.

TRANSPORT

GETTING THERE & AWAY

CAR & MOTORCYCLE
CONTINENTAL EUROPE

When driving in Europe, always carry proof of ownership of a private vehicle and evidence of third-party insurance. If driving a vehicle registered and insured in an EU country, your home country insurance is sufficient. Theoretically, the International Insurance Certificate, also known as the Carta Verde (Green Card), is no longer required for EU-registered cars. Unfortunately, in case of an accident, police may still ask for it!

Ask your insurer for a European Accident Statement (EAS) form, which can simplify matters in the event of an accident.

A European breakdown assistance policy is a good investment. If for whatever reason you don't have one, assistance can be obtained through the **Automobile Club d'Italia** (see p401).

You can book a car before you leave home (for multinational car-rental agencies see p402), but you can sometimes find better deals by dealing with local agencies as you go (check individual chapters for contact information). Check with your credit-card company to see if it offers a Collision Damage Waiver, which

RAIL PASSES

The InterRail Pass is available to people who have lived in Europe for six months or more. It can be bought at most major stations and student travel outlets.

Eurail passes are for those who have lived in Europe for less than six months and are supposed to be bought outside Europe. They are available from leading travel agencies and online at www.eurail.com.

Seniors travelling from the UK should ask at the Rail Europe Travel Centre about possible discounts on rail travel in continental Europe (see p400).

InterRail Pass

InterRail (www.interrail.net or www.interrailnet.com) are for people who have been resident in Europe for more than six months. A Global pass encompassing 30 countries comes in four versions, ranging from five days' travel in 10 days to a full month's travel. These in turn come with three prices: Adult 1st class, Adult 2nd class and Youth 2nd class. The one-month pass costs, respectively, €809/599/399. The InterRail one-country pass for Italy can be used for three, four, six or eight days in one month. For the eight-day pass you pay €309/229/149/154.50/114.50 for Adult 1st class/Adult 2nd class/Youth 2nd class/child 1st class/child 2nd class. Children's passes are for kids aged 4 to 11, youth passes for people aged 12 to 25, and adult passes for those 26 and over. Children aged three and under travel for free.

Eurail Passes

Eurail passes are good for travel in 20 European countries (not including the UK), but forget it if you intend to travel mainly in Italy. People aged over 26 pay for a 1st-class Global Pass and those aged under 26 for a 2nd-class pass version.

covers you for additional damage if you use that card to pay for the car.

Italy is made for motorcycle touring, and motorcyclists swarm into the country in summer to meander along the scenic roads. With a bike you rarely have to book ahead for ferries and can enter restricted-traffic areas in cities. Crash helmets are compulsory. The US-based Beach's Motorcycle Adventures (☎ 1 716 773 4960; www.beachs-mca.com) can arrange two-week tours around various parts of Italy in May and October. Riders need to have a motorcycle licence – an international one is best.

UK
You can take your car across to France by ferry or via the Channel Tunnel on Eurotunnel (☎ 0870 535 3535; www.eurotunnel.com).

TRAIN
Depending on distances travelled, rail can be highly competitive. Those travelling from neighbouring countries to northern Italy will find it is frequently only marginally longer and/or more expensive. You avoid all the airport hassle and generally can rely on trains being on time.

Passes are valid for 15 days, 21 days, or for one, two or three months; the 1st-class adult pass costs €511/662/822/1161/1432. The 2nd-class youth version comes in at €332/429/535/755/933. Children aged between four and 11 pay half price for the 1st-class passes.

The 1st-class Saver is for groups of two or more and brings a 15% reduction in the standard Global pass adult prices. Another option is Global Pass for 10/15 days' travel within two months, which costs €603/792. The 15-day version costs €675/515 for the Saver/2nd-class youth versions.

Eurail Selectpass
This provides between five and 15 days of unlimited travel within a two-month period in three to five bordering countries (from a total of 23 possible countries). As with Global passes, those aged over 26 pay for a 1st-class pass, while those aged under 26 can get a cheaper, 2nd-class pass. The basic five-day pass for three countries costs €324/275/211 for the 1st-class adult/Saver/2nd-class youth versions.

Regional & National Passes
Eurail also offers an Italy national pass and several two-country regional passes (France-Italy, Spain-Italy and Greece-Italy). You can choose from three to 10 days' train travel in a two-month period for any of these passes. Single-country and regional passes come in five versions: 1st and 2nd-class adult, 1st-class and 2nd-class adult saver, and 2nd-class youth. The 10-day regional pass for Italy and France costs €442/386/386/338/295. The 10-day Italy pass costs €335/271/285/231/221. As with all Eurail passes, you want to be sure you will be covering a lot of ground to make these worthwhile. Check some sample prices in euros of where you intend to travel on the Trenitalia (www.trenitalia.com) website to compare.

It is also a much greener way to go – the same trip by rail can contribute up to 10 times less carbon dioxide emissions per person than by air.

CONTINENTAL EUROPE

Thomas Cook's *European Rail Timetable* has a complete listing of train schedules. The timetable is updated monthly and available from Thomas Cook offices worldwide and online (www.thomascook publishing.com) for around UK£14. Some of the main international services include transport for private cars.

UK

The passenger train **Eurostar** (☎ 08705 186186; www.eurostar.com) travels between London and Paris, and London and Brussels. Alternatively you can get a train ticket that includes crossing the Channel by ferry.

For the latest fare information on journeys to Italy, including the Eurostar, contact the **Rail Europe Travel Centre** (☎ 08448 484064 in the UK; www.raileurope.co.uk). Another source of rail information for all of Europe is **Rail Choice** (www.railchoice. com).

SEA

The helpful search engine **Traghettionline** (www.traghettionline.com, in Italian) covers all the ferry companies in the Mediterranean; you can also book online. Tickets are most expensive in summer, and many routes are only operated in summer. Prices for vehicles usually vary according to their size.

GETTING AROUND

You can reach almost any destination in Italy by train, bus or ferry, and services are efficient and cheap; for longer distances there are plenty of domestic air services.

Your own wheels give you the most freedom, but *benzina* (petrol) and autostrada (motorway) tolls are expensive and Italian drivers have a style all their own: the stress of driving and parking in a big Italian city could outweigh the delights of puttering about elsewhere in the country. One solution might be to take public transport between large cities and rent a car only for country drives.

AIR

The privatised national airline, Alitalia, is the main domestic carrier. Smaller airlines have brought competition, although tough times have seen some close. Among others, **EasyJet** (☎ 899 676789; www.easyjet. com) and **Meridiana** (☎ 892928; www.meridi ana.it) operate domestic flights. **AirAlps** (A6; ☎ 06 2222; www.airalps.at) has short-range domestic flights – book through Alitalia.

Alitalia is generally fairly expensive, but you should enquire about possible discounted rates for young people, families, seniors and weekend travellers, as well as advance purchase deals.

BICYCLE

Cycling is a popular pastime in Italy. There are no special road rules, but you would be wise to equip yourself with a helmet and lights. With good reason, you cannot take bikes onto the autostradas.

Bikes can be taken on any train carrying the bicycle logo. The cheapest way to do this is to buy a separate bicycle ticket (€3.50, or €5 to €12 on Intercity, Eurostar and Euronight trains), available even at the self-service kiosks. You can use this ticket for 24 hours, making a day trip quite economical. Bikes dismantled and stored in a bag can be taken for free, even on night trains, and all ferries allow free bicycle passage.

HIRE

Bikes are available for hire in most Italian towns, and many places have both city and mountain bikes. In Florence, for instance, there are several private outlets and a municipal scheme. Rental costs for a city bike start at €10/30 per day/week.

PURCHASE

If you shop around, bargain prices for bikes range from about €100 for a standard women's bike without gears to €210 for a mountain bike with 16 gears.

BOAT

Navi (large ferries) service Sicily and Sardinia; *traghetti* (smaller ferries) and *aliscafi* (hydrofoils) service smaller islands. The main embarkation points for Sardinia are Genoa, Livorno, Civitavecchia and Naples; for Sicily they're Naples and Villa San Giovanni in Calabria (near Reggio Calabria). The main points of arrival in Sardinia are Cagliari, Arbatax, Olbia and Porto Torres; in Sicily they're Palermo and Messina.

For a comprehensive guide to all ferry services into and out of Italy, check out Traghettionline (www.traghettionline.com, in Italian). The website lists every route and includes links to ferry companies, where you can buy tickets or search for deals.

For other relevant destinations, see the Getting There & Away sections of individual chapters. Most ferries carry vehicles.

BUS

Buses are not always cheaper than the train but are often the only way to get to smaller towns.

It is usually possible to get bus timetables from local tourist offices. In larger cities most of the intercity bus companies have ticket offices or operate through agencies. In some villages and even good-size towns, tickets are sold in bars or on the bus.

Although it's usually not necessary to make reservations on buses, booking is advisable in the high season for overnight or long-haul trips.

CAR & MOTORCYCLE

Italy boasts an extensive privatised network of autostradas, represented on road signs by a white A followed by a number on a green background. The main north–south link is the Autostrada del Sole (the 'Motorway of the Sun'), which extends from Milan to Reggio di Calabria (called the A1 from Milan to Rome, the A2 from Rome to Naples, and the A3 from Naples to Reggio di Calabria).

On most of the motorways you pay a toll. You can pay by cash or credit card as you leave the autostrada. For information on road tolls and passes, contact Autostrade per l'Italia (☎ 840 042121; www.autostrade.it, in Italian), where you can also get information on the latest traffic situation.

Off the beaten path you'll be doing most of your travelling on the larger system of *strade statali* (state highways). On maps they're represented by 'S' or 'SS' and can vary from toll-free, four-lane highways to two-lane main roads. The latter can be extremely slow, especially in mountainous regions. Two other categories, in descending order, are the similar *strade regionali* (highways administered by the regions, coded SR or R) and *strade provinciali* (administered at provincial level, SP or P), which you'll find in rural areas and connecting small villages. Finally there are *strade locali,* which might not even be paved or mapped. You'll often find the most beautiful scenery off the provincial and local roads.

AUTOMOBILE ASSOCIATIONS

The ever-handy Automobile Club d'Italia (ACI; www.aci.it; Via Colombo 261, Rome) is a

TRANSPORT

GETTING AROUND

driver's best resource in Italy. To reach the ACI in a roadside emergency, dial ☎ 803116 from a landline or ☎ 800 116800 from a mobile phone. Foreigners do not have to join but instead pay a per-incident fee.

BRING YOUR OWN VEHICLE

Cars entering Italy from abroad need a valid national licence plate and an accompanying registration card. All vehicles must be equipped with any necessary adjustments for the Italian market; for example, left-side-drive cars will need to have their headlamps adjusted.

DRIVING LICENCE

All EU member states' driving licences are fully recognised throughout Europe. Those with a non-EU licence are supposed to obtain an International Driving Permit (IDP) to accompany their licence, which your national automobile association can issue. It's valid for 12 months and must be kept with your proper licence. Many non-EU licences (such as Australian, Canadian, New Zealand and US ones) are generally accepted by car-hire outfits in Italy. If you want to hire a car or motorcycle you'll need to produce your driving licence.

FUEL

Italy is covered by a good network of petrol stations. Prices are among the highest in Europe and vary from one service station (*benzinaio, stazione di servizio*) to another. Lead-free (*senza piombo;* 95 octane) costs up to €1.11/L. A 98-octane variant costs as much as €1.20/L. Diesel (*gasolio*) comes in at €1.06/L. Prices fluctuate with world oil prices.

HIRE

CARS

Most tourist offices and hotels can provide information about car or motorcycle

rental. To rent a car in Italy you have to be aged 25 or over and you have to have a credit card. Most firms will accept your standard licence or IDP for identification purposes. Consider hiring a small car, which you'll be grateful for when negotiating narrow city lanes.

Multinational car rental agencies:

Avis (☎ 199 100133; www.avisautonoleggio.it)

Budget (☎ 199 307373; www.budgetautonoleggio.it)

Europcar (☎ 199 307030; www.europcar.com)

Hertz (☎ 08708 44 88 44; www.hertz.it)

Italy by Car (☎ 800 846083; www.italybycar.it)

Maggiore (☎ 199 151120; www.maggiore.it)

MOTORCYCLE

You'll have no trouble hiring a small Vespa or scooter. There are numerous rental agencies in cities where you'll also be able to hire larger motorcycles for touring. The average cost for a 50cc scooter (per person) is around €20/150 per day/week. Note that many places require a sizable deposit, and you could be responsible for reimbursing part of the cost of the bike if it is stolen.

Most agencies will not hire motorcycles to people under 18.

INSURANCE

You need insurance when bringing your own car to Italy. See the Continental Europe section, p398.

Car-hire companies offer various insurance options. Be careful to understand what your liabilities and excess are and what waivers you are entitled to in case of accident or damage to the hire vehicle.

ROAD RULES

In Italy, as in the rest of continental Europe, cars drive on the right side of the road and overtake on the left. Unless otherwise indicated, you must always give way to cars entering an intersection from a road on your right. If you are caught not wearing a seat belt, you will be required to pay an on-the-spot fine.

A warning triangle (to be used in the event of a breakdown) is compulsory throughout Europe. If your car breaks down and you get out of the vehicle, you risk a fine if you neglect to wear an approved yellow or orange safety vest (available at bicycle shops and outdoor stores).

Random breath tests take place in Italy. If you're involved in an accident while under the influence of alcohol, the penalties can be severe. The blood-alcohol limit is 0.05%.

The speed limit on the autostradas is 130km/h (on some motorways with three lanes in either direction, the limit can be raised to 150km/h), and on all other highways it is 110km/h. On minor, non-urban roads, it is up to 90kmh. In built-up areas, the limit is 50km/h. Speeding fines follow EU standards and are proportionate with the number of kilometres that you are caught driving over the speed limit, reaching up to €2000 with possible suspension of your driving licence.

You don't need a licence to ride a scooter under 50cc but you should be aged 14 or over and you can't carry passengers or ride on an autostrada. Indeed, you should not venture on to an autostrada with a bike of less than 150cc. On all two-wheeled transport, helmets are required. The speed limit for a scooter is 40km/h. To ride a motorcycle or scooter up to 125cc, you must be aged 16 or over and have a licence (a car licence will do). Helmets are compulsory. For motorcycles over 125cc you need a motorcycle licence.

You will be able to enter most restricted traffic areas in Italian cities on a motorcycle without any problems, and traffic police generally turn a blind eye to motorcycles or scooters parked on footpaths.

All vehicles must use headlights at all times (day and night) on the autostradas. It is advisable for motorcycles on all roads at all times.

LOCAL TRANSPORT

All the major cities have good transport systems, with bus and underground-train networks usually integrated. In Venice, your only options are by *vaporetti* (small passenger ferries) or to go on foot.

BUS & UNDERGROUND TRAINS

You must buy bus tickets before you board the bus and validate them once on board. If you get caught with an unvalidated ticket you will be fined on the spot (up to €50 in most cities).

There are *metropolitane* (underground systems) in Rome, Milan, Naples and Turin (which has built the country's first automated metro line). You can get a map of the network from tourist offices in the relevant city.

Every city or town of any size has an efficient *urbano* (city) and *extraurbano* (city, suburbs and outlying areas) system of buses that reach even the most remote of villages. Services can be limited (or nonexistent) on Sundays and holidays.

STAMP IT!

Countless foreigner travellers in Italy learn the hard way that their train tickets must be stamped in the yellow machines (usually found at the head of rail platforms) just before boarding. Failure to do so usually results in fines, although the cry of 'I didn't know' sometimes elicits an indulgent response from ticket controllers. So stamp that ticket!

TRANSPORT

GETTING AROUND

TRAIN ROUTES

Principal Train Lines
Local Train Lines

Tickets can be bought from a *tabaccaio* (tobacconist), newsstands, ticket booths or machines at bus stations and in underground stations, and usually cost around €1 to €1.20. Most large cities offer good-value 24-hour or daily tourist tickets.

TAXI

You can usually find taxi ranks at train and bus stations or you can telephone for radio taxis. It's best to go to a designated taxi stand, as it's illegal for them to stop in the street if hailed. If you phone a taxi, bear in mind the meter starts running from when you've called rather than when it picks you up.

Charges vary somewhat from one region to another. Most short city journeys cost between €10 and €15.

TRAIN

Trenitalia (☎ 892021 in Italian; www.tren italia.com or www.ferroviedellostato.it) is the partially privatised, state train system that runs most services. Other private Italian train lines are noted throughout this book.

There are several types of trains. Some stop at all or most stations, such as *regionale* or *interregionale* trains. Intercity (IC) trains are fast services that operate between major cities. Eurocity (EC) trains are the international version. High-speed *pendolini* and other fast services are collectively known as Eurostar Italia (ES), and some make fewer stops than others.

Quicker still, the Alta Velocità (High Speed) services (variously known as AV and ESA) that began operation on the new Turin–Milan–Bologna–Florence–Rome–Naples–Salerno line in late 2009 have revolutionised train travel on that route. Nonstop trains between Milan and Rome take three hours, at least 2½ hours less than any other standard service (an Intercity train takes 6¼ hours)! With stops in Bologna and Florence, the time is 3½ hours. Prices vary according to the time of travel and how far in advance you book.

CLASSES & COSTS

There are 1st and 2nd classes on most Italian trains; a 1st-class ticket typically costs from a third to half more than the 2nd-class ticket.

Travel on Intercity, Eurostar and Alta Velocità trains means paying a supplement, determined by the distance you are travelling. This is included in the ticket, but if you have a standard ticket for, say, an *interregionale* and end up hopping on to a faster IC train, you will have to pay the difference on board. You can only board a Eurostar or Alta Velocità if you have a booking, so the problem does not arise in those cases.

For longer trips, the faster trains are generally worth the extra paid. On the Rome–Milan run, for instance, the difference in price in 2nd class between the 6¼-hour IC train and the 3½-hour run on the AV is €22.50.

For shorter hops (say, Venice–Padua or even Milan–Turin, for which there is at most a half-hour time gain for up to three times the price of a *regionale* ticket), the time gain is often not worth the extra money.

RESERVATIONS

Reservations are obligatory on Eurostar and AV trains. Otherwise they're not and, generally, you should be fine without them. You can do this at railway station counters, selected travel agents and, when they haven't broken down, at the automated machines sprinkled around most stations. Reservations generally carry a fee of an extra €3.

↘ GLOSSARY

abbazia – abbey

affittacamere – rooms for rent in private houses

agriturismo – tourist accommodation on farms; farm stay

AIG – Associazione Italiana Alberghi per la Gioventù (Italian Youth Hostel Association)

(pizza) al taglio – (pizza) by the slice

albergo – hotel

alto – high

anfiteatro – amphitheatre

aperitivo – before-evening meal drink and snack

APT – Azienda di Promozione Turistica; local town or city tourist office

autostrada – motorway; highway

AV – Alta Velocità, high-speed trains that entered service in 2009 between Turin, Milan, Bologna, Florence, Rome, Naples and Salerno

bancomat – ATM

battistero – baptistry

bianco – white

biblioteca – library

biglietto – ticket

borgo – archaic name for small town, village or town sector (often dating to Middle Ages)

camera – room

campo – field; also a square in Venice

cappella – chapel

carabinieri – police with military and civil duties

Carnevale – carnival period between Epiphany and Lent

casa – house

castello – castle

cattedrale – cathedral

centro – city centre

centro storico – historic centre

certosa – monastery belonging to or founded by Carthusian monks

chiesa – church

città – town; city

città alta – upper town

colle – hill

colonna – column

comune – equivalent to a municipality or county; a town or city council; historically, a self-governing town or city

contrada – district

corso – boulevard

duomo – cathedral

enoteca – wine bar

espresso – express mail; express train; short black coffee

est – east

ferrovia – railway

festa – feast day; holiday

fontana – fountain

foro – forum

funivia – cable car

gelateria – ice-cream shop

giardino – garden

golfo – gulf

grotta – cave

IC – Intercity; fast train

interregionale – long-distance train that stops frequently

isola – island

lago – lake

largo – small square

lido – beach
locanda – inn; small hotel
lungomare – seafront road/promenade

mar, mare – sea
mercato – market
monte – mountain
municipio – town hall
nord – north

osteria – simple, trattoria-style restaurant, usually with a bar

palazzo – mansion; palace; large building of any type, including an apartment block
palio – contest
parco – park
passeggiata – traditional evening stroll
pasticceria – cake/pastry shop
pensione – guesthouse
piazza – square
piazzale – large open square
pietà – literally 'pity' or 'compassion'; sculpture, drawing or painting of the dead Christ supported by the Madonna
pinacoteca – art gallery
ponte – bridge
porta – gate; door
portico – covered walkway, usually attached to the outside of buildings
porto – port
posta – post office; also *ufficio postale*
presepio – nativity scene; also *presepe*

questura – police station

reale – royal
regionale – slow local train
rifugio – mountain hut; accommodation in the Alps
ristorante – restaurant
rocca – fortress

sala – room; hall
salumeria – delicatessen
sassi – literally 'stones'; stone houses built in two ravines in Matera, Basilicata
scavi – excavations
servizio – service charge in restaurants
spiaggia – beach
stazione – station
stazione marittima – ferry terminal
strada – street; road
sud – south

tavola calda – literally 'hot table'; pre-prepared meat, pasta and vegetable selection, often self-service
teatro – theatre
tempietto – small temple
tempio – temple
terme – thermal baths
traghetto – ferry
trattoria – simple restaurant
Trenitalia – Italian State Railways; also known as Ferrovie dello Stato (FS)
trullo – conical house in Perugia

vaporetto – small ferry (Venice)
via – street; road
viale – avenue
vico – alley; alleyway
villa – townhouse; country house; also the park surrounding the house

↘ BEHIND THE SCENES

THE AUTHORS
CRISTIAN BONETTO

Coordinating author, This is Italy, Italy's Top Itineraries, Planning Your Trip, Naples, Pompeii & Amalfi, Italy in Focus, Directory & Transport

Much to the chagrin of his northern Italian relatives, Cristian's loyalties lie with Naples. Such affection seems only natural for a writer of farce and soap with a penchant for running red lights. Based in Melbourne, Australia, Cristian makes regular trips to Campania and its capital to indulge his weakness for *mozzarella di bufala* and hot-blooded locals. His musings on the region have appeared in print from Sydney to London, while his Naples-based play *Il Cortile* toured Italy in 2003. Cristian's other Italian Lonely Planet titles to date are *Naples & the Amalfi Coast, Rome Encounter* and *Italy*.

Author thanks An epic *grazie* to my very own San Lucano, his partner in crime, Silvana, Valentina Vellusi and Francesco Calazzo for their incredible generosity and insight. Also, a heartfelt thanks to Santiago Faraone Mennella, Valerio Prodomo, Fulvio Salvi, Luca Cuttitta, Sally O'Brien and Denis Balibouse, Penelope Green, Antonio Romano, Carmine Romano, Daniela Ibello, Mario Spada and Daniele Sanzone. At Lonely Planet, a big thanks to Paula Hardy for the commission and support, and to Josephine Quintero and Duncan Garwood for their sterling research.

DAMIEN SIMONIS

Milan & the Northwest, Italy in Focus, Directory & Transport

Damien still remembers listening to crackly shortwave Italian broadcasts years ago on many an Australian midsummer night. It all started in Rome, part of a typical backpacking tour, and carried on as a university obsession. Damien has explored Italy from Bolzano in the north to the island of Lampedusa, way south of Sicily. He has lived in Milan, Florence, Venice and Palermo, and returns frequently for work and (especially) pleasure. Involved with the *Italy* guide since its 2nd edition, Damien also wrote the

---

LONELY PLANET AUTHORS

Why is our travel information the best in the world? It's simple: our authors are passionate, dedicated travellers. They don't take freebies in exchange for positive coverage so you can be sure the advice you're given is impartial. They travel widely to all the popular spots, and off the beaten track. They don't research using just the internet or phone. They discover new places not included in any other guidebook. They personally visit thousands of hotels, restaurants, palaces, trails, galleries, temples and more. They speak with dozens of locals every day to make sure you get the kind of insider knowledge only a local could tell you. They take pride in getting all the details right, and in telling it how it is. Think you can do it? Find out how at **lonelyplanet.com**.

original editions of Lonely Planet's *Venice, Best of Venice, Florence, Tuscany* and *Sardinia* guides. He was last seen working on *The Italian Lakes,* a new regional guide.

ALISON BING   Venice & the Northeast, Italy in Focus
Alison contributes to Lonely Planet's *Venice, USA, San Francisco* and *Tuscany & Umbria* guides, and architecture, food and art glossies, including *Architectural Record, Cooking Light* and Italy's *Flash Art*. Currently, she divides her time between San Francisco and a hilltop town on the border of Lazio and Tuscany with partner Marco Flavio Marinucci. Alison holds a bachelor's degree in art history and a masters' degree from the Fletcher School of Law and Diplomacy, a joint program of Tufts and Harvard Universities – perfectly respectable diplomatic credentials she regularly undermines with opinionated culture commentary for newspapers, magazines, TV and radio.

GREGOR CLARK   Venice & the Northeast, Sicily & the South
Gregor caught the Italy bug at age 14 thanks to a year living in Florence, during which his professor dad trundled the family off to see every fresco, mosaic, church and museum within a 1000km radius. He's been making regular return visits to Italy ever since, including longer stints in Venice and Le Marche, leading bike tours in the Po Valley, and huffing and puffing up every major pass in the Dolomites while researching Lonely Planet's *Cycling Italy*. A lifelong polyglot with a degree in romance languages, Gregor is a regular contributor to Lonely Planet titles, including *Brazil, Argentina, Portugal* and *New England Trips*. He lives with his wife and two daughters in Vermont, USA.

DUNCAN GARWOOD   Florence & Central Italy
Duncan never set out to become an Italy buff – it just sort of happened after an encounter in a London pub and a subsequent move to Bari. More than 10 years later he's still in Italy, now based in the Alban hills outside Rome. He got his first Lonely Planet commission in 2002 and has since contributed to a raft of Italy guides, including the country guide, the *Rome* guide, *Naples & the Amalfi Coast, Sardinia* and *Piedmont*. As he travels he's constantly revising his best-of lists, which currently have Rome as top city, Sardinia as best beach hangout and Abruzzo as most resilient region in the face of natural disaster.

ABIGAIL HOLE   Rome
Chaos, beauty, endless summer, effortless cool, handsome inhabitants, the ice cream of your dreams and picture-book countryside on your doorstep: Rome fits Abigail's view of an ideal city, and since she visited in 2003, she's never really left. She's married to an Italian, her first son was born in the Eternal City and her Italian *famiglia* live here. She's written on Rome for various newspapers, magazines and websites, and contributed to Lonely Planet's *Best of Rome, Italy,* and *Puglia & Basilicata* guides. A freelance writer, she nowadays does her best to divide her time between Rome, London and Puglia.

ALEX LEVITON   Florence & Central Italy
Alex first visited Perugia in 1998, and has returned to work, live and travel throughout Umbria and Le Marche a dozen times since. Alex received a master's degree in journalism from the University of California at Berkeley in 2002 and has been freelancing and writing

for Lonely Planet ever since. She lives mostly in San Francisco and sometimes in Durham, North Carolina, but one day dreams of buying a farmhouse in the Umbria hills.

VIRGINIA MAXWELL   Florence & Central Italy, Italy in Focus

After working for many years as a publishing manager at Lonely Planet's Melbourne headquarters, Virginia decided that she'd be happier writing guidebooks rather than commissioning them. Since then she's written or contributed to Lonely Planet books about nine countries, eight of which are on the Mediterranean. Virginia has covered Rome and Florence for Lonely Planet's *Italy* and the north of the country for *Western Europe*. She is also the coordinating author of Lonely Planet's *Tuscany & Umbria*.

JOSEPHINE QUINTERO   Sicily & the South

Born in England, Josephine started travelling with a backpack and guitar in the late '60s (didn't everyone?), stopping off in Israel on a kibbutz for a year. Further travels took her to Kuwait, where she was editor of the *Kuwaiti Digest* and was held hostage during the Iraqi invasion. She moved to the relaxed shores of Andalucía, Spain, shortly thereafter, from where she makes frequent trips to Italy to visit family and deepen her appreciation of the finer things in life.

BRENDAN SAINSBURY   Milan & the Northwest

An expat Brit now living in Vancouver, Canada, Brendan first visited Italy as an inter-railer in the 1980s when he ran out of *soldi* in Venice and ended up falling asleep outside the ticket office at Milan railway station. He returned on his bike in 1992 and sprinted west out of Turin just in time to see Italian cycling hero Claudio Chiappucci nab a legendary Tour de France stage victory in Sestriere. As well as updating three chapters for the *Italy* guidebook, Brendan is also the author of Lonely Planet's *Hiking in Italy*.

CONTRIBUTING AUTHORS

Content for the section on Health was originally written by Dr Caroline Evans.

THIS BOOK

This 1st edition of *Discover Italy* was coordinated by Cristian Bonetto, and researched and written by him, Alison Bing, Gregor Clark, Duncan Garwood, Abigail Hole, Alex Leviton, Virginia Maxwell, Josephine Quintero, Brendan Sainsbury and Damien Simonis. It was commissioned in Lonely Planet's London office, and produced by the following:

Commissioning Editor Paula Hardy
Coordinating Editor Daniel Corbett
Coordinating Cartographer Valentina Kremenchutskaya
Coordinating Layout Designer Yvonne Bischofberger
Managing Editor Bruce Evans
Managing Cartographer Herman So
Managing Layout Designer Laura Jane
Assisting Editor Paul Harding
Assisting Cartographers David Kemp, Alex Leung
Assisting Layout Designers Nicholas Colicchia, Margie Jung, Jessica Rose, Cara Smith

SEND US YOUR FEEDBACK

We love to hear from travellers – your comments keep us on our toes and help make our books better. Our well-travelled team reads every word on what you loved or loathed about this book. Although we cannot reply individually to postal submissions, we always guarantee that your feedback goes straight to the appropriate authors, in time for the next edition. Each person who sends us information is thanked in the next edition and the most useful submissions are rewarded with a free book.

To send us your updates – and find out about Lonely Planet events, newsletters and travel news – visit our award-winning website: lonelyplanet.com/contact.

Note: we may edit, reproduce and incorporate your comments in Lonely Planet products such as guidebooks, websites and digital products, so let us know if you don't want your comments reproduced or your name acknowledged. For a copy of our privacy policy visit lonelyplanet.com/privacy.

Cover research Jane Hart, lonelyplanetimages.com
Internal image research Sabrina Dalbesio, lonelyplanetimages.com
Project Manager Rachel Imeson
Language Content Annelies Mertens

Thanks to Sasha Baskett, Glenn Beanland, Eoin Dunlevy, Jane Hart, Suki Gear, Joshua Geoghegan, Mark Germanchis, Chris Girdler, Michelle Glynn, Brice Gosnell, Imogen Hall, James Hardy, Steve Henderson, Lauren Hunt, Chris Lee Ack, Nic Lehman, Alison Lyall, John Mazzocchi, Jennifer Mullins, Wayne Murphy, Darren O'Connell, Naomi Parker, Trent Paton, Piers Pickard, Howard Ralley, Lachlan Ross, Julie Sheridan, Jason Shugg, Caroline Sieg, Naomi Stephens, Geoff Stringer, Jane Thompson, Sam Trafford, Stefanie Di Trocchio, Tashi Wheeler, Clifton Wilkinson, Juan Winata, Emily K Wolman, Nick Wood

Internal photographs p4 Outdoor cafe on Piazza Bra, Verona, Glenn Beanland; p10 Revellers at Trevi Founain, Rome, Greg Alms; p12 Hiker above Vernazza, Cinque Terre, John Elk III; p31 Museo Archeologico, Naples, Greg Alms; p39 View from Villa Rufolo, Ravello, Glenn Benland; p3, p50 Piazza della Rotonda, Rome, Russell Mountford; p3, p103 Galleria Vittorio Emanuele II, Milan, Bethune Carmichael; p3, p155 Grand Canal, Venice, John Hay; p3, p207 Piazza del Duomo, Florence, Martin Moos; p3, p263 Positano, Amalfi Coast, Glenn Beanland; p3, p297 Greek temple, Sicily, Izzet Keribar; p342 Basilica di San Giovanni in Laterano, Rome, Will Salter; p379 Streets of Giovinazzo Vecchio, Isabella Lettini

NOTES

↘INDEX

INDEX

A-C

INDEX

D-F

000 Map pages
000 Photograph pages

INDEX

R-T

000 Map pages
000 Photograph pages

INDEX

T-Z

GREENDEX

It seems like everyone's going 'green' these days, but how can you know which businesses are actually ecofriendly and which are simply jumping on the eco/sustainable bandwagon?

The following attractions, tours, bars, shops, festivals, courses, restaurants and accommodation choices have all been selected by Lonely Planet authors because they meet our criteria for sustainable tourism. While many restaurants in Italy serve seasonal, locally sourced produce, we've highlighted those that chose to go the extra mile and are accredited by the Slow Food Movement. We've also highlighted farmers' markets and the local producers themselves. In addition, we've covered accommodation that we deem to be environmentally friendly, for example for their commitment to recycling or energy conservation. Attractions are listed because they're involved in conservation or environmental education, have been given an ecological award or are World Heritage–listed by Unesco.

We want to keep developing our sustainable-travel content. If you think we've omitted someone who should be listed here, or if you disagree with our choices, contact us at www.lonelyplanet.com/contact and set us straight for next time. For more information about sustainable tourism and Lonely Planet, see www.lonelyplanet.com/responsibletravel.

MAP LEGEND

ROUTES

Tollway	One-Way Street
Freeway	Mall/Steps
Primary	Tunnel
Secondary	Pedestrian Overpass
Tertiary	Walking Tour
Lane	Walking Tour Detour
Under Construction	Walking Path
Unsealed Road	Track

TRANSPORT

Ferry	Rail/Underground
Metro	Tram
Monorail	Cable Car, Funicular

HYDROGRAPHY

River, Creek	Canal
Intermittent River	Water
Swamp/Mangrove	Dry Lake/Salt Lake
Reef	Glacier

BOUNDARIES

International	Regional, Suburb
State, Provincial	Marine Park
Disputed	Cliff/Ancient Wall

AREA FEATURES

Area of Interest	Forest
Beach, Desert	Mall/Market
Building/Urban Area	Park
Cemetery, Christian	Restricted Area
Cemetery, Other	Sports

POPULATION

✪ **CAPITAL (NATIONAL)**	◉ **CAPITAL (STATE)**
● LARGE CITY	● Medium City
● Small City	● Town, Village

SYMBOLS

Sights/Activities
- Buddhist
- Canoeing, Kayaking
- Castle, Fortress
- Christian
- Confucian
- Diving
- Hindu
- Islamic
- Jain
- Jewish
- Monument
- Museum, Gallery
- Point of Interest
- Pool
- Ruin
- Sento (Public Hot Baths)
- Shinto
- Sikh
- Skiing
- Surfing, Surf Beach
- Taoist
- Trail Head
- Winery, Vineyard
- Zoo, Bird Sanctuary

Information
- Bank, ATM
- Embassy/Consulate
- Hospital, Medical
- Information
- Internet Facilities
- Police Station
- Post Office, GPO
- Telephone
- Toilets
- Wheelchair Access

Eating
- Eating

Drinking
- Cafe
- Drinking

Entertainment
- Entertainment

Shopping
- Shopping

Sleeping
- Camping
- Sleeping

Transport
- Airport, Airfield
- Border Crossing
- Bus Station
- Bicycle Path/Cycling
- FFCC (Barcelona)
- Metro (Barcelona)
- Parking Area
- Petrol Station
- S-Bahn
- Taxi Rank
- Tube Station
- U-Bahn

Geographic
- Beach
- Lighthouse
- Lookout
- Mountain, Volcano
- National Park
- Pass, Canyon
- Picnic Area
- River Flow
- Shelter, Hut
- Waterfall

LONELY PLANET OFFICES

Australia
Head Office
Locked Bag 1, Footscray, Victoria 3011
☎ 03 8379 8000, fax 03 8379 8111
talk2us@lonelyplanet.com.au

USA
150 Linden St, Oakland, CA 94607
☎ 510 250 6400, toll free 800 275 8555,
fax 510 893 8572
info@lonelyplanet.com

UK
2nd fl, 186 City Rd,
London EC1V 2NT
☎ 020 7106 2100, fax 020 7106 2101
go@lonelyplanet.co.uk

Published by Lonely Planet
ABN 36 005 607 983

© Lonely Planet 2010
© photographers as indicated 2010